THE MORE WE WIN THE BETTER IT WILL BE

Front cover photo:
(L-R) Dan Spence, Ben Strevens, Michael Green, Ben Wright,
Glen Southam, Ross Flitney and Dan Wishart finally drag
themselves from the field after Eastleigh's crunch late season
game at fellow promotion chasers Bromley.

"The *More* we *Win* the *Better* It will be"

A Year with
Eastleigh Football Club

Paul McNamara

Matador
9 Priory Business Park
Kibworth Beauchamp
Leicestershire LE8 0RX, UK
Tel: (+44) 116 279 2299
Fax: (+44) 116 279 2277
Email: books@troubador.co.uk
Web: www.troubador.co.uk/matador

ISBN 978-1784620-592

Photographs courtesy of Tony Smith and John McNamara

British Library Cataloguing in Publication Data.
A catalogue record for this book is available from the British Library.

Typeset in Bembo by Naomi Green, Troubador Publishing Ltd
Cover design by Terry Compton, Troubador Publishing Ltd

Printed and bound in the UK by TJ International, Padstow, Cornwall

Matador is an imprint of Troubador Publishing Ltd

TO FOOTBALL FANS EVERYWHERE

CONTENTS

THE BEGINNING

The idea of living and breathing everything Eastleigh Football Club, for an entire season, first formed in my mind well over two years before that hazy concept became a reality.

By the campaign of 2010/2011, I was finding myself gradually and willingly falling for this charming and homely institution. Moreover, the entire experience of watching football in comparatively reduced surroundings had become infinitely more pleasurable than the Premier League Groundhog Day to which I had become accustomed.

I had long since wearied of traipsing from my home on the south coast to Goodison Park, the home of my lifelong football love, Everton. Elements of my creeping disenchantment with all things top flight can be apportioned to familiar laments – expense, complete disregard for 'customer' care, and the arduous ticket-buying process, which has become something akin to completing a university application form.

I had my last season ticket at Goodison in 2004. In the years since, my attendance, even when the Blues are playing nearby, has lapsed. Shorn of the habit, the nadir came in David Moyes' final year in charge when I didn't attend a single Everton match.

A £35 fee to sit in Southampton's St Mary's Stadium, only eight miles from my home, on a bitterly cold Monday night, to watch a game that was being screened live on television would once have been paid as a matter of duty. Quite simply, I realise now that I was slightly barmy. I viewed that 0–0 draw between Southampton and Everton in January 2013 from my warm front room. A month previously, Everton's Under-18 side had played an FA Youth Cup fixture at the same ground. A seat for £5 and a highly entertaining contest made for an evening well spent.

Any self-respecting football supporter will look askance if confronted by an individual who purports to have switched their loyalties. That isn't what I have done.

I remain prone to seething bouts of fury when hearing news relayed such as that in February (2013) while standing in the clubhouse after watching Eastleigh play a game at the ground of Woking FC. Norwich City's arch-plodder Grant Holt had scored a 94th-minute winner against the Blues and I was raging. Conversely, a Goodison dismantling of Manchester City one month later, witnessed from the comfort of home, was a prompt for days spent walking on air. The mere sight or mention of anything Liverpool FC sets me off listing countless reasons why I find that particular club so unpalatable.

Nevertheless, I have been forced to admit that Eastleigh have taken pride of place in my affections. When I first stepped inside the Silverlake Stadium as a spectator on Tuesday, August 18th, 2009, to watch a 6–1 thumping of Bromley, I couldn't have imagined quite how much of a hold the 'Spitfires' would come to have on me.

To the same degree, as enthusiasm for draining my energies and already pitiful bank balance in the name of Everton was dwindling, my fascination and downright obsession with all things football continued to head in the opposite direction.

The need to get my viewing fix led me to a few other outposts before the Eastleigh bug gripped. A number of Saturdays in the 2008/2009 season were spent travelling with my dad to watch AFC Bournemouth at Dean Court.

The Cherries were playing in League Two and had been hit with a 17-point deduction by the impotent FA, which was determined to show one of the little guys just who is boss. Bournemouth's financial strife had similarly incurred a ten-point penalty a year earlier – a punishment without which the club would still have been competing in League One.

What looked destined to be a fortnightly 45-minute drive to see a doomed team accepting its fate turned into something altogether different with the appointment of Eddie Howe in the new year.

Watching that team burrow its way clear of trouble was a captivating affair. The atmosphere in the ground on match days quickly transformed. Crowds swelled and the late-career brilliance of Darren Anderton was complemented by a group of players imbued with fresh belief. When survival was assured, it felt as if I'd witnessed a 'proper' football story over the course of nine exhilarating months.

Despite being pleased at the subsequent upturn in the fortunes of a fine club, I haven't set foot back inside Bournemouth's Dean Court Stadium since the day when, in front of a sold-out crowd on a balmy April afternoon in 2009, their football league survival was confirmed with a 2–1 home win against Grimsby Town.

Sure, I enjoyed the ride and I've looked on approvingly as Bournemouth have won two promotions since I last darkened their door. Furthermore, I always cast an eye towards the progress of Howe and other men of the Cherries' 2009 escape. The advancing careers of Jason Pearce, Rhoys Wiggins, Danny Holland, and Brett Pitman at least allow me to indulge my belief that I can spot a player.

Prior to my brief flirtation with football in Dorset, my post-2004 'hit' had to be taken at Southampton. Portsmouth were in the midst of their Premier League years – no, really. The Saints, beset by fiscal trouble of their own, had plunged into the depths of League One. That suited me perfectly. It was possible to rock up on the day and pay for a ticket to watch a match of decent standard.

Never having really taken to what had traditionally been my local top-flight team after moving to the area in 1986, I tended to sit on my hands and hope the day's visitors took the three points – unless they happened to be called Leeds United. That eventuality actually only ever occurred once. Thank you, Brentford.

Still, prices weren't cheap. It was actually cash that indirectly halted the regular journey to Bournemouth. My match-going accomplice – the old man – retired in 2009. Being rather fond of a pound note he contested that being a destitute 60+ male he could no longer justify a fortnightly 80-mile round trip just to watch football.

'Have you seen the price of petrol lately, Paul?'

When the longing to watch a game took us to a non-league ground, the usual destination was Havant & Waterlooville's Westleigh Park. The club had achieved national renown through their FA Cup run in 2007/2008, which finished with a 5–2 defeat at Liverpool in the 4th round.

Perhaps more impressive than the Hawks' big day at Anfield was their 3rd-round replay win against Swansea City. The Welsh team – who would go on to top that campaign's League One table and were managed by Roberto Martinez (gulp) – were thumped 4–2 on a night that stood as testament to all that remains wonderful about the FA Cup.

I can clearly recall listening to updates on Radio 5 Live as the latest goal was stuck past a Swansea team containing a few men who would go on to be integral to their club's surge up to the Premier League. I wasn't best pleased, as it goes.

There was always something about Havant & Waterlooville that didn't sit right with me, and still doesn't. It's a personal thing, but it isn't likely to change. Even my attitude towards Southampton has softened – firstly, owing to the adventurous and exciting football they have played under Mauricio Pochettino and, secondly, watching the Saints enchanting Under-21 team play a series of home matches at the Silverlake last season was a real treat.

Lee Bradbury, a likeable member of the Bournemouth team that overcame their 17-point impediment, was appointed manager at Westleigh Park in October 2012. No matter. The Hawks will need to hire Howard Kendall as boss, play in Royal Blue, and change their nickname to 'The Toffees' before my outlook softens.

At this stage I should confess that my grudge goes back to my teenage years. I was spirited away from my local side to play for Havant Town's youth team – pre that club's 1998 merger with Waterlooville. Due to circumstances largely of my own making – an extremely stereotypical 17 year old's devotion to pubs and fruitless pursuit of members of the opposite sex – and a back injury I was too lazy to pay enough regard to, I didn't make the most of my own football opportunity.

My very first venture into Eastleigh's Ten Acres ground – and last before that night in August 2009 – came with Havant's Under-18s. If the line-ups were to have been recorded in a newspaper my name would have been found under 'unused subs'.

Why did I take it so personally? I didn't realise I had until many seasons later when I first went and watched a few games at the pleasant enough but sterile Westleigh. I found myself inwardly cheering on the opposition. The desire to witness an away victory was only heightened by some of the 'characters' who inhabited the main stand.

I wouldn't for one minute suggest this bunch are entirely reflective of the whole club's support. It just so happened that the vicinity of my chosen spec – a seat close to the half-way line – was populated by some of the worst kind of know-it-alls. There were only three or four of them, but theirs were the voices that spoke loudest. Not a piece of action could unfold without it being subject to the acerbic wit of said individuals.

The final nail was driven into my, one way, unhappy relationship with Havant & Waterlooville by their momentous 2008 day in front of the Match of the Day cameras.

It is an occasion that the club's supporters have no intention of letting anybody forget. Furthermore, it spawned a preponderance of Liverpool apparel on match-going locals. That's not a rare sight down south, granted, but the grating 'half-and-half' scarves and repellent red shirts were a little too much for my tastes. Add in a shirt-sponsorship arrangement with Carlsberg and I was never likely to adopt Havant & Waterlooville as a new favourite.

Jamie Collins was the captain of that Hawks FA Cup side. He has been signed this summer (2013) by Eastleigh's manager, Richard Hill, as a key component of the team that is being constructed with the intention of winning the Conference South title.

Still giddy after his Anfield outing, Jamie reflected thus.

'It was the greatest day of my life – apart from when my little boy was born. It was an absolutely unforgettable experience and we'll be replaying it time and again both on our video players and in our minds.'

So far, so understandable. But he continued.

'I had my eye on getting Steven Gerrard's shirt at the end of the match on Saturday – skipper's perk and all that – but I was beaten to it by "Harry" [inspired footballer's nickname alert] [Alfie] Potter. But I am a West Ham supporter and was delighted to come away with Javier Mascherano's shirt in the end.'

An ex-Havant & Waterlooville player with an avowed admiration for Steven Gerrard and Javier Mascherano does not point towards a man destined to become one of my favourites.

Of course, such judgements are the prerogative of any football supporter. Regardless of how utterly inaccurate they might prove to be, it doesn't prevent the same criteria being applied time and again.

When assessing the personal credentials of a more celebrated footballer we are at least afforded the advantage of the insatiable sports – and on occasion news – media's appetite for reporting every quote and action of these individuals.

Their public portrayal shapes our view of the subject's personality. That, despite the relatively miniscule level of access we have into any footballer's 24-hour existence. The same is actually true of a player's football competence – or otherwise. Unless they happen to play for the team we watch week in, week out, we can only draw limited conclusions as to their ability.

It is not uncommon on mentioning to another club's follower an admiration for one of their players to be instantly shot down while you listen to a lengthy list of that individual's short-comings. Likewise, with so much access to live football on television, it is easier than ever to see a player suffer a poor 90 minutes and write them off as a waste of space. Announce that belief to somebody who has watched the same performer with rather more clarity and regularity than once or twice through the medium of a screen in the corner of his lounge and you might just be treated to a contrary opinion.

Indeed, the blanket coverage of elite football – both on and off the field – enabled me to conclude that Don Hutchison and Sylvain Distin would be woeful additions to Everton's playing resources. Wrong – startlingly so, in fact.

If you digest your football at non-league level, impressions of players, other than those at your own club, are formed purely by a blend of seeing them operate twice a season, random tittle-tattle, and the printed word.

Typically, unless you are a dedicated away-game traveller or happen to frequent the bar/clubhouse post-match, any clue as to the personality of your own players, those who hold your football dreams in their gift each week, is deduced wholly from their on-pitch demeanour.

A mild fascination with that scenario was one of the triggers for my wanting to spend a season with an eclectic bunch of non-league footballers. By January 2011, the previous one and a half seasons had involved my backside taking its routine place in the main stand at the Silverlake for every Eastleigh home match.

Any pretence that Westleigh Park could be my habitual football haunt had been dispelled. We'd also spent sporadic afternoons at Gosport Borough, but that local club had fallen a long way since their heady late 1980s days competing in the upper reaches of the Southern League's Premier Division.

THE BEGINNING

Watching Southern League Division One South & West football at a perennially cold and dark Privett Park venue was never likely to tempt me into becoming a Gosport regular. Furthermore, the seats in their antiquated stand are distinctly uncomfortable. There can be no denying that the event of my 30th year expedited the emergence of my softer side. Therein lies another explanation for the surroundings in which I watch football taking on increased importance.

I remember being absolutely incredulous at my dad being narked with standing in the rain at a match. His obvious irritation at being crushed in a queue for the toilet or the inability of any number of Premier League clubs, due to their undermanned service counters, to take his £2 for a tea bag and some hot water was, to me, baffling. The football was all that mattered.

My attitude has turned 360 degrees. Living in a time when, theoretically, a firm emphasis is placed on agreeable customer service, top-class football plainly deems itself excluded from that specific responsibility. It is part of the deal that loyalty is one factor these enormous entities don't have to worry about, as they consider how to prize the next penny from their grateful 'consumers" grasp.

Sadly, the manner in which a high proportion of this country's biggest clubs take their supporters for granted is unlikely to change. When someone like me disappears, there is generally another body ready to follow in my stead.

I, though, had, like my dad, reached the tipping point. I valued being guaranteed a cup of tea at the match, rarely paying above the comparatively bargain price of £1 for my drink. Being able to reach the Gents, without needing to fight my way there while wondering if I'll make it back to my seat in time for the start of the second half, brings dual relief. (My stress levels are never higher than when I'm confronted with the prospect of missing even one second of a football match.)

And that seat. I could take my pick. Now, I love the buzz and exhilaration of a full and partisan, atmospheric football ground. Not the happy-clappy culture of many of today's stadiums, with the latest witty ditty being belted out to the tunes of 'Sloop John B', 'Bread of Heaven', 'That's Amore', or the otherwise forgotten Pigbag. No.

Being an active part of a raucous crowd, contesting every decision, living each second of action, becoming hopelessly immersed during 90 minutes (plus an extra ten if you happen to be one up against Liverpool) that feel like the most important of your life, is one of the world's great offerings.

I have come to learn, however, that the ability to savour that experience needn't require you enter a contract to forego your basic human rights for an afternoon.

One of the great joys of the Silverlake is the grandstand running down one touchline, which caters for a wonderfully panoptic view of the action. It holds 371 people and is on the same side of the ground as the (rudimentary) toilets and a 'van' serving hot drinks and food.

Strangely, despite their locality and a league status corresponding with Havant & Waterlooville's, Eastleigh hadn't even been discussed as an alternative when my dad and I ruminated over where we should take footballing root. Not even the presence in their team of a personal friend for the five years up to 2008 persuaded me to drive the required 12 miles to watch him.

Retrospectively, I can appreciate that my first taste of watching football at the Silverlake made a positive dent in my subconscious. A clement late summer evening, a friendly ambience – most notably a welcome absence of the contemporary Saint & Greavsie's that narked me at Havant – and, essentially, an easy on the eye team with an appetite for goals; albeit that latter impression was comparable to the assumption made by my seven-year-old self that Everton probably win the league every year. Additionally, there was something intangible I liked about the environment. That feeling holds true every time I walk through the gates to this day.

I can actually pinpoint the match that spiked my curiosity about the men who I was regularly handing over £10 to watch.

It was on January 3rd, 2011 against, rather predictably, Havant & Waterlooville. These Bank Holiday local derbies are a focal point of the non-league calendar. There is much to query about the administration of the game at this level, but the scheduling of fixtures against a local adversary over the Christmas, New Year, and Easter periods is unmistakably wise. Attendance numbers are swelled by punters desperate to get out and watch some football. The 822 who showed up for this game though represented a slightly disappointing figure – especially when considering the preponderance of replica Hawks (and Liverpool) jerseys evident.

After a typically feisty first half, the men who had travelled from another world altogether – in spite of it being only 25 miles away – held a 2–1 lead. In truth, there was an air of inevitability about the manner in which they would efficiently see out a clinical victory. But then, football did what football does best. It produced a final 20 minutes of mayhem. The game was on the brim of boiling over when, with 18 minutes to play, Tom Jordan rose imperiously to head an equaliser – during his over-four years playing for the Spitfires, the words 'Jordan', 'headed', and 'goal' could be found together in countless match reports.

Jordan's goal on that afternoon had the twin effect of rendering apoplectic a sprinkling of the visiting contingent and sparking a thrilling conclusion to the contest.

Brett Williams, an excellent young forward whose capacity to flourish on a higher stage than Conference South football was screamingly obvious to all but Eastleigh's then manager Ian Baird, started this game. He had already made a case for his regular selection by scoring the afternoon's first goal, but he trumped that with a 90th-minute strike to give his team the lead. (Within weeks Williams had signed for Reading and he has since bounced around the Football League and Conference Premier.)

The free-scoring Jamie Slabber had entered the fray with half an hour to play – god forbid the two Spitfires strikers be fielded from the off – and he put an extra gloss on the day by contemptuously dispatching a stoppage-time penalty.

The last 20 minutes of that cold afternoon at Ten Acres, when any outside worries or duties were placed on pause, the home crowd formed as one in support of a stirring fight back and the floodlights shone through the gloom on a home team in the ascendancy over their near neighbours, elevated me onto a cloud from which I didn't descend for a good 72 hours.

Suddenly, I was gripped. I could feel a sense of belonging. I'd not roared so enthusiastically in response to a Spitfires goal as I did strikes two, three, and four, since Chris Holland, Jordan's central defensive partner, had headed an equaliser deep into injury time in the season's first derby at Westleigh Park. Even then, the high had taken me through the remainder of the day, but ebbed away soon after.

I think my delight on that previous afternoon owed as much to the abject desolation of certain individuals sat nearby, as it did the hard won away point, earned by a distinctly under-strength Eastleigh team.

It was while scaling the post 4–2 euphoria that I wondered how many other people out there were feeling similarly buoyed in the wake of both the result and the rousing style in which it was earned.

I was no less intrigued as to the effect the match would have on its victorious participants. We know that if a league club's players had enjoyed such a high, the next day would likely consist of nothing more taxing than a late-morning mosey into the training ground for a warm down and plenty of joshing and happy reflecting on their triumph.

What of their non-league counterparts? Eastleigh were, at that time, a wholly part-time outfit. A little over 12 hours after trooping off the pitch to a rapturous ovation, those same players were faced with the same grim reality as many who were heartily cheering their efforts. It was January 4th. It was cold. The mornings were dark. The holidays were over. It was time to return to work.

By definition, that is the lot of a part-time footballer. The only dressing room insight to which we might be privy after such a tumultuous afternoon would usually arrive via a few words delivered by the manager for publication on the club website or in the local press. A very rare treat comes with the recording of a few printable quotes from a key player.

I wanted to know much more. What jobs were these fellas getting up to tackle so soon after their starring roles in a spine-tingling afternoon? How long did it take for the adrenaline to disappear? Had winning a derby match seen off the return to work 'blues'?

My musings inspired by that single afternoon set the ball rolling. I became increasingly fascinated by both the lifestyle that is incumbent upon a non-league footballer and the array of personalities contained in the dressing rooms of these clubs.

I wanted to know about the humdrum. What motivates the semi-pros, with no chance of any national kudos for their efforts and a pay-packet that corresponds more closely to the paying fan than that of a world-renowned film star, to drag themselves into training and apply eyeballs-out intensity to their football on a miserable winter's day?

What is the thought process when climbing into the car or boarding a coach bound for a midweek game at Staines or Dover – in the knowledge that all there is to look forward to upon the final whistle is the return journey, introspective reflection during the night on their personal performance, and the dawn of another day that will involve a return to work or looking after the kids?

It was all these unanswered questions that stimulated the first green shoots of my book idea.

Continuing to ruminate on his armband-wearing day at Anfield, Jamie Collins captured the reality of both his own and his colleagues' existence.

'Apart from the football at Old Trafford [a sponsor had provided the Hawks players with tickets to watch that Sunday's tie between Manchester United and Spurs], my mind has been concentrated on getting back home in time for work on Monday morning. I have to be at Yeading at 9:30 to continue my other life, which is that of a football coach. And if I don't make it I will be in trouble. It's back to real life for everyone now, the bin man and the cabbie, the courier and the builder and the plumber.

'Anything you want done in your house we can get done. So if anybody needs any work done they should give us a call and we will get it sorted.'

Collins went on to win the Conference South division with Newport County in 2010, before following his manager at the Welsh club, Dean Holdsworth, in to the Football League with Aldershot. His return to Hampshire didn't last long and, prior to signing up for the high expectations that now prevail at the Spitfires', he spent a season and a half with Forest Green Rovers.

Everything about that itinerant career path is entirely in keeping with life outside the league. Budgetary restrictions mean the majority of clubs will offer one-year contracts only. Every close season is illuminated by a captivating merry-go-round. Each team's prospects for the forthcoming campaign are implicitly declared by their player trading.

I am writing in June 2013 with my journey laid out in front of me. The ten months through which I am preparing to live Eastleigh Football Club will deliver a series of events – good and bad, exhilarating and disheartening – that simply cannot be foreseen. The benefit of experience tells us that nothing is certain in this chaotic sport. It is possible to deduce, however, that freshly relegated Ebbsfleet United will be a serious threat to any side with title aspirations.

'The Fleet' have been, somewhat incongruously, purchased by a Kuwaiti investment group. Suddenly, a club that was confronted with a winding-up order, and seemingly on an unerringly downward spiral, has been transformed into the Chelsea of the Conference South.

To date, the new manager – Steve Brown, the ex-Charlton Athletic player – has hoovered up five players from Dover Athletic, where he was formerly assistant to their boss, Chris Kinnear. It is safe to assume the Ebbsfleet spend won't end there.

That is how quickly the landscape can change. Those Eastleigh supporters – and they weren't in a complete minority – who believed the club's development might benefit from another year at this level before breezing to the 2014 title, will be re-considering their confidence.

For Dover's part, they broke Eastleigh hearts in last month's play-offs and, after losing an engrossing final against Salisbury City, would have been considered strong favourites to challenge again. Not now.

Sutton United, who finished the last campaign like a train, are another outfit to have started their recruitment at the higher end of the accessible market. Chelmsford City, having recently appointed Dean Holdsworth to their helm, can be expected to do likewise.

If anything, the non-league transfer market holds greater fascination than the swollen spending and ceaseless rumour-mongering of its Premier League equivalent. The transient nature of many a player's relationship with his present team is best demonstrated by a scan through the pen pics in a match-day programme.

Take Glen Southam, captain of Eastleigh, a terrific footballer and a man who will feature prominently in the year ahead. His profile, which appeared last season, read:

'July 2012 signing from fellow Blue Square South side Dover Athletic. Experienced midfielder who has also seen service with Fulham, Tottenham Hotspur, Enfield, Bishop's Stortford, Boreham Wood, Dagenham & Redbridge (201/24), Hereford United (6/0), Histon, and Barnet (33/1). Glen also has 13 appearances to his name with 2 goals for the England 'C' side. Born in Enfield. August 27th, 1980.'

Glen, therefore, joined the Spitfires as a 31 year old with ten clubs already on his CV. A comparably nomadic resume would make any suitors higher up the food chain think twice about an individual's viability for recruitment.

Down here, it is accepted. Glen was sensational for the entirety of his first season at the Silverlake – culminating in the play-off second leg at Dover, in one of the finest, most dynamic, midfield performances I have ever witnessed.

He is very much considered to be 'one of us' and left the end of term presentation night weighed down by personal awards.

I picked out a random programme from one of last season's home matches – it was from the game with Bath City. Turning to the player opposition page, Charlie Griffin's profile stood out.

'Bath born, Charlie finally joined his home town club after a career that has been spent mainly in the high echelons of non-league or the lower reaches of the Football League.

'His CV includes spells with [deep breath] Chippenham Town, Swindon Town, Yeovil Town, Woking, Havant & Waterlooville, Forest Green Rovers, Wycombe Wanderers, Newport County, Salisbury City, and Stevenage. A consistent goalscorer throughout his career.'

That succession of sides took me long enough to type. Consider the time that is necessary to get around to playing for all of them.

The football world is claustrophobic, but, in the realms of the Conference Premier and below, it is a small village. Those on the inner circle thirstily drink in every minor detail that is available, not only concerning their own team, but any snippet that can be ascertained about its divisional counterparts. That enduring interest, for many devotees, often extends right across the non-league pyramid.

Non-league football is an esoteric attraction. For its supporters, however, their team's success or failure means every bit as much to them as Manchester United's and Chelsea's results do to their followers.

That statement, for some readers, will be confirmation of the blindingly obvious. Others will view it with a degree of incredulity. I have almost imperceptibly moved from the latter category to the former.

I can effortlessly recall leaving one of my formative matches at the Silverlake, an October 2009 FA Cup 3rd qualifying round win against Basingstoke Town, and ear-wigging a conversation between two disconcerted away fans.

They were scathing in their assessment of their team's display. The players didn't care, the manager was clueless and new blood was needed. The griping was no different from mine after many a past Everton defeat, nor from what you hear from myriad post-match phone-in drones decrying the hapless boss 'unable to take his side to the next level'.

I have to admit, I was somewhat confused by the passion of two blokes for Basingstoke Town. My original bewilderment, across the passage of the next year, gave way to sympathy, if not empathy. I was, gradually, growing to understand that the results and displays of a team that isn't crammed full of millionaires can matter. My attitude shift extended as far as realising it was acceptable to care beyond 5pm on Saturday about how Eastleigh had fared – despite 'knowing' that Everton were the prime concern.

My eureka moment occurred when I was simultaneously intoxicated by Eastleigh's 4–2 vanquishing of Havant & Waterlooville and cogitating over its emotional effect on the players.

How much exactly did such a victory mean to the Spitfires long-standing fans? Could it possibly provide the inner glow that I experience every single time Everton beat Liverpool (admittedly not something that happens with any regularity)?

The logical next step in my thoughts was to ponder how many of those Silverlake loyalists follow the team on its travels, wherever that might take them. What must life be like when away trips are not to West Ham United and Sunderland, or even Leyton Orient and Oxford United, but Weston-super-Mare and Bromley?

I now know, but back in what feels like the mists of time – although it was actually a mere two and a half years ago – I had not the slightest clue.

The premise for a season with the Spitfires was crystallising, then. I was becoming wrapped up in Eastleigh to the stage where I was ready to make a firmer commitment – when Howard Kendall spoke of his respective affiliations to Everton and Manchester City in terms of marriages and affairs he hit upon a perfect analogy.

I wanted to find out much more about life at a small, amiable, hesitantly aspirational, semi-professional football club.

To the broadest degree possible, I wanted to detail a Conference South season through not only my eyes, but those of the management, a selection of players, people who earn their living out of sight at the Silverlake, and a couple of devoted home and away attendees.

When I initially took my idea to the club's hierarchy, I was greeted with a cautiously positive response. There was enough encouragement to spur me into writing an analysis of each member of the first-team squad, based solely on my perception of each individual's personality. A large part of my original concept for a book was based on assessing the disparity that exists between on-pitch persona and the 'real' character of the same man before he steps across the white line.

As the 2010/2011 campaign played out, I was aware of how much the

Eastleigh bug was taking hold. I took a last-16 FA Trophy defeat against lowly Northern Premier League outfit Chasetown particularly personally – with a Wembley final becoming a teasing possibility, the team turned in a thoroughly supine display and were well beaten.

That flattening defeat was in keeping with a close to the season when the Spitfires flirted with the play-off positions, only to be undone by a series of poor home performances when the stronger sides came calling.

Such a moderate finish, combined with the necessity to rein in an inflated wage bill, had a destructive effect on the playing squad. No fewer than nine were released. Those included: Pete Adeniyi, Jamie Brown, Anthony Riviere, Richard Graham, and Shaun McAuley, players of whom I had undertaken my own form of (very) amateur psychoanalysis – and was eagerly readying myself to discover much more.

With my wasted efforts not amongst his list of concerns, Eastleigh's then Director of Football, the flamboyant Dave Malone, was busy explaining a change of philosophy at the club.

The idea, in brief, was to 'bring in and help to develop talented younger players'. The lure of working as 'full-time professionals' was the carrot on offer, as the club endeavoured to attract promising tyros to the Silverlake. This move was, Malone said, 'part of our medium-term plan to both achieve promotion and to change the ethos and culture of the club'.

So far, so exciting. I was actually taken with this bold blueprint. My older and wiser dad believed it to be the dressing up of a pressing need to drastically cut the budget. Time would prove him correct.

The opening to 2011/2012 cruelly exposed an inexperienced side that, in plain speak, was not fit for purpose. Still, the evidence was mounting that I cared more than I ever expected to. When Eastleigh won their first point of the season, at the fourth attempt, it came through a heroic backs-to-the-wall home performance against the eventual champions, Woking.

That goal-less draw owed much to the talismanic Brown – whose early season re-signing was testament to the complete lack of coherent thinking during a confused period at the Silverlake. My fraying nerves as the minutes ticked down on a notable result were eerily similar to those I have endured on countless Everton-watching days.

The older heads in the team, boosted by intermittent contributions from the fledglings, were just about keeping Eastleigh out of trouble when, in November 2011, came the news that would condemn the Spitfires' muddled strategy to the dustcart.

Stewart Donald, owner of Bridle Insurance, was to acquire a majority shareholding in Eastleigh FC and he had a plan all of his own.

A five-year vision was widely reported to include the achievement of Football League status – with development of the ground to match.

Subsequently, it seemed as if each week brought a fresh body into the team. Progressively, all but the very best of the callow 'full-timers' either drifted away or found themselves cast as reserves.

In February 2012, and after playing his part in overseeing the smooth transition of the Bridle takeover, Malone resigned. With him went my book. More important, admittedly, was the fact that Eastleigh were, by that time, competing on the pitch.

There was something of a scattergun approach, once he was furnished with a few quid, to Ian Baird's player-recruitment policy. I had long tired of his management. That was a further sign that I was taking Eastleigh to heart. How can anyone be a true fan if they haven't tackled the initiation process of calling for the head of at least one boss?

Included in the players to be enticed by the Silverlake revolution were: Damian Scannell, Daryl McMahon, and Bradley Bubb (on loan), an exceptional trio at this level. The Spitfires had a competitive team again and the buzz at the club had taken on an authentically optimistic tint.

(Incidentally, player recruitment was not problem free. One of Baird's early December 2011 purchases, Ali Fuseini, played one match before disappearing off the radar – leaving his manager explaining to the local radio station that he wasn't sure why the player hadn't reported in for a home game. It later transpired that a scrape with the land's traffic laws would curtail his availability for a while. He would not be seen in an Eastleigh shirt again.)

I was, by then, a home match regular. A casual relationship was becoming a binding commitment. Weekend plans were worked around Eastleigh, as opposed to the reverse. My enthusiasm hadn't yet spilled over into following the team on the road.

Indeed, the only game I'd been to as an Eastleigh away supporter – with the exception of the annual derby at Havant & Waterlooville – was the previous season at Basingstoke. I'd attended with my best friend of over 20 years standing, who was living in that area at the time.

I can picture to this day the baffled, almost sympathetic, look on his face when I leapt in the stand to greet each of the Spitfires' two goals and again as I squirmed through a late onslaught on their goal while they clung on for a victory.

I had been blindsided by Eastleigh Football Club and there would be no going back.

2

CROSSING THE RUBICON

Despite being replenished with various illustrious additions to their unit, Eastleigh had limped to the 2011/2012 finishing tape in 12th place. There was no dissuading me from my belief that the seven defeats suffered in the final 13 games, of which only three were won, should have resulted in a change of manager.

The new regime, however, had its own view. They opted to give the man in situ a chance – the argument being that he deserved a fair run, buoyed by the financial backing that he'd never previously known.

When the team kicked off against Boreham Wood on August 18th only two of its 11 starters – and not one of the five substitutes – had survived from the very first Eastleigh side I had watched three years earlier. One of those, Andy Forbes, had spent a chunk of that period at Woking and then Sutton United. The other was the dependable Tom Jordan.

Having grasped a marvellously generous £99 'early-bird' offer, I could now claim to be an Eastleigh season ticket holder – another definitive step on my initiation course.

Yet – the prospect of giving up a large part of a sweltering day, for hours spent aboard a mini-bus, had proven enough to stop me acting on any tentative thoughts I'd had of joining the jaunt to Hertfordshire.

Stewart Donald, the Bridle figurehead of the club, had announced subsidised travel for supporters to every one of the season's away days. No matter, on this day my £10 stayed rooted in my pocket.

I was somewhat astonished when news came through that Baird's expensively assembled team had been brushed aside 3–0 by 'The Wood'.

Ah well, teething problems. An opinion confirmed by a few brighter performances that followed. The apogee of that brief August 2012 flourish was undoubtedly a 3–0 clobbering of our local rivals at their Westleigh Park coliseum.

In many minds, this one included, the overwhelming nature of that victory was confirmation of Eastleigh's merit as bona fide promotion contenders. Furthermore, it was grist to the mill for wasp-chewing Hawks and other grizzly onlookers with a keen interest in all things Conference South, who viewed the Spitfires as that year's non-league big-spending bullies.

That stroll in the Havant sun took place on August 27th, 2012. The next away victory, in the belting rain and howling wind of Weston-super-Mare, would have to wait until February 5th, 2013.

The intervening months did not lack for drama. Subsequent to their derby win, Eastleigh suffered three straight defeats. The last of those, an ignominious 4–0 spanking at Billericay Town, did for Baird. It would also be the last away game I would miss during a topsy-turvy campaign.

I had contacted Stewart Donald during the close season to raise the prospect of reviving my idea for a season spent 'stalking' his club. That led to a chat with Mark Jewell – the man who was hired as Commercial Manager shortly after the formalities of the Bridle takeover were completed in February 2012.

I hadn't made sufficient headway to get the green light for a book, in readiness for what everybody at Eastleigh was hoping would be a momentous campaign. Nevertheless, the potential project's lustre never diminished in my mind.

Meanwhile, the supporters club (TSSC) was asking for volunteers to provide match reports for their 'dedicated' page in the programme. I jumped at the chance and filed my first synopsis after the win at Havant & Waterlooville.

My eagerness for becoming involved on the Eastleigh scene was hurrying along unabated. Along with my football-watching side-kick, I boarded the mini-bus for a short September trip to Dorchester Town. On the same day, we both became registered members of the Spitfires Supporters Club. That latter act was again, in part, due to my dad's eye for the bottom line – we would qualify for a cheaper seat on our maiden official away trip.

That night ended in a manner to which I had become accustomed over years spent travelling the country with Everton. After passing up a string of gilt-edge openings, Eastleigh conceded a free-kick deep into injury time 25 yards from goal. When Jamie Reid, a handy substitute, stepped up to take the set-piece, I knew the script. From the second Reid hit the ball it was only going to end up in the top corner.

I was utterly deflated. The journey home was dominated by discussion about the pros and cons of Baird and his latest raft of signings. I was hooked.

Four days after Dorchester came the aforementioned Billericay surrender. When the Spitfires next took to the road for a league game, 24 days later, Richard Hill was the club's manager of three weeks. Owing to a couple of comprehensive home wins, Mr Hill's reign had started prosperously.

My dad and I were back on the TSSC mini-bus journeying to Farnborough, both full of anticipation for what a revived team, back on their travels, might summon. That transpired to be an utterly abject performance, on a filthy night, which brought home to the new boss the size of the task he had signed up to.

Kudos to Richard, though, for shaking the hand of every travelling fan in the clubhouse post-match – albeit bear in mind our mode of transport and you'll have an inkling as to how long that took him.

In common with many Spitfires at that time, an FA Cup 3rd qualifying round tie at Gloucester City really captured my imagination. Again, with Dad in tow, I joined the substantial support bound for the West Country. The prospect of a first-round meeting with a football league club quickens the pulse of many a non-league club's supporters. I now belonged to this category and so was suitably despondent after a limp 1–0 defeat. Not as crushed as Mark Jewell, however, who had witnessed a budding source of ample revenue disappear down the tubes.

The test of my growing attachment would come the following weekend. Would I have the appetite for a 270-mile round journey to Chelmsford, in order that I could sit in a stand on a scathingly cold afternoon, with little hope of seeing an Eastleigh win?

I didn't need to think twice. We were there, revelling in a doggedly earned 1–1 draw, heading and kicking every ball clear as late pressure on the Spitfires' goal became near unbearable to watch.

And so it continued for the remainder of the season. My reporting evolved from a collection of musings based on my memory of the 90 minutes of action to detailed recollections of the match with a sprinkling of my own thoughts thrown in. Depending on your tastes, I produced either an accurate and in-depth review of events or a long-winded re-hash. If Eastleigh were playing football I was there, notebook and pencil in hand.

A consequent and welcome by-product of my writing was a developing, tangible connection to the club. I took on the mantle of 'official website reporter' and in turn was treated to free entry to games. You can imagine who was even more pleased about that than me.

A feature of being part of the official away troop is the 50 minutes or so spent in the opposition clubhouse once the game is over. It's something I had envisaged would be a necessary burden – to be tolerated rather than enjoyed.

That brief excursion into enemy territory is actually another enamouring facet associated with watching your football away from the bright lights of the Premier League. The very same men you've spent 90 minutes encouraging, cheering, and yes, chastising, mingle as part of the throng.

Plenty are happy to chat with their supporters – although, with the exception of infrequent cordial exchanges with the current boss, I've not, as I write, spoken with any of Eastleigh's playing or management troop.

I have become a recognised face though, to the point where this summer (2013) I was asked if I would take on responsibility for much of what is intended to be a refreshed and comprehensive match-day programme for season 2013/2014.

Bingo. In a meeting with Bridle's freshest off-field recruit, the Sales & Marketing Manager Owen Clark, to discuss content for the new magazine, I broached the book subject once more.

In an instant, an agreement was struck.

It was a perfect pick me up after the fashion in which season 2012/2013 had reached its brutal climax. As a rule I avoid football clichés, but the preceding nine months had transpired to be the definitive 'rollercoaster ride'.

The inability to pick up even the remotest scrap away from the snug environs of the Silverlake, allied to an unprecedented streak of weather-enforced cancellations, had Eastleigh sitting in 21st place on January 5th, 2013.

The transformation sparked by that low, which was plumbed after a 3–1 humbling at Bromley, began a stirring rise all the way to an eventual 4th-place finish.

On that grim afternoon at Bromley's Hayes Lane ground, I was sat a few seats away from Farnborough's manager – one Spencer Day. Formerly Spencer

Trethewy, he was, in 1992, the teenager who rode to the rescue of Aldershot Town, only for some pesky problems, well reported at the time, to thwart his ambitions.

My gripe with Day at Bromley was in the extent of his apparent satisfaction at watching Eastleigh disintegrate – losing an early lead to be well beaten by a side whose midfield was bossed by a certain Ali Fuseini (he turned up on that day alright).

If I and my mini-bus accomplices – no coach required for this one – were fed up, that was nothing compared to the dark mood that had beset Richard Hill.

The discontent of both manager and owner was evident in the fresh bodies subsequently rushed in through the door and from some individuals on the Hayes Lane pitch either rarely, or never, being seen in Spitfires blue again. By the time Billericay were at the Silverlake, just over 72 hours later, Eastleigh were fielding a brand new central-defensive pairing. The starting 11 contained six changes from that of three days earlier.

That single match at Bromley is viewed through many Spitfires' eyes as *the* watershed moment in the club's fortunes.

From dishing out a 5–0 hiding to Billericay to winning the final home match against Truro City in front of a 1,320 crowd – a figure boosted considerably by the innovative decision to grant free entry to all – the tidings between January and April were predominantly of the happy variety.

When Dover Athletic turned up and scored within 20 seconds of the first leg of May's play-off semi-final, then, it came as something of a shock. A visiting goal in the dying minutes – made all the more painful for being scored by Daryl McMahon, who had left the Silverlake under a cloud earlier in the season – left Eastleigh with a mountain to climb in the return fixture.

They so nearly managed to surmount that peak and recover a 3–1 deficit.

If you still have any doubt, or are given future cause to do so, regarding how much their football club means to any group of supporters – not only those who follow the game's pre-eminent outfits – I would implore you to search the internet for footage of Damian Scannell's 90th-minute equalising goal at Dover's Crabble Athletic Ground.

Firstly, the sheer audacity and class of the finish represents proof that there are some exceptional footballers operating in the perceived backwaters of the game.

Essentially though, the joy of watching that goal comes with savouring the wholly unconstrained and loopy collective reaction of the band of Spitfires congregated on the terrace behind.

Delirium doesn't begin to describe it. I was sat, predictably, in the ground's main stand and, along with my dad, celebrated with an abandon that wouldn't be wise in among the quietly simmering home support at a Premier League stadium.

In fact, our response and that of Richard Hill's son, Dan, who was sat nearby, would have had only one consequence had it occurred at say, Newcastle United's St James' Park: we'd have been subjected to some tasty abuse and immediately ejected.

That conundrum had exercised my mind as the season was drawing to a close and promotion was becoming a realistic prospect. As I have described, one of the real joys for me in finding this spiritual home at Eastleigh, and in the Conference South, is the freedom to watch, unencumbered by aggravation, from a prime viewing spot.

I was well aware that if I were to position myself in with the home masses at, for example, Kenilworth Road or The Racecourse Ground, sitting on my hands would be a necessity. Nevertheless, such concerns had, by now, been well and truly usurped by my fixation with Eastleigh's on-pitch destiny. Inevitably, results had become king.

When I had re-composed myself, I hastily scribbled down details of Scannell's effort, which had levelled the tie at 3–3 on aggregate. My notes were rammed full of details of a slew of Spitfires' chances. For 120 minutes they absolutely dominated a side that had consistently proved itself one of the strongest in the league.

When it came to recording the penalty shoot-out particulars, I was compelled to note that Dover converted four of their spot-kicks to Eastleigh's two.

My after-match feelings, and those of virtually every single Spitfire present, were a mixture of immense pride and absolute dejection. The players, some still in tears, trudged over to their band of followers, shook hands, and shared consolatory words. It was a scene you could only witness at a non-league ground. Southam, especially, was distraught.

Over the following week, with that epic afternoon in Kent still fresh in the memory, I kept my chin up. Cliché alert here again, but it was a case of 'taking the positives'. In my report's summing up I said:

'For Eastleigh's part, a talented, spirited, confident, and driven group, led by an astute manager, can only inspire excitement and great anticipation for when we come back and do it all over again.'

There have been days since when the stinging reality has hit hard. The team was so close to, yet so incredibly far from, achieving the first aim in the club's grand plan.

The reality stretches out before us. Forty-two matches, in an ultra-competitive league. Title rivals with no less desire than Eastleigh – and whose actions are solidifying their ambition. It will be an irresistible, exciting, gut-wrenching, and bumpy ride.

3

WHERE ARE WE NOW?

While I write today (June 19th, 2013), the sporting headlines are concentrated on the release of the fixtures for the looming Premier League season. This focus overshadows news of the England cricket team competing in a global one-day international semi-final (the Champions Trophy match against South Africa) and latest missives from the British & Irish Lions rugby tour of Australia.

Further confirmation then of the remarkable global commercial monster that England's foremost football division has become. I have cast a cursory Evertonian glance towards the traditional standout dates – recognisable to football devotees the land over – first match, Boxing Day opposition, when are the dreaded derby games?

It is the fixture announcement in little over a fortnight, though, that will prick my interest to a far greater degree. I will be able to pore over the clashes that lie in wait, knowing that they are destined to affect my day-to-day existence.

That list of names and dates will dictate when I will travel to each of the eclectic bunch of Conference South venues. It informs me of the 21 days on which I am due to consume my football at the Silverlake.

I am sure that a personally hitherto unknown sense of belonging and shared experience has expedited my immersion in Eastleigh FC. However extreme the emotion Everton aroused in me on any given day, I was consigned to a long and lonely journey home. The adrenaline-charged high, or temporarily debilitating low, rapidly gave way to the solitude of hours on the motorways of England.

Even on the infrequent occasions when my dad or sister accompanied me on the 500-mile round trip to Goodison, 5pm always seemed like the time when we were prematurely departing the hub of an event – leaving everybody else to indulge in tribal celebration or post-mortem, or to simply drag match day beyond its frenzied 90 minutes.

Living on the south coast and actively supporting Everton do not form a sociable combination. With the exception of family members, there is nobody with whom to drink in the thrill of victory or to turn to in the wake of a decidedly soul-sapping afternoon.

Now, as a fully paid-up member of the Spitfires Supporters Club, every element of fortune visited upon my/our team is felt as part of a like-minded group.

In brief, Eastleigh have taken precedence in all things football.

Now, if, in the name of Eastleigh, I have to sacrifice watching Everton on the television, so be it. It is hard to enunciate quite what a shift in attitude even that represents.

4

THE SEASON IS COMING

The internet message board is the modern-day gauge of fan opinion – and home, it has to be said, to the airing of some bizarre thoughts.

Foremost, and typical of the fan-base of any football team, dialogue centres on the side itself. Beyond the enduring contemplation of the relative merits, or otherwise, of the manager and players, there is microscopic inspection of every minor detail surrounding the club. And at Eastleigh, thanks to the continuing Bridle revolution, there is a lot of that.

Of more clout than its virtual world equivalent was the real life 'Fans Forum' – hosted by the club on June 4th. Stewart Donald and Richard Hill placed themselves at the mercy of approximately 50 inquisitors. The range of matters on which they were challenged illustrates the broad canvas of worries borne by any fan in the deeper reaches of football.

The first question of the night centred on the progress of Stewart's attempts to purchase the ground. He was able to confirm that a deal had been concluded three days earlier – Stewart and four fellow directors had become the new owners of the Silverlake Stadium.

As fans of any club will attest, if underlying worries exist about who might potentially hold the deeds to the stadium that their team calls home, it is a matter of overwhelming concern – above even results. Without a ground to call its own, a team loses its identity, at best, and faces extinction, at worst.

Assurances that the Silverlake is in safe hands and, moreover, that the fiercely ambitious owners will not have their lofty plans stymied by an inability to implement necessary ground improvements were welcome and re-assuring.

Asked about what those improvements might encompass, and when dealing with enquiries about sponsorship agreements and enhanced stadium accessibility, the chairman tackled every query with the openness for which he has become known (indeed, at times it is a trait that has attracted criticism; particularly after he publicised a proposed transfer deal, which subsequently collapsed, on the aforementioned supporters message board).

I've made clear my fondness for Eastleigh's characterful home. It is, however, reflective of a club that has come a long way in a relatively short space of time.

I was playing for the local Hampshire League team, Pirelli General, in the late 1990s when the bigger side down the road were only operating at one level above – the Wessex League.

Under the management of Paul Doswell, who is now in charge at Sutton United, the Spitfires began their surge up the football ladder with promotion into Division One East of the Southern League in 2003. A 4th-place finish there was no bar to further progression. The FA's 2004 re-structuring of their pyramid resulted in Eastleigh jumping up into the Isthmian League's Premier Division.

On something of a roll, Doswell's team won that league's promotion play-offs. In the space of three years, a club from the lowly Wessex League had gained Conference South status.

During their incipient Silverlake tenure, the Bridle newcomers have found it's not just the ground that betrayed Eastleigh's relatively recent standing.

There has, therefore, been a firm commitment to increased professionalism in every area of the club's operation. It is a thankless task. Changes in personnel or custom are a jolt to the folk who are comfortable with the status quo. Stewart even received some mild laments about staff changes from one forum attendee who missed a friendly face, now departed.

I can empathise with the fear of change. When tickets were gratis, and the Silverlake consequently overflowing for the final home match of last season, I had my reservations about the stand – *my* stand – being choc-full. The half time queue for a tea crept so far along the touchline I didn't bother joining it. Getting away from the car park was a more demanding exercise than usual.

Stewart spoke on stage of his acute awareness of how much it means to Eastleigh supporters to feel fully involved with their club. He understands the 'we're all in it together' mentality and believes it crucial that no division is ever allowed to form between owner and fans. He also has an insatiable appetite for success. He wants the '500 of us' to expand in number. There will be further free entry matches this coming season and a determined drive to recruit new fans.

For me, and plenty of others, aspects of this promised growth will be uncomfortable – in some cases, painfully so. Inherently, we don't like change. Notwithstanding that, there are occasions when it is a necessary process, after which we wonder what we were afraid of.

That is the case with Eastleigh FC now. This is a club that is thoroughly geared up to 'kick-on'. If it does just that, every sacrifice will be worthwhile.

Stewart's honesty is mirrored by that of Richard Hill. The manager told his rapt audience of a hankering to get the team out of the 'sh★★ league' they are in. His frustration with the Conference South owes much to the manner in which he believes Eastleigh are treated by some 'disrespectful' opponents, jealous of his club's perceived 'riches'. The standard of officiating is Richard's perpetual gripe, an annoyance he shares with an overwhelming majority of his team's supporters.

The manager spoke of his plan for the year ahead. He intends to work with a bunch of 13 or 14 high-class, largely versatile players. Many of those were integral to last term's storm to the finish line. That eminent bunch will be supplemented by any youngsters emerging through the ranks.

These men, the squad being formulated by the Spitfires' boss, are those I hope to get to know and, in turn, tell you all about. In corresponding manner to the pre-conceived ideas I had developed about the personalities of the Eastleigh class of 2010/2011, I have developed my own impression of each of the current group.

Off-field advances at Eastleigh include players and management being put forward to offer their thoughts on the day's game for the delectation of 'Spitfire TV'. The ever burgeoning world of social media, and its allure for footballers, means we learn more about their lifestyle and character than was possible before.

All these insights, though, are afforded at specific standpoints in time. We never know what is really said in the dressing room after a sloppy defeat or a sterling win. There is little access into the hangover from either scenario.

Players, manager, supporters, chairman, and other Eastleigh staff will come together to form a story that begins with pre-season training on July 1st and ends... where?

One certainty is that Richard will make a wonderful subject. Candid, passionate, and fiery, but with a dry sense of humour, he is a manager with a breadth of football experience.

Our first extended conversation occurred at the June 4th forum. I was astonished at how receptive he was to my wish to get up close and personal to his team, and deliver a blow-by-blow account of their impending campaign. It is a privilege most football managers would not be willing to extend.

So, what do I expect to encounter? Who are the men charged with defining the next chapter in the history of Eastleigh FC?

Speaking at the forum, Richard expressed a belief that his team was limited by their 'one-dimensional' style of play last season. That description evokes images of a side's goalkeeper, or its burly centre-halves, smashing the ball to an area in the vicinity of their immobile striker.

For the Spitfires, however, the manager's contention was that for his unit to function at full capacity, every on-field move had to flow through their exceptional playmaker Jai Reason.

Reason's back-story is one that is representative of many footballers at this level. He was a trainee at a professional outfit – in this instance, Ipswich Town – before being forced to pursue his career outside the league. When he signed for Eastleigh, Jai took the calculated gamble of dropping a division from his former home at Braintree Town.

His prime reason for seeking a move away from that club was their insistence on positioning him on the left of their midfield. What a waste. Jai is blessed with ability on a par with his attacking counterparts at numerous Football League clubs.

I don't say that lightly. His vision, touch, intelligence, and football intuition blend to set him apart. Opposing fans are wont to see his bulky figure and dismiss as no threat the 'fat ba★★★★★' in Eastleigh's midfield. Their preconceptions are routinely washed away with Jai's first sweet pass or sublime touch of the day.

As for the individual, I have little idea. His Twitter account reveals someone who takes his football extremely seriously, enjoys a holiday in the sun, and invests huge stock in the art of motivation. Jai's match persona doesn't offer even a trace of the real person inside the 'trequartista'. Whatever the state of play, he often bears the look of a man who has just been gazumped on his dream home.

Jai's on-pitch maturity belies his 23 years and, assuming – and fervently hoping – he isn't spirited away by a bigger gun, he will be fundamental to the cause if the Spitfires are to achieve their soaring ambitions.

When things were apparently unravelling at the mid-point of last season, and a few of the higher-profile players were jumping ship, my prime worry in life – beyond trivialities such as global peace and the health and well-being of family and friends – was that I would flick on Eastleigh's website to be greeted by news that Jai was the club's latest absconder. With the side struggling, his classy presence provided a beacon of joy at a testing time – akin perhaps to Matthew Le Tissier decorating a seemingly forever relegation-threatened Southampton outfit with his otherworldly talent.

Jai was the only authentic threat to Glen Southam's anointing as last term's 'Player of the Year'. While Jai's outward nature is introspective, Southam is as expressive an individual as you will see on a football pitch. His will to win is second to nobody. After some of the more horrible displays away from home in 2012/2013 it was all Glen could do to drag himself off the pitch, so forlorn was he at the latest setback.

Another whose social media communication offers a glimpse of the personality within, Glen strikes me as having limitless energy – an attribute that is replicated in his effervescent play – but alongside his jovial bearing there is a serious side.

Every set of fans holds in common one player in whom their collective eyes will never see any wrong. At the Silverlake, that privilege – deservedly – belongs to Glen Southam. His obvious desire, commitment and undoubted quality are a beguiling mix.

Glen's popularity at Eastleigh is nothing new. On occasion during his first season with the Spitfires, supporters of one of his former clubs, Barnet, showed up solely to watch their old favourite.

Glen gave probably his finest individual performance at Eastleigh, to date, for the play-off second-leg tie at Dover. As captain he is an impeccable ambassador for his club.

I might be a bit old now – 35 – to count footballers as heroes, but it is certainly acceptable to hold them in high esteem. There is an oft repeated adage that you should never meet your heroes, for you can only be disappointed. That is the real risk that is attached to an undertaking such as this. For all the intrigue of unpeeling the layers that separate the supporter from his football team, there is a co-existent worry that once you delve beneath the skin you might not like what you find. With Glen, I am confident that such concern is unwarranted – even if his tweeting does disclose a fondness for reality television.

One of Eastleigh's better known 'names' is that of Craig McAllister. The centre-forward has had a transient career that reached its peak when he was part of the Crawley Town team, which won promotion into the Football League in 2011. In that same year he played for the Sussex club in their FA Cup fifth-round game at Manchester United – a match they lost by a single goal.

Now then, there will be an elevated degree of personal interest when I encounter Craig. He first signed for Eastleigh in 1999 during their Wessex League days. It was Craig's goal-scoring prowess for Pirelli General that captured the Spitfires' attention. To this day, my football claim to fame is that said flood of goals wouldn't have been possible without this author's unerringly consistent and accurate left-foot delivery.

I'll continue to state that as fact for ever more because, quite frankly, there is no available evidence to the contrary. And we all love to ponder regretfully on our own individual tales of 'what might have been'.

There is a possibility, probably measured somewhere between 95 and 100 in percentage terms, that Craig will fail to recall my cultured left peg of yore. Hey-ho.

Craig was one of last summer's top-end purchases and he splits supporter opinion like none of his current colleagues. There are those who appreciate a selfless forward, one who never shies away from the weekly physical battering to which he is subjected; the alternative view being that he doesn't consistently fulfil the foremost requirement of a striker – scoring goals.

I am in the former camp and value the contribution of a man who I remember as a shy, gangly teenager turning up at Pirelli in the hope of finding a game. His rather more powerful frame was, for the final months of last season, accompanied in attack by Chris Zebroski.

Zebroski had been released by Cheltenham Town and was snapped up this summer by Newport County. It is one of the wonders of football, that different pairs of eyes can watch exactly the same action and see something entirely different.

If the weight of McAllister's effectiveness arouses a variety of views, then Zebroski provoked sentiment at extreme ends of the 'approval-rating-ometer'.

He was either lazy and disinterested or hard-working and possessed of an ability rarely seen in Conference South football.

Nobody will dissuade me from the fact that the latter description is correct. That is why Zebroski has landed straight back in league football despite a, shall we say, chequered – and well-documented – off-field history.

Yemi Odubade has been recruited in Zebroski's stead. In keeping with the manager's desire to have in his ranks men who are accomplished in more than one role, Yemi can play as a striker or out on either flank. His is a name I recognise owing to its regular appearance in *The Non-League Paper* and from sporadically chugging through Sky's *Soccer Saturday* vidiprinter. He has made the long trip to Eastleigh from Gateshead, and was previously with Oxford United.

When I tuned in to ESPN's coverage of an FA Cup tie between Cheltenham Town and Hereford United in December 2012, I was hugely impressed by Will Evans and his Hereford midfield cohorts, Harry Pell and Sam Clucas. Pell quickly moved on to AFC Wimbledon and is surely destined to go even higher. Only yesterday (June 20th), news broke that Clucas is destined for League Two newcomers, Mansfield Town. I didn't expect for one minute to be seeing the third of that excellent triumvirate at the Silverlake. Will's signing this summer is authentic proof of Eastleigh's drive to get out of this 'sh★★ league'.

Two acquisitions that administered an equivalent statement of intent arrived, in quick succession in January 2013, after what will henceforth be known as 'the Bromley game'.

Dean Beckwith is a tough and unyielding centre-half who has played in the Football League for both Hereford and Northampton Town. In the traditions of many of the game's 'stoppers', he principally concerns himself with his number one duty: defending his goal, be that via winning a series of aerial duels, throwing himself in the way of shots or doing whatever else is required to keep his opposition out.

That is not to say Dean lacks 'football ability'. He is composed on the ball and has a gratifying knack of passing it to a team-mate. I expect to meet a man who is a consummate professional and, perhaps, a touch reserved in character.

Chris Todd's name will be familiar to many football watchers. He has formed a superb partnership with Beckwith. I am especially looking forward to finding out more about Chris. Him being somebody who devotes a portion of his existence to modelling, I am unlikely to happen upon a man of shrinking disposition.

Chris has a story to tell of far more import than anything that has happened in his professional life – which has been spent on both sides of the league/non-league divide. He has detailed that story in his own tome – *More Than Football in the Blood*. The book is an account of Chris's encounter with, and happily subsequent recovery from, the chronic myeloid leukaemia with which he was diagnosed in 2008.

From afar, Chris appears to have crammed a lot into his 31 years. He operates on the pitch with command and authority and, I imagine, would be the sort of man you'd be delighted to share a pint with.

Nervous, Me?

I haven't sought to disguise my excitement and anticipation at being granted the freedom to become ingrained with all things Eastleigh for a year.

At this stage, however, days from the start of pre-season training, I should admit to feelings of nerves and trepidation.

Embedding into any new environment can be a daunting prospect. A football training ground and its dressing room relation are unforgiving places. Outsiders are habitually viewed with an initial degree of suspicion. I imagine any wariness has the potential to be exacerbated by the reason for my presence. It is here that I hope my balanced outlook – something I strive to make a feature of every match report – wins trust.

Then there is the human desire, which exists in all of us, to be accepted. That particular longing grows ever more intense as I prepare to become absorbed into the routines of a group of men that I am used to monitoring from a safe distance.

Any crack at kidding myself that I am perfectly relaxed about that prospect is undermined by the recurring dreams that involve me taking part in training and playing for the team. Now, that is a scenario to have us all running for the hills.

Transfer gossip is the summer lifeblood for all football supporters and myriad prospective signings continue to be bandied about by excited Spitfires

– in addition to the cloak-and-dagger, 'can't say who, but we're after a striker who's played at a much higher level' internet declarations.

We keenly await news of the next arrival, but first, a word about the rest of the men already in place.

First-choice goalkeeper, Ross Flitney, had his day on the back pages in 2005. Unfortunately, Ross's headline-grabbing act was to be sent off 80 seconds into a League Cup match when playing for Barnet at Old Trafford.

Nevertheless, he is a fine 'keeper. Ross was signed by Richard to replace previous Number 1, Jack Dovey. Jack was fantastic when he came to Eastleigh on loan from Southampton in October 2011. When that temporary deal was made permanent ahead of the 2012/2013 season, it was a move greeted with some acclaim by fans of his new club.

After Jack had endured a testing period, something to be expected with a rookie 20-year-old goalkeeper, Richard decided that he owed men like Beckwith and Todd a comparably sure presence behind them. He has that in the man brought in from Gillingham.

Similar to Jai Reason, there is nothing in Ross's inscrutable bearing to inform of his broader personality. Notwithstanding that, occasional pictures of our 'keeper in a social environment do reveal his singular dress sense.

Eastleigh goalkeeper musings complete, I switched off my laptop. Within half an hour my dad was on the phone.

'Have you read about Eastleigh's latest signings?'

An hour after writing about my expectation that there were legs left in Richard Hill's trading, the club released news about both Ben Strevens' arrival and Sam Wilson's return.

The wary tone in my dad's voice when he mentioned Strevens' age – 33 – was my daily cutting reminder that any personal aspirations to smash a winning goal for Everton at the Kop end or even, more prosaically, make a living in the less salubrious environs of a Southend United or Rochdale – barring re-incarnation – are gone.

I knew Strevens' name and associated it with Dagenham & Redbridge. A scanning of his Wikipedia page, the refuge of the lazy, confirmed his more notable scoring feats had come when playing for the Daggers and, before that, Barnet. He was released at the end of a short second stint at Dagenham & Redbridge in May.

Sam is at the other end of the age-range and is coming back to the Silverlake after a year away. He made a few fleeting appearances as a 17 year old under Ian Baird in 2011/2012 and is good enough to have spent a trial period at Fulham. I remember a wisp of a lad with cunning movement. He is a yard of pace and a few pounds of red meat away from being a seriously dangerous centre-forward.

As a rule, football supporters love to see a local lad flourish. The heights of elation reached upon watching your team score can be indescribable. When the goal is delivered by the boot of a hometown boy the high comes rocket-fuelled. Sam has been at Poole Town and Gosport Borough during the past season. I hope – and believe – he can prove what a waste of talent that was now he's back where he belongs.

Speaking of talent, Dan Spence was signed on a cold Tuesday in February this year (2013). The first that any Spitfire, other than those within the 'inner circle', knew of Dan's arrival was when we set eyes on the team-sheet for a match that night against Salisbury City and saw his name pencilled in at left-back.

He played like he'd been part of the team for an eon. Dan is one of those footballers whose every action radiates an impression that the game comes absurdly easy. His touch is exemplary and positioning uncanny. Perhaps his extreme comfort on the pitch should come as little surprise. Dan was reared at Reading – and subsequently spent time with Glenn Hoddle's football academy in Spain.

In only his fourth Spitfires appearance, Dan suffered a shoulder injury, which ended his season. All we've seen of him since has been his sitting among us civilians in the stand or adroitly manipulating a ball on the field at half-time.

My research into his personality – yes, ok, following him on Twitter – unearths a man (I can barely believe he is merely 23 years old) with a zest for life, nay, a bon viveur. Recent pictures attributed to Dan's account have included an action shot of his diving into a tropical sea and then dressed to the nines at Royal Ascot.

What is for certain is that Richard Hill believes Dan will be a valuable presence in the coming year. Judged on initial impressions, I agree.

Michael Green was the collateral damage on Dan's debut night – his being the spot nicked by the new boy. That, from my vantage point, was the harshest of all the calls Richard had to make during his first term in charge.

When Ian Baird still controlled team matters, the touchline cry of 'GREEEEENER' would reverberate around my skull for about three days following any game. A cultured full-back, who when playing with an uncluttered mind has no peers in the division, Michael never seemed to fit the Baird bill.

If I were cynical, I'd put that down to both 'Greener's' innate tendency to pass the ball on the floor and his aptitude for stealing possession off an opposing winger by applying certain finesse to the process without any need to upend said rival. But I'm not.

Make no mistake, Michael has an on-pitch nasty streak – evidenced by his needless sending-off in the first leg of the Dover play-off.

There are three clues, available for public consumption, regarding 'Greener's' character.

He clearly thrives on confidence and never played with the same freedom when subjected to the constant chuntering of Baird – or the erstwhile manager's assistant of the day.

In 2011, the defender's form for AFC Totton in their Southern League South & West Division Championship winning team earned him a move to League Two side Port Vale. Michael had no trouble adapting to the increased footballing demands. Away from the game though, and to Eastleigh's considerable benefit, the yearning for home was too much. He came back to the Silverlake that October – having previously been released by Baird without playing a game in 2009.

If you believe his bolt from the Potteries displays a character flaw (although depending on personal tastes you might consider it a sign of supreme wisdom), Michael's reaction to being demoted to the bench against Salisbury City would set you straight.

When he returned against Havant & Waterlooville a fortnight later, Greener was one of the best players on the pitch in a fiercely contested 2–2 draw.

Damian Scannell's first Eastleigh coming was in the opening half of the 2007/2008 campaign. His sparkling attacking play (so I'm told) was rewarded with a move to Southend United in League One.

By the time of his popular re-signing – an early statement of Bridle's intent – Damian was a Dagenham & Redbridge player, discontented with the constraints imposed on his game by then Daggers' manager John Still's rudimentary brand of football.

When he is in rude health, there is little that can stop 'Scans'. Unfortunately, that fitness caveat is all too relevant. The stout Wayne Rooney is often described as needing a continual diet of match action in order that he is wholly primed. Damian is no different.

The sight alone of him at full throttle, and with ball at feet, can incite mayhem in opposing defences. It would be easy to interpret Damian's, at once, expressive and languid style as symptoms of an easy-going personality. I wouldn't be particularly taken aback, though, to happen upon a man who cares deeply about his game and how it is perceived.

I've detected that serious aspect to Scans' persona by dint of his isolated, but unmistakably angry, ripostes whenever he has taken umbrage at his manager's touchline appraisals. Brave man.

That then, is our starting cast. With a fair wind, all will roll up on July 1st prepped and ready for what everybody associated with Eastleigh FC profoundly hopes will be an epochal ten months.

5

THE INSIDE TRACK

Wednesday, June 26th

Offered three wishes, many is the football fan who might use one of those to request that they be privy to all the inside information at 'their' club. There is a keen sense of satisfaction that comes with knowing, long before anybody else, which players might be on their way in or heading in the opposite direction. The day-to-day soap opera that is life behind the scenes at any football club is eternally gripping for many of its followers.

To have access to that wider daily script is something the mere man in the stand can only dream of. When we hand our money over at the gate, it buys us the right to watch the 90 minutes of football. Any peripheral information or action – be that the manager's latest transfer target or a dressing room incident – is kept in house. We are left to speculate and indulge in animated conversations, all fuelled by hearsay or personal theories and prejudices.

I could never have imagined when I was progressively falling under the spell of Eastleigh FC that I would one day have the first-team boss's phone number saved in my own handset. Little more, that when I – slightly anxiously – punched in that number to discuss my attending the opening day of pre-season training, it would prompt a returned call that stretched beyond an hour.

As we closed our conversation, Richard was extremely apologetic for not getting back to me instantly. In fact, I was surprised his reply was so rapid – it came within two days during an exceptionally busy period and with him having already made contact via e-mail.

A large part of Richard's time had been taken up by trying to secure the purchase of Elliot Frear, a winger who spent a chunk of last season on loan at Salisbury City from Exeter City.

Frear was a perpetual menace in his two appearances against the Spitfires during that spell in Wiltshire and would have provided a perfect solution to the present attacking left-sided hole in the team. Having agreed to sign, and had his requested wage agreed to (more than Exeter could offer, a testimony to the financial predicament of many Football League clubs if ever there was), Frear began playing for time.

Then, the enemy of many a football manager reared his head – the football agent. Frear's deal-maker wanted extra cash for his client and a contract that lasted two months longer than the ten originally stipulated.

Richard's immediate response was to say, 'Deal off.' Or at least I think that's the phrase he told me he used.

There was another twist to come, however. The apologetic player was soon in touch, desperately sorry for his representative's demands and avowing his desire to move to the Silverlake. After some consideration, Richard gave Frear a second chance.

For his willingness to put the money man's intervention to one side, Richard was rewarded a day later with news, from the player, that Salisbury were prepared to match Eastleigh's offer.

'Deal off' were most certainly not the words used this time.

That is the lot of a manager in the market for players. For every successfully concluded deal, there are countless blind alleys to walk, near misses, and knock-backs.

Damian Scannell, meanwhile, had told his manager that he would not be able to commit to day-time training. Sessions are held on Monday, Tuesday and Thursday mornings. Without being completely full-time, everything about the Spitfires' operation fits strictly professional criteria.

Last term's revival coincided with the implementation of this new training regime. It swiftly produced a fitter, more cohesive unit.

There was, initially, a degree of leniency extended to players unable to meet the extended hours. Now, with a fresh campaign ahead, and having had six months to make necessary lifestyle adjustments, there can be no leeway allowed. With a heavy heart, Richard began looking for a new home for one of his star players – a task all the more frustrating for the fact that it was likely to conclude with the strengthening of a promotion rival.

That was until a swift change of mind, which provided a cheering antidote to the Frear saga. Scannell wants to stay.

The extra hours spent together have forged something deeper than a keenly drilled football team. There is time to sit and eat in one another's company and to chat freely before and after the hard work of the day. A greater camaraderie exists between colleagues, tightly bound during each 90 minutes of combat. The close-knit feel that has developed within the squad is plainly identifiable from the side-lines.

It is the significance that Richard places on his players being of the 'right character' that rules Corey King out of Eastleigh's future plans. Corey is a teenage winger, who has already been employed by Reading, Yeovil Town and Macclesfield Town. He is a scintillating footballer with extraordinary potential.

When we have been treated to bursts of Corey's play, he has exhibited flashes of outrageous skill and blinding pace, which, crucially, he knows how to utilise in a game environment. Still, there was another side in the slumped shoulders and dropped head after a misplaced pass or stalled break.

Richard has arranged for the player to train at Maidenhead United. That club are managed by Johnson Hippolyte, a gentleman perfectly suited to honing this youngster's energies and abilities to maximum effect.

I sincerely hope that the player, who rendered a plethora of AFC Bournemouth academy tyros scared of their own shadows during a Hampshire Senior Cup match in January, and in April entered the field with five minutes left on the clock at Bath City to twist the blood of his direct opponent and lay on a joyous 94th-minute equaliser, can fulfil his vast potential.

Richard, then, is still casting around for the final cogs in his promotion spinning wheel.

There is what the manager confesses to being a 'cheeky' £2,000 bid lodged with Maidenhead for their 20-year-old left-winger Harry Pritchard. He is a player of whom I wrote after Eastleigh faced him in March:

'It was evident from the early exchanges that Pritchard was central to the Magpies' game plan. At every opportunity the left-winger's colleagues sought to either spring him in behind [Mitchell] Nelson or feed the ball to his feet so allowing him the freedom to run at the Spitfires' right-back.'

Alex Lacey, another January 2013 acquisition – on a temporary basis from Luton Town – and a player who made his debut on the same night as Dean Beckwith three days after the Bromley horror show, may yet be back.

Alex is a sublime defender and I, in common with every other Spitfire, had long since written off any possibility of seeing him in the blue of Eastleigh again. Richard accepts that Alex's return would leave him top-heavy in defensive areas, but there is simply no passing up the opportunity to have a player of that calibre on the books – it is surely a long shot, however.

Richard happened upon Alex's initial availability by chance. During his discussions with the then Luton boss, Paul Buckle, regarding the Beckwith transfer, Buckle mentioned his intention to send the young centre-back away for a loan period. The boss was straight on the case, speaking to his contacts across the football village's garden fence.

Richard will not consider a player fit for his club without first engaging in a series of background checks. The comparatively enormous catalogue of names in the lower and non-league brochure makes this a particularly exacting task. The capacity to tap into a variety of trusted sources therefore is invaluable.

Jason Bristow, in charge at Basingstoke Town, was informed on Lacey and provided a glowing testimony. When Bristow chooses to cash in his return favour, he's due.

I have my fingers crossed that John Still, now at the Luton helm, gives Lacey's move his blessing before watching over the stylish 20 year old during the Hatters' pre-season.

I did cautiously ask Richard if Weston-super-Mare's left-winger, Dayle Grubb, a player who caught my eye on a rain-lashed night in February and whose terrific range of passing and ceaselessly accurate crossing stuck in the memory, was somebody he had considered for his left-wing vacuum.

Yes, but he wasn't prepared to pay a fee, which Weston were sure to want for an accomplished 21 year old.

(Or, if you prefer, 'Wind yer neck in and leave the managing to me.') Fair point. My place on the scouting staff is on hold for now.

David Wheeler, the standout midfielder at Staines Town, is another player to interest Richard. Wheeler's recent two-week trial at Exeter, and his stated intention to move to a Football League club, makes his signing unlikely. An enquiry for Wheeler is, nevertheless, affirmation of Richard's determination to attract the very best footballers possible to the Silverlake.

I also broached, with Richard, the latest message-board maelstrom, which surrounds the wisdom of Eastleigh's reserve/development team being withdrawn from the Suburban League and entering only the weaker Wyvern League (the previous preference was to field a team in both).

I understand the club's thinking. One-off matches will be arranged against contemporary academy outfits in order to provide the competitive action required by any fledglings with first-team pretensions. The decision also ends the nonsense of the second string playing at the same time as their senior counterparts.

If I had needed any further convincing that this change is for the good, Richard's reference to the £40,000 invested to run the 'stiffs' last season would have been a clincher. Lads of 17 and 18 were in receipt of upwards of £100 each week to play in a Conference South team's reserve 11. Madness.

I am still to see, with my own eyes, the excess of demands that add up to the load of managing Eastleigh Football Club, but the frenetic and all-consuming nature of the job is rapidly becoming very clear.

A 'football tragic' being personally treated to the insight and thoughts of *his* team's manager is akin to a wine connoisseur having an unimpeded lifetime run of Bordeaux's galaxy of vineyards. My 'pass' into the players' first day back next Monday is, metaphorically speaking, appreciatively clutched tightly to my chest.

It might not be many people's idea of a dream, but, here and now, I am living the Spitfires' version.

Speaking to my dad soon after chatting to Richard, I told him of my hour-long conversation with Eastleigh's boss.

'What – on your phone bill?'

6

THE NEW BOY

It's Monday, July 1ˢᵗ, and the country's collective sporting eyes are cast towards Wimbledon, where both Andy Murray and Laura Robson are attempting to reach the quarter-finals at the All England Club (with a 50% success rate, as it happened).

Football is featured as far inside the back pages as I can ever remember. The British & Irish Lions series levelling defeat in Australia two days ago and fall-out from yesterday's British Grand Prix are hogging the non-tennis headlines.

The only newsworthy story around the national game is today being David Moyes' first day in his new job at Manchester United.

If the former Everton boss was nervous on his morning drive to Carrington, I experienced a few butterflies of my own as I travelled to the Silverlake Stadium.

I was on my way to take in the opening day of Eastleigh's pre-season training. It is hot and I can count myself extremely fortunate not to have been subjected to the exertions imposed on the 20 players present.

While waiting for the squad and management to emerge from their 'what I did over the summer' chat in the comfort of the dressing room, I was able to luxuriate in being the only soul in what has become my football home.

With the sun shining on a lush green pitch – albeit one that, despite much recent attention, a few players expressed continuing concern about – and the empty stand at my back, it was a pleasure to stand idle for ten minutes and, in a wonderfully serene atmosphere, thrust my mind back to some of the more epic games I've been entranced by in that very arena. There is something inexplicably evocative about an empty football ground.

When Glen Southam emerged he augmented my impression of him as being an affable soul. Without yet knowing my identity or why I was stood incongruously alone next to the players' tunnel, he stopped and chatted happily.

The Spitfires captain was hankering to get back to work. Indeed, he confessed that within weeks of the holiday period starting his feet were growing itchy.

I did wonder how many of Moyes' players would, in the last few minutes before their annual physical torment kicked off, be replicating Glen's fuelling strategy – a Mars Bar, washed down by a can of Red Bull.

Through my research (Twitter again), I was aware that a few of the squad were fervently hoping they would see plenty of footballs during this elongated pre-season period – as opposed to being force-fed a diet of 'old school' running.

My concerns for the day were more prosaic. I simply wanted to turn up on time and then slip comfortably into the background while the players started work. Being introduced as the individual who would be on the team's tail throughout the next ten months was a daunting prospect, but thanks to Richard's easy nature – and demand that his men be completely honest in their discussions with me – it was a painless experience. The manager's short explanation to his players, that I was writing a book detailing their efforts across the season, was rounded off by his saying, 'We all know what's going to make it successful.' The message is clear from day one.

Long gone are the days of footballers waddling out, full of holiday indulgence and stiff from long afternoons on the sun lounger, to start the summer slog. There was the odd minor paunch on display, but certainly nothing irreparable with August 17th (the season's opening day) so far away. Actually, the importance these players place on maintaining a robust physical condition was striking.

On the green expanse of the Wellington Sports Ground, located within a Ross Flitney punt of the Silverlake, and with Southampton's Academy side training in the distance – a buzz of fast and sharp movement, and all replete with customary heart rate monitors – Eastleigh's finest indulged in a leisurely jog with balls at feet.

During the first directed discipline, Richard interjected with punchy instructions and clarification of his wider expectations.

'I like my players to know what I'm thinking. I believe we're back a week too early, but I couldn't turn down the friendly with Wycombe next week. You don't need to impress me today. It's a long pre-season. We start at 60% and build.'

The reason for this extensive preparation period is the strange – actually, plain daft – decision of the Football Conference to begin their season two weeks after the Football League gets underway.

There are innumerable arguments to be made against their thinking – assuming there has been any. The chief complication of the staggered starts, on a practical note, is provided by league clubs being at entirely different stages of readiness to non-league adversaries when friendly fixtures are played. A consequence of every league team's need to be ripe by August 3rd is that warm-up matches against higher-ranked opposition have to be scheduled earlier than preferred.

That is why Richard faces the situation whereby, eight days after their first workout following an eight-week break – and a full one month and eight days ahead of their first meaningful fixture – he will send his team out for a game against Wycombe Wanderers.

The lack of competitive early August football vexes Stewart Donald. He and his 21 league counterparts are irrationally deprived of a banker home late summer Saturday fixture; a veritable money spinner when compared to a re-arranged Tuesday night match in February.

When the players, all with running shoes on their feet – an express directive in close season correspondence sent out by the manager – first gathered today, the air of collective apprehension was unmistakable. Regardless of each man's individual status – veteran, apprentice, or anywhere in between – the day of their reconvening plainly inspires the type of nerves we all remember from early Septembers and the trudge back to school.

There is a keen anticipation to catch up with friends and swap stories about their respective weeks away. But there is also the self-doubt; 'Have I prepared enough?', 'He looks like he's been keeping well.' There is mild dread regarding the work ahead. It will hurt. Ergo, human nature dictates there must be an element of fear. Finally, every individual wants to hit the ground running, to catch the boss's eye early.

As the day's demands were steadily ramped up, a few of the men with some way to go in terms of hitting their required fitness levels began to blow. Jamie Collins is going to need his hours on the training ground. That much was quickly apparent to Richard, who quietly disclosed that Collins's is a character that might, on occasion, benefit from some managerial 'encouragement'. No sooner had Richard uttered to that effect than he wandered over and said the same thing to the player, at that moment, red-faced and a tad distracted by his endeavours to complete the 30 seconds demanded on the latest arduous exercise of a ten-station circuit.

Scannell doesn't relish the grind of putting work into his legs. He does, though, bear the burden with a smile and a certain sense of fun that is in accord with his personality. The winger, a favourite of his 'gaffer' (a moniker for the manager that I can confirm stubbornly, and rather charmingly, endures in a football environment), was one of the first to approach me and ask about the book.

Jack Dovey and Craig McAllister were similarly forthcoming. And, lo and behold, McAllister remembered my cultured left peg at Pirelli – well, he recalled playing in the same side anyway. Same thing, surely?

There was a marked communal sense of relief when the real hard work kicked in. If the worst part of requiring painful dental work is the time in the waiting room beforehand, minutes spent anticipating the ordeal ahead, then the pre-season equivalent is the calm before the intense storm of energy-stripping, oxygen-thieving exercise.

Completion of the session's first serious running drill acted like a pin, inserted to deflate the tension of every participant. With endorphins flowing and a few of the players reassured about their condition after hurdling a first physical barrier, the chatter over water bottles became decidedly more animated. Holidays, individual fitness and, of course, girls were all enthusiastically discussed, before two minutes was up and it was back to the mill.

Reason, Todd, Beckwith, McAllister, Southam and the youngster, Matt Gray, stood apart for their ability to focus on each new task in an instant. Like the batsman who trains his mind to devote complete concentration to every ball he faces and can switch off for the precious seconds in between, those men displayed a canny knack of being right 'at it' on the sound of a prompting whistle.

The huge slice of trust that Richard places in his players is obvious. There is an onus on his men to accept a degree of personal responsibility. If Collins is still off the pace – and quite so laid back – in mid-August then it becomes a problem. This is a player, though, who is well versed, after nine previous professional pre-seasons, in how best to manage his body.

The manager spoke individually to Beckwith and Strevens, telling both that if at any stage of this period they'd benefit from reining in their efforts they were free to do so – as long as they 'don't take the mick'. There is no danger of that. My first look at the players working away from the glare of match day told me that this is not a bunch interested in cutting corners.

When the group was split into two sets of ten – one completing a couple of trips around their training circuit, the other, under the watchful eye of Richard's assistant, Guy Butters, being kept on the move while familiarising themselves again with the football – a discernible hum of industry hovered overhead.

That's not to say there was an absence of humour. McAllister, in particular, is ready with a quick retort to any gentle ribbing. Not many of my erstwhile team-mate's (that's the last time I'll mention that fact, I promise) comebacks are suitable for reprise here, but they unfailingly draw a laugh.

When it was time for the day's final slog, the circle of football boots optimistically carried out by each player for later use remained redundant. As weary legs followed Richard to the starting point for one more lung-bursting run, Southam's mild frustration betrayed him.

'First day back, take it easy, yeah, Pinocchio.'

If he heard it, Richard actively ignored the barb.

Green completed his lap of the field, which was looking bigger with each passing minute, his face decorated with a gleaming smile. McAllister and Scannell suffered, but drove to the very last yard nevertheless. Ross Flitney was one of the early finishers and encouraged his colleagues until the end.

Ross jovially suggested that I join in a future session to add an extra dimension of insight for the book. I brushed that idea aside with a lame – well-rehearsed – excuse about my Achilles.

With their two hours of graft at an end, and drinks – all bar Scannell's who had unwittingly left his idling in the changing room – and untouched boots being collected, Jai Reason muttered along the lines of being a member of 'Eastleigh Running Club'.

He – and the rest – will have been delighted when the balls took centre stage on Tuesday. Not so much with the order of play on Thursday, which, it was agreed after a brief meeting of Richard, Guy, and Andy Cook's (the club's Sports Therapist/Fitness Guru) minds, will consist of repeated running drills – and, when they're finished, a bit more running by the sounds of it.

It is all structured work, however. When he was manager at Sheffield Wednesday during the mid-1980s, Howard Wilkinson sent his players out every Tuesday for a 90-minute run, the Yorkshireman's misguided thought process being that his charges would then be fully prepped on match day. Mercifully, advances in sports science (and common sense) have enabled evolution beyond such ill-conceived notions.

I will be back next Monday – and I am already counting the hours. This now feels real. It undoubtedly felt odd to be rubbing shoulders with the men who were, until now – even allowing for the inclusive nature of non-league football – set apart by their respective roles as player to my supporter.

It was only chatting to McAllister that I heard any mention of Dover and last season's cruel conclusion. With a sudden steely edge to his voice, the big striker told me that there was no desire on his part to be forced into the unpredictable play-offs again. This is a team bent on being champions.

Seven days' distance will throw light on any changes in training ground dynamic and industry. Will a further week's physical labour under the players' collective belts result in evidently improved strength and endurance? Has Will Evans – a peripheral and slightly shy presence on his first day but, unquestionably, a very good footballer – be emerging from his shell? Is Collins stepping on the gas? The only certainty will be a prevailing work ethic.

'It is impossible to be good in training every day. It is impossible to play well every single week. There is never an excuse for failing to work hard and falling below your standards.' Richard Hill. July 1st, 2013.

After my day as one of the 'new boys', I am more excited than ever by the prospect of being front row for this next instalment in the history of Eastleigh Football Club.

7

STEREOTYPES

Bare pitch, an oppressively baking sun, full water bottles quickly becoming handy stand-ins for failing kettles, and footballers bent to the knee vomiting on the unforgiving ground, which has been jarring at their bones for the preceding two hours.

This is the image that readily springs to the mind of anybody cognisant with football's pre-season traumas. Steadily, those dated perceptions are being washed away.

Nature initially looked to be serving up a miserable summer for 2013. That particular weather prediction, however, has proven premature. Yesterday, Andy Murray astonished the nation by beating the world's number one tennis player, Novak Djokovic, in a brutal Wimbledon final, played in Centre Court temperatures that peaked at above 40 degrees.

Today, Monday, July 8th, the sun is back. Fantastic news – for those of us who treasure every sizzling summer's day. Purgatory for Eastleigh's footballers, consigned to completing a fourth training session since returning after their break and the second to come under my transfixed gaze, in severely testing conditions.

Attached to the profusion of tributes heading in Murray's direction is widespread awe regarding his physical prowess. It is no less extraordinary watching a group of men, who it should be remembered are employed to play in the sixth tier of English football, train so ferociously in the furnace-like heat. The relentless energy levels on display are astonishing.

As the squad congregated prior to the final exercise of the day – a ten-a-side match played on a small-scale pitch – Chris Todd mentioned that he was feeling stiff as a board.

That was enough for Richard to declare that the players could finish for the day, right there and then, and head inside. The manager actually began striding purposefully away from the playing area.

A chastened pack followed and, in the manner of cheeky schoolboys having stepped uncharacteristically out of line, persuaded their boss that they wanted to continue to the end of their scheduled day's work.

It was a telling vignette. At once it was immediately clear who the authority figure in this environment is and evidence of a team ethic, which has at its core the principles of hard work.

By this time, every individual was worn by nearly two hours of high-intensity labour. Nobody dropped to their haunches, or worse, tailed off to re-produce their morning's food – or indeed anything else a fatiguing system could no longer hold down.

Not only does professional pride and competitiveness dictate that a sizeable majority of players would no sooner clock back in after their holidays carrying a rogue extra half-stone than they would trade their job for a career down the pits; there is a purpose, an end result to be achieved with every drill that is performed.

Eastleigh's Sports Therapist and the brain behind many of the more punishing elements of training, Andy Cook, enjoyed a professional playing career, which began, in 1997, with a home debut for Southampton against Manchester United and encompassed further stops at Exeter City, Swansea City, Portsmouth, and Millwall.

While Guy Butters led the team through three gentle laps of the cavernous field – 'Southam won't like this, he'll be on the phone later asking what the point of that was,' chimed Richard – Andy regaled me with tales of horrific-sounding ordeals Frank Burrows, at Swansea, used to dress up as pre-season running.

Sam Wilson confirmed as he gratefully tied his boots that however rigorous the demands placed on a player's body, it never feels quite so strenuous when a ball is involved. Not dissimilar to resourcefully hiding some snippets of carrot or courgette in your child's pizza.

There is an instinctive tendency imbued in some to whinge about any non-football graft demanded of them. The reality is, footballers love playing football, but they are keenly aware of what needs doing. Reason might mutter about being part of a 'running club' – and he did again today – but this is the same man who was tweeting about having finished his gym session last Thursday night – when the side had been put through their limb-shredding paces only hours earlier.

This is the man who, instead of eating the lunch fare on offer, chooses to pack his own fastidiously pre-prepared meal.

The discipline at the post-training feed is remarkable. I can still recall the voracious hunger that followed a particularly enthusiastic workout – just. Not for this lot though plates stacked high with the pasta, rice, bread, and potatoes on offer. Southam's fist sized portion of pasta in tomato sauce wouldn't kill the pangs of a boisterous juvenile fresh from charging about the playground.

Scannell, who has vowed abstinence from red meat and alcohol until the year's end, was ready to make do with salad and yoghurt, until coerced by the men charged with feeding the playing staff into trying a slice of vegetarian quiche.

Whatever unique diets those two men are adhering to, they would be wise to copyright the contents. 'Effervescent' is a word I repeatedly attributed to Southam when detailing his performances last season. Scannell is cut from stone, mainly.

Today's initial hard running involved a complex exercise, which required all participants to be as sharp of the mind as in their feet. A lazy aspersion cast on footballers is that they have been blessed with the ability to play this game in some sort of compromise, whereby they must pay for their gifts with significant rations of brain cells.

Witness a slickly managed training pitch and that wayward theory will be wiped from your mind for good.

With cones spread across the ground in various bewildering – to all but the trained eye – patterns and having received the most cursory of explanations, delivered in clipped, crisp, and forceful speech, every player flies into action.

I consider myself capable of understanding and following instructions. As the more intricate elements of the session commence, though, I am as in the dark regarding what is about to unfold as I had been prior the commands of Messrs Hill, Butters, or Cook.

What's more, there isn't the luxury of taking a back seat and watching what your mate does first, no switching off at the back of the classroom and turning to your more attentive neighbour for a personal description of the task in hand.

Suddenly, there is a torrent of movement, footballs fizzing hither and thither. Every pass is struck with an implicit question affixed for its recipient. 'How good is your touch?' The answer, almost invariably, is positive.

Watching a match from on-high in supporter mode, the touch and clean striking of the ball on display are taken for granted. Sure, we wish we could do the same, but in the same way it is possible to become complacent about having a proficient family doctor, we don't think too much about the hours of work that have gone into delivering the end product.

Thanks to the factor 50 lathered over any exposed skin on my body today, I won't be hurrying to my GP with severe sunburn. My pale frame drew a few jocular comments from Scannell, a sign at least of my presence being accepted.

'Training ground banter.' Three words that strike directly at the worst fears of some of the game's quieter personalities. Football is littered with sombre tales of men of sufficient talent to have established a professional career, if only for a thicker skin.

I don't mind confessing that the reputed 'boys' club' mentality of the dressing room had ingrained a few unfavourable pre-conceptions in my mind. I wasn't expecting the Eastleigh branch of Club 18–30, but I have been surprised by the low-key nature of any light-hearted exchanges. I'm sure that as individuals grow into the season and training slants away from its fitness-building emphasis, laughter and loud voices will fill the air to a greater degree.

From the idle chit-chat that it is impossible to avoid over-hearing, Green is a target for some gentle prodding when the team are clustered within four walls. A blossoming new relationship is a matter of keen interest for a faction of his colleagues.

Haircuts and dress-sense are fair game, although that didn't prevent Will Evans being confident enough to bestride his new workplace in a pair of risky pink shorts. The signing from Hereford looks to be gradually settling into his new surrounds.

First-time observers of Will's midfield play could interpret his lolloping and lazy on-pitch stride as that of a man without the necessary bite to operate in the heat of a midfield battle. That would be a hasty – and inaccurate – judgement. Of the four major arrivals to date – the other three being Yemi Odubade, Jamie Collins, and Ben Strevens, it is the raw 21 year old who is hitting his straps the quickest.

Nevertheless, watching Strevens at close hand, every one of his 15 years spent higher up the ladder – nine of which came in the football league – is reflected in his lightning movement and a ferocious shot. If he misses the target it is not for lack of conviction.

Strevens' imprecise radar was not uncommon in a session that, for all the composure, pace, and intelligence exhibited, was marked for its erratic finishing.

It is a truism that the hardest feat in the game is to actually put the ball between the two white posts. That's a task Flitney wants to make even more daunting for opposing forwards this season by wearing an all-white kit – 'If a forward glances up and sees a big white c★★★ coming at them, the goal will look smaller.'

Typical eccentric goalkeeper's bluster? One of the greatest custodians in history, Everton's Neville Southall, reverted to wearing all black late in his career for the exact same reason – and he took his guide from the most legendary of shot-stoppers, the Russian Lev Yashin.

The premium on those men who can be relied upon to complete what is, ultimately, the object of football is reflected right throughout the game.

Tonight, Christian Benteke, Aston Villa's young Belgian striker, submitted a transfer request. That act will inevitably spark the interest of every club with aspirations towards winning the Premier League. Benteke's demand is further reason for lament among those people – me included – disenchanted by the widening gap between the Premier League's elite and the rest.

It is only fair to acknowledge, then, that exactly the same circle of life is a feature right throughout the football world. Once the Eastleigh bug took hold, I was quickly resigned to the club's better players being destined for brighter lights – and wholly accepting of that reality.

Now that I'm sitting on the other side of the fence, with the Spitfires being one of the gilded Conference South minority who can offer a mix of competitive terms, near full-time football, and authentic table-topping potential, I plan to enjoy it. Nevertheless, nobody will be taking Stewart or Richard for a ride.

During today's training match, I remarked to Richard that one of the young players was particularly apt at finding space and taking up smart positions on the field. His four-word reply? 'He's not good enough.' Additionally, the player in question, yet to wear a first-team shirt in competitive action, wants £200 every week. Not on this manager's watch.

There are numerous players whose progress has been checked by their own misguided demands. Equally, a footballer can fall short entirely because one man with a stack of experience, stockpiled across a long career, has detected deficiencies in his game that are unclear to the less-trained eye.

'Our Friends from Surrey'

We now know that Richard and his team will, this forthcoming season, be first placed under scrutiny in a match against Sutton United at the Silverlake – where, in my solitary pre-training ten minutes today, I tip-toed onto the pitch in the cautious fashion of a civilian walking onto the wicket at Lord's, unable to resist the urge of treading hallowed ground when the opportunity arose.

When the fixtures were released last Wednesday (July 3rd) I was sat at my laptop, a mix of excited anticipation and nerves.

Why any anxiety over the publishing of the dates for 42 football matches? My sister's wedding is taking place on Saturday, August 24th. The very prospect that a derby against Havant & Waterlooville might be taking place during the nuptials was of chief concern.

I frenziedly scrolled down to find the opponents for that day and saw the name Basingstoke Town. A nice local trip and one I'd ideally not miss, but, with the Hawks rolling into town two days later, I would have shaken on that deal.

The prospect of Sutton first up delighted me and, judging by message board consensus, a good deal of fellow Spitfires.

Richard was less enthusiastic. My argument is that having a blockbusting opening tie – for Sutton, with their cavalcade of former Eastleigh men (including a certain Mr Doswell at the helm) and collection of extremely good footballers, are a genuine title rival – is sure to keep minds focused ahead of 'kick-off'.

The boss is of the view that his side will not be taking a definitive shape until ten games in. He would rather take on the league's big-hitters when the team has a familiar look and everything is clicking – we hope.

There, in microcosm, is the contrast between the clinical mind of a pragmatic manager and a supporter's short-term, less-reasoned, outlook.

There is no denying that, for us fans, the prospect of an immediate skirmish

against serious competition, and the return of Dale Binns, Mitchell Nelson –
'he's bound to have one good game before the end of August,' Richard
lamented – Tom Jordan, Jamie Slabber, and the rest, is one that has you counting
the sleeps.

For now, Wycombe Wanderers, fresh from a win in the sun at Westleigh
Park on Saturday, arrive for the Silverlake's first football since Daryl McMahon's
ugly, but crucial, play-off semi-final goal for Dover on April 30th.

That occasion remains so fresh in the memory, but here we go again.
Despite the manager's initial reluctance to be playing so early into his
preparations, the players are already straining at the leash. They want to play
football. This game will enable them to iron out stiff bodies and satisfy a craving.

The pre-season friendly is a curious thing, no more than a public workout.
This edition, Richard believes, will be to the benefit of Doswell who, still living
locally, is a banker presence at the Silverlake if his own side are not in action.

The inclusion of trialists in the mix only adds to the confusion. Most will
prove to be transient souls. They may turn up in different colours during the
course of the season and ignite on the terraces a 'didn't he turn out here once'
discussion.

Already, a few aspirants are included among the Eastleigh training ground
number. One, a defender, for now known as 'Chris', is progressively playing his
way into Richard's thoughts. Another, a right-winger let go by Queen's Park
Rangers in 2011, and who despite his mere 23 years has experience of football
with another 10 (ten) clubs, has speed of foot and the skill to match.

At this stage of his work, Richard must also contend with sporadic left-
field situations thrust upon him. One such happening occurred last weekend.
After some persistent badgering of Stewart by an acquaintance, said
acquaintance's son, with no contract on the table from the Football League club
where he has been on the books, was given the chance to be assessed by
Eastleigh's management.

T. Rialist is a good footballer, no doubt. He is not, though, befitting of his
father's grand sell during a telephone conversation with Richard, which
suggested the lad is a genetically modified replica of a 1970s Dutch
international. Nor will he be to the standard that Eastleigh desire.

Nevertheless, no stone can be left unturned in Richard's pursuit of a
promotion-winning formula. As the manager polished off lunch there was a

letter – with DVD enclosed – to peruse over. It had been sent by a player who is eager to join this burgeoning club.

As I was set to leave after Monday's session, I happened to casually mention to Richard that I was hoping to speak with Owen Clark in the coming days and would confirm my willingness with the Sales & Marketing Manager to ghost-write the manager's programme notes each week.

'Owen?'

'Yeah.'

'Owen Clark?'

'Yeah.'

'He's left the club.'

Wow. I didn't see that one coming. Details of Owen's departure are not for here, but suddenly the man with whom I'd established a host of ideas for the programme and, crucially, who had given the club's consent to the publishing of this book was gone.

E-mails to Ray Murphy (Club Secretary) and Mark Jewell (Commercial Manager) were dispensed forthwith.

Stewart has other concerns. The beleaguered chairman has taken to the Spitfires internet forum, on the day of the Wycombe match, to express his exasperation at some of the moans concerning admission prices for friendly games (£8 adults, £5 concessions, Under 7s free).

Before later explaining that prices need to be at a certain level to satisfy the visiting club and their desire for a healthy gate receipt sum to share in, Stewart concluded his opening post with the following plaintive statement:

'Sometimes these threads make you realise you will never please everybody, so why make the financial and emotional effort?'

It isn't only on the training pitch that temperatures are broiling at Eastleigh FC.

8

THE PHONEY WAR

Not so long ago I'd have earnestly nodded along if anybody dismissed attending pre-season friendlies as a futile exercise.

Spending money to watch an open training session is undoubtedly an extravagance (some of my dad's pecuniary conscience must be rubbing off). It is far too early to be watching football – July 9th, two days after the Wimbledon Men's final and with the first ball of an Ashes series to be delivered the following morning. On an emotional level, the unmistakable first-day buzz is neutered somewhat when you have already seen the new signings in action and the team performing in their glistening new strip.

In fact, Eastleigh took to the field in the change version of their sparkling Nike number, only after some serious panic and foot to the floor industry ensured the away kit's arrival earlier in the day.

The perpetually harangued Mark Jewell revealed as much in a post-match conversation, during which I embarked upon my re-selling job for the book.

Across the quarter-hour I spent with Mark, he was interrupted on at least four occasions – each time to be confronted with a question about a different subject that falls under his remit. If you are employed by Stewart Donald, you earn your wage.

With a share of the responsibility for bringing every last drop of cash possible into the Silverlake coffers, Mark wouldn't have been greatly enamoured by a paltry attendance of 150 for the run-out against Wycombe.

In gift of a free press-admission – a privilege I'll never take for granted – I didn't count among the official number of spectators. Until this year, I would not have been inside the ground at all.

I can't remember the exact moment when I decided that these warm-up 'clashes' were not for me, nor when I last paid into one.

In the naivety of youth, I'd experience the same pang of excitement at the prospect of watching some mid to late summer football as I would when clutching a prized ticket for a full-tilt league encounter or cup-tie.

Twenty-one years on from the event, I can recall the thrill upon realising that a July family stay in Liverpool would coincide with the visit to Goodison Park of Borussia Monchengladbach. The swathe of empty seats mattered little to me, as I sat rapt by Everton's 1–0 win.

I was no less keen to watch Real Sociedad go through the motions on a balmy Friday night at The Dell – chuckling inwardly at the Spaniards' 1–0 win.

As recently as 1997, I traipsed up to L4 to watch the first day of the now defunct, and not remotely missed, pre-season Umbro Cup. Everton's spectacularly underwhelming match against Ajax Amsterdam was won through a goal scored by the late, great, Gary Speed.

If you ever find yourself wondering how much to read in to pre-season form, consider that Howard Kendall's side went on to escape relegation on the ensuing campaign's final day.

The Dutch masters, who boasted in their ranks the calibre of Edwin Van Der Sar, Danny Blind, Jari Litmanen, the De Boer brothers – Frank and Ronald – Michael Laudrup, and Shota Arveladze, went on to win their domestic league by a margin of 17 points and smashed their nearest challengers, PSV Eindhoven, by five goals to nil in a landslide Dutch cup final win.

Another precautionary tale to be drawn from that day on Merseyside is that, in the afternoon's second match, Newcastle United's Alan Shearer, then the England national team's talismanic striker, sustained the ankle ligament injury that wrecked his and, in turn, his club's season. Easy does it, boys.

It might be that, sub-consciously, the pallid offering served up at Goodison by such an illustrious European football name as Ajax swore me off going to any more of these games.

Even when considering this book's undertaking, I viewed the imminent cluster of pre-season fixtures as a series of appointments in the diary – obligations to fulfil as a matter of duty. But, in common with the players I've been watching train, my unseasonal sighting of footballs had whet my appetite for something resembling the 'real' stuff.

When I spoke to Southam on that first day back, he meant every word of his assertion that July 1st was a particularly early return and that this meeting with Wycombe would arrive too soon.

Richard told me on the morning after the match that his captain, as well as Reason and McAllister, was 'grumpy' about being left on the side-lines for kick-off. The manager had considered that a game being played five and a half weeks before Sutton rock up provided the scope to look at trialists and tinker with formations.

I had noted during Monday's training, which made no concessions in its intensity for the fact there would be a match approximately 32 hours later, that there had been no work carried out specifically with Wycombe Wanderers in mind.

The absence of anything tangible riding on the result drew none of the sting from Southam when he entered proceedings for the second 45 minutes. He began by upending the League Two team's tricky forward, Junior Morais, and competed throughout with a ferociousness that would not have been out of place in a Champions League match.

Not one for suppressing his feelings, Eastleigh's captain let his simmering frustration rise to the surface when Ramone Rose (our contract-seeking ex-QPR man) ignored his 40-yard run and opted, wastefully, to shoot on goal.

That is the lot of many a trialist – unable to resist trying to go the extra yard to impress. I was interested to get Richard's take on how his three job-seekers had fared.

Danny Smith, he of the DVD and letter, started the game. Wheels can be made to turn very quickly when there is even the remotest potential chance to improve the playing unit. Rose and the third trialist, once of Oxford United, both had their chance in the second half.

It was fascinating to hear Richard empathise with the situation of these three individuals. He considers their predicament to be no different to that of anybody else looking for work in any competitive industry. The manager, therefore, believes that he owes his hopefuls more than just a cursory look at their wares on the training field. They should be allowed the opportunity to showcase their abilities in battle – or at least in something that resembles a contest.

It is then up to the manager to scrupulously assess what he sees. In the stand we can afford to lazily pass our opinion before moving on to the evening's next topic of discussion.

I am no less guilty of this than my fellow supporters. To me, Rose's final ball and decision-making continue to cancel out the pace and directness he offers. Smith was one-paced and without any single 'trick' that would elevate his game to the standard required here. The man from Oxford needed too many touches and had an unfortunate habit of playing 'hospital balls' to Dan Spence – a man whose renewed fitness is a serious boon for the Spitfires.

All write-offs then? Not so. It must be considered how these men's 'trialist' status affected their product – be that a dazzling display that won't be mirrored with a contract safely tucked under the belt or a nervy outing with its roots in angst relating to where the next pound is coming from.

In a pure footballing sense, Richard said he may see just one aspect in an individual's play he believes to be worthy of perseverance. Attention to detail must be meticulous in order to guard against the passing up of a potential jewel.

Aside from a wisp of exasperation regarding the confusion of some supporters when presented with his starting 11 (the exclusion of Reason and Southam, even at this early stage, had the conspiracy theorists all aflutter), the manager was cautiously satisfied with the night's work.

The 3–0 reverse was of no consequence – especially with, as anticipated, the League Two side's comparatively earlier start to pre-season being apparent in their superior game sharpness.

Richard did acknowledge that if similar lapses were repeated four matches down the line then he would be vexed. As a man with wisdom amassed from upwards of 25 previous pre-season campaigns as player, manager, and coach, however, Richard knows what he wants, and when, from this period.

The accuracy of the boss's foresight was confirmed on Tuesday by the watching presence of Paul Doswell. Even with Doswell's Sutton team not due at the Silverlake until mid-August, Richard was not about to offer up any clues about what he will face. A rudimentary 4-4-2 system was employed – a formation that is not on the agenda when we start to play for points.

Whether Doswell's apparent preference for watching the Spitfires when his own team are not in action, as opposed to viewing more imminent adversaries – RH 'You can bet that if Sutton were playing Basingstoke Town on the first day and they were playing a friendly on Tuesday, Doswell wouldn't have been at that' – will cost his club, we'll know in April.

In truth, it is unlikely. Doswell's body of work at the Silverlake was remarkable. Success has followed at Gander Green Lane, where a revival of the outfit who enjoyed their day in the national spotlight after beating Coventry City in the 1989 FA Cup is well underway.

Standing in my shorts and t-shirt (another reason why pre-season friendlies might just be winning me over) and talking to Kieran James – a young Eastleigh devotee – prior to the match, I learned another piece of news that confirmed football's food chain to be in full working order.

Michael Kurn, the club's enthusiastic and slick PA man for the past year, has been enticed away by the glamour of the mic at Crawley Town. There's just no loyalty left in the game.

By the time an hour had elapsed on Tuesday, I was already considering the possibility that Gareth Ainsworth in the visitors' dug-out would be wondering whether Will Evans might improve his squad. The introverted new recruit was colossal. A definite victim of white-line fever – Will's personality was transformed into ultra-competitive, spiky football monster upon the sound of the first whistle – if his outing was a preview of what we can expect for the next ten months and beyond, Eastleigh Football Club has a gem in its ranks.

So, it has begun. Ruminating over team selection, forum debate gradually homing in on a season that is creeping ever closer and a manager keeping his cards close to his chest.

Any outside notion that members of the football fraternity have it rather 'cushty' with their long, lazy summers is mistaken. Saturday (July 13th) will see the players put through the motions for the benefit of supporters at Eastleigh's Family Fun Day – a vital initiative with its eyes on long-term gain and for which a now former employee printed 50,000 promotional flyers marked with the wrong date.

The news of this weekend commitment was jarring for an incredulous Ross Flitney who had designs on his Friday night at the 'Wireless Music Festival' being a thirsty occasion. Ah well, he can soberly sing along to Justin Timberlake. There will be time for drinks aplenty when the year's mission is accomplished.

9

A PECKING ORDER AND PRIORITIES

A telephone call to Richard on Sunday (July 14th), which was intended merely to confirm details of tomorrow's training session, gleaned far more than 'usual time, usual place'.

The conversation brought the seriously exciting news that Stuart Fleetwood, a player whose phenomenal goal-scoring for Forest Green Rovers in season 2007/2008 earned him a move to Charlton Athletic, is expected at the club tomorrow to agree terms on a contract.

He may be just released by Luton Town, but the mention of Fleetwood's name drew from me a sharp intake of breath. This would be a 'statement' signing that, when allied to that of Strevens, stands comparison with Ebbsfleet's twin-capture of Ben May and Billy Bricknell, and Jamie Taylor and Jamie Slabber's fresh and potentially productive pairing at Sutton United.

The trading of these three teams, widely considered as the triumvirate set to fight for the division's top-spot, is further testament to the premium placed on men who put the ball in the net.

Interestingly, Richard has left much of the negotiation with Fleetwood to Chris Todd. I had chosen to pass a blazing hot Saturday sitting in the sun and reading Todd's book, *More Than Football in the Blood*, in preference to spending an afternoon in the vicinity of a flood of hyperactive whippersnappers, drunk on heat and the excitement of their close proximity to Eastleigh's footballers at the Silverlake's 'Family Fun Day'.

Chris's tome is an inspirational tale of one man's will in the face of being struck, while in the prime of youth and health, with a pernicious illness. Todd's diaries, which detail the year of his life post-diagnosis, disclose why he is an individual of whom Richard says, 'If I get any good at this management and move on, I would want Toddy by my side.'

Viewed in that light, Todd's responsibility for assisting with the smooth completion of a conceivably 'game-changing' transfer will surely aid his prospective transition into a post-playing career – although, at just short of 32 years old, he'll hope that's a while off yet.

As indicated by the manager's statement with respect to what will happen if he becomes 'any good', supporting a Conference South team requires a deal of stoicism. No matter how big a fish your club might be in these modest surroundings, there is a vast pool of possible suitors out there, all ready to snap up your key men – players, management, or both.

A sole worry after last week's run out against Wycombe Wanderers could have been the potential for Will Evans' dynamic performance to act as a siren call to any Football League club on the lookout for a midfielder blessed with a multitude of attributes (so most of them).

In fact, it was another of our players who sparked the interest of Wanderers' boss, Gareth Ainsworth. Typically honest, Richard assured Ainsworth that, for a probable £20,000 fee, purchasing the man in question would be terrific business for him.

That advice was extended by a man who is both wholly conscious of his employer's place in the pecking order and loath to block the progress of any aspirational footballer. There is a warning, though, for those players who believe that a step into the league comes with a guaranteed upgrade in lifestyle.

Richard shed more light on Michael Green's time at Port Vale. He believes it was more than a desire to be back in home environs that cut short the player's League Two experience. A blend of his lowly wage and the necessity to pay for 'digs' left Green with a daily existence restricted to training and killing time within the constraints of a suffocating four walls.

It has to be frustrating as a manager to work with the enduring knowledge that vital components in your meticulously crafted plans could be snatched away in the blink of an eye. Nevertheless, unless you hold the top job at Barcelona or Real Madrid, that is the reality of the job. Moreover, like Chris Todd, Richard has been provided with a newly clear perspective on what matters in life.

Unbeknown to all but those closest to him and, it must be said, without offering any clue that beneath his usual animated exterior he's been churning with anxiety, Richard was undergoing tests to determine whether he had cancer. Mercifully, the all-clear was received late last week.

'When people are getting agitated about losing a friendly to Wycombe Wanderers, I'm thinking there are far more important things for you to worry about.'

For now, it will take more than footballing travails to disturb the manager's ability to doze off at night.

10

THE HEAT GOES ON

Monday, July 15th, dawned in conditions that Richard likened to those that prevailed in Kazakhstan during his spell assisting John Gregory at FC Kairat. Eastleigh's footballers knew they were in for another unforgiving workout.

This would also be the day of my first player interview. My aim was to extract, from Glen Southam, some quotes that would make for a good match-day programme read, while simultaneously discovering a little more about the individual who dons the Spitfires' captain's armband.

Before that meeting could take place, Glen and his colleagues were put through a session that, although moderately tailored for the excessive temperatures, was taxing in the extreme. Included in the hard-working collective was Sanchez Ming, a wide player previously with Bromley and the latest man to attempt to play his way into Richard's plans.

They certainly don't provide post-training grub at Sanchez's former club and he wasn't about to be short-changed on his share of that particular perk. His plastic plate was in danger of buckling under the strain of his king-size helping of spaghetti bolognese.

The feed had been well earned. Ming was no timid new boy. He drove into tackles and was committed to his every action. Furthermore, he was not afraid to voice his anger during a practice match if one of his off the ball surges went ignored.

The ferocity of these sessions, the extra pace, competitiveness, and intensity on display, as compared to that on day one a fortnight ago, is readily discernible. There was no junior school style picking of teams for today's 11v11 either (when Todd and Beckwith were granted captain's privileges seven days ago it was no less painful watching the final few, stood longing not to be last man left standing, than it was years ago in the school playground).

The countdown to Sutton is beginning and Richard is sowing the seeds for the system he intends to adopt – primarily concentrating on his deployment of a three-man forward line.

Not that the emphasis on that element of the manager's formation spared those elsewhere on the pitch from Richard's all-seeing gaze. Green, in particular, was urged to apply more confidence and authority to his forward raids.

'I don't want players attacking and looking over their shoulder, worrying what's going to happen if the move breaks down.' It was an instruction delivered towards 'Greener', but intended for the ears of all.

The commitment to attack with conviction sits comfortably alongside the boss's desire for his team to focus on playing quick-witted, one- or two-touch, mobile football – so making maximum capital on possessing one of the league's strongest squad of players.

During a prior drill Richard carefully chose his moments to interject. He concentrated on reinforcement of his belief in the players' quality, alongside the delivery of specific coaching points. One aspect of his tutelage centred on a deficiency that reared when the team came under pressure last term. The easy option, often taken in such circumstances, was to hit the ball forward to Craig McAllister. That, in Richard's view, is 'isolating one of your mates'.

'The crowd may clap and gasp and say what a great ball, but, in reality, you've left your team-mate dealing with a pass coming for his head or neck and with nobody anywhere near him to help. All that's going to happen is he'll be upended and the opposition have got the ball back.'

The manager's avowed preference for his players to use two or three passes to work the ball forward, rather than taking a more direct route, makes for entertaining viewing.

Still, so many players crave the feel of the ball at their feet. It was striking that, when the players were permitted just one touch in a possession-based training game, the ball was zipped about, being retained to far better effect by each team than it was after the reins were loosened.

As the watching joint-reserve team manager and Academy Head Dan Wright observed, Reason was exempt from that failing of surrendering possession, which afflicted some of his colleagues when allowed more time on the ball – this is an individual of serious talent.

'He can receive the ball and already know the picture that surrounds him.

He'll choose the best option and can execute it in one touch. That is very difficult to coach.'

Being the side's chief artisan, however, doesn't spare one the manager's wrath. With the oppressive heat setting off a few rising tempers, Reason snapped at what he considered to be a poor refereeing decision on the part of his boss. So ensued an expletive-riddled exchange – the type of which is a feature of football training grounds across the world.

A marked hush descended over everybody in the vicinity – players, coaching staff, and most certainly me – as respective bootlaces, studs, and water bottles became objects of fascination, to be studied in the most microscopic detail.

Manager and player later indulged in a light-hearted social-media exchange. Richard is comfortable engaging in laid-back chat and ribbing with his players. When it comes to business time, he is in charge – and everything is executed exactly as he wants.

A similar deferential atmosphere to that which descended during the verbal ruckus outside took over the cool clubhouse once feeding time was over. Christian Roberts, himself a former professional footballer, most notably with Swindon Town, was in the room to extol the virtues of his present employer's player insurance cover.

Roberts' career was ended abruptly in 2008, at the age of just 28, after he sustained an irreparable knee injury. The story of his inability to manage that unforeseen twist in his professional life was a stark reminder for every man sat listening intently as to the capricious nature of their occupation.

Richard, whose career was ended at 26 by his own knee problem, added credence to Roberts' zeal for his subject. Roberts had preferred to routinely spend what would have amounted to his monthly insurance contributions on 'a crate of Stella'. Richard, by contrast, had taken care that he was insured personally and by his club. He believes that, without such prudence, his capacity to move on and pursue a coaching and managerial career would have been hopelessly obstructed.

When the floor was opened for questions, Eastleigh's bar and club was momentarily transformed into something akin a classroom of reticent adolescents.

Once Scannell had broken the ice, though, a series of perceptive enquiries were thrown at Roberts and his colleagues. Todd, Southam, and Beckwith were as sure of mind in their queries as they are of foot on a Saturday afternoon.

Roberts' words delayed my chat with Southam. I know that, two weeks ago, the extra 30 minutes of waiting would have been time spent trying to suppress frothing nerves.

Already though, I feel more comfortable in these surroundings. McAllister had earlier been happy to share in relaxed conversation as we took the five-minute stroll from changing room to training field. It was encouraging to hear him assert his faith that, despite turning 33 last month, he can function at a high level for at least three more years.

'Crikey, Kevin Davies [at 36 years of age] has just been given a two-year deal by Preston.'

Equally illuminating, and gladdening, was 'Macca's' professed commitment to looking after his body. I hadn't yet seen this serious side to one of the jokers in the pack. He also confessed that he is making a concerted effort to break the habit of taking his football worries home with him.

'Even after the Wycombe game last week I was totally fed up. I went home in a right mood.'

McAllister's predictable nickname actually allows me the occasional moment to dream that I'm fulfilling my own futile ambitions. Whenever the shout of 'Macca' echoes out around the training expanse on Stoneham Lane, it brings back memories of answering to the same moniker when playing at various football outposts – after initially looking up to see who's calling me, that is.

Yemi Odubade was forced to withdraw early in this latest session having jarred his side. While the increasingly charged practice match was in process and as he wrestled with the ice pack affixed to his stricken body region, Yemi was full of questions for yours truly about various members of his new team.

Who is the first choice 'keeper? Where's Dan Spence from? He imparted his high opinion of Sam Wilson and admiration for McAllister whom he played alongside at Oxford United.

Despite Southam's regular exhortations, during that game, for team-mates to work harder and with more quality, and his chiding of anybody who loses concentration or misplaces a pass, I had seen enough by now to suspect that the skipper's off-field manner wouldn't be so confrontational.

So it proved. An engaging interviewee, Southam spoke about his hatred of losing, the difficulty of shaking away the sense of grief after last season's cruel climax, and his fastened determination to ensure that disappointment will not be repeated. The elongated list of clubs our captain considered might jostle for top spot gave another indication towards quite what a tough season this will be.

A day after I had recorded 'Suvs" thoughts, the small, aesthetically delightful ground of Hellenic Football League team Wantage Town was the setting for Spitfires' friendly number two.

The players' first test came by way of a navigation exercise, namely finding the home of the night's opposition. In bygone days, when in-car sat-nav was a luxury, it is quite possible that my modern-day sweat-laden dreams of turning out with the Spitfires badge on my chest would have become reality.

As it was, all were present and correct and, despite a first-half lull after scoring twice in the opening seven minutes, the side completed a competitive evening's work with the 6–1 score-line a pleasant postscript.

I had the briefest of after-match chats with Richard who merely declared that 'he'd learned a lot'. When gently pressed on whether the fresh knowledge concerned individuals or tactics, the response was identical.

Now, on Thursday (July 18th) it is likely that the boss's mind will have moved on. A morning look at the club website reveals the top story to be my report on Tuesday's fixture, i.e. no news of Fleetwood's transfer.

True to his word, on Tuesday Richard continued to offer his trialists every possible opportunity to prove their worth. Ming, Rose, 'Chris' and the Oxford youngster – the last two scored for good measure – all took some part in the action at Wantage.

A day earlier, the manager was faced with the conversely unpleasant task of informing youth team graduate, Matt Gray, that there would be 'nothing for him' at the Silverlake.

Matt's decision to progress his game by training in Eastleigh's professional environment was rare among last season's development group. As Dan Wright explained to me, a number of his brood – many of whom demonstrated genuine promise – preferred to seek first-team involvement lower down the ladder and, by extension, guaranteed financial return.

One can't help wondering how many of those tyros will, when taking a retrospective view, wish they had exercised a mite of added patience. Contrarily, they may consider their erstwhile colleague's fortunes as validation of their respective decisions.

The only summer hopeful not on show at Wantage was Danny Smith. DVD on Monday, signed and played on Tuesday, disappeared on Wednesday. I think that's how the old nursery rhyme reads anyway.

Watching this latest 'tune-up', it dawned on me just how absorbed I was in its every intricacy. The understanding, taken from time spent watching the manager work with his players on the training pitch, of exactly what the team is trying to achieve, provides an entirely new perspective. When Green pushed on without a backward glance and scored from 20 yards, it was a moment that any coach in any sport would cherish — that when one of their charges reaps the rewards of his willingness to listen and learn.

Dan Wright had favourably compared Richard's pro-active coaching with other bolshy, 'bollocking' training field manners that he's encountered. That goal endorsed the assessment.

Talking with a Wantage Town die-hard after Tuesday's game (since my adoption of an 'Eastleigh Supporter' mantle, this was the first occasion on which I have spoken with a peer who would view my team as a relative 'giant'), he expressed admiration for his side's fitness levels, with their having played in the fierce heat as recently as three days ago.

I resisted the urge to recount the 90 minutes of purgatory the visiting players had been subject to the previous afternoon. When that session had culminated with a series of punishing sprints, I was wide-eyed in admiration for 'poor-trainer' Scannell's diligent approach. The bare-chested duo of Ming and Southam pushed themselves to extreme limits, while Green coasted five yards ahead of his mates in the graceful style of a Kenyan middle-distance master.

Once a demand is set on Eastleigh's training field, it must be complied with exactly as requested. When, at the outset of the final running exercise, there was a collective tailing off below the instructed 90% capacity, a halt was called and the stop-watch rewound to zero.

During an earlier possession assignment, what looked to the untrained eye to be a laudable readiness to take the ball in tight areas was interpreted by Richard as laziness — a lack of desire to push bodies and use the wide spaces available.

'Always remember, I've been where you are. I can see that you don't want to run.'

But this team does want to run. They are already counting the days until they can do so for real.

11

IT'S ALL IN THE NUMBERS

The first leg of my sister's ill-timed wedding fiesta crashed in on my Eastleigh plans for Saturday, July 20th. While the team were involved in their third pre-season encounter, against an Aldershot side whose supporters are simply relieved to still have a club to follow, I was over 30 miles away at Newbury races.

My soon to be brother-in-law's stag day – thankfully not some monstrous 72-hour extravaganza in a European 'party capital' – condemned me to complete ignorance with regard to events at the Silverlake until a post-match text, provided by said sister, informed me of the result.

Even allowing for my renewed enthusiasm for these warm-up games, I was astonished at the extent to which I longed to be able to transport myself into *my* usual seat for the two hours between 2:50pm and 4:50pm on a match afternoon.

When I read the afternoon's plain fact, 'Eastleigh 2 Aldershot 1' the Johnny Nash composition 'There Are More Questions Than Answers' wormed its way into my mind.

When, on Sunday, I viewed the five minutes of highlights available by dint of Spitfire TV, I fastidiously studied every second – having already trawled through the Twitter feed updating the afternoon's action.

I had been surprised by Richard's displeasure, expressed when he phoned me last Thursday, with respect to how his new attacking triumvirate had operated at Wantage two days earlier.

The original catalyst for the manager's call was an ironic ten-point list of Eastleigh FC concerns that had been posted on the fans' internet message board. He has a blunt and uncompromising exterior – watch any post-match interview on the club's website for confirmation – but the manager takes personally any criticism he deems unfair.

I think the reason for that is twofold. Firstly, Richard has a burning work ethic. Any suggestion that he could be doing more, then, leaves him bristling. Additionally, and in common with plenty of people 'inside' the game, the boss is frustrated by extremely simplistic solutions many supporters proffer as remedy for a perceived shortcoming in their team.

A favoured analogy of Richard's describes a woman who buys a new dress every week for her Saturday night out. Eventually, the wardrobe is full. What happens to the obsolete garments? Correspondingly, if a football manager were to rush to the transfer market every time fans clamour for new blood, he will eventually end up with a bloated squad and heinous wage bill.

The recent confirmation of Stuart Fleetwood's purchase has crystallised Eastleigh's standing as bookies' favourites to win the division. This high-end acquisition also fits perfectly with Richard's preference for bona fide quality acquisitions over 'wardrobe stocking'. Even more importantly for the club's followers, it underlines the owner's commitment. That is a commodity whose value cannot be understated in the present day.

Stewart is a familiar face in clubhouse bars pre- and post-game and will happily mingle with his supporters, in the process dealing in good spirit with the inevitable interrogation he receives. He didn't immerse himself in Eastleigh FC to savour the straitened hospitality of myriad boardrooms. His match-day custom is more full-English and a few pints of Guinness – before watching the team from among the fans who owe him a deal of thanks.

Indeed, listening to some 'behind-the-scenes' chit-chat, it is possible to believe that without Stewart's timely intervention, this club might no longer exist – or if it did, it would not be as a member of the Conference South.

My investigation into the Aldershot friendly showed the side to have played some excellent football and, most positively, suggested that the attacking trio functioned well. Fleetwood applied some sheen to the afternoon by making a substitute appearance and tapping home the winning goal.

Watching the marquee signing for the first time during Monday's session (July 22nd), his destructive goal-scoring potential was glaring. Richard is particularly effusive about his new acquisition's inherent ability to strike the ball with minimal back-lift, so leaving an opposing 'keeper with feet still helplessly planted as a shot flies beyond him.

'Fleets' is settling into the group effortlessly. Will Evans, meanwhile, is becoming progressively more demonstrative. It is far too early to make a comparison in playing style between Will and Steven Gerrard in the match reports I file, but, I'm happy to place on record here, the way he exudes complete authority over whichever part of the pitch he bestrides is eerily reminiscent of the Liverpudlian (whose retirement, with my Evertonian specs on, can't come soon enough).

My first extended interaction with Jai Reason centred on those match reports. On Monday, Jai asked whether I had written up the Aldershot clash yet. I actually felt a pang of guilt when I explained my absence. My ego was boosted when Jai not only confessed to reading my dispatches, but declared that his parents, unable to travel to many games, rely on them for news of their son's progress.

(As an aside, my earlier reading of Jai as a man who conforms to his manager's description of 'grumpy' – Richard's favourite term for anybody in a dark mood – is shaping up to be off beam. I have, thus far, encountered an affable chap who smiles far more off the pitch than on it.)

Surely even the most hardened hack feels some satisfaction when hearing that their scribblings are well received? It is with one reader in mind – Paul Doswell at Sutton – that Richard has requested I omit any information concerning his strategy and assorted formations when I write about the four remaining warm-up fixtures. That measure might not be required this coming Friday when a Southampton XI visits the Silverlake – after all, Sutton aren't playing at the same time.

That game could provide a first start for the man hitherto known as 'Chris' and since revealed to be Chris Dillon – now the lone trialist still standing. If the centre-back continues his impressive integration into the unit, then his return to English climes after a period living abroad – which included time spent on a football scholarship in the USA – will be off to a prosperous start. That, in all likelihood, with defensive cover assured – and no indication that Luton Town will again loan out Alex Lacey – will end Eastleigh's incoming trading.

Who knows the next destination for our Oxford friend as he seeks his break – and the means to finance his next personalised car registration plate?

The voracious Sanchez Ming will not be a Spitfire and Richard's final duty before setting off for home on Monday was to take Rose to one side and inform him there would be no contract at Eastleigh.

The concentrated summer spend on five high-calibre recruits, combined with the retention of every one of his leading men from last term's revival, has caused Richard to overshoot the agreed playing budget.

A cup run would be more welcome than ever, then, but – 'Don't bank on it. I never have any luck in the FA Cup.' Richard can recall with startling clarity the finer points of a quarter-final replay defeat against Millwall in 2004 when he was working under Brian Little at Tranmere Rovers.

The decreasing squad numbers gave rise to a charged air at Monday's training. Just 16 men took to the field, including the goalkeeping pair of Ross Flitney and Tom Coffey. There will be the scope, throughout the season, to involve extra youngsters from Dan Wright's developing ranks – a priceless opportunity for the chosen individuals.

On the day when the country recorded its highest temperatures for seven years, another hour and a half of near perpetual motion concluded with a sprinkling of shattered Spitfires dropping to the floor, overcome by exhaustion.

The only troubling aspect of the fiercely fought session-closing eight-a-side was the number of balls sprayed far and wide behind each goal. With no Guy Butters on hand for the day, it was up to Richard, and occasionally myself or the on-looking and injured Damian Scannell (Scans' troublesome groin, which he hinted to me last Monday was being adversely impacted by the hard ground, failed him late on at Wantage), to collect footballs, which sat anything up to 60 yards from their intended target.

It is unlikely that many of Richard's exalted counterparts multi-task to the extent of concurrently refereeing and analysing a training game, while periodically dashing off to retrieve the consequence of its participants' erratic shooting. (Likewise, it is against all odds that Messrs Wenger, Mourinho and Villas-Boas et al. ever instruct their players with a dead pigeon adorning the day's training pitch.)

Jamie Collins, whose initial conditioning had been, shall we say, below par, is rewarding the manager's trust in his experienced midfielder to nurture himself to fitness. Collins, of whose personality I have much to discover, took responsibility for urging his colleagues to spend every grain of energy throughout their 8v8 game.

With each passing week, the combative instinct and hatred of losing imbued in every player at this club becomes clearer. When Richard enquired as to the half-time score of this 'friendly' practice match (of which I had no idea and didn't expect any of the 16 men involved to be keeping tally), he was met with numerous voices announcing the standings as '4–3 to the blues'.

It was the loudest noise that had been heard during any of the session's latter breaks – the earlier joviality and discussions about Phil Mickelson's Open golf win and resultant cash prize and, of course, the fairer sex long having given way to shattered contemplation and recovery.

Yet, even after training was declared finished, only for Andy Cook to then lead ten minutes of upper body work, the consequent moans were all in jest. Sam Wilson's less than enthusiastic attempt at completing a set of press-ups, though, was immediately picked up by his manager.

Turning to me, Richard said, 'What you don't realise, Sam, is I see everything. You can't get away with a single thing – unless your name is Beckwith or Todd.'

12

YOU WILL LIVE WITH GREAT EXPECTATIONS

By the time a 'Southampton XI' (actually, make that 21 players with an attendant coaching and support staff numbering nearly half that number and fighting for space in the visitors' dugout) arrived at the Silverlake on Friday (July 26th), Richard had been embroiled in a touch of off-field strife.

Dan Wright, despite the player's release from the club, included Matt Gray in a reserve match last week. Undeterred by his manager's wrath at the time, Dan has since repeated the trick, wanting to field the strongest team he can muster. Having to then placate a confused parent on the other end of his telephone line is not something the boss subscribed to as part of his remit.

It transpires that another parent, our Oxford hopeful's father, was not so much confused as incandescent that his son was not offered a Spitfires contract. His offer to cover the boy's wages for a year was politely rejected. Dad believed his lad was the best player on the pitch at Wantage. He wasn't.

Unlike the rejected rookie, Chris Dillon is now in possession of an Eastleigh playing contract and, due to Chris Todd's absence against Saints, the centre-back was handed his first start against the attacking duo of Lee Barnard and Billy Sharp – two first-team fringe men who seemingly have no part in the plans of Mr Pochettino. In his 45 minutes on the pitch, the Spitfires' new defender was a match for his more celebrated adversaries and displayed a marked poise on the ball.

Without excelling, Eastleigh gave the Premier League side (albeit a second string) a serious test. If it wasn't for the team's shooting mirroring their wild thrashing of Monday's training, then Tadanari Lee's late penalty would have been a Southampton consolation strike and not the night's only goal.

Richard was more enamoured than of late with the effectiveness of his trio of forwards. One of those three, Ben Strevens, was simply magnificent – equally so when, for the second 45 minutes, he dropped into midfield.

The portents for my 'old friend' McAllister weren't so good. He was left on the bench. Richard unfailingly speaks in glowing terms about the workaholic centre-forward – even drawing a comparison between his player and one of the chief lieutenants in the triumph of the British cyclist Chris Froome at this year's Tour de France.

Richard likened Craig to Richie Porte, the 'domestique' who sacrifices himself in the mountains for the benefit of his team leader. McAllister performed a similarly selfless role last season, taking the hits and doing the 'ugly jobs', thereby freeing the road for Jai Reason to impose his broad range of skills on a game.

As an unashamed Macca fan – and somebody who repeatedly championed his brave endeavours throughout last term – I hope we'll be seeing plenty more of him this year.

Craig's straightforward and direct manner are traits that endear him to his boss. Reason is a more complex character. When in his football togs he is wont to bouts of temper and introspection, but, after observing him closely for a month, I am sure Jai's serious nature can be attributed entirely to an intense and deep-rooted desire to produce everything of which he is capable.

While taking a breather during the first training session since the Saints match – and with the Premier League club development group's complex and modern prop-laden workout taking place on the horizon – Reason quietly elucidated his concern to Fleetwood that pre-season has yet to feature any specific shooting practice. It is a decision beyond his compass, but the thought shows he is clearly an individual with the team's welfare high on his agenda.

Prior to the day's work (Monday, July 29th), Richard told me that Brian Howard would be taking his place among the group. Perhaps my earlier assertion that the summer's inward trading is complete was premature?

Being the man who scored a 90th-minute FA Cup winner for Barnsley at Anfield in 2008, leaving the risible, whey-faced Phil Thompson, watching on in a Sky Sports studio, utterly unable to coherently express his seething fury – Brian is alright with me.

Alex Lacey will most certainly not be donning the Spitfires' royal blue. That much can be deduced by the classy centre-half's 90-minute outing for Luton Town in a friendly match against Aston Villa last week. The Hatters won 2–0 and the now pacified Christian Benteke – it's amazing what an extra year on the contract that you agreed just 12 months previously, and the associated considerably boosted remuneration, can achieve – was withdrawn at half-time.

If a man of Howard's distinction does become an Eastleigh player (unlikely, but even the hint of that possibility demonstrates the club's progress and ambition), the incredulity and jealousy among some followers of our divisional counterparts will climb ever further.

When, this week, the Twitter account of Radio 5 Live's *Non League Show* asked for season's predictions a reply from the account of a Bromley FC fan, posting under the label of @MashHuey, stated:

'Skrill South League winners: Eastleigh. More money than sense but prob [sic] enough to guarantee promotion.'

Setting aside the obvious contradiction in Mr Huey's statement – that if the powers that be at Eastleigh have taken leave of any rational thought when spending their cash, they would not be recruiting players capable of topping the league – the underlying contempt for our club's ambitious spending shines through.

That feeling of resentment ensures that wherever the Spitfires go this year, theirs will be considered a prized scalp.

It is unlikely that Woking's footballers and supporters were experiencing the extremes of jubilation after their July 30th 4–2 friendly victory at the Silverlake that will be attained by, for example, Eastbourne Borough should they triumph over the Spitfires in similar style during the forthcoming nine months.

The Conference Premier team provided a first-hand example of the playing standard to which Eastleigh strive. A blend of power, skill, athleticism, movement and cunning was all, ultimately, too much for our 'work-in-progress' side.

Indeed, coming away from the game it felt as if the Spitfires had been on the end of a good old shellacking. It was only when trawling through my notes that I realised, in terms of scoring opportunities, how even things had been for much of the 90 minutes.

Nevertheless, Woking discernibly held the upper hand throughout. When the first tune-up game was lost against Wycombe Wanderers, Richard said that he'd be annoyed if the same mistakes were repeated three weeks down the line.

They were, so I will be all ears when we next talk. I don't expect the result to be of concern, more the fashion in which Eastleigh's opponents were able to find space all over the pitch – and tear through our side every time they embarked on one of their jet-heeled counter-attacks.

For the second time since Richard asked me not to detail his tactical manoeuvrings, in my pre-season reports, the purpose of that request was compromised by the on-looking Mr Doswell. Continuing on Richard's theme, it would be enlightening to know whether Sutton's manager has been equally assiduous in his studying of Staines Town, Bishop's Stortford, and Concord Rangers – all slated to face Sutton over the nine days following their visit to the Silverlake.

Meet the New Me; Same as the Old Me

As I gradually come to know the men whom I watch every week, my match-day feelings remain unaltered. I had pondered on whether becoming so ingrained in Eastleigh might throw a little too much light on the magic and, consequently, rob me of some of the emotion that hijacks us all when watching our team in action.

It is still exceptionally early, but that scenario has not transpired. I have, though, noticed a developing inclination for keeping a keen eye on the performances of individuals who have struck me, during my first month with the group, as particularly open and affable.

Yemi (back playing against Woking after his side strain) fits firmly into that category. My training ground conversation with the former Stevenage man a fortnight ago was followed by his merrily spending half an hour speaking to my dad and me ahead of the game at Wantage. As well as offering up some vignettes about his career to date, Yemi was enthusiastic to learn more about his new club. Our new signing's crash course in all things Eastleigh illustrates the polar opposite relationships that player and fan have with their club.

For the dedicated supporter no detail is too small to be of the utmost importance. All die-hards are steeped in their club's history. Matters such as kit colour, badge design, ground improvement and location, ticket prices, and holding the ascendancy over historic rivals are all afforded gravity almost on a par with current team selection and results.

The player is, first and foremost, an employee. That is the stark reality and, despite the links forged between fans and their team being incrementally stronger as you drop through the leagues, the men on the pitch are doing their jobs. Their concerns, by definition, must be selfish. Earn a place in the side, perform to your best, and hope that is enough to keep the money flowing into the bank – be that at their present place of work or elsewhere.

A day prior to the Woking fixture I interviewed Dan Spence. He was no less candid than Yemi in expressing a longing to return to full-time league football. Here lies the conundrum for followers of any club outside Europe's elite – never mind those whose heart belongs to a non-league outfit. Do supporters want men in their team who are happy to drift along, with no ambition beyond maintaining their status quo? No.

A player hungry to succeed will be fully committed to his club's cause, no matter how transient his stay. That is all we, as fans, can ask for. In identical fashion to the manager himself, if Yemi or Dan is wrenched away from the Silverlake, the likelihood is that they will depart having made a notable contribution to Eastleigh FC.

One player who regrets leaving the Silverlake is Sam Wilson. The forward told me on Monday that he believes he should have stayed around in the summer of 2012, rather than seek game time elsewhere. Sam's spells with Poole Town and Gosport Borough didn't bring the regular action he craved. Notwithstanding his relative lack of football, the teenager has come back a changed specimen from the raw and slender would-be prodigy of a year ago.

Richard doesn't expect to be counting Sam as one of his attacking options any time soon, but, with a bulkier frame to complement his burgeoning movement, touch, and vision, the local lad will be investing everything he has to try and force his boss to re-consider that initial forecast.

While Sam focuses on inching into his manager's thoughts, Jamie Collins continues to win me over. The excess weight is slipping away. Correspondingly, the real footballer is emerging. Collins was exceptional in his use of the ball and positioning against Southampton – although at this early stage his mobility was occasionally exposed by Woking's fleet-footed style. Having witnessed the calculated precision with which Jamie has managed his physical advancement,

I share Richard's confidence that come August 17th he will be wholly primed.

Elsewhere this week, the Football Conference has agreed a three-year title sponsorship with Skrill – an organisation described as 'a global online payment company'. The bean counters at all 68 member clubs will be delighted.

During an interview on TalkSport, Dean Holdsworth, now manager at Chelmsford City, made no mention of that financial boon when he professed to be operating within the confines of a restrictive budget at the Melbourne Stadium.

In the next breath, the man whose Newport County team achieved a record 103 points when winning this division in 2010 revealed that his team have added an extra day to their training schedule and now employ a goalkeeping coach – that job at Eastleigh is fulfilled by first-choice stopper Flitney. The manager is not the only person multi-tasking and improvising on the Spitfires' training ground. Furthermore, it is at Chelmsford where Mark Hughes, a midfielder who spent last year with the Spitfires, but whose salary demands Richard was unwilling to meet this time around, has landed up.

The art of publicly lowering expectations and pleading mitigation ahead of time is not the lone preserve, then, of Harry Redknapp and his likeminded contemporaries in the Premier League, or rather the Championship.

13

ECHOES OF THE LEGENDS

As I have grown to learn more about Richard Hill during my first six weeks closely tracking Eastleigh FC, I have come to recognise a number of attributes that the manager shares with a historical master of his profession.

It might not sit well for a man of Leicester being compared to a counterpart who won his legendary status with first Derby County and then, primarily, Nottingham Forest, but there is more than a touch of Brian Clough in both Richard's brusque manner and absolute confidence in his own knowledge and aptitude for his job.

Richard is happy to debate any facet of his team. Selection, player form, the team's match-day performance, and potential signings are all open for discussion.

During some of our recent chats, one of the more famous quotes associated with Clough has sprung to my mind. When asked about dealing with any player who might disagree with him, Clough responded thus:

'We talk about it for 20 minutes and then we decide I was right.'

Comparably, any dialogue with Richard – especially one regarding an individual player's strengths or weaknesses – will conclude only one way. We both agree with the boss's initial viewpoint.

There is an element in Richard's strong headedness of the inimitable Danny Baker – the media heavyweight who claims his opinions to be 'sometimes right, sometimes wrong, but always certain'.

The arts of decisiveness and clear thinking are essential in order to prosper in Richard's occupation. Hesitancy, uncertainty, and a mind that is easily swayed are not features in the make-up of any successful football manager.

If Eastleigh's boss does go on and forge a notable career in the dugout he would be scoring a point against Clough on behalf of the denizens of his home city, who were witheringly dismissed by the wonderfully eccentric two-time European Cup winner with the line:

'Anybody who can do anything in Leicester other than knit a jumper has got to be a genius.'

It is not only Clough, of the game's managerial greats, with whom Richard's style is reminiscent. Sir Alex Ferguson, throughout his 26.5 years in charge at Manchester United, was renowned for his vehement protection of his players.

However heated the atmosphere behind closed doors and regardless of whether or not an individual had just been in receipt of Ferguson's fabled dressing room hairdryer, Sir Alex would not countenance uttering a word against one of his own for public consumption.

Richard has no qualms about expressing his views, good or bad, commending or chastising, to his players in private – no matter how painful that might prove for any of them. He is yet to give a local paper or radio station a tasty lead by selling out one of his men – and never will.

Equally, the manager is loath to castigate his collective playing unit during our talks. When we spoke a couple of days on from the Woking defeat, Richard articulated some surprise that there had been an overall positive reaction to his side's showing in that game.

I agreed, and went further by declaring that I felt his midfield had been overrun. A mistake. The manager was not on the same page – and you can probably guess the course that that part of our conversation ran.

In that instance, I'm not totally sure that Richard didn't share my conviction – although maybe not to the same degree. Like Ferguson, though, when it comes to his group, only one man can criticise.

The same prickliness is existent if the 'gaffer' detects, among the Spitfires' support, unrest or discord with his methodology. I spoke in praise of Dan Spence and alluded to the fact that the right-back had proved unfounded any fans' concerns that he would not provide the attacking qualities of his predecessor, Mitchell Nelson.

That was enough to cause a mild tremor on the other end of the phone line. Taking my intended affirmative statement as an implied slight on his decision to allow Nelson to leave for Sutton United, Richard forcefully reiterated just why Spence provides an upgrade in that position. He was preaching to the converted.

Richard had been unhappy with his players' off-the-ball work against Woking and so commenced his next training session by using a DVD recording of the match to highlight a selection of identified failings. This was another incidence when the disparities between life in the Conference and the Premier League – or even Football League – were exhibited.

Eastleigh's is a part-time operation. With three get-togethers a week, time is at a premium. There isn't the luxury of a full day yawning ahead to be filled at leisure.

More prosaically, the Silverlake Stadium is not replete with a plush video room, decked out with big screen television and various gadgets of the type you see Gary Neville wielding on Sky Sports' Monday night football coverage. There is a grainy television. A DVD player. And a remote control.

Additionally, and this holds true anywhere, there is a distinctly limited timespan in which you will hold rapt an assembly of highly charged males by showing and scrutinising a replay of a football match.

When the team returned to action on Saturday, August 3rd, for their penultimate friendly against Salisbury City, Jack Dovey was handed the gloves. Newly promoted into the Conference Premier – having beaten Dover in last season's play-off final – the visitors from Wiltshire presented another stern test, without being the all-round package that we saw in their divisional rivals from Woking.

In terms of the score-line, then, Eastleigh could have done without Dovey's absolute howler giving their opponents a goal start. There is something compelling, bordering on sadistically so, about watching a sports person in the public glare undergoing a miserable personal ordeal. Concurrently, it is rather uncomfortable.

Individual competition shines the harshest light on its players. Collapses that replaced certain victory with failure are recalled as readily as some of sport's greatest feats. Golfers Rory McIlroy at the 2011 US Masters and Jean Van de Velde at the 1999 Open Championship suffered a high-profile loss of nerve and technique to throw away the prize that was within their grasp.

By extension, the footballer most prone to falling victim of a comparable unravelling is the loneliest man on the field – the goalkeeper. When the Number 1 is having a bad trot, there is no place to hide, no team-mate to bail him out. As Ross Flitney commented last week, 'A 'keeper can make nine great saves, then make the smallest mistake that costs a goal and that's all anybody will remember.'

A midfielder misplacing a pass can look on as a colleague retrieves possession or perhaps chase back and rectify his error. For the misfiring forward, if a scoring chance comes and goes without conversion, the next opening could be seconds away.

There was nothing Jack could do about Salisbury's second goal in their 2–1 win. Notwithstanding that, our number two stopper's endeavours in this game will only be recalled for his hitting the ball into Ben Wright and forlornly watching it loop back past him and into the net. Jack was replaced late on by Flitney – who is causing his manager some consternation for his perceived 'chippiness' of late. (To this observer, Ross's training ground mind-set is not dissimilar to the ex-Manchester United player Roy Keane's pursuit of perfection – in himself, his team-mates, and the execution of every exercise undertaken.)

Jack was absent from Tuesday's (August 6th) flogging. His income is supplemented by work as a green-keeper at a local golf course. The extra salary is particularly important, given that Jack's contract, which he signed when Ian Baird was still in charge, stipulates that he is not paid during the summer months. His attempts to renegotiate have not so far been fruitful.

Yet another 'keeper, a teenager called Lewis, was integrated into Tuesday's session. He could have chosen a better day to be invited. The closing 30 minutes, which comprised an unrelenting tide of various gruelling sprints, visibly drained the last vestige of energy from every 'runner'.

Lewis fought his way through the unforgiving speed-work, having already startled a few people with his shot-stopping in an earlier eight-a-side contest. Within five minutes the teenager had been christened – and here, this group did conform to the footballer stereotype regarding training ground imagination – 'The Cat'.

Another man missing from training is Will Evans. Early in the Salisbury friendly, Will, after an innocuous coming together with an opponent, collapsed to the floor in apparent agony. We wait to know the extent of the damage. Richard has said that a good version of that will dictate a 6–8 week lay-off. The worst case alternative is that one of the summer's leading acquisitions will not be seen at all this campaign.

Richard accepts this setback as philosophically as he would any other. Without being able to adopt a phlegmatic mind-set when necessary, a football manager would rapidly lose the way to rational thinking. This manager has interpreted Evans' absence as a 'sign'. Richard is not fully convinced by his players' application of the 4-3-3 system. Complete with genuine wingers, 4-4-2 could be the battle-plan by the time Mr Doswell makes his appearance as 'visiting manager' on August 17th.

Room for one less out-and-out striker in Richard's first choice 11 will impact further upon McAllister's potential involvement. Craig's paucity of pre-season starts is causing the man himself some anxiety. He admitted, on Tuesday, 'I can't see it changing. I'm not looking forward to the season anymore.'

Notwithstanding his chagrin, Macca is vowing to continue working as hard as possible to prepare for any opportunity that comes along. I would expect nothing less from a fiercely professional and dedicated individual. Craig could probably have done, then, without my erasing out of one of his training match goals. I executed that deed in my guise as 'linesman', not a responsibility – however fleeting – I expected to have bestowed upon me when starting out on this adventure.

Meanwhile, one of Macca's striking counterparts, Stuart Fleetwood, appears primed and ready for action. Top discarded and grinding through Tuesday's running ordeal, 'Fleets'' upper-body exhibited the sculpted frame of a man who takes his conditioning seriously. Catching sight of the post-training food, however, Fleetwood wasn't instantly won over. 'Pasta and bellyache then.'

The riches from which Richard has to choose in those attacking berths – such a powerful troop that when discussing his original plan to play three up-front, the manager didn't include McAllister in the four-strong list of strikers at the front of his mind – was emphasised this week. Ollie Palmer, a prolific 21-year-old forward with Havant & Waterlooville – and, with 25 goals, the division's leading scorer last term – has been enticed away from Westleigh Park by League Two outfit Mansfield Town.

It's a terrific move for the player, but a serious kick in the teeth to the ambitions of our friends down the road. Of course, I couldn't help but smile at the Hawks losing arguably their most potent weapon less than a fortnight before the season's opening day. On the flip side, Palmer's move is a sharp reminder of the reality that is life for clubs at this level.

Eastleigh are in a very select band of two or three in the Conference South (along with Ebbsfleet and possibly Sutton) whose finances dictate that, in lower league terms, they can be considered a buying as opposed to a selling club.

It is a fine margin. David Wheeler, the Staines player who was on Richard's radar, has been snapped up by Exeter City. Elliott Frear, he of the labyrinthine early summer transfer saga, emerged from Salisbury City's bench at the Silverlake on Saturday to produce a cameo of some quality. Surely a campaign as a 'super-sub' is not what a talented 22 year old is aspiring to.

Speaking of gifted youngsters, Corey King is back and playing for Eastleigh's reserve team. The second shot handed him by Maidenhead United has slipped away. Richard remains adamant that Corey will have no part in his plans. Where next for this precocious talent?

Right now, the interminable pre-season build-up concludes tomorrow (August 10th) in Oxfordshire, with a fixture at North Leigh FC of the 'Southern League Division One South & West'. Is it only in England where these lower football tiers have titles wordier than a line from a Shakespearean sonnet? Bring on Sutton, please. Eight more sleeps is a long time to wait for a shot of the real stuff.

14

LIFE ON THE OTHER SIDE

An interview I conducted with Ben Strevens after the first training session of the seventh and concluding week of pre-season, and a conversation with Craig McAllister minutes later, summed up the truth of post-football life for men who pursue their trade in lower or non-league surrounds.

The two individuals have much in common. Both are 33 years old, have spent well over a decade in Leagues One and Two, as well as in the upper echelons of non-league, and are very aware that a future for them without the game as its focus is coming.

The end of the 2012/2013 English season was as notable for the retirement of a clutch of its foremost players as for anything that occurred on the pitch.

Paul Scholes, Jamie Carragher, Phil Neville, and Michael Owen – all players who can be considered as standard-bearers during the evolution of the monstrous Premier League era – announced that they would be moving on to new phases in their respective lives.

That foursome have, in no particular order, found employment as football pundit, Manchester United coach, newspaper columnist, football agent, and racehorse owner. Of course, their individually well-stocked bank accounts would enable any of that number to devote their free time to travelling the world, sitting on a beach, or lying in bed all day.

There is a further group of footballers, still playing but busy carving out a niche for when their bodies give way. No human being is ever more than six feet away from a radio that is giving air time to the thoughts of Reading's striker Jason Roberts. Rio Ferdinand is making a tentative transition into the analyst's chair.

Strevens and McAllister are bound for relatively real life vocations. Nevertheless, there is a definite excitement that emanates from both men when they discuss their respective futures outside the game.

Ben is set to embark on the final year of a Sports Science degree at the University of Roehampton. Starting out with Barnet at the age of 18, it would have been easy to become wrapped in the comfort blanket of an existence that McAllister acknowledges 'millions of children dream about'.

Instead, Ben has always been aware that after football he 'has to do something'. That something, he hopes, will be working as a PE teacher – his original ambition in life. It is sobering to realise that a man with such a transparent aptitude for his current trade is approaching the moment when he must look elsewhere for his weekly wage.

Quite understandably, sympathisers will be few and far between. For every Steven Gerrard and Frank Lampard, though, men in their twilight footballing years, there are hundreds more like Ben and Craig. Yes, even outside the avaricious Premier League, players seek to maximise their earnings. Nevertheless, witness them at work and you believe that they genuinely love and appreciate what they are doing.

McAllister is especially sanguine about his likely career switch into the world of plumbing. His own on-going studies for his qualification use up a chunk of the spare time he didn't have when employed by Exeter City or Crawley Town.

If Macca feels any resentment that years of 'real work' await, it isn't perceptible. When Craig came to Pirelli General he was already earning a crust elsewhere. Unlike some of his Eastleigh colleagues, there was no upbringing in a cushy academy environment to savour. His wider-world experience determines that Craig is ceaselessly thankful for the professional life he has carved out by virtue of his inherent ability and persevering application.

On the subject of bodies, Damian Scannell's will not play ball – literally. I had noted – from Twitter naturally – that Scans' absence from last Tuesday's training was down to his presence at the 'Scannell Academy' – Damian's summer football project.

His participation in Saturday's friendly at North Leigh was restricted to a late run-out and, despite being the first to greet me with a cheery hello on Monday, Damian's characteristically outward high-spirits were betrayed by the missing customary sparkle in his eyes.

Richard took the post-session walk back towards the Silverlake's changing rooms with his player. When I arrived, a short while later, the two men were pitch-side and still engaged in earnest conversation. 'Scans' was, plainly, mildly distressed. I could only assume that, in that moment, his second spell as a Spitfire was over.

Richard confirmed as much to me the following day. The manager had told Damian that he would not be starting against Sutton United and, furthermore, that he will not in the foreseeable future be displacing any of his attacking contemporaries from the team.

Damian had no desire to stay on those terms, a decision with which Richard had no problem. A lesser man could have contentedly stayed put for another nine months, collecting a decent pay packet, and turning out for 20 minutes here and there. Damian loves playing football. Good luck, Scans.

My own stroll back from the training pitch – its lush green surface standing out amidst the still parched Wellington Sports Ground's fields – to the stadium was taken in the company of Dean Beckwith. It was the first occasion on which I'd had the opportunity to exchange more than pleasantries or small talk with a reserved man – described to me by Richard as 'this club's best ever signing'.

Dean's working side-line takes the form of operating as a 'distributor' for – unavoidable product placement alert – Herbalife. A healthy professional interest in fitness and conditioning make the promotion of a 'well-being' nutrition range the ideal way for Dean to supplement his income.

The defender's avowed faith in the company's products is backed up by his actions. A meal replacement shake is a staple of Dean's lunch – although, amid much mirth, on this specific day it was slurped down after a generously piled plate of 'real' food. Jai Reason is trying out his team mate's diet, but, not having the same voracious appetite as a towering centre-half, gets by on a banana and a salad to stave off any residual hunger-pangs.

Similar to Yemi Odubade's steep learning curve in all things Eastleigh, Beckwith betrayed a lack of insight relating to Sutton United. I mentioned the testing centre-forward duo – Jamie Slabber and Jamie Taylor – with which he would be in direct combat five days later. Dean knew Taylor's name, but nothing more (the striker has a stellar reputation in non-league circles).

As for Slabber, there was a slight recollection that the player had started out at Tottenham Hotspur. Regarding the fact that Slabber is something of a Spitfires legend – not a clue. There was no disguising the surprise in Dean's voice when he learned that Slabber had played for the club, let alone that his goal-scoring feats made him one of the more popular men to pull on the blue shirt in recent years.

There lies another example of players' and supporters' contrasting outlooks. Any fan watching their team up against a former hero – or villain – is resigned, from the off, to their scoring or making a decisive contribution on the match.

We'll sit there, biting our nails and waiting for the 'inevitable'. Dean Beckwith will take to the field, do his 90 minutes of work and, if he maintains the exacting standards he has set for himself since coming to Eastleigh in January, not put a foot wrong. The identity of the opposition is irrelevant. They are just that day's nuisance.

Regardless of how immune to such forces the Spitfires players might be, the pressure from outside the club is being steadily ramped up. *The Non-League Paper*'s (the 'go-to' publication for news and statistics at this level of football) guest columnist, Jamie Day – last year's title-winning manager at Welling – has tipped Eastleigh to be this season's champions. It is little wonder that 'expectation' is emerging as a rival to 'grumpy' for the honour of being the most commonly used word in Richard's vocabulary.

When alluding to his confidence regarding the campaign ahead, Strevens confessed to 'not knowing much about any of the other teams in the league'. And there's nothing wrong with that. Put simply, you and I, the people consigned to live our football dreams through others, see the weekly drama from a very different perspective from that of those who play its lead roles.

Tuesday (August 13th) brought the final chance for us mortals on this side of the fence to interrogate Richard and Stewart at another 'fans forum'. Given both the air of expectation (I have been prone to overusing the term myself) that pervades the club and the proximity to the season's kick-off, an attendance of approximately 20 was decidedly underwhelming.

The small numbers didn't prevent the two men on the stage facing a two-hour barrage of questions. Danny Butterfield's participation in training was divulged. The right-back, recently released by Southampton and with a history of playing at the very top end of English football, notably with Crystal Palace, is hunting a taker for his skills.

When the singular Stan Ternent had seen his then Burnley side turn in what he considered a 'woeful' performance, he argued that even 'a blind man on a galloping horse' would agree with his verdict. That same sight-deprived jockey would swiftly arrive at the conclusion that Butterfield is a seriously good footballer – just like his fellow 'unattached' pro, Brian Howard. The latter, who sports the whitest set of teeth I have ever seen, is still a regular on the Eastleigh training ground.

Both men were discussed with the fans, but rather than being held up as potential recruits, their requesting to train with the Spitfires was portrayed as confirmation of the club's blossoming status.

Moreover, having watched Butterfield and Howard work, I would not hesitate in saying that there are plenty of Richard Hill's players who do not suffer by comparison with their transitory comrades.

No matter the strength of a squad, though, that is soon diminished when several of its members are struck lame. In the blink of an eye, Southam, Collins, and Todd are all doubts to face Sutton. The game at North Leigh was played on a sticky surface, with overly long grass. Against competitive opposition – Richard insisted that 'they have never played that well before and won't again this season' – the game was an energy sapper.

The first half especially, when Jai Reason scored the afternoon's only goal, was a battle for a group of players who are desperate to get on with some meaningful action. (When Fleetwood was asked earlier in the week by Brian Palmer – a keen supporter, committee member and ubiquitous helping hand at the club – if his team might consider winning a game, his forceful response disclosed the value placed on pre-season score-lines: 'When does the league start? We'll win then.')

A hamstring niggle forced Todd off, while Collins and Southam picked up what appear to be fatigue injuries. All three were in good spirits when, having been put through a swimming pool workout by Andy Cook, they bounced in for Monday's (August 12th) lunch.

The preceding outdoor session, with only 13 outfield players taking part, had involved yet more elaborate – that is to my eyes – fleet of foot and fast of thought ball work. Mannequins, a whirr of legs, precise dribbling and close control, and crisp/venomous passing all combined to make another impressive sight.

Back to the forum and Stewart's twin priorities remain his desire to connect with the fans and to maximise the paying numbers coming to the Silverlake every week. That ambition has clearly struck a chord with the manager, who responded to one ponderous passage of play during a training exercise with the withering verdict, 'That won't bring the f****** crowds back, will it?'

The chairman was grilled further on ground expansion plans – we are awaiting council approval for 'terracing'. Said terracing, which would be installed behind either goal, amounts to roughly six steps in each case. Any promotion will require rather more grandiose upgrading. When individuals put their finances into a football club, it would be safe to assume they don't do so with the vision of becoming entangled in planning-permission battles.

Stewart and Richard were in firm agreement that Eastleigh is now assuredly a club that some very good players want to be involved with. Fleetwood's name was cited as the obvious example, but also that of a former Bath City striker, who persistently badgered Richard to sign him, before giving up and switching to a Conference North team.

The only issue on which owner and manager weren't entirely in concert concerned the latter's contract – or lack of. One cheeky inquisitor – hello Dad – asked Stewart if the club had safeguarded itself against having their manager stolen away by tying him to a lengthy deal.

A feisty riposte indicated that the Chairman didn't deem that a necessary measure, his reasoning being that there are very few non-league clubs that would represent a step up from this one. Additionally, if Richard found himself the recipient of a genuinely attractive proposition, Stewart declared that, as with any playing staff in a similar situation, he would 'not stand in his way'.

There must be an element of risk in allowing one of your key employees to work without any binding agreement of his terms. Nevertheless, Stewart and other shrewd operators of his ilk do not bring about their notable business success without making a calculated judgement call here and there.

Now, as I write, there are less than 24 hours to pass until a shrill blast of a referee's whistle will spring Eastleigh FC's management, players and followers from their leash. If there's a more restless bunch of people anywhere in the country right now, they probably wouldn't make for soothing company.

At Tuesday's forum, Richard admitted that he and his players are 'bored'; an emotion they share with many of us whose football fix is drawn from this league.

There has never been greater excitement ahead of a football season at the Silverlake. Into the breach we step. Bon voyage.

15

COME ON, YOU BOYS IN BLUE

Ah, the first day of the football season. Clear blue skies, glaring sun, and a rock hard playing surface. Well, not exactly. In fact, drizzly, misty, miserable conditions heralded the dawn of a new era at Eastleigh Football Club.

To the delight of every man, woman, and child of a Spitfire persuasion, the grey backdrop to their big day couldn't have been in starker contrast to the end result.

Any needling anxieties about a Slabber-inspired Sutton putting a spike in this most anticipated of days were rendered a complete waste of energy when the prospective bogeyman aggravated a strain in the pre-match warm up. Among the other ex-Spitfires, Dale Binns was similarly less than 100% and it would appear that Tom Jordan is some way short of fitness.

So, not quite the prickly affair we all expected then? Wrong. This Eastleigh-centric opponent still boasted four former Silverlake men in their starting 11 and another two on the bench (including Binns). The irrepressible Paul Doswell was serving a touchline ban from two separate locations: a seat in the stand and a spot rather close to his coaching troop that was surely sailing close to the wind with regard to the stipulations of his censure.

Richard spent his own 90-minute touchline embargo sat a few rows in front of me. Beside the boss was Chris Todd – any temptation to risk his dicey hamstring was resisted. It was a chance for Richard's 'future assistant' to inject his thoughts on proceedings. The following Monday, the manager delighted in telling a high-spirited group that Toddy's most tactical insight of the afternoon was his exclaiming, 'F****** h***, gaffer, Yemi's got their left-back on toast.'

It was Yemi, making his full home debut, finishing smartly from close range that decided an absorbing match. Jai Reason laid on the chance with a cameo of his skill – a two-second exhibition that would have graced any of the Football League contests concurrently playing out across the land.

The game really bubbled up during the second half. Reason was on the end of some rough treatment from his good mate, Mitchell Nelson – the recipient of a fair degree of stick from the Spitfires faithful – and, typically, responded in kind.

Another confrontation involving Reason and an opponent – sparked by Jai having the temerity to put the back of his head in the way of a forearm smash – culminated with the Sutton player (no names here) threatening to bite his adversary's nose off. I am happy to relate that Eastleigh's playmaker has no need for rhinoplasty. He did confess, however, that his initially amused reaction to the flare-up gave way to some concern upon noticing the riled visiting player foaming at the mouth.

When, on Monday at training, I cheerfully asked Richard if he'd enjoyed his Sunday, I anticipated a response in the affirmative. That being a day after a match against a Paul Doswell outfit I should have known better.

Richard had, by entering the dressing room at half-time, unknowingly flouted the constraints that his ban placed on his match-day contact with players. A miffed Doswell, who had spent half-time kicking his heels by the food van – the Premier League alternative of reclining in a plush executive lounge not being an option – was, on Saturday night, warning that he planned to report his counterpart's transgression to the FA.

A night's sleep gave the Sutton manager time to take a more conciliatory stance – that was until he took in Richard's post-match interview broadcast on the club's website. As he had promised to, Eastleigh's boss drew attention to Doswell's attendance record at the Silverlake. Not wanting to stop there, Richard questioned whether or not Mr Doswell had been as keen to study his other early season opponents.

That was enough to invoke the fury of our ex-boss, so renewing his appetite for taking Richard's contravention of the laws to a higher power. With the tit-for-tat episode at its apogee, Ray Murphy, Eastleigh's indefatigable secretary, produced his photographic evidence of Doswell's positioning close to his own bench during parts of the match.

By Monday morning, Richard and Ray had decided to be pro-active and take control of the situation. A letter was sent to the FA explaining what had happened and that any breach of the rules was made in ignorance. The matter now rests with our game's governing body – a guaranteed swift outcome to follow then.

Elsewhere, Farnborough are making the national news for a barmy sponsorship deal they have struck with a bookmakers, which requires the management and playing staff to change their names to those of football 'legends'. The publicity-hungry Spencer Day ('Jose Mourinho') and his midfielder Scott Donnelly ('David Beckham') were both interviewed on Radio 5 Live about the gimmick. The pair appeared completely unaware of what a tawdry scheme they were subscribing to.

It is the latest chapter in a sorry story. Farnborough have, so far, not deposited the membership bond with the league that is required to participate this season and their opening matches have consequently been postponed.

The whole mess is causing a series of problems. From an Eastleigh perspective, I can already envisage our neighbours from Havant & Waterlooville turning up for their Bank Holiday date at the Silverlake a game lighter than would be the case if they meet Farnborough on August 19th. (I should confess that I had a sneaky look at Everton's fixture on November 9th – the date on which 'Mourinho' is set to bring his team to play the Spitfires. Crystal Palace away. Very handy indeed – until I discover the price of a ticket undoubtedly.)

A final turn up for the books on Saturday was the sight of Damian Scannell among the home substitutes. Scans didn't make it onto the pitch and was again absent from Monday's training. My enquiry as to his whereabouts was met by a typically blunt Richard Hill response, 'He won't play for me again.' It was obvious that this was not an issue the manager was in a mood to discuss much further.

A starter for ten:

Within three days of his valedictory bench-warming appearance, which fellow Conference South club did Damian Scannell sign for?

If you're struggling to answer, they are awash with players who Scannell will know well from their days playing together in the Spitfires blue. I'm wondering when the big money bids for Eastleigh match reporters and supporters will begin.

I was staggered that the 16 outfield players on duty for training two days after a seriously gruelling opening fixture could put one foot in front of another. Indeed, after deliberately loosening their bodies, all managed to complete a bout of short, sharp running exercises with some vim. Included in the troop was Danny Butterfield. Four days later he was making his Carlisle United debut in a League One match at Colchester United's banally named Weston Homes Community Stadium.

Brian Howard, meanwhile, was in the sultry climes of Sofia, having put his signature to a contract with the once mighty CSKA. 'Professional Footballer' has few rivals for the title of 'most precarious/unpredictable/fickle – take your pick – of all possible livelihoods'.

Monday's usual practice game was played with some intensity. Todd was able to take part in everything and finished up by undergoing some individual sprinting under Cookie's instruction.

While 'Toddy' zoomed between cones, Odubade, Spence, and Collins sat icing niggles that had either sprouted in the hour previous or two days earlier. Spence had limped off mid-session, allowing me the chance to catch up with our classy right-back. As well as showing welcome interest in the book, he tapped into my knowledge of the Conference South circuit – which teams will be strong this year, who are the promoted clubs, and who has moved where?

My first duty upon arriving in the morning – prior to helping Guy Butters lug goal frames into their correct position – was filling the assistant manager in on Saturday's other results. Fans and players: same hopes/different worlds.

The constant tending to limbs and other body parts is another sight unfamiliar to the regular fan. Once a player is on the pitch in our team's colours we expect them to operate at full tilt. There is rarely, if ever, any leeway granted for the possibility that an individual might be fatigued or dragging an uncooperative body through the 90 minutes.

The daftest theory I've heard regarding elite footballers is that, owing to the money they earn, they can have no excuse for ever feeling jaded. I am yet to meet the human being whose bank balance has any direct correlation to their health. If personal wealth were any guarantee of physical well-being then Steve Jobs would still be walking the earth.

The former Scotland centre-half, Richard Gough, was still playing in the Premier League at the age of 39. His philosophy was simple – 'a footballer's body is his bank'. The stratospheric fitness demands imposed on players in today's game decree that conditioning is a round-the-clock burden. There are few days during each season on which any one footballer pulls on his boots fully ailment free.

When Todd returned, in chipper mood, from his shuttle running, his usual Monday night hotel accommodation became the hot topic of conversation. Toddy would be travelling home today due to the following night's trip to Bath – a journey he can more easily make from his Devon home. Reason, Beckwith, and Odubade, though, were taking their turn to have an overnight stay in Southampton – Twitter posts later revealing that Beckwith pulled senior rank and condemned the other two to a sharing arrangement.

Most enlightening was Todd's nose for a bargain. He could not have been more enthusiastic when extolling the Slug and Lettuce's cut-price meals. Upon hearing of that snip, Yemi's tail was up. When the two moved on to laud the savings that can be reaped by shopping at Aldi, you could have been ear-wigging a conversation at a coffee morning.

I did ask the pair whether they thought that comparable discussions would be taking place 8.8 miles away at the Staplewood training base of Southampton FC. Unlikely, they surmised.

Prior to this crucial debate, the team had undergone specific shape work with Bath City in mind. Richard had received the lowdown on the Somerset side's opening 2–1 win at Bishop's Stortford.

Ahead of the Sutton clash the manager had overseen a defence-focused exercise, centred on incorporating Chris Dillon into his back-four. The former trialist completed his charge up the outside of the race for places by taking a starting berth on day one. It was a challenge he rose to just as effectively as he had the task of earning a contract. Dillon could prove one of the non-league bargains of the year.

With the narrow margins that exist between so many clubs in this league, addressing the minutiae is essential – no less so than is the case for Manuel Pellegrini or Sam Allardyce. I referred to the attention paid by the manager pre-season to pushing Green up the pitch. From that early period onwards, a recurring aspect of training ground matches has been the requirement for players to fill a variety of positions. Richard believes that if, for example, Yemi is back covering at right-back and makes a costly horlicks of the job, the fault would lie with the manager if he had never asked the winger to fulfil that duty as part of his practice.

They perhaps fall short of 1970s Holland's total football, but when these players are asked to operate outside of individual comfort zones their game intelligence shines through. The standout is McAllister's frequent turns at centre-half – so much so that, in my admittedly layman's eyes, the forward's desire to prolong his career could be bolstered by a newly discovered versatility.

After carrying out my Monday (August 19th) interview with Craig, my wish that he achieve his playing objectives rocketed further still. His attitude is the antithesis to that applied by many a miffed footballer. Not for him the sulking and stirring now routinely utilised by players unhappy with their lot.

Craig is irked to find himself cast to the side-lines. His reaction, with the sole aim of winning back his treasured Spitfires Number 9 shirt, has been to expend every ounce of available energy within his 6ft 1in frame towards meeting that target. Despite his frustration, Craig's training ground demeanour has not suffered at all. It is the same bubbly and quick-witted man who takes the field when he's first-pick who has turned up for work throughout this bumpier period.

It is only two and a half years since Craig was playing for Crawley Town in that FA Cup fixture at Old Trafford. He is now approximately 18 months from being fully qualified to work as a plumber. What price Wes Brown or John O'Shea, Macca's direct opponents that day, considering a trade?

On to Bath City, a 'big ask' coming a little more than 72 hours after the draining clash with Sutton. First and foremost, I am more than a touch grateful that I am here, and in one piece, to continue writing.

My dad and I had taken a late decision to drive to this game. As we made our way home, heartened by a 1–0 win – Strevens '68 for the statisticians – and the assured style in which it was accomplished (I have never seen as controlled and savvy a performance by an Eastleigh team), our choice of transport for the night could have ended in disaster.

Having eased his Honda Civic into the overtaking lane just south of Salisbury, the old man was suddenly confronted by a car hurtling the wrong way up the dual carriageway towards meeting us in a head-on collision. The potential smash was avoided with a swift move back inside. Only in retrospect did we appreciate what a near miss we'd had.

A high-speed car crash would have been an unfortunate end to a very good day. As well as seeing an excellent Eastleigh display, a 100-minute interview I had carried out with Richard the previous week had earlier appeared on the club's website.

The manager had spoken extensively about the unhappy ending to his time at QPR, something that enabled supporters to learn a lot more about the man in charge of their team. He was typically honest when covering a range of other topics – including his opinions on the league's authorities (not high) and his season's ambitions (very high).

The value of Richard's quotes, in tandem with his readiness to open up, made it a challenge to pare the final piece down to 3,000 words. All feedback on the final edit was appreciative and enthusiastic – proof of the fans' thirst for knowledge about the major figures at their club.

All the spirit and togetherness in this evolving squad were called upon to overcome a feverishly motivated and tireless Bath side. Those intangible qualities, common to every Spitfires player, are exactly what any manager – whether in sport or industry – craves in their team.

The fact that Richard's players are 'as one' is no accident. When recruiting a fresh face, he looks beyond the footballer, instead assessing the whole individual. His signings all have in common a totally professional attitude, as do those players retained from the previous regime.

I came away from Bath's Twerton Park fully convinced that not many sides will collect three points from that venue this year. Richard was rather more cynical. 'They won't play like that again this season.' That is the reality for a team who are up there to be shot at – be they defending champions or, as in Eastleigh's case, a club with bold ambition stated by deed and word.

Pressingly, it is why Basingstoke Town, with two wins from two, will be rabidly fired up as they hunt the scalp of their eminent Hampshire rivals on Saturday. That, of course, is a match that will play out away from my gaze. I will be undertaking my wedding usher chores – on a Saturday afternoon, I ask you.

Then, on Monday, I shall slink nervously back into my seat for Eastleigh vs Havant & Waterlooville, or 'El Clasicoast' (copyright Ade: high-profile Hawk, currently controversially banned from the Spitfires fans' internet forum – a decision that has split opinion no less than did England's then manager Glenn Hoddle when he discarded the magnificent, but patently unfit, Paul Gascoigne for the World Cup of 1998).

16

THREE MATCHES AND A WEDDING

A banner, omnipresent at Old Trafford, proclaims, 'Utd Kids Wife In That Order.'

The declaration raises a smile, but really, deep down, despite anything we might say to the contrary – particularly in the wake of our team winning a huge game or suffering a defeat of such gravity that it feels as if the world's end is nigh – football has its place in the hierarchical structure of life. Barbs about the poor timing of my sister's wedding were, of course, made with tongue in cheek. Nevertheless, I can confess to being more than a mite miffed at having to miss the Spitfires' visit to Basingstoke.

When, just past 5pm on Saturday, August 24th, I was able to pounce on a magic half-hour of phone signal availability and peruse the Conference South scores, Basingstoke 2 Eastleigh 0 leapt prominently from the screen. Through a squinted and glazed eye, I leaned in for a closer view as if that might cause the result to change. No joy. The phone was placed back in my pocket, with Everton's humdrum 0–0 draw against West Bromwich Albion barely registering, and the world kept turning.

While the newlyweds were planning to jet off to Borneo for a three-legged honeymoon (three separate destinations that is, they weren't tying their legs together for the duration), a disappointing 753 people were at the Silverlake for a Bank Holiday Monday (August 26th) afternoon in the sun. In fact, the game against Havant & Waterlooville was played in punishing, suffocating, and evidently draining heat.

Coming 48 hours after Basingstoke, and with the labours of three attritional battles already in the players' legs, it was somewhat predictable that this would not be 90 minutes for Conference chiefs to record and use as a marketing tool.

My own concerns about this derby encounter had been raised when I spoke to Richard on Sunday. He made no secret of the fact that his players are a fatigued group. Dean Beckwith had admitted as much to his manager earlier in the day, saying that the efforts at Bath had come insidiously home to roost during Saturday's blip.

A 0–0 stalemate was, in truth, a better outcome for our own Spitfires than the visiting Hawks. Despite the lack of fluency and zest in Eastleigh's play, there was no shortness of commitment and willingness to do the 'ugly' jobs – never more vital than during a parochial contest.

Beckwith had been forced to pull out of the starting 11 after aggravating a groin niggle – something he first felt on Saturday – during the warm-up. Chris Todd's readiness to return, then, was rather opportune. That was until, after just ten minutes, he informed the boss that his hamstring was playing up. Toddy manfully fought on until mid-way through the second half, until the arrival of Havant & Waterlooville's lightning striker Sahr Kabba expedited the need to get a centre-half who was operating on one leg off the pitch.

Todd's replacement? Ramone Rose. Yes, the very same Ramone Rose who weeks earlier was told his services would not be required at the Silverlake. With Scannell's wage no longer an Eastleigh concern, there was scope to bring in the speedster.

'Have you ever played right-back before?' was unlikely to have been the prompt that Ramone expected to herald his first Spitfires appearance. 'A couple of times,' was a compelling enough response for him to be handed a significantly tricky baptism in front of his own fans.

Richard places great stock on the need for any new recruit to hit the ground running. He considers himself to be operating with similarly limited latitude for error. Owner and supporter demand is, he contends, a bar to the type of settling in period that might be granted his own managerial rivals or players finding their feet elsewhere.

Jesse Kewley-Graham, at Havant & Waterlooville on loan from Wycombe Wanderers, had his first stay at Westleigh Park last term. Richard had first dibs on taking the player, but declined. The midfielder was impressive on Monday, but the manager recalls his contribution during that initial Hawks stint as 'bang average'. Afforded the time to integrate, Kewley-Graham has flourished.

Richard believes that had he taken the player, everyone at the Silverlake would have expected a positive impact from day one.

That tale illuminates the severity of Ramone's immediate examination. Happily, he passed with flying colours. Without the label of 'trialist' hanging burdensomely around his neck, we saw the real player – and he is a 'real' player; one newly in receipt of a one-year contract at that.

Both teams did strike the goal-frame during the second 45 minutes. Strevens' header came back off the bar, but Christian Nanetti's 25-yard free-kick smashed against an upright with such venom that the ball flew away for a home throw-in. Nanetti's sparkling performance stood out amid his more workmanlike colleagues and opponents.

Ollie Palmer, who is making a good early impression at Mansfield, was watching on from the stand. I've come to suspect, though, that Palmer's eve of season departure, which had me chuckling away, is not going to prevent Lee Bradbury's team from threatening the League's top five spots.

At training, three days after the meeting with Bradbury's men, Richard expressed to me his admiration for Kewley-Graham's midfield partner, Perry Ryan. My thoughts on the ex-Pompey scholar's abilities haven't always been complimentary. I did, though, thanks to his combative display in the match, gain a modicum of respect for him after last February's 2–2 draw. That has elevated further following Monday. However, to ape another of Richard's favoured lines, 'not for me'.

A player who would be 'for me' is Nic Ciardini. The Havant & Waterlooville attacker was mighty impressive on the three occasions I watched him last season (playing for Farnborough) and is blessed with the proverbial 'cultured left foot'. He is someone Richard had considered as a potential Spitfire before Lee Bradbury nipped in early in the summer.

I did, during a 3,000-word match-report (my longest ever – a result of my bright wedding-inspired mood, enthusiasm for being back at the football and, it must be said, relief at getting out with a point), make mention of Ciardini's lack of pace. The man himself posted a good-humoured comment on Twitter in response. His later description of my chronicle as a 'fair write-up' is praise indeed coming from a member of Eastleigh's local adversary.

With Todd's injury, and Beckwith's current struggles, Richard is back in the market for another addition. The ridiculous 'Transfer Window' is days from closing. Fortunately, that specific restraint of trade is not imposed on clubs below the Conference National.

Ergo, while the daft Gareth Bale saga is nearing its conclusion, Luis Suarez is locked in the 'famous boot room', handcuffed to a replica European Cup while being forced to listen to 'You'll Never Walk Alone' on a loop, and David Moyes scratches away at the last vestiges of his popularity at Goodison Park with 'derisory and insulting' bids for Leighton Baines and Marouane Fellaini, the same urgency does not exist in Conference South environs.

Richard did make a Wednesday afternoon enquiry about the availability, or otherwise, of Salisbury City's towering centre-half/holding midfielder, Brian Dutton, only to discover that the player is injured. Having had his defensive numbers tested before the season's opening fortnight has elapsed, cover in that area is becoming a priority. Chris Dillon is looking a better buy every day.

The ability to bring players in throughout the campaign is instrumental to Richard's ability, when hiring on a permanent basis, to focus on quality over quantity. Adam Watkins and Alex Lacey – both brought in from Luton in the second half of last season – were testament to the boost a top-end loan purchase can provide an entire club. Crucially, the annual wage-bill is more manageable to boot.

Witnessing the unseemly transfer scramble through Eastleigh eyes will be something of a relief. While the self-regarding Scotsman Jim White convulses away on *Sky Sports News*, there is no danger of the Spitfires' name being drawn into any clandestine shenanigans.

One issue that continues to gnaw at Richard is the harsh early season hand, with its abundance of demanding away trips and meetings with potential top-five outfits, he perceives to have been dealt his team. When we spoke the day after Basingstoke, the issue was bugging the manager again. By Wednesday morning, when some message board criticism had needled him, Richard's fires were burning.

Our 40-minute telephone conversation on that day had roughly an 80/20 split with regards words spoken. The manager was raging. Some fans, after the derby match, had questioned why the Hawks weren't summarily dispatched. Remarkably, a few took their gripes further and asked the manager why more cash wasn't being spent on new players. That, along with a lack of wider recognition concerning Eastleigh's demanding start, had stoked Richard's ire –

a lot. He confessed that, after a cooling off period, he had asked Jamie Graham – the chap who records post-match reaction for 'Spitfire TV' – to refrain from uploading a 'rant' that Richard had embarked on after Monday's draw regarding the league's administration.

The majority opinion is that seven points from 12 represents a solid start. The dissenting minority, though, have the loudest, and most grating, voice. I was moved to write a defence of the team on the forum; a rare occurrence indeed – and a crazy situation after four matches.

It was when constructing my message that it dawned on me just how defensive I have become of this bunch of players. I have seen with my own eyes their dedication, professionalism, and appetite for old-fashioned graft. It has, to be honest, blown me away.

What's more, I find it difficult to comprehend how anybody watching the side can have failed to notice that on-pitch commitment and drive are delivered as standard. Yes, the anticipated attacking fluidity is still to emerge, but, crikey, four games.

A regular antagonistic poster on the internet forum argued that there can be no excuse for the 'team not turning up'. I was dumbstruck – that is one fault that Richard's men will never be guilty of.

It cheered me when, on attendance at my maiden 'Spitfires Supporters Club' (TSSC) meeting, the closing 'any other business' included a discussion about the poor uptake of away travel so far this season – in marked contrast to last year's spiralling numbers. There was undisputed agreement that, expressed kindly, any fan who is discontented with this team is quite frankly barmy.

Every football club has its supporters who couldn't honestly list tolerance as one of their virtues. At Eastleigh, the impatient souls are outnumbered by their more even-handed counterparts. It is one of the things that drew me to the Spitfires in the first instance.

Next up was my first TSSC mini-bus trip of the season. All seats were taken with the exception of a spare left by the late withdrawal of Dan Mays, an Eastleigh follower of one year who endures more than his share of ribbing for a lifelong affiliation to Southend United. Dan called off, citing his dodgy Friday night Fajita dinner. The rest of us clambered aboard our 'well-used' mode of transport, consigned to negotiate the stop-start M25 – albeit one impromptu 'stop' was made under duress from an already well-refreshed minority, all watering eyes and straining for a break.

The same crew that had availed itself of industrial amounts of lager, and divvied up 64 flavoured shots of vodka to be dispatched en route to Boreham Wood, was in fine voice on the return leg.

I don't use the word 'fine' lightly. The noise generated may have rendered any communication with my dad – squashed into his seat beside me – impossible, but Eastleigh FC's impassioned barbershop quartet is surely one of the more harmonious mobs of songsters returning from all corners of the land on a football Saturday evening.

A deal of the Beach Boys' back catalogue was given an airing, as were tunes by The Eagles and Meatloaf. We were even 'treated' to some Irish Folk.

Andy Everitt is deserving of a proportion of credit, blessed as he is with a melodic spectrum. Callum Smith, a 23 year old with a fondness for Inverness Caledonian Thistle to sit beside his fanaticism for Eastleigh FC and who had marked one away goal earlier in the day by placing a bin over his head and running around the terrace behind the goal, was another making a hefty contribution to the lyrical elixir.

Callum's mode of backing for his team is exceptional, but far from unique among many individuals for whom attending football matches is a way of life. I have always been baffled by those people who pay good money to get into a football ground, only for the action to completely pass them by in a haze or for 'banter' with opposition supporters to spike their curiosity over and above what is unfolding on the pitch.

Callum freely claims he is sometimes unaware of which players have turned out for the side, the identity of any goal-scorers and, on occasion, the full-time score. In Callum's case it is a complete paradox, given he regularly arrives for an away trip with a copy of *The Non-League Paper* under his arm and has a deep knowledge of, and obvious interest in, the game at this level.

The tone of the trip home's vocal efforts was more guttural when the familiar Eastleigh FC ditties were roared in approval of what had been a clinical 3–0 away victory.

At the previous Thursday's training session, Richard had informed his players, based upon his scouting of the Wood against Bishop's Stortford a week previously, that Saturday's opponents were 'completely f★★★★★★ average'. The evidence proved him correct. Boreham Wood's appetite for the contest was not in doubt. They were simply completely outclassed – not that the Spitfires reached the fluency of which they are capable. It is, nevertheless, coming closer. All in all, it was a perfect riposte to the few disgruntled mutterings in the week.

The 'privilege' of watching the final training ground work ahead of a game was brought home to me, once again, when the team lined up for the match in Hertfordshire exactly as they had on the preceding Thursday for a concentrated 45-minute schooling on shape and tactics. That is, apart from Southam and Beckwith. Glen arrived late onto the training ground, flip-flops on his feet after some time spent under Cookie's care. Dean was taking it extremely easy to protect his dicey groin.

That session had also been notable for other reasons. Beckwith wasn't in need of his Herbalife drink for lunch, but that was nothing to do with his minimal level of energy outlay. Sharon Cavill, a familiar face to all Spitfires fans – along with husband Andy and daughter Lianne – had been on post-training cooking duties during the summer holiday from her job at a secondary school. This was her final day and she went out with a bang, bringing an irresistible collection of cakes to mark the event. (Mr Cavill did declare on Saturday that a week ensconced in his family's household would add much needed meat to the bones of Sam Wilson.)

Having seen off his main course, Dean took the measured decision to dig in to two slices of cake. He wasn't the only one. Jamie Collins isn't a man who will ever go hungry.

In an age of sports science and nutritionists, this pair might have hit upon a more advantageous formula. They were the standout players at Boreham Wood and have been the nascent season's stars – along with Ben Strevens.

My day one assessment of Collins is being made to look more inaccurate by the day. In fact, initial judgement of a player hasn't been as wide of the mark since Ian Wright was deemed not up to the mark by a series of professional talent-spotters during his first football coming – yes, the same Ian Wright who went on to score 185 goals for Arsenal during a rather distinguished career (including, in front of my eyes, a hat-trick on his Gunners league debut at The Dell in 1991).

Conspicuous during Thursday's preparation was the deployment of Craig McAllister as a central striker and the importance placed on his full-backs providing the former Pirelli General (and Exeter City, Crawley Town et al.) man with high-quality service.

When Dan Spence teed up the opening goal for Craig at Boreham Wood, the scorer's fusion of pent-up frustration and desire to play football were plain to all 202 people in the ground (there is some serious competition for support in this corner of North London). Olivier Giroud, celebrating striking the only goal for Arsenal against Tottenham 24 hours later, was no more exuberant in his subsequent expression of joy than his Eastleigh counterpart had been at Meadow Park.

Craig's hearty kick of the advertising hoardings, on his way to receiving the adulation of the buoyant travelling Spitfires, did not possess Temuri Ketsbaia's wild-eyed and uncontrolled fury when the Georgian reacted in similar vein to scoring a goal for Newcastle United in 1998, but it spoke volumes for a keyed-up individual.

Sat away from the hoi polloi in the relative luxury of a main stand seat, I wasn't privy to any of the 'Anglo Saxon' vocabulary that might have come from the mouths of some of the mass of players congregating to salute Macca's effort. It had struck me for the first time on Thursday quite how much swearing takes place in a football environment.

Of course, having played and watched the game for years, it had just not registered. In a quiet moment, I found myself pondering what a lay-person might make of the use of what Americans would term 'curse words', as exclamation marks, full-stops, sentence fillers, or as an emotional response to any event – good or bad. Chat with the players on a more casual basis and you're less likely to hear anything of that type – with a few exceptions.

When I spoke to Craig in the clubhouse after Saturday's match, he confirmed his delight at the day's work – personally and on behalf of the whole team, before beating a hasty retreat to a home-cooked meal. Sunday, he assured me, would be far from relaxing with a two year old to keep entertained.

Richard, in laid-back mode before kick-off, told myself and my dad that, in addition to Dutton, his search for a central defender had led to ultimately vain enquiries for David Artell at Northampton Town and Reading's young prospect Matthew Partridge.

After his team's victory the manager was delighted, although I wouldn't agree with his immediate euphoric assessment that it had been the leading performance of his reign. Notwithstanding that, the contemptuous style in which the game was wrapped up by Stuart Fleetwood's first goal as a Spitfire and a Jai Reason penalty both bode nicely for what lies ahead.

Already, Danny Butterfield's future is comparably less settled. Lost among Transfer Deadline Day headlines about Gareth Bale, Mesut Ozil, and Kaka, the news that Danny's contract at Carlisle had been cancelled – after two appearances – caused my eyebrow to raise even higher than the revelation that West Bromwich Albion are prepared to fork out £6m for Everton's occasional striker Victor Anichebe.

At the conclusion of the pre-Boreham Wood session, Richard had led a group de-brief during which he asked his players if there was any subject they wished to raise. There were no takers. Given the freedom to voice any concerns or request some training ground work be focused in a specific direction, the ensuing silence was interpreted as an expression of general accord.

Richard was especially clear that any discontent or worry should be addressed as a group. Again drawing on his own experience in the mechanisms of a footballer's mind, the manager is determined to guard against any muttering behind hands or splintering of his squad into separate factions all pursuing disparate aims. Collins, McAllister, and Strevens did hang around for a talk with their gaffer, focusing on tactics and everything that has passed so far this term. It was a treat to listen in as real 'football men' enthusiastically discussed their trade.

The boss's final message for the day was one to file under 'professionalism'. It certainly wasn't a directive to meet with the approval of the puritans.

'You need to start getting in referees' ears. By that, I don't mean like Suvs [Southam] and Strevs [Strevens] telling him he's a ******* ******. You need to be clever. Remind him he's not given us anything. "Come on, ref, you haven't given us a free-kick for ten minutes." Keep at him.'

It was a command prompted by two incidents against Havant & Waterlooville, when Richard believed his team were denied obvious free-kicks because they had 'made it easy for the referee to ignore them' – decisions that came close to costing Eastleigh the game. No detail is left to chance.

August is over. The dark nights are looming. But, at Eastleigh FC, September signals only a fight for 12 valuable points – and the magic of the FA Cup.

17

LEAVE IT TO THE PROS

'Hi Rich. Just in case you haven't seen, [Charlie] Clough at Dorchester has asked to leave – although I'm sure they'll be after a decent fee!'

'I knew last week.'

'I thought you'd be in the loop on that one.'

'Sutton want him…'

'But he's never played for Eastleigh! I rate him – and Walker who used to play next to him.'

'What positions are they?'

(Anticipating having my head placed in a metaphorical guillotine ready for its clean removal.) 'Both centre-halves. Big and strong, read the game well, and fairly young.'

Then, the tone of a breezy text conversation shifted.

'I'll sign them and move Beckwith and Todd on.'

Ahem. I might have stamped on the manager's toes here.

(Scrambling back – especially given my high regard for both Eastleigh players; as already stated Beckwith has been a standout performer over the season's opening weeks.)

'Haha. I was thinking more in terms of your recent need for another body in that area. I appreciate Clough would cost though… and want to play. The way Beckwith is playing, I think anybody would do well to find a better centre-back outside the league.'

'You stick to journalism!'

'Haha… good idea. I think I'm right about Beckwith though!'

And there, at 13:28 on September 3rd, 18 minutes after it had started, ended that particular conversation.

Notwithstanding my appreciation at being implicitly considered a 'journalist', I could consider myself to have been put back in my box.

My original text was sent without a second thought – and with genuinely helpful intentions. I was logged in to my Twitter account – natch – when I saw the story break regarding Clough's desire to move on. Fully versed in Richard's potential requirement for an additional defender, and knowing he probably had better things to do with his day than be sat trawling through his social media timelines, I considered it worth ensuring he was aware that one of the league's better centre-backs could be available.

Mindful of the lure of Eastleigh for any footballer at this level, and that Richard is on good terms with Clough's manager at Dorchester's Avenue Stadium, Phil Simkin, I knew that it was odds on that the manager would have been informed of the situation.

As we walked over to the Wellington Sports Ground training fields two days later, I did my best to clarify the fact that I hadn't appointed myself de facto scout for Eastleigh FC.

My next text exchange with the manager took place on Sunday (September 8th). I happened to ask if, with Dan Spence having hobbled off with what looked a serious hamstring injury against Bromley 24 hours earlier, the need for that defender had become ever more pressing.

After being initially chastised once more, 'Stop being a supporter!', a subsequent message disclosed that the Spitfires' ranks have been boosted once more.

'Keep this to yourself and ya dad. Please don't tell anyone else, but Damian Batt has just agreed to sign.'

Batt's pedigree is strong. He has won promotion to the Football League with both Barnet and Oxford United – and spent the past three years playing in League Two with the latter. Intriguingly, earlier this week, at the tender age of 28, Batt declared his intention to retire.

'After turning down some fantastic opportunities and offers, I have had to make the hardest decision of my life and retire from full-time professional football. I appreciate all the messages I have received and I understand people wanted to know where I was signing. But I am looking forward to the future and focusing on my businesses.'

Despite the caveat that his retirement is from the 'full-time' game, it still represents a coup for Richard and the club to persuade the player, three days after he had released the above statement, to put his name to a Spitfires contract.

It would be stretching a point to say that Spence's injury rendered Saturday's (September 7th) 2–1 win over Bromley a Pyrrhic victory. It is, nevertheless, a kick in the teeth – for team and player. Dan offers the side much more than just his reliable defending at right-back. Some of his attacking play this season has been fantastic and, moreover, his presence was integral to the successful functioning of the set-up employed by Richard during the Boreham Wood and Bromley matches.

This book is not intended as a tactical thesis so, put plainly, the team are playing 4-3-1-2. Fleetwood is operating centrally, alongside the restored McAllister, and suddenly looks like the striker who should be playing higher up the football pyramid. That midfield three is narrow. Ergo, the full-backs are charged with providing width. Dan Spence is extremely proficient at doing just that, and equally adept at wreaking havoc once he gets forward.

Ironically, or sickeningly for the man in question, the interview that I conducted with Dan prior to the campaign's starting was published in Saturday's match programme. The underlying theme of the piece was the player's delight at being fit again after sustaining an injury in February four games into his Eastleigh career and his consequent determination to showcase his quality throughout the forthcoming campaign.

A sample line: 'I just want to have a good run of games, stay injury free and show the fans what I can do, help the team push on and have a good start to the season.'

If Batt is to sign on for the term, and performs to the standard expected, there will be a delicious scrap for the full-back spots.

Having spoken to Dan for that article, and gradually begun to know him a little better during the past couple of months, a conspicuous element of his make-up is his marked intelligence. Indications are that the apparent steep average on-pitch IQ among Richard Hill's ranks shouldn't suffer for Batt's inclusion.

After being released by Oxford in the summer, Damian was close to making a move to Vancouver Whitecaps. The Canadian press made great play of the fact that, when he boarded a flight to their country to discuss his prospective move, the 'well-read right-back' was armed with a copy of the Nelson Mandela autobiography, *Long Walk to Freedom*.

Whatever next; 'Footballer settles down to watch *Panorama*'? No. That would be preposterous.

The Bromley outfit, which was vanquished 2–1 by way of some of the most enterprising and captivating football you could hope to see – on what was the official 'Non-League Day' – came to the Silverlake having won four of their first five games. Their team included the man who had been named as the Conference South's 'Player of the Month' – Pierre Joseph-Dubois. The decision confused Richard, who believed that Beckwith should have been a shoo-in for that particular award.

League leaders or not, Mark Goldberg's side were outclassed during a first half that could conceivably have seen the Spitfires construct an advantage well in excess of their two-goal lead.

Goldberg, however, a man famed for his whittling away a personal fortune when owner of Crystal Palace, exhibited a huge degree of tactical nous by making a series of changes that altered the tide of the game. Nails were being chewed all round as we watched our team hanging grimly to their three points, but hang on they did, thanks in no small part to Flitney's goalkeeping – which is currently hitting serious heights.

For the entire 90 minutes of any game the Number 1 can be heard urging, driving, and yes, bollocking his colleagues. He told me that this is a conscious tactic, employed to guard against his mentally knocking off. So far as his 'keeping attributes go, Ross's vigilance tops the list. I have long since lost count of the number of times my match reports have mentioned him racing from his area to swipe a ball clear of an onrushing attacker.

Whomever the day may bring as Eastleigh's adversary, Richard is fond of saying that it is incumbent on him to win every match. During tactical preparation for Bromley he drummed that message into the players. 'You play for a football team that has to win matches, so you have to take gambles.'

In the wider football world, millions of pairs of eyes are fixed towards England's World Cup qualifier in Ukraine. The big debate centres on whether Roy Hodgson should revert to his pragmatic self and prioritise the avoidance of defeat, as opposed to going on the front-foot and seeking to earn what would be a colossal three points. If Richard Hill was manager, one imagines there would only be one way to go.

This isn't a group of players that is perturbed by the broad expectation resting on their shoulders. When, days after the draw with Havant & Waterlooville, I was chatting to Beckwith about his fitness issues and resultant pre-derby pull-out, Jamie Collins suggested with a smile that his team-mate 'was too scared' to play in front of a big crowd. That humour was typical of the prevailing cheery atmosphere throughout a lighter first half-hour of Thursday's pre-Bromley session, time that included an interesting debate about the value in the £42.4m Arsenal had shelled out for Mesut Ozil's signature earlier in the week – over the top was the consensus.

The first discordant Eastleigh voice of the day was saved for lunch when Fleetwood, freshly showered and coming inside from the day's searing heat, saw that chicken curry was the dish of the day. If the choice of fare didn't agree with him, then the sight of it only further disturbed our resident food critic. You're entitled to your opinion, though, when you then go out and score a goal of the blistering nature that 'Fleets' hit, to add to McAllister's smart headed effort, against Bromley on Saturday.

Fleetwood's finish was of the 'violent' variety. It will have delighted a manager who had grown progressively more exasperated during Thursday's shooting drill. Demanding his players apply 'violence' to the skill, Richard instead bore witness to some frankly awful efforts.

After Collins had nonchalantly lifted a ball wildly over an open goal from two yards (and I'm being generous), the boss's patience snapped.

'This is not good enough. It's lazy. Set your standards. It matters as much here as it does on a Saturday.'

Akin to the classrooms of the country's schools, now back from their summer break, the lesson's tone became more hushed, while chastened pupils endeavoured to please their master.

At the same session, I discussed with Richard the reserve team's showing the preceding Monday (September 2nd). He agreed with my interpretation of the performance against Sholing's second string. Entertaining, but the players – most of who are still finding their way around a razor – are some way from being ready for any first-team action, notwithstanding their 2–1 victory on the night.

One midfielder, Jamie Bulpitt, bravely contested a host of tackles that many bigger, stronger players would have baulked at. Jamie has trained with the first team, but, on this competitive outing, he was strangely shorn of the composure in possession I had seen on the practice field. His was the display that Richard picked out as worthy – alongside that of Lewis (aka 'The Cat', and since revealed as Lewis Noice). Jamie took his place on the bench for Bromley's visit. It was reward for the youngster's reserve exertions, but, more pertinently, exposed the dwindling numbers on which the manager can presently call.

Chris Dillon continued his epic emergence, starting again, but was responsible for handing Bradley Goldberg – Mark's excellent striking son –a chance to score, which he duly took with some aplomb. Chris has proved something of a hit with supporters. When my dad and I went to tick our chosen name for August's TSSC 'Player of the Month' award, we both wholly expected to be supplementing Beckwith's runaway triumph. Not so. Chris was steaming ahead. No matter. If he wins the vote, I can't imagine there'd be a more grateful recipient.

I had asked Chris, on Thursday, when he was (uncomplainingly) eating his curry, how the standard of football he is experiencing compares to that which he tasted on his travels in the USA and Australia. He had no hesitation in saying that this is a considerable step-up. Still, a man who took himself off to Alabama at the age of 18 to pursue a four-year sports scholarship is unlikely to be overly vexed by his current challenge.

Richard did, while watching Thursday's eight-a-side training match, throw me a figurative bone after the Clough debacle. The manager agreed with my analysis of Sam Wilson's 'ressies' outing. Sam would be far better utilised as a striker working on the last defender's shoulder, rather than operating deeper and having to thrust his slender frame into a procession of physical battles for possession as happened on Monday.

Then suddenly, the boss was off. Something in the eight-a-side action didn't meet with his approval. I'd been able to absorb what was happening in the match, but the manager's digestion of every single occurrence, all while holding a conversation, was remarkable.

His coaching points were imparted with reference to a series of incidents that had unfolded across the previous five minutes. Be it a player's slightly poor positioning at a specific juncture, somebody having embarked on the wrong run, or a passing option being ignored in favour of an inferior choice, nothing had escaped the gaffer's eye.

I don't know if it's due to Richard's intuitive coaching, or my own sheltered existence, but I can scarcely remember anything holding me quite so rapt as do the tactical intricacies of Eastleigh's training sessions.

Michael Green's decision-making continues to fall under his manager's scrutiny. Greener playing a sideways pass, during a team shape exercise, rather than open his field of vision to spark a more enterprising sortie, provoked one of the boss's more excitable interventions of the week.

When the left-back made that particular pass, I instantly sensed that it would not meet with approval. Six weeks ago, I'd have considered it a good ball. Time spent in this environment can't help but evolve personal game appreciation – a by-product of this venture that I hadn't anticipated.

Richard wasn't the only person bending Green's ear on Thursday. Beckwith, who looks to be thriving on his football as only a man in such authoritative form can, spent the duration of the 8v8 contest loudly demanding the unbending concentration and application of his defensive colleagues. The centre-back's focus embodied that of a 'real pro' – training as one would play. Green was Dean's chief target for a tongue lashing – lambasted for not meeting his senior team-mate's rarefied standards.

Surrounded by the likes of Flitney, Beckwith, and Todd, all coaxing him along, and blessed with a talent for his position, Greener has the potential to mature sufficiently for a successful future return to the Football League.

A prosperous week for Eastleigh FC was supplemented by the training ground sight of Will Evans, with Andy Cook watching on, completing an onerous workout. It may just be that Will is going to avoid the surgeon's scalpel. The initial diagnosis of cartilage damage was errant. Will actually suffered severe bone bruising and could be back with us by the time September is out.

Needless to say, there can be no positive spin placed on a 21 year old having his knee opened up and meddled with. If all goes smoothly from here, it will be a considerable boost to the Spitfires' prospects of topping this league – and for a prospective stellar Football League career.

Sprinting and stretching with Will were Chris Todd and Glen Southam. Todd is tentatively optimistic that his second come-back isn't far off. Southam has not taken part in full training for some weeks, dogged as he is by a misbehaving thigh. Notwithstanding his discomfort, Glen has refused to miss a game. This is a man who would be absolutely lost without his weekly fix. It doesn't take a psychologist to recognise a character who will, one day, find it hard to replace the twin buzz of competitive football and dressing room camaraderie.

18

THE RIGHT STUFF

One of the joys of non-league football is the underlying friendliness – even respect – that exists in many of its traditional rivalries. Havant & Waterlooville might be Eastleigh's most local adversary, but the relationship between the two clubs – and their respective sets of supporters – is more cordial than antagonistic.

There are exceptions and, disappointingly, the game outside of the league is, on occasion, used as a vehicle by Neanderthals bent on re-creating 1970s- and 1980s-style mayhem – particularly now that such backwards behaviour is so passé at Premier League venues.

In the modern day, any incidence of football-related violence – especially inside a ground – comes as something of a shock. That was certainly true when a brief kerfuffle broke out during the second half of the Spitfires' latest win – by three goals to one at Maidenhead on Saturday (September 14th).

A few of the more refreshed travelling fans took it upon themselves to celebrate the game's progress, by exuberantly running the length of the touchline towards the end occupied by most of the home support. That, predictably, provoked any irascible personalities among the Maidenhead faithful, with inevitable consequences.

The ensuing stramash was over within 60 seconds, but that was plenty long enough to cast a cloud over an otherwise – from a football perspective – ideal day.

First and foremost, Eastleigh were magnificent. They responded to going behind just after the quarter-hour, having been in charge up until that point, by replying two minutes later. Yemi Odubade put the team ahead with his second goal of the game and McAllister, having come off the bench, added a third. It was a 90-minute performance that, for its dominance of possession, quick passing, and astute movement, illustrated quite how good this side is.

Their opponents had until now boasted the league's only unbeaten record and were, in spells, impressive. Yet, when the Spitfires put their foot to the floor, there was an obvious chasm between the sides.

This was the first day of the campaign to throw up an Eastleigh–Everton conflict. As alluded to earlier in this book, the Toffees on the telly would once have meant, without question, a week's break from watching my 'non-league team'.

The pendulum has swung, though, and talkSPORT's commentary was my medium for following the first half from Goodison. When Steven Naismith scored on the stroke of half-time, with my dad and me still two minutes from home, celebrations were as much of the shocked variety as anything too wild. I 'enjoyed' the second half from an armchair – only fitting for my new Everton-supporting status – and pondered afterwards on how Roberto Martinez is progressively winning me over. I'm sure the savvy Spaniard will be thrilled.

Forty-eight hours before that doubly satisfying day, I interviewed Chris Todd. 'Toddy' spoke about his diagnosis, at the age of 27, with chronic myeloid leukaemia. It wasn't a subject I dwelt on, but there is little doubt that experience has had a part in forming today's personable, ebullient man – one who plainly relishes and appreciates the manner in which he earns a living.

Now free of the illness for two years, an indication of Chris having returned to a more 'normal' way of life is his confessed irritation at sustaining an early season injury. 'I'm gutted I'm not playing and I still feel left out in my own head because as a footballer you want to be a part of it, and when you're not involved you feel like you're drifting away.' Football has crept its way back up the priority list. For those bitten by the bug it always will.

There is, though, in Chris's day-to-day existence, one remnant of his encounter with ill health. 'I just take my tablet – one tablet a day – my "super pill". It's incredible. I take it each night and it keeps me alive because it keeps away the badness of the leukaemia. Luckily, for the last two years, there's not been a speck of it showing.'

The Welshman was fit enough for the bench at Maidenhead and is likely to make a full return soon. When he does, that is likely to be at the expense of Chris Dillon, described in Saturday's local paper as the 'Spitfires' surprise package' – and confirmed as the supporters club's August player of the month.

Three days prior to the shenanigans at Maidenhead, I had accompanied my dad to Westleigh Park to watch Havant & Waterlooville entertain Farnborough. The match was re-scheduled after the Football Conference, in an act of self-preservation on September 5th, authorised Farnborough's continued participation in the Conference South. Gratifyingly, their membership was permitted on condition that the players are registered under their birth names – one in the eye for Boro's shameless bookmaking sponsor.

A transfer of the club's ownership from 'Farnborough Football & Social Club Limited' to 'Boro FC Limited' enabled the football team to carry on. Whatever their off-field predicament, Spencer Day's side looked slick and organised. The Hawks were fortunate to win the game 2–1. It was an entertaining way to spend a wet, miserable, typical November (in September) English evening.

Watching Havant take on Farnborough, along with a flock of Conference South bosses – our very own Mr Hill, Paul Doswell (fresh from signing Charlie Clough), Tommy Widdrington, and Phil Babb – were a few of the Silverlake hard-core. Committee men, Mike Wimbridge and Stuart Solly, director John Russell, and man of many parts, Mike Andrews, couldn't resist 90 minutes of midweek football.

I was up bright and early the next morning for what is currently my routine Thursday training ground visit (September 12th) – the day of my Todd interview and the team's final preparations for Maidenhead.

While waiting outside for the players to emerge from the changing rooms, I was treated to the sustained noise perfected by groups of footballers everywhere – a cacophonous, piercing sound that evokes mental pictures of an agitated aviary.

Stewart Donald popping his head in briefly calmed things down, but so high are spirits in this winning team, the din quickly returned. The chairman and Mark Jewell both later ate lunch with the players – and pontificated merrily on whether they would win by three or four at Maidenhead.

During the intervening session, Richard had informed his charges of Stewart's light-hearted promise to buy his first-team manager an Aston Martin if they progress as far as the third round of the FA Cup and then draw Liverpool. 'Been and done that already,' said Jamie Collins.

On the day I am writing (Monday, September 16th) Eastleigh have pulled out Mangotsfield United at home in the competition's second qualifying round.

Mangotsfield play in the same clunkily named 'Southern League Division One South & West' as one of our pre-season opponents, North Leigh. Moreover, they've only won one of their first five fixtures. 'We're on the march with Hilly's army… etc.'

I was still kicking my heels on Thursday when a harried-looking Damian Batt, now officially an Eastleigh player, scurried past at 10:52am. I didn't hear any paint being torn off the walls, so I assume one late mark early in his Spitfires career was forgiven. Batt played 'within himself' at Maidenhead – understandable for a man making his maiden outing of the campaign.

A merry and boisterous training atmosphere was no bar to Southam losing his rag during early shooting exercises. These drills, again, kept the spare goalkeepers excessively busy scurrying off to collect footballs sprayed far and wide. A lot of the digs at goal were the polar opposite of what Yemi and Macca would produce two days later – and we'll all settle for that.

It shouldn't pass without mention that Fleetwood went on to retain the cloak of the Silverlake's resident Gregg Wallace. The cottage pie was 'dry' and needed washing down with a vat of orange juice. I had shared my first extended conversation with Stuart that morning. He was far more amiable than I had imagined when studying his manner from afar, and is obviously delighted to be starting matches in his favoured centre-forward spot.

It is enchanting to encounter a footballer who so plainly loves the game he is paid to play. When I broached the subject of Stuart spending his childhood Saturday afternoons watching Gloucester City there was an appreciable softening in what is a guarded exterior. I had harboured niggling doubts about whether 'Fleets' was in this Spitfires revolution for the long haul. All it took was that five-minute chat for my scepticism to be dispelled – as much as can be possible in this fickle world anyway.

After later teasing down his mince and potatoes, Stuart was discussing with colleagues his latest business venture. My curiosity got the better of me and I enquired what said business involves. I should have known. Herbalife. Another training ground revelation had come in the form of Richard admitting that he is sampling these magical elixirs.

The evidence in front of my own eyes suggests, though, that whichever your Herbalife product of choice, there is nothing in the ingredients to dampen a fiery temperament. I am writing three days after my last despatch and, in the meantime, the Spitfires took on and beat another of the season's quick starters, Eastbourne Borough (on Tuesday, September 17th). When Tommy Widdrington, the East Sussex club's manager, demanded the referee book Jai Reason for a trivial offence, Richard snapped.

I discovered today that the verbal pressure being applied from the visiting dugout on the man in the middle had started in minute one and continued unabated. Reason receiving his card under those circumstances, early in the second half, sent his manager into a state of apoplexy.

Richard, evidently seething, began a march towards his opposite number – only to change direction and head for the tunnel, while beckoning/imploring Widdrington to follow him. The target for the Spitfires boss's rage declined the invitation, but would spend the remainder of the match intermittently goading the man whose team were striding out to a 2–0 victory.

The away side were kept on the field for a post-match warm down – a move that Richard believed had its motives fully in providing an excuse for their manager to avoid the dressing room area. Perhaps mercifully, the Geordie disappeared stealthily into the night, not to be seen again at the Silverlake until next year at the earliest. The return fixture later this term is already one to whet the appetite.

It will be extremely tough as well. Borough were a gritty, expansive outfit. With a more favourable run of the ball they would have gone into half-time with a lead. As it was, Eastleigh reached the break at 0–0 and, after Reason had hit a 49th-minute penalty so far over the bar that the local air traffic control centre was plunged into chaos, went on to impose their class on the visiting team. After his erratic Chris Waddle-esque 12-yard effort, Jai came to the fore, taking on responsibility for righting his error, scoring one and creating the other.

Training today (September 19th) was, naturally, another rambunctious affair. Numbers were sufficient for nine-a-side to be the order of the day (19 trained in total, which is as healthy a turnout as I've witnessed since the days of trialists and scorching July sun).

Will Evans took part in his first full session since pre-season. After a careful recovery process under the expert guidance of Andy Cook, Will is back and moving freely. His renewed mobility must be a colossal relief for an ambitious 21-year-old footballer who, less than seven weeks ago, feared he had suffered anterior cruciate ligament damage.

Today's stricken men formed a very exclusive group. Jamie Collins, having sustained a niggle in his groin against Eastbourne, expects to miss Saturday's free-entry home fixture against Hayes & Yeading United. Dan Spence is still nursing his torn hamstring back to health, but expects to be ready for action soon.

As his stock of fit players rises, Richard might just have some tough decisions on his hands. Whichever way he goes, the issue of team selection is sure to exercise some locals. Not to the same degree, though, as a refreshing thread initiated by Callum on the ever-intriguing Spitfires internet message board.

One of the more 'lively' members of the away support, Callum had, after a bout of introspection and self-flagellation, concluded that his on-the-road behaviour might be portraying Eastleigh FC in a bad light. That prompted reams of forum posts expressing a range of views on the twin subjects of drinking on away trips and conduct inside grounds – a hot topic after the Maidenhead contretemps – and subsequently, the resultant effects of these issues on travelling numbers.

In light of my dad and me opting to drive to more fixtures away from the Silverlake this year (a happening I would never have foreseen when I first boarded a TSSC mini-bus 12 months ago), it was fascinating, and enlightening, to discover how many other supporters choose to journey separately from the raucous 'official' transport.

Adding to the debate, the Maidenhead game had been the first at which a 'fancam' was operated. This was a camera aimed for 90 minutes directly at the Eastleigh following congregated behind the goal. If we didn't already know it, this confirmed that there are some supporters who prioritise the away-day high-jinx over watching the on-pitch action.

Nevertheless, it has to be appreciated that everyone has their own way of enjoying their football experience. For many, the promise of replicating my match day would appeal no more than walking to every away game with a nail in their shoe. There is a balance to be drawn and it will be intriguing to track the forthcoming narrative.

While a section of their followers relish a liquid lunch – again, not a criticism, different strokes, etc – the players' edible variety today came in the form of pizza slices eaten in the club shop. The unusual dining venue was due to a large electricity company staging a health and safety training day for 150 employees at the stadium. Every single revenue source is being mined.

I had spoken to a 'rusty' Sam Wilson ahead of Thursday's training. The youngster was downbeat after what he felt was a poor personal midweek reserve outing, when only a late goal saved a 2–2 draw against the second string of Wessex League outfit, AFC Portchester.

As the players walked off the field, having completed their nine-a-side and prior to another intriguing directed exercise centred on the shape of the side, Glen Southam took Sam aside. 'Sam. You've got to work harder in these games, son. You've got all the ability in the world. I need more from you.'

With Chris Todd over his hamstring trouble, Chris Dillon found himself in a group separate to that working towards Saturday and Hayes & Yeading. It is a harsh, harsh game – and it tests its combatants' characters. 'Dills', in common with so many of his colleagues, exudes the air of a man who is made of the 'right stuff'. The tactic adopted by any individual fighting for his place in this Spitfires unit, as already laudably embodied by McAllister, is to get their head down and work like mad.

That widespread attitude could be a determining factor in this book having a very happy ending.

19

TWO CUPS AND A DOUBLE DECKER BUS

Prior to the clash with Hayes & Yeading on Saturday, September 21st, I was due to conduct a semi-formal interview with Chris Blake, the tireless chairman of the TSSC. With the debate concerning both the away-day antics and fancam having gathered pace over the preceding couple of days, Chris declared his heart not to be in his role at present – to the extent that he didn't feel he'd do justice to his 'Fans Head' status in any chat. Moreover, Chris was considering resigning the post that he has held for two and a half years.

The bunch that likes a match-day tipple consider themselves to have been painted as lager louts and took to wearing ties to the game – a forthright answer to perceived criticism and, most hurtfully, accusations that some of their away-day behaviour has besmirched the Eastleigh FC name.

This unforeseen outbreak of inner conflict indicates how many elements, many of them away from what happens on the pitch, contribute to the enjoyment of any one person's football experience.

Andy Cavill has volunteered his services for what I consider to be *the* most thankless of all Eastleigh FC related tasks – driving the mini-bus on those away trips that attract smaller numbers. With laundry now being aired, in what has started to feel like a Spitfires version of world cycling's mooted 'truth and reconciliation committee', Andy has felt liberated to say that anybody behaving inappropriately on his watch will be dumped at the next service station.

Still, the debate raged. Once in my seat – well before kick-off, of course – a long-time Eastleigh follower, Paul from nearby Romsey, and somebody I often spend time at games dissecting the action with, told me that he and his young son, as well as two regular match-going friends, feel ostracised by a bulk of fellow supporters owing to their travelling to away matches by train.

For this scenario to develop, it is evident that there is an issue to be addressed. This fella, a Southampton fan by birth, was a Spitfires devotee before me and before many of his detractors. He was at the Silverlake when more trees than stands surrounded the pitch. The team were playing in the Wessex League (three tiers below the level at which they operate today). If he wanted to know of any team changes, he would simply ask Mr Eastleigh (the club's founder and Life President) Derik Brooks for the information.

There was no doubting the fans' backing for the club and its team during this latest match: 1,202 patrons took advantage of the opportunity to take in some free football – although the late re-arranging of a Southampton Under-21 fixture at St Mary's to a Saturday 3pm kick-off was causing Mark Jewell some early consternation. Leyton Orient are currently living with an omnipresent fear about the effect on their very livelihood when, in 2016, West Ham United move into the nearby Olympic Stadium. Any threat to attendance figures, no matter how small, is a serious issue here. Nobody feels the loss of every single pound more keenly than 'Jeweller'.

If one of the prime motivations of this brave initiative was to attract any hitherto Silverlake virgins back for more, then Phil Babb did his bit to nip that intention in the bud. With his Liverpool connections, Babb doesn't readily spring to mind as one of the football men I hold in any great esteem. Nevertheless, I do have a flicker of admiration for a former Premier League footballer who, with, one imagines, oodles of cash already in the bank, is prepared to put in the hard yards to make a go of his maiden managerial job.

The now Hayes & Yeading boss was at the Spitfires' game against Eastbourne on Tuesday and, after witnessing the ultra-cautious manner in which he asked his side to play when it was their turn to take on the league leaders, one can only conclude that the way in which Tommy Widdrington's team walked away with nothing, after a spirited and adventurous performance, sent a shiver down his spine.

Babb's side came to the Silverlake in rare form and the manager patently did not want a heavy defeat to damage the upbeat mood in his squad. It made for ugly viewing, an aesthetic work not helped when the visitors were reduced to ten men before half-time. Craig McAllister's goal minutes after that dismissal eventually proved the decider. Indeed, there were some shaky moments near the end when the visitors' inevitable point-seeking charge arrived.

I was at the training ground two days later (September 23rd) and was immediately struck by Sam Wilson's application. The bit was firmly between the teenager's teeth. Whether that is a direct consequence of Southam's word in his ear it is impossible to know, but the skipper's intervention has certainly done no harm.

I know that Sam is yearning to feature in the FA Cup on Saturday, but I would expect his first-team chance to come in a less glamorous Hampshire Senior Cup tie against Wessex League side, Whitchurch United, the following Tuesday.

Yemi, injured after half an hour on Saturday, Southam, and Collins – who against Hayes & Yeading made a return in Yemi's stead from what amounted to a 75-minute absence, after being forced off against Eastbourne – were all off working in the swimming pool, and 'Greener' ill, but there were enough bodies for a Monday nine-a-side.

When that game was over would there be reward for the team's sparkling run of results, off to lunch and home for the day? No. Richard had a surprise up his sleeve, which could only have been less popular among his players if he'd told them they were all up for transfer and would be having their pay withheld.

In two bunches of eight, all of the first-team unit in attendance, including Flitney and Dovey, performed eight penalty-box to penalty-box – and back – sprints, the rest period in between each run lasting as long as the other group took to complete their dash.

By the time five shuttles had been performed there wasn't one man, resplendent in shiny new blue training gear, not bent double with a mix of exhaustion and raw pain. Yet, before they could begin to recuperate, the sound of heavy feet and heavier breathing grew louder as colleagues approached, and it was time to drag burning legs and pale faces off the starting line once more.

It is the most enervated condition, inclusive of pre-season, that I have witnessed these players reach. Sam struggled, perhaps due to his earlier exertions. He wasn't alone. With honorary Kenyan Green on his sick bed, it was Fleetwood who emerged as the morning's thoroughbred.

Jai Reason was making plain, as early as three runs in, his feelings regarding this start to the week. For his energy-wasting complaints, he was assured that everybody would be subjected to an extra run. In the clubhouse, and still miffed, Jai harked back to something he believed Richard had once said: 'You do alright on the pitch and when it comes to training I'll look after you.'

Yet, for all that, I suspect that Jai loves the graft. It is what allows him to bring his exceptional skills to the main stage.

The root of Richard's disgruntlement this week – some internet criticism for the keep-ball approach to seeing out Saturday's match aside; a few wanted to see Hayes & Yeading torn to shreds – was that Phil Babb game-plan.

During a text chat on Sunday, the manager had already made clear to me his disillusion with respect to the 'anti-football', bus parking tactics employed by the West London side. Continuing that discussion face-to-face, it didn't take long to discern the extent to which the manager was annoyed.

It was only Babb's status as a rookie boss that spared him Richard's public criticism. The manager's opprobrium was reserved for Babb's assistant, Tristan Lewis – a man who also holds the posts of Reading FC's Academy Director and Eton College's First Team Coach. Neither of Lewis's gilded positions in the game, nor his avalanche of qualifications, prevented him from unleashing on the referee a 'spirited' half-time critique. That would be usurped when, at full-time, he turned his verbal barrage towards the opposing dugout. Richard's colourful description of an ensuing confrontation in the tunnel hints towards another future tasty return contest to add to that at Eastbourne.

Listening in, and contributing when I dared, to a conversation between the boss and Flitney, the final verdict is 'we got the win and that is all that matters'. It is. Eastleigh had been in the ascendancy against the same opponents away from home last season when, late in the first half, they found themselves up against a team reduced by a red card to ten men. We expected, from there, a cake walk. What transpired was a 2–1 defeat.

Yes, Saturday was a dour watch, but the discipline of Babb's players, which at once speaks well of them and the faith they have in their new boss, made Saturday a true test. Eastleigh's goalkeeper and manager agreed that it is unlikely their team would have come through a similar examination before this campaign. Notwithstanding the victory, Richard confessed to his overriding sentiment in its wake as being one of 'anger', purely because of the opposition's negativity.

There was no such downbeat mood during another raucous mealtime.

Generating significant curiosity was the arrival in the clubhouse of the freshly released autobiography of one Ian Baird. Aside from the customary index searches for individual citations, there was some incredulity regarding the £14.99 cover price.

This led to Jamie Collins chastising Chris Todd for re-releasing his own diaries (Chris initially self-published) and cashing in again for the same product – overlooking for the benefit of his verbal prodding that all proceeds from the book's sales are funnelled towards a leukaemia charity. Referring to an extra chapter, which updated events in his life since the original edition, Chris explained that the book had a different ending. Now Collins was really on his man. 'How on earth can it have a different ending?'

'He died,' said Richard.

Cue a lot of laughter, especially from the published author in our midst. Football managers everywhere love to talk about the 'great spirit and togetherness of the lads'. Richard went one further in an interview with the *Southern Daily Echo* this week. 'My players all love each other to bits.'

They don't, though, all put the same price on the local derby as their supporters. One of the questions I put to Richard during an interview I carried out on behalf of his former club, Stevenage, alluded to that club's rivalry with Woking, and asked whether he and his players understood it.

The typically blunt answer was that, for them, it was just another game and that, fantastic duel though it was, it didn't concern players or management to the degree it did the fans. I couldn't resist asking if his present crop buys into their own local conflict with any more relish than his Stevenage class.

'Nah, not really. If Havant & Waterlooville had six or seven players with a PO [Portsmouth] Post Code, and we had seven or eight with an SO [Southampton] Post Code it would be far more intense. That's the problem you get nowadays, isn't it?'

I shouldn't have asked.

By the time Eastleigh's youngsters took to the Silverlake pitch for their FA Youth Cup first qualifying round tie against Wimborne Town that night, the manager was long gone. There is presently a chasm between the under-18 and first team operations – Richard prefers to assess any advanced rookies in the more exacting environment – mentally, physically, and technically – of his day-time training.

The 132 hardy regulars taking a look at the 'next generation' of Spitfires will have seen that this group has a way to go before they give Richard additional options for his squad. A lack of young English players forcing their way into Premier League first 11s is a contemporary hot topic. With the exception of the nationality specification, the situation is no different at any ambitious football club. Eastleigh top their league, in large part, due to their assiduously amassing a collection of individuals that have the requisite quality and knowhow for the risk of 'failure' to be minimised. With every youngster added to the team, however gifted, the end result becomes less certain.

Ross Barkley was held back by David Moyes at Everton simply because the cautious, presently floundering, now Manchester United manager perceived the player's indisputable attacking talent to be outweighed in its benefit to the team by his immature decision-making.

Richard knows his remit allows no room for bargain. He has to win the league. As such, sitting through a ponderous, occasionally incohesive youth cup defeat would have been of little use to the first-team boss. Wimborne, despite their lowlier footing, grew as the game progressed and thoroughly deserved a 3–2 win.

As a viewing experience it was refreshing. Aside from watching Everton's version in a later stage of the same competition last season, it was the first under-18 football that I have watched since I was embarking on my own playing 'career'.

It feels like I am swallowing something jagged and hard upon realising that is a gap of roughly 17 years. In the early stages of the game, it was instinctive to judge what we were seeing against our usual Silverlake fare; noticing the comparably looser touch, reduced vision, and slower speed of movement and thought. The fairer parallel would be drawn with the standard of football I knew.

Eastleigh, with their academy and its six hours' weekly contact time with UEFA-qualified coaches, would expect to be turning out well-drilled, progressive young footballers. That wasn't consistently evident on this night, but, even as they began to toil, the organisation and understanding within the side remained above anything I encountered throughout my aspirational teens.

Exceptionally impressive was the highly coached, but still daring and free-willed display of a teenage group that plays in the hinterland of the Dorset

Youth League. I can say with a good deal of surety that the coaching and playing of football at under-age levels is on an upward trajectory. The talent is out there. We just need patience – and a touch of extra faith in these developing footballers.

The very next evening (Tuesday, September 24th) I was taking in some action from right at the other end of the scale. For the first time since I forlornly trudged away from Wembley, in the wake of Everton finding a way to lose an FA Cup semi-final against a bog average Liverpool team in April 2012, I was at a Toffees match.

My sister (back from extensive honeymoon and still married), my dad, and I all surprised ourselves by quite how stoked up we became by a Capital One Cup tie at Fulham's Craven Cottage. For the 90 minutes when Everton play, I am as immersed as was ever the case.

When the whistle blew on a 2–1 defeat, for a much changed side from the one that has started this campaign so well (Mr Martinez is bestowing my inner Evertonian with a touch more confidence than I may have previously expressed), the fist-clenching anger dissipated in seconds.

The top end of English football offers us all plenty about which to gripe. There can be no argument, however, that the pace and skill on the pitch are mesmerising. It is, in truth, a different game from the one I have latterly fallen in love with. Yes, watching Everton arouses a taste for more. Nevertheless, before long I'm ready to get back to my 'home', which is exactly what I did for the Spitfires' next training session (September 26th). On Saturday, the big boys' FA Cup qualifying gets underway and the first team is in no mood to suffer the same fate as their under-18 counterparts.

While I was in West London, eating pizza, looking at mobile phone photographs of elephants in Borneo, and pontificating on what great value £20 for a match ticket is, Richard had been watching Mangotsfield slump to a 2–1 loss against Taunton Town. Those, again, are the unseen hard-yards that must be run, lest any corner-cutting bites you on the backside.

The boss revealed his opposition-scouting methods to Chris Todd and myself during the walk back from Thursday's training. Rather than sit comfortably in one speck for the entire match, like, erm, me and likeminded football civilians (although non-league regulations don't preclude against the practice whereby supporters switch ends at half-time in an attempt to suck the ball into the net that their team is attacking), Richard takes up a series of vantage points. This, he says, provides the scope to study each facet of a side.

What's more, in addition to a close-up of how a back-four functions and whether wide players 'cheat' or track-back, there is a chance for some surreptitious ear-wigging of what is being said on the home bench – what they believe is going right or wrong and, therefore, a morsel of insight into the manager's intentions.

So simple – much about football is – but I had never even considered that scouting duty might require one to leave a princely main stand seat for anything other than some free tea and biscuits.

Richard's message to his men was that their underdog opponents are limited, but full of endeavour and fight – 'a group of players you'd be happy to have, as a manager in their league.' The wingers were singled out as a threat, although not one that will trouble Eastleigh if their collective attitude is 'spot on'.

Dean Beckwith, recalling the day with sharp clarity, told me how a Luton Town team in which he was playing were given a cup tie fright by a Swindon Supermarine outfit that was labouring two divisions below. Jamie Collins knows only too well about the potential for an FA Cup turn-up – as does the manager himself.

As if to ensure that his players had further cause for motivation, Richard slipped in the fact that he'd been made aware how hard done to Mangotsfield felt regarding the draw – for reasons other than Eastleigh's markedly superior quality. 'They're not happy they've drawn us. We've got a playing budget of over £20k a week apparently and we're all on huge money.'

The overriding message was clear: if the visiting players think that they'll be up against a team of prima donnas, then it should be plain to them from the first whistle that the prima donnas work bloody hard and fight for every ball.

The session was concluded with Richard declaring that all 17 players present would be required for duty on Saturday. That number included Ryan Fuller, a right-back used, to Richard's dismay, at centre-half in Monday's youth cup tie. Jamie Bulpitt was the other tyro to benefit from the freedom to name seven substitutes in the FA Cup.

Of the regulars, Spence is ready for a squad berth and Collins, much to Cookie's relief, is back and fully immersed in all training activity, bar shooting drills. When Richard explained, to the man responsible for restoring Collins to health, that he was keen to guard against one of his key men aggravating his troublesome groin, Cookie hastily expressed a confidence that Jamie could participate in the practice match. 'Keep him out there, will you? He's a bloody nuisance.'

It was said with plenty of affection, but it would be fair to surmise that our ex-Havant & Waterlooville skipper has a more relaxed approach than some of his spritely team-mates.

The previous exercise from which Jamie was excused did not take off at a tempo that pleased the manager. In short, the conclusion to each routine would see a player cross the ball from one side of the pitch. Two colleagues, making unopposed runs into the area, would attack the ball and, in theory, the recipient would score.

Five minutes in (barked, and every word teeming with anger), 'Start scoring some f★★★★★★ goals. Come on, don't make me nag you.'

After announcing his active involvement in the day's work, Richard, in a flash, metamorphosed from passive onlooker into exhorting, demanding, and coaching leader. The calibre and cadence of what was being produced rocketed in accordance.

There would be no repeat of Monday's running horrors – something that a masochistic Beckwith admitted to having enjoyed – thrust upon the players 48 hours ahead of the cup kick-off. Nevertheless, a curious glance in the bin that sits outside the changing rooms while I waited for the inhabitants to surface divulged the 'liveners' of choice. No need for the doping authorities to intervene here until sachets of Dioralyte and cups of Starbucks take-away coffee are added to the 'banned list'.

Ritual and superstition have equal billing in the mind of many a sportsperson and I guess there are plenty of footballers who wholly believe they would be below par without their double shot espresso or if forced to detour from their customary route to the ground.

A battle-hardened, seen-it-all character such as Richard would surely be immune to such nonsensical flimflam. Not quite. As he made off to lay out his training mannequins, unable to decide which end of the pitch to direct his attacking players towards, the boss opted for 'the usual, because we've been doing alright when we've been going that way' (that despite the opposite penalty area being in better playing condition). It isn't only a winning team that a manager is reluctant to change.

I suspect the form and capability of that team, not any hocus-pocus, was the reason for Mangotsfield being clinically dispatched 4–0. By half-time it was 3–0 and Jamie Reid, a chippy and vociferous visiting midfielder, had moulded those two traits to pick up the yellow cards that saw to his dismissal. The second 45 minutes was a stroll.

On a straightforward afternoon there were two highlights. Will Evans returned and played 79 minutes at right-back – comfortably – before being replaced by an outwardly nervous but efficient Jamie Bulpitt. The biggest worry about Will's appearance was him being bestowed with the jinxed Number 2 shirt. Spence, that jersey's principal owner, continues to wait patiently for his return while, on Saturday, Damian Batt, Dan's fellow right-back, was unavailable due to illness.

Late in the game Sam Wilson was given a run-out, and how he responded – putting the cap on an energetic outing with a delicious finish for the day's final goal. Richard was quick in his post-match interview with the in-house TV station to extol Sam's goal-scoring attributes, but concurrently cautioned that the ambitious rookie has enormous strides to take before figuring in a Spitfires starting line-up. Nevertheless, 'Sam can be what he wants to be' is rich praise indeed coming from his exacting manager.

I am gradually learning how much of a wider influence that same manager wields on his players. During our talk about his time at Stevenage, I came to understand more about the attributes an individual must possess to be considered one of those 'right characters' Richard wants in his dressing room. He doesn't lean towards the head-banging cheerleaders, favoured by some 'old-school' gaffers. I have discussed how Eastleigh's footballers have, without exception, struck me for their respectful, polite and dedicated dispositions. That is no coincidence. When he recruits, the manager investigates further than merely ensuring he is not inviting a divisive personality into his camp. Anybody working under Richard's charge knows that courtesy, respect, and manners are expected in every walk of life.

Those shared characteristics translate into the real bonhomie that prevails at the club. It also brings about vignettes such as Richard gently censuring Chris Todd for tweeting while driving. Toddy had posted a message expressing his sadness at the death of a friend. No matter the subject. 'You've escaped death once, so don't tempt fate and end up getting hit by a juggernaut.'

The opportunity to interview Jai Reason on Thursday (September 26th, two days before Mangotsfield) confirmed my initial judgement about him – that he might not meet all of his boss's personality demands – was well off beam. If, in the fortnight prior to our conversation, I had been limited to watching Jai during matches or training, I'd have seen nothing to change my mind.

He possesses a fiery temper, which triggers the occasional outburst – physical and verbal. That might be at his manager for asking him to finish training with a series of runs, at a referee for missing the latest kick at his calf, or at Ramone Rose – who I thought last week Jai was about to punch as they tangled for a ball during a practice game.

At ease and talking in the clubhouse while eating his home-packed lunch (he told me he has shed over a stone since pre-season began), Jai couldn't have been more cordial or effusive. His stormy competitive edge is borne of his release at the age of 19 by Ipswich Town. Jai confessed that for the ensuing two years he 'didn't live or train right'. A further two years down the line he is back on track and desperate for a second go at the Football League.

Like many of his colleagues, though, Jai needs a release away from Eastleigh FC and manages his own coaching school, which puts on multi-sport sessions in schools. Any of the pupils landing this 'trequartista' as their football guru will correspondingly receive a boost to their chances of being part of England's World Cup winning team in Qatar.

20

THE GREEN, GREEN GRASS

A perfect football scenario has me at the Silverlake Stadium on a Saturday at 3pm. Compliant cup draws and the switch of the Hayes & Yeading game from its original slating as an away fixture – owing to the Tour of Britain cycling race passing by Woking's Kingfield Stadium, which Phil Babb's team continues to share – have led to this becoming a recent weekly ritual. Now, having come out of the hat first for an FA Cup tie, which pits the Spitfires against Conference North (honestly) Oxford City, the home game run will continue.

I didn't click onto the club's official website, or the supporters' internet message board, for news of our next opponents – on what the majority of Spitfires seem to be hoping is the road to Molineux. Rather, I headed for the FA's home domain and read through the draw, line by line. That enabled me to mirror as closely as possible the thrill of watching the balls pulled from the bag, so to speak, while anxiously and excitedly awaiting 'our' fate.

Oxford City actually came to the Silverlake two years ago at the same stage of the same competition and coasted to a 3–1 win. In football terms that is a day from another age. Eastleigh's opponents were then in the midst of what would be a promotion-winning season from the Southern Premier League, while the words 'Bridle' and 'takeover' were yet to form part of any Spitfires' lexicon.

One of the City goal-scorers on that flat occasion was Steve Basham. The forward, as somebody who played with moderate success for Southampton, Preston North End, Oxford United and Exeter City, will be on the radar of plenty of football fans.

Personally, the name Steve Basham is another reminder of what could have been (in my mind anyway). As schoolchildren we were direct opponents in many a battle for our respective club sides. More than once, playing in my left–

back role, I kept the darling of Southampton youth football quiet. Conversely, on a few less than glorious Sunday mornings I was taken to the cleaners, but that happens to the best of us (them), doesn't it?

Consequently, I've charted Steve's progress with both a vicarious fascination and a bit of the green-eyed monster. When, in August 1996, he made his Southampton debut in a match against Chelsea at the Dell, coming onto the same field as men of Gianluca Vialli and Roberto Di Matteo's ilk, the watching experience was surreal. Later that same Sunday I was off to 'Pilkington Barnes Hind' to put in my night-shift as a contact lens inspector.

Regardless, I was delighted when, over two years later, my former adversary scored a 'Premiership' goal at Blackburn Rovers – one of two in a Southampton win that sealed the fate of Rovers' then manager Roy Hodgson. Where ever did he end up? Actually, by the time this book reaches publication that could be a particularly pertinent question.

The Hampshire Senior Cup is a long way removed from the world-renowned English FA equivalent. As mentioned early in these pages, the humble county competition threw up a riveting game at AFC Bournemouth in January and eight months earlier had provided the club with a valued piece of silverware – and moment in the national spotlight.

For the manager and his promotion-seeking squad, however, this trophy sits somewhere on the priority list between the choice of red sauce or brown sauce on a sausage sandwich and catching up with the latest episode of *Neighbours*.

Some Sunday evening Twitter repartee between Stuart Fleetwood and Michael Green, which hinted towards a lack of appetite to be involved in a Tuesday (October 1st) floodlit clash with mid-table Wessex League side Whitchurch United, gave the game away somewhat. No more than the reaction of Chris Todd when Richard had informed him of the impending fixture – 'Oh f****** h***.'

A confession. If I wasn't writing this book, and resultantly nosing into every facet of the season at Eastleigh FC, I would have been tempted to spend 90 minutes at Westleigh Park hoping to see Gloucester City larrup our Havant-based neighbours in their FA Cup replay, rather than watching an understrength Spitfires team up against opposition from three leagues below.

One man's poison, however, is another man's pleasure. Any chance to impress Richard is manna for Sam Wilson, Jack Dovey, Jamie Bulpitt, and now

Chris Dillon. I was expecting to include Ramone Rose in that list. The former trialist is missing out, though, due to a dental appointment. Even in what has become a distinctly professional environment, that is a magnificently 'non-league' reason for being 'unavailable for selection'. It is, nevertheless, a peculiar diary conflict for a man who Richard has told me is 'very unlucky not to be starting at the moment'.

It's still early days, but, the mild controversy over what constitutes acceptable match-day behaviour aside, life for all concerned with Eastleigh is trundling along agreeably enough. At Ebbsfleet, tipped by many, including me, to be our chief rival at the top of the league, discontent is rife. The club have shut their online supporters' forum due to 'unacceptable levels of personal abuse and negativity of postings'. In this world, where we all get to have our say, one win in nine will do that.

Night of the Damned

A stodgy Spitfires Hampshire Cup display merited what it got – nothing. Whitchurch, who their boss Jim Macey described as 'awful', won 1–0.

These nights offer extra intrigue for being able to run an eye over which of the regular supporting faces is present. Unique to the football fan is the badge of honour worn for being at the most mundane of matches or having loyally stuck around throughout the darkest days.

Swansea City followers who kept turning up at their old Vetch Field ground when their team were battling for football league survival right up until the season's final day in 2003 can rightly set themselves apart from the newer breed attracted by a re-born club and the beguiling football produced inside their plush new Liberty Stadium. Every single set of supporters has their own reference point, which sets apart the fair weather attendees from the 'real' loyalists.

For Eastleigh, you need only go back to some of the hapless trips undertaken during the last campaign, notably to Bromley. Whitchurch at home was the first 'die-hard' test of this term – and among the 116 crowd there were plenty of familiar Silverlake inhabitants.

It was the perfect opportunity to catch up with Chris Blake – chairman of the TSSC. I have known Chris for a little over 12 months and have always assumed that he, his sons Mark and Craig, and daughter Kirsty had a long-standing affiliation to the club. I was astonished, therefore, when he revealed that the family connection to Eastleigh is only six years old. The Blakes, wanting to take in a match, decided on a whim that the Spitfires' home meeting with Havant & Waterlooville might be worth a watch. They were hooked from that day.

Once a Southampton follower, and among the Saints supporters who watched their team win the FA Cup at Wembley in 1976, Chris's loyalties are now firmly with the smaller club five miles away from St Mary's. He cites the November 2009 FA Cup first round trip to Barrow as his most treasured memory as a Spitfire – an occasion I severely regret dipping out on, that date being in the embryonic phase of my absorption into Eastleigh FC. I certainly share the longing, then, of Chris and a host of others for our incipient run in this year's competition to become something rather more serious.

There is not a great deal different in this mind-set from that of Manchester City or Chelsea fans, who demand substantial Champions League progress, while expecting their respective sides to sacrifice nothing of their Premier League form. When we already have something, we want more of it. Even when we haven't yet received what we wish for, we're greedily plotting for what we can grab next.

In common with many of his fellow fans, Chris is now cock-a-hoop with the giant strides being taken by his side – on and off the pitch. In fact, he declared that he 'just can't see them losing a game'. For the moment, despite knowing full well it'll happen, I agree.

With his high-profile TSSC role, Chris's perspective on all things Eastleigh does reflect the views of a good proportion of the supporters' club's members. Whatever their disparate takes on many smaller issues, there is one overriding belief in the outlook of any Spitfires follower. This is their time. As such, we (and I include myself in this) want to achieve as much as we can right now.

The low-key attitude towards the 90 minutes we watched after our chat could be best ascertained by Chris, Mark, and many other regular 'behind-the-goal' heads saving their voices for another day, instead sprawling out in the stand for the first half – 45 minutes that ended with Eastleigh a goal behind.

Richard's attempt to assume a back seat and cast an eye from on high over the mix of reserves, fledgling hopefuls and, for 55 minutes, Will Evans was short-lived. This manager was never going to sit idle while a team under his control were performing so limply. His half-time intervention inspired only a brief arousal though. The first period's apathy quickly returned and there was no further score.

When I spoke to Glen Southam two days later, he reluctantly admitted that not having the Hampshire Cup clogging up their calendar will aid the side's wider ambitions. He won't have many dissenters, manager included.

What did trouble Richard was the lack of fitness and guile exhibited by the next rung of players below his trusted main group. Whitchurch United at home had seemed a fixture to tick off, to put some minutes into lightly run legs and provide a rare 'first-team' chance for teenaged aspirants. It might transpire to be something more seismic than was foreseen.

The result was certainly not the talk of the training ground on Thursday (October 3rd). Apart from 'Suvs" comment, I didn't hear a single reference to the club's exit from a competition that, only 16 months ago, was providing all the glory one could imagine would come the way of Eastleigh FC.

Now, in the driving rain, which had me cowering under the trees to one side of the pitch, the club's main men were engaging in a hotly contested shooting drill. Ross Flitney's reaction to Jamie Collins casually rolling a ball into the corner of his net was to bellow 'f*** off' at a volume that would have been heard over in Havant – where the local team were ruminating on their FA Cup defeat against Gloucester City – before planting a boot into his right post.

Unlike my four layers – five short of the record number I've crammed on – t-shirts, shorts and a smattering of training tops were the order of the day for those at work. While I took the incessant downpour and every single gust of wind as a personal affront, the filthy conditions didn't register with any of the players. Anyone with their love of football, and the fortitude of character required to reach even this level of the game, does not gripe about the cold and wet.

The game does, though, turn out men prepared to participate in their intermittently physical practice matches without wearing shin pads. It only dawned on me within the past fortnight that this happens. 'Ah, you soft ?*?*' is a fan's reflex reaction when one of his side's players comes off second-best in a tackle – the words spat out while peering from underneath a heavy duty woolly hat and cradling a cup of tea for warmth.

At matches I watch in wonderment at Craig McAllister getting kicked to pieces or Chris Todd throwing his head at a ball with no thought for the threat posed to his safety by a looming 6ft 4in, 15 stone, chiselled centre-forward. More than anything, I am grateful. Grateful that, for our entertainment, there are men ready to embrace that combat as a feature of their weekly routine, but also grateful it's them and not me.

When Richard was hollering his mid-training game instructions, fighting to make himself heard against the conditions, I did bravely creep forward from my temporary shelter to listen in. The manager's commands are consistent. Speed and intelligence of movement, readiness to accept individual responsibility, high tempo of play, and positivity in every act are qualities this boss wants stamped across his team.

He said during a phone conversation the previous day that he considers his currently employed 4–3–1–2 formation to be proving apt for this group of players. Fleetwood is one of the 2 and McAllister is deserving of the highest praise for the way in which he has, by sheer force of will, demanded selection alongside his old Exeter City colleague. Craig is, accordingly, piqued by the recurrence of his hamstring niggle earlier in the week. That injury condemned him on Thursday to working with Cookie, alongside Yemi and Dan Spence – and ultimately, a return to bench duties for Saturday's (October 5th) clash against Concord Rangers.

Richard spoke in public about his huge regard for Ben Strevens this week and the man who received my September 'Player of the Month' vote (the award was won by a no less deserving Flitney) took McAllister's striking role. The hole left in midfield was filled by Will Evans. Still, manager's praise notwithstanding, Ben wasn't spared a verbal lashing for a lazy chip at goal during Thursday's training. 'Strevens, that's not you, Strevs. You're better than that.' The words were snapped with gusto. 'Never drop your standards' was the implied message, delivered for the benefit of all.

Strevs, Southam and Collins joined Dillon, Batt and Green in choosing the 'knock it on the head' option when the players were left to their own devices for the concluding minutes of that session, all hovering for a short while before deeming it safe to beat a stealthy retreat for their changing room sanctum.

Fleetwood, utilising the mannequins that had acted as markers for a running drill, meticulously lined up a defensive wall and devoted some time to the art of free-kick taking. Reason, Evans, Wilson, Ramone Rose and James Jennings – invited to work with the big boys after a promising cameo on Tuesday (perhaps even benefitting from not having started that night) – took on a fresh shooting exercise.

Evans and Reason dispatched a selection of murderous efforts that tore into the back of the net – and a few that were rather more awry. Reason would repeat the former feat on Saturday to score an equaliser against Concord. Evans, with the chance to hit a winner late on in the same match, couldn't match his colleague's accuracy, missing by inches. A 1–1 draw was, though, a fair outcome to a tight game.

The remarkable Essex Club, which were playing in that county's Senior League in 2008, were an obdurate opponent – and one which could plausibly have sent the wheels careering off the Spitfires' formidable run.

Richard suggested that his opponents' modus operandi echoed that of Hayes & Yeading a fortnight previously. I saw an away side that was minded to form an imposing barrier behind the ball when out of possession. If a chance to attack opened up, that is precisely what Rangers did – and with conviction.

As the clock ticked down on the match, so anxiety among the home faithful went in the other direction – an unfamiliar occurrence through these serene times at the Silverlake. I was moved to a state of incredulity by some of the audible displeasure expressed at Eastleigh merely heading for a single point.

The howls that greeted the otherwise rock solid Dean Beckwith hitting a pass into touch or an initially well-constructed move breaking down were grating. Furthermore, as is often the case when a team is considered to be performing below par, the prospective replacements and stricken squad members gained increased worth in the eyes of some.

It was a point towards the cause, and should be accepted as such. The standout result on the afternoon was forum-less Ebbsfleet winning 6–0 at Weston-super-Mare. Nobody saw that coming. It sets up beautifully our trip to Kent on Tuesday night. I will be making that journey with my loyal chauffeur (Dad) in his Honda Civic (the mini-bus leaves Eastleigh train station at 4:15pm; a potential recipe for serious 'we'll miss the kick-off' angst) and will travel with words of praise ringing in my ears.

Danny Cowley, the plainly perspicacious manager of Concord, delivered the following verdict on my match report: 'Without doubt the most accurate, articulate & football intelligent match report that I can remember reading!' Now I know where to go for a strapline for this book.

My dad's desire to guard against the tiniest possibility that we'll be strangled by rush hour traffic is determining a departure time roughly six hours prior to the 7:45pm kick-off at Ebbsfleet. The anticipated early arrival will apparently precede some time spent in the Bluewater shopping centre. Hell. On. Earth. But preferable to what would be the horrendous scenario of missing any of the evening's action.

A similar fear of being absent from an Eastleigh match day, although with a different underlying explanation, is inherent in our captain 'Suvs'. He discussed at length during another interview with me after last week's training (October 3rd) the way in which he has been managing a legion of tweaks and twinges through the season's opening stages. For Glen Southam, it seems that the prospect of being prevented from playing football is unthinkable – bordering unmanageable.

There was plenty in our chat – primarily the sharp intake of breath and answer to the negative when I enquired if he had considered what lies beyond football – to confirm my suspicion that when he can no longer go on, it will provide a true life challenge for a good man.

There was no detectable hangover, on the day of that interview, from a falling out that had occurred between Richard and Suvs when the manager withdrew his skipper during the Mangotsfield cup tie. The gaffer had told the player to stop chirping at the referee as he made his way off. That instruction provoked, in the heat of the moment, a curt response. Predictably, Richard exploded and, when we spoke on Wednesday, was still unhappy with his captain. Hopefully, Glen's stellar 90 minutes against Concord on Saturday has put a lid on the proverbial 'storm in a teacup'.

Richard's response to his September 'Conference South Manager of the Month' award was equally pointed – believing it overdue recognition for his results across the last 12 months. This was the first time he'd received the gong. Fortunately, he both resisted the temptation to tell the league to 'shove it' and avoided the traditional curse associated with the prize.

So then, off to a tinderbox of a clash at Ebbsfleet. Steady as we go.

21

IF I HADN'T SEEN SUCH RICHES

Making for the exit of a 'tinpot' ground – as Stuart Fleetwood in an interview with me this week described some of the less salubrious Conference South venues – having watched Eastleigh turned over by the hosts, was as much a part of following the team on the road during a phase of last season as getting out of bed and heading for the motorway in the first place.

Ebbsfleet United's Stonebridge Road home certainly does not fit Fleets' evocative portrayal of some non-league arenas, but, for the first time in this campaign, I paced back to the car stewing on a Spitfires defeat (I was otherwise engaged when the side slumped at Basingstoke). The action across the 90 minutes, though, played out in a fashion entirely contrary to that which I had expected.

Eastleigh went to the relatively grand abode of one of – notwithstanding their sluggish start – the division's strongest teams and dictated terms. The section of home support housed in the magnificently titled 'Liam Daish Stand' – named in homage to the club's former manager – furnished their side with a distinctly irascible backing, contesting every refereeing decision. Furthermore, no opportunity to lavish their assorted judgements on various individuals within the away team was declined.

The Daish Stand denizens' studied approach to balancing encouragement for the 'Fleet' with visitor baiting was detectable from its slightly mellower 'Main Stand' equivalent. That is where I sat with my dad, having enjoyed a fine Wagamama Japanese meal in the otherwise sprawling vapidity of the Bluewater shopping centre. That's not to say that we weren't stationed among a few opinionated types – one poor young lad in particular incurred our already riled manager's ire for his 'wise-cracking'. Nor were we spared the monotonous pre-conceptions of our side as being one rammed full of individuals raking in salaries that would make a City trader blush.

As Fleetwood writhed in agony after being cynically sliced to the floor by Eastleigh boo-boy Daryl McMahon, he was greeted with the standard quip, 'Get up, Fleetwood. What's the matter with you, tripped over your f★★★★★★ pay packet?'

The evidence, as posted on Twitter and shown to me two days later by our goal-scorer on the night, revealed a grotesquely swollen ankle and array of ugly cuts. McMahon's punishment? Nada. That oversight was by no means the low point of the night's refereeing. I have never before, in a match report, gone in especially hard on an official. It's a job I wouldn't do for Fleetwood's wage, nor for his imagined one.

When composing my write up on this game I broke my self-imposed rule. Not to do so would have been neglecting to mention one of the match's chief influences. Two convincing Spitfires penalty appeals were turned away, one of those for a glaringly obvious handball. Just after half-time, and with the score at 1–1, Ebbsfleet were awarded a highly contentious spot-kick, which was scored by Billy Bricknell. For good measure, as time drifted away referee O'Brien watched on idly as the home team adopted a flagrantly ponderous approach to re-starting play.

A generous proportion of Ebbsfleet devotees, laudably so ardent in support of their team and elated with the result, were vocal in praise for the vanquished Spitfires. Beckwith, Collins, Southam, Strevens, and Fleetwood were absolutely terrific. Indeed, the whole display, despite what was eventually a 3–1 defeat, was the epitome of everything that the Eastleigh football team, and the club itself, has become – energetic, exciting, ambitious, confident, and loaded with desire.

McMahon barely got a kick, apart from the one that tore through Fleetwood's sock and de-faced his ankle. Until, that is, a late free-kick won on the break, which the midfielder, who had the brass to leave the Silverlake for greater financial reward with Dover, bent round a defensive wall and a weak Flitney glove to settle the destination of the three points. For a few of the travelling number – players and fans alike – that was the final straw on a night when it was possible to believe the football gods had decreed in advance that we would come away with nothing.

It is an inbred trait of high-achieving sportspeople that they will only pause briefly to savour the good moments. Confronted by disappointment, the pain and resultant introspection lasts for an extended period. Notwithstanding that, Richard remained upbeat the next day and, although still seething about the erratic refereeing of which his men were victim, the manager's opinion of his team as 'the best in the league' had deepened.

Richard confessed that the 'attack at all times' policy employed by this Eastleigh team, home and away, leaves them 'sailing by the seat of their pants defensively'. Interestingly, he lamented a missing killer instinct. A cutting edge that would have avoided the referee becoming the main talking point on this occasion and, perhaps, prevented the two defeats suffered to date.

I expected to find the players in good cheer on Thursday (October 10th) and I wasn't disappointed. The issue of Tuesday's game, however, seeped through much of the early chat. I held my first post-mortem with Chris Todd – the penalty-conceding 'culprit' at Ebbsfleet; a decision that the linesman, at the time, told Todd and Dean Beckwith he disagreed with, before denying any knowledge of that confession when Richard was granted a post-match audience with the officials.

We were musing on how the result had slipped through Eastleigh's grasp when I declared that I knew McMahon was going to score his free-kick (I had experienced that customary sense of foreboding when watching an erstwhile favourite in opposition colours). Ross Flitney, walking a few paces ahead, instantly spun on his heels. I hadn't intended to criticise a man who has produced a string of assertive displays this term, but, in plain speak, the goalkeeper made a hash of McMahon's strike. Fortunately, 'Flits' just wanted his say on that goal and the team's progress in general.

Ross, perhaps unwittingly, provided an intriguing insight into the workings of a goalkeeper's mind. How many times have you watched a 'keeper fumble the ball into their own net and sat uttering words to the effect of 'what was he playing at?' I had suppressed any inclination to react in such fashion on Tuesday, not least because Ross's dad was sat directly in front of us. What's more, it was only right to cut our Number 1 some slack given he's bailed the side out plenty of times since his arrival. Still, the question ran through my head.

The explanation for the 'keeper's error lies in the goal conceded to Concord Rangers the previous Saturday. In that instance, Ross was unhappy with the way he had pushed a long-range shot directly into the path of an onrushing Leon Gordon, who casually tapped in. The swerving, dipping ball had caused our stopper to be conflicted about whether he should turn the strike around the post or attempt to clutch it to his chest. He did neither and it was his desire to avoid a repeat that held sway in Ross's mind when he tried to push McMahon's mediocre attempt away from danger – instead only succeeding in pushing the ball high into his net. However random football might appear at times, there is a reason for most of what happens during any given 90 minutes.

Ross went on to bemoan the goalkeeper's lot – noticeably, without a trace of bitterness. If a ball slips fatally through a Number 1's fingers, it really doesn't matter what else he contributes to a game. We remember his display for one thing.

Turning conversation towards what is happening at the other end of the pitch, Ross expressed the view that his goal-scoring colleagues might be devoid of a clinical streak, due to their conviction that another chance will arrive quickly around the corner. He could be on to something. There is an analogy in the world of cricket. Many a stellar batting line-up has been blown away, with all its components undone by loose shots that were born of a misplaced sense of freedom, attributable to the knowledge that another top-notch player was next in.

Nevertheless, it is those very strikers and their out-field allies who have Ross echoing his manager's bullishness. 'We'll run away with this league.'

Craig McAllister returned to the starting 11 at Ebbsfleet, but was back out of the picture after 45 minutes. The hamstring he had hoped was ready for the off on Saturday recovered in time for Tuesday – or so he had thought. When, on Thursday, he emerged from his treatment with Cookie, Macca joined me on the side-lines during the training match that was being contested at frantic pace in front of us.

He was simultaneously philosophical and fuming about his latest dollop of misfortune, admitting that he took home a sore after-game mood to go with his painful upper leg – something that his 'missus' wasn't too chuffed about when he came stomping through the door late at night. (I neglected to ask if he'd been regally stitched up en route by roadworks convoy vehicles on the A3 – apparently de rigueur among the after-dark crews charged with improving our transport conditions. That was 40 minutes added to the homeward journey.)

Macca, thankfully, has an understanding partner. Her father is Martyn Rogers, a former player with Exeter City and Weymouth and, between 1992 and 2010, manager of Tiverton Town. If anything I have become even more of an advocate of Craig McAllister's importance to the team this season – and not solely because he remembered me.

His bravery comes as standard, while his presence and intelligence bring the best out of the array of speedy and enterprising forwards that Richard has at his disposal. Additionally, Craig's readiness to stare down and overcome what initially resembled the impossible task of reclaiming his place in the side has exhibited an estimable character. He is resigned to resting the irksome hamstring for 'a few weeks' now. I'm not alone in keenly anticipating his full recovery.

At the conclusion of another windswept and freezing cold – for me stood doing nothing anyway – training session, Southam came over for a talk. Tuesday still hurt, but our captain added his name to the list of those whose confidence in his team has been bolstered after the trip to Kent. Particularly vital for 'Suvs', and something that Fleetwood highlighted when I interviewed him, was just how hard this group works on the pitch – a virtue that has caught cold peddlers of the 'Eastleigh will be a team of show ponies' myth.

Fair to say, I'm not sure that Suvs would have contributed to any Daryl McMahon testimonial fund had the Irishman settled anywhere long enough to warrant such a tribute. Notwithstanding that, he wouldn't have eschewed the chance to play in an opposing midfield during any celebratory match for his former 'team-mate', given the relish with which he runs all over him.

Richard actually participated in this session's (October 10th) focused passing and shooting drill. Despite still bearing the scars and gait of the knee injury, which prematurely cut short his playing career, the boss still knows how to score – one-headed finish especially brought the house down. Richard's desire to be right in among the players was his way of retaining the harmonious, boisterous atmosphere that prevails whenever these players are together. It was a display of fine man-management – a skill that is as essential as tactical savvy and player recruitment to make a go of this job.

There was a quieter than usual dining room when the players congregated for their sweet and sour pork – almost a contented air in the wake of two hard but refreshing hours outside, which had acted to banish any last thoughts of Ebbsfleet.

Oxford City is now the focus. Fleetwood, with fresh memories of his part in Luton Town's double giant-killing feats against Wolves and Norwich City last term, alluded in interview to his enthusiasm for the imminent cup tie.

It was a talk that provided a lot of copy. Stuart candidly admitted that he thought he had 'made it' before he'd actually achieved anything at Cardiff City. The habit of going out drinking with first-team regulars didn't help either his personal development or reputation. His involvement in a car crash, which ended the career of a colleague – Nicky Fish, a Wales under-21 international – and his release from the club he'd been signed to since the age of 14 inspired a change of outlook – towards both his life and his profession.

I had suspected that Fleets, even at the age of 27, had given up the ghost so far as returning to league football goes. Not so. He declared that Eastleigh were the only team at Conference South level he would have joined – in large part due to both the club's ambition and the quality of players already in situ.

The dabbling in Herbalife, a job coaching football in a local school, and some journalistic leanings (he has his own blog) are stimulated by the requirement to plan for his years beyond football and, of course, a want to bring in an extra few quid. Fleets smiled when he spoke of 'having a finger in a few pies', but there was definite steel in his voice when he discussed a return to football's higher echelons being at the apex of his current agenda.

As I was leaving the clubhouse, Chris Todd had returned from his car with two pairs of Ugg boots. In return for ready cash, Mike Andrews and Mick Geddes (Director, Stadium Manager, 'man responsible for completing any number of chores around the club' and another all-round Mr Eastleigh) became the proud owners of said footwear – on behalf of female partners, they assure me. Toddy says he sells the Uggs for 'a mate who imports them from Australia'. There is a pronounced shade of entrepreneurialism in this Spitfires squad.

In sardonic frame of mind, I would be tempted to state that I wish comparable inventiveness was evident in Eastleigh's on-field set-pieces. Fleetwood's assiduous free-kick practice has, so far, yielded only a clip of the woodwork and a few digs floated narrowly over the bar.

A host of corners are routinely being wasted. That failing is something Richard sought to hone during his preparation work for Oxford City. Frankly, there still wasn't a huge deal on show to suggest that we'll suddenly see a raft of goals from these situations. There was no repeat, though, of a fortnight previously when McAllister responded to Jamie Collins, unusually, hitting consecutive poor deliveries with a cheerily mocking scolding: 'Come on. Do you want me to get the f****** groundsman over to do it for you?'

And So It Goes

The lure of FA Cup third qualifying round day on Saturday, October 12th, drew only 434 people to the Silverlake (Mick Geddes, with foresight gained from years spent in the non-league world, had foreseen the paltry turnout: 'There won't be many there when they've got to pay'). While not quite bad enough for home supporters to demand that the groundsman lace up his boots, this was a team performance to frustrate on par with some of the notable Eastleigh let-downs in years gone by.

The same opponents two years previously, Gloucester 12 months ago, Chasetown in the 2010/2011 FA Trophy. All were occasions that left even the hardiest of Spitfires feeling hopelessly flat. That is exactly how the mood of me and many others, meandering away from the ground in the wake of a 3–2 defeat, could be accurately described.

Would we prefer Wolves away in round one or a facile route through to a national interest third-round tie against a Premier League monolith? That particular debate was rendered obsolete for another year by 90 predominantly despairing minutes. The despondency is still too raw to roll out the 'at least we can concentrate on the league' line, to which all supporters – bar those of the two clubs that ultimately reach May's final – revert upon the point of their own team's exit.

Our visitors were two up inside ten minutes and anybody who wasn't au fait with the characters in this squad might have suspected that they had taken their comparatively lowly opponents lightly. Whether that could be true on a sub-conscious level we'll never know. It is certainly not beyond the realms of possibility, though, that a few legs were still heavy with Tuesday's exertions at Ebbsfleet.

The inability to kill off Concord Rangers, followed by a failure to make the most of our dominance at Ebbsfleet has already roused discussion among fans concerning whether Richard would be well advised to add a 'goal-poacher'/'fox in the box' – whichever parlance you choose – to his squad. A personal view is that such a move would be premature and that the players we have are capable of scoring goals in droves.

Nevertheless, the manager did make reference to the emerging clamour for a new striker when he spotted Yemi back among his group during last Thursday's (October 10th) workout; 'F★★★★★★ h★★★, I know I keep being told to sign a striker, I didn't realise I had one already.'

Richard continued, in reference to having 18 bodies on the training ground (although Dan Spence remains fit enough only to dip in and out, dependent on the demands each exercise places on his delicate hamstring), 'We'll need two training sessions to fit them all in at this rate, Guy [Butters].'

The sight of a busy and bubbly training ground influences my take on the lack of a need for reinforcements. Nevertheless, McAllister's absence left the side with a slightly one-dimensional look against Oxford. Most disconcertingly, having battled back to 2–2 shortly after half-time there was never a feeling that a head of steam was building, with a dogged but limited opponent on the verge of being blown away.

Moreover, when City had grabbed their lead with 13 minutes to play, and subsequently strung five across the back with a stubborn line of four placed in front of them, Eastleigh didn't have the craft or vision to pick their way through the blockade. Any equaliser was going to arrive via a long-range effort or a fortunate drop of the ball to home feet around the penalty area.

There was some consolation to be drawn in the shape of Yemi playing the final quarter of this game and, in that time, serving up one of the afternoon's brighter Spitfires displays. Fingers crossed that this insouciant, genial figure, not to mention one with the potential to be key in achieving the season's overwhelming aim (ah b★★★★ to it, at least we can concentrate… etc.), can now enjoy a prolonged run of football.

If Richard does decide he wants the insurance of extra goals there won't be a shortage of players hankering to act as the spur in Eastleigh's promotion charge. The boss admitted a couple of weeks ago that – predictably given both the club's early delivery on their pre-season billing and the fanciful rumours of extravagant wages on offer at the Silverlake – he routinely answers his phone to agents hawking their respective clients' services.

That circumstance is a side-effect of success – or more precisely in this instance, prospective success. As such, the boss is happy to accept it. Nevertheless, he is astonished by the 'arrogance' of the players' representatives who stipulate that their man would need to be starting matches. Richard points to the case of Chris Todd who, after regaining fitness, had to bide his time to replace Chris Dillon. If 'Toddy' – a real manager's favourite – has no guarantee that he will start on a Saturday, it is exceedingly unlikely that Richard would blithely accede to the request of somebody wishing to breeze in and upset the equilibrium in his squad.

Back to Oxford City, and the void left by McAllister saw Damian Batt restored to the line-up (Will Evans, progressively bringing new meaning to the title 'utility-man', started up-front). There is plenty of time for a Damascene conversion regarding my initial assessment of Damian, which is that he possesses undoubted ability, but doesn't appear to have subscribed to the single-minded drive that is expected in this group – an attribute that, at Eastleigh, is a 'must-have', with no room for compromise. His outings have thrown up a mix of lax moments and glimpses of easy talent. Damian was in part culpable for both of Oxford's early goals, but contributed to Jamie Collins commencing the Spitfires fight-back.

On the training ground, 'Batty' can appear passive. That is not a criticism, but there is none of the gusto naturally transmitted by his colleagues. Whenever Southam, Beckwith, McAllister and the rest speak, their words are laced with desire and zeal for the task – and the club. I haven't exchanged much more than a 'hello' with Damian, so I am casting judgement from my old standpoint as 'supporter' only, but I haven't read him as an individual whose mind is fully invested in his Eastleigh career.

His September retirement perhaps hinted towards a loss of appetite for the game – not merely the full-time version. Damian has wider business interests – and my word, his dress ensemble on Thursday ahead of leaving the training ground for wherever his ventures were taking him was dapper in the extreme. It could be that this is a man whose priorities lie elsewhere. Equally, I could be very, very wrong. Only the unfurling of time will reveal the truth.

Tuesday, October 15th

A telephone conversation with Richard soon after finishing my previous book dispatch (written on Sunday) quickly disproved my theory that recruiting an extra striker is absolutely not necessary. Richard expanded on his thinking by saying, 'I have to win the league.'

From the other end of the phone line, I sensed that Richard was stewing to an extent I'd not previously encountered – although I'm sure it was as nothing by comparison to some of his Sunday moods at the lower points of his early tenure. The manager has been relentlessly supportive and defensive of this group of players, until now. He considered that Oxford had deserved to beat his team, and was both mystified and angered by the entire performance – right down to the last detail.

As we discussed Oxford's second strike, which featured some distinctly careless home defending, Richard went right back to the goal's origin and an unnecessarily quick throw taken by Southam. I study the game avidly, but, as I continue to discover, the eye of somebody who has spent a life ingrained in football sees so much more than that of even the most enthusiastic – and 'nerdy' – layman.

I could spot that Batt, Green, and a few others were horribly out of position to defend the break that precipitated the goal. I hadn't absorbed the fact that it was 'Suvs' re-starting play with undue haste that had left a string of his colleagues spread wide and, therefore, irreparably stretched when possession was conceded.

Eastleigh's footballers know that if they put a foot out of place, the misdemeanour will not go unnoticed. Their 'punishment' for falling short of what the manager demands actually speaks very well of the entire squad. Richard cancelled the training sessions planned for Monday and Tuesday. 'They love coming in, having a laugh and working together, so I'll take it away from them.'

That minor episode provides the surest confirmation of the impression I have captured, across three and a half months of steadily becoming acquainted with the squad. This is a terrifically committed and professional set of players – and they will be hurting. That much was obvious by both the manner in which Southam and Reason dropped to the floor on Saturday's final whistle and the remainder of the vanquished bunch dragged themselves, heads bowed, from the field.

Richard, in the wake of defeat, had resisted a glance at the online forum for fear that he would read criticism to exacerbate his ire. I was able to tell him that, had he poured over the fans' dissection of events, he wouldn't have encountered any outright opprobrium – more a sense of an opportunity lost.

The boss asked what it was that people really wanted from the FA Cup. When I responded to the effect of it being a day in the spotlight, seeing their team pitted against esteemed opposition, something that devotees of non-league clubs commonly lust after, I realised I was treading dangerous ground. I inserted the caveat that, when pondering over the defeat, I had reconciled myself to the fact that a prospective 'big day' was all we had lost. Oxford City would have no tangible bearing on the season's only real objective.

Too late.

'Why do fans want a day out? F★★★ me. If they want a day out, I'll book a coach and take us all to the races or on a trip to Old Trafford.'

I took the point, but there is, of course, a difference. People want Eastleigh FC at the centre of their 'big day'. They want to bask in an occasion when their football club grabs the nation's attention, perhaps even attracting the television cameras and associated loot.

It is that difference between supporters and staff again. Richard has had these days as player and coach. Jamie Collins and Craig McAllister have strutted their stuff at Anfield and Old Trafford respectively. A cup run would be great, but the manager and players have been hired with one job in mind. And, if they accomplish their assignment, a potential 'big day' is replaced by a plethora of them.

Indeed, the manager hopes that this setback will re-focus minds on the task in hand. He declared that he has detected the first signs of complacency among his players. A title-winning celebratory jaunt to Las Vegas has already been mooted. The announcement on Thursday, October 3rd, of Amir Khan's planned fight in the self-styled 'Entertainment Capital of the World' against Floyd Mayweather triggered plenty of animated lunchtime chat on that day.

Richard even confided that he had, more than once, fallen into the trap of referring to the day 'when' we win promotion. The confidence among fans has also drifted perilously close to arrogance – and I include myself in that. Predictions are no longer based on whether the side will win, but by how many goals. I already had my sights cast on Monday's FA Cup fourth qualifying round draw before a ball had been kicked against Oxford.

Now, says the boss, it is time to deal in reality. 'Winning championships doesn't just happen, you actually have to go and do it.'

He expanded on his point by referring to the Sir Alex Ferguson reign of dominance at Old Trafford. 'When did you ever hear anybody from Manchester United getting carried away when Ferguson was in charge? Players or management, or even supporters, coming out and saying that they would win the league? They just won a game then concentrated on the next one. If they lost a game, they made sure they didn't lose the next one. The rest takes care of itself.'

If Richard wants to model his Eastleigh set-up on the premier British football club of our age he will not meet with many objectors.

Continuing in confessional vein, the boss conceded that he might have made a mistake by adopting a relentlessly offensive game plan once his side had pulled level on Saturday. Sat in the stand it had appeared, at 2–2, that the Spitfires had wrested the momentum from an opponent now ripe for the beating there and then. The boss's call at the time had its merits – and found no argument.

I hesitantly broached the Batt subject with the manager and extracted enough to infer that the 'three doesn't go into two' dilemma, which Richard had hoped to face with regards to his full-backs when Dan Spence is ready to go, will not be an issue just yet.

Our chat was over 48 hours ago now. Two days for Eastleigh's conscientious boss to put his feet up and take stock?

Frankly, I would be amazed. I have very rapidly become cognisant with the daily grind that is required to manage a football team – let alone one that 'must win' every week. When Richard told me a fortnight ago that he'd had a busy couple of days, I enquired if that had been the result of Eastleigh business. 'Always.'

And so the story goes on.

22

ELEVENSES

Not elevenses of the type that well-to-do retired folk enjoy – a cup of tea and a slice of cake, the need for sustenance all the more acute for having been out of bed since 5am. This was elevenses that kept Guy Butters and myself, kicking our heels out on the training ground, wondering as to the whereabouts of Eastleigh's manager and, goalkeepers aside, his entire first-team squad.

When the missing troops surfaced at midday (Thursday, October 17th), one hour after work routinely begins, everybody was in one piece. The players had, however, been subjected to a video analysis of the gorier elements of their FA Cup demise. It transpired that Richard's focus had fixed on a combination of the defending at each of the three goals shipped, slack positional play during the game and the absence of any tempo to his team's passing.

Exchanging a brief 'are you well?' with Southam, the Spitfires skipper muttered along the lines of his brain being 'frazzled', before plodding off for his warm-up with a set of individuals who were straining at the leash. Being starved of their raison d'être has proven a stringent measure, one that is having the desired effect.

When the intensity of training was ramped up – the first 'competitive' action for any of the players since they trudged away from the Silverlake pitch on Saturday – verve and resolve oozed from every move and every touch. There was a snap, bordering on venom in tackles. And this was a game of 'keep-ball'.

One lunging, but fair, Beckwith challenge on Todd brought about Guy's instruction for contact to be eliminated from the drill, followed swiftly by a blow of his whistle to signal a drinks break. While the players were 'cooling off', Fleetwood was urging that they 'work out there like we want to on a Saturday'. 'Suvs' had walked, bristling, from the field. 'F★★★ that no contact bo★★★★★★, f★★★ that.'

The comparably downbeat hue to proceedings wasn't overbearing, but it was perceptible nonetheless. When the 'keep-ball' came under a 'one-touch' rule, the playing standard was astonishing. Touch, movement, awareness – all of it drew the breath of this lucky observer. I was inwardly debating whether there is another Conference South squad capable of producing what I was watching.

One poor afternoon's work, which, with a clear mind, we can console ourselves had no direct impact on the year's primary objective, has elicited internal recriminations that are surely beyond anything that would occur at another club playing 'tier-six' football. If any of Eastleigh's playing staff had forgotten the burden they are carrying throughout this campaign, their 11am meeting would have handed them all a substantial reminder.

And yet, these are men who must juggle the expectancy of their Spitfires existence with broader goals and responsibilities in life. Jamie Collins, my next interviewee, asked if it was ok that we speak next Thursday, rather than Monday. His request was due to Ben Strevens, a member of the 'Hertfordshire Car School', needing to be home in time to attend his university course at the start of the week.

Chris Dillon today left the clubhouse clutching a slice of French baguette – the late finish that spilled over from 'trial by tape' leaving him no time for lunch ahead of a shift at the leisure centre where he works. Greener continues to earn an extra buck whenever possible. McAllister, who is delighted that he will miss just one more match before he is fit to play again, is eager to 'get stuck back into' his plumbing course after a hiatus in his studies due to a house move. That upheaval took place with a third child on the way and his summer wedding to organise.

Macca's new residence will have him situated even closer to his football home – the football home to which he is contracted only until this season's conclusion. It is little wonder he is desperate to be out playing and contributing to the cause. A switch of club is not something that fits snugly with Craig's maturing life circumstances. All he can do to guard against that eventuality is don his boots and perform. That is a very real pressure.

McAllister was the lone injury absence from today's session, making do with passing the time of day with yours truly after he had completed his rehabilitation work with Cookie. Yemi and Dan Spence are on the brink of full fitness.

Macca is of the view that the FA Cup, great as it is – and he knows after his adventures with Crawley Town – won't matter a jot if promotion is achieved. It is time to pull a veil over that aspect of the season, although I won't be able to resist keeping tabs on the progress, or otherwise, of Oxford City.

I sat rapt, on Monday lunchtime, listening to Colin Murray overseeing the fourth qualifying round draw on his talkSPORT programme. It was a throwback to days of yore, so fondly recalled by the older generation, the age demographic towards which I am reluctantly tip-toeing. Listening on the radio, as balls were pulled from a velvet bag to reveal simply who would play who in a set of football matches, was once the most exciting thing imaginable.

With no Eastleigh involvement there was a sense of 'here's what you might have won' regarding this specific edition – until, that is, our conquerors were presented with a trip to Dover Athletic. I did smile. It was the identical reaction to that I had when Richard told me he's been asked to give a talk to the Hampshire FA Referees' Association, not least because he passed on that little gem two days after the hapless officiating we endured at Ebbsfleet. That could be a lively evening.

Richard's wisdom was exclusive to his players during their lone session last week (it is now Tuesday, October 22nd). Jai Reason was locked in conversation with his manager for ten minutes, while the rest of the squad engaged in their warm-up. It was clear that a range of tactical issues was being discussed. Whether or not his boss's advice included the instruction, 'When Stuart Fleetwood sends over a terrific deep cross from the right, burst into the box and plant your head on the ball to send it flashing high into the net', I couldn't ascertain, but that is exactly what Jai did 14 minutes into Saturday's (October 19th) match against Staines Town. It was enough to win the game.

The side could conceivably have scored more than their one goal, but the tension that clings in the air when any team has a narrow lead remained until the final whistle. That whistle blew after seven minutes of injury time had been played – a period required due to Will Evans being stretchered from the field late in the game. Will landed awkwardly after jumping for an aerial challenge and remained grounded until he could receive treatment. An effort to walk from the pitch was abandoned within a couple of paces. The last we saw of Will he was on his back with his hands covering his face, being lugged down the tunnel.

I read a tweet from the player himself an hour ago that stated, 'That feeling like you're back at square 1.' To be honest, if the message can be interpreted as Will having suffered a recurrence of his twisted knee then that's better news than I feared.

If Saturday was a bad day for Will (even though he was impressive until his involvement was prematurely halted), then the opposite is true for Jai. Richard had intimated, during the week's lead up to the game, that the Spitfires' playmaker is not presently reaching the exalted standards of which he is capable – citing a couple of examples to back up his assertion. I replied that I thought Jai had, at the very least, been working extremely hard in games. When will I learn?

When asked to provide my evidence for the defence I referred to the back-tracking and hard running that Jai routinely undertakes.

'Yes, but where does he do it?'

'Back in his own half.'

'Exactly.'

In Richard's mind that is easy. It is work that catches the eye and 'looks good', but he is asking Jai to spend his energy within a specific area where, by applying his armoury of creative skills, he can cause any opposition a host of problems.

The criticism sounded, on first hearing, harsh. But, on Sunday (October 20th), no less a judge than analytical maestro Gary Neville unwittingly confirmed Richard's assessment of his player's efforts. In his role as match summariser, Sky Sports' star turn discussed the lack of impact Tottenham Hotspur's Lewis Holtby, operating in Reason's 'Number 10' position, was exerting on his team's game at Aston Villa. Neville went on to explain that, instead of seeking to dictate play near his opponent's goal, Holtby was concerning himself with defensive responsibilities, i.e. 'taking the easy option'. On the first occasion that the German imposed himself in Villa territory Tottenham scored, before going on to win at a canter.

Our premier football broadcaster pays a hefty whack for that intuition. I am receiving it for nowt. Furthermore, opportunities such as that to speak at length with Guy Butters, while we waited for the chastened group to emerge on Thursday, are wont to crop up at any time. The freedom to tap into even a handful of the Eastleigh Number 2's stories, accumulated across a 20-year professional playing career – which included being at Spurs during Paul Gascoigne's first two years with that club – is a personal bonanza.

What stands out when talking to Guy and Richard, as well as other members of the ex or current professional football fraternity, is how utterly normal they can make the job sound. Many of those who are good enough to make the grade simply always knew that they had what it takes. It follows that any line of work will, in time, become a way of life. That's not to say there is no awareness among these individuals of how blessed they have been. Guy did concede, though, in common with all players whose days were numbered by the time being a top-level footballer reaped such ginormous financial dividends, that he'd have appreciated earning today's rewards for his uncompromising defending.

Presently, Guy's boss is in the unusual situation of managing a relatively early-season break – although a couple of elongated weather enforced lay-offs during his first Eastleigh term provided Richard with some practice in this sphere. No FA Cup tie this week means we don't go again until Saturday, November 2nd, when, with indecent haste, we reconvene with a Sutton United side that is frankly flying – and up in third. The trip to Dover – originally scheduled for cup weekend – has been slotted in on bonfire night. It already promises to be a big four days although, with incessant rain lashing down and causing tonight's reserve match at the Silverlake to be canned, it is wise to use a pencil when marking fixtures through to February in the diary.

Five Days On…

…(October 27th) and that postponed second-string fixture will never be played. Eastleigh have relinquished their membership of the Wyvern League. The consequences of that Hampshire Senior Cup defeat against Whitchurch, although by no means the single reason for this decision, have proved far-reaching. The league is not considered the correct breeding ground for young players at a Conference South club (last Tuesday's opponents were due to be the 'stiffs' from New Milton Town, whose first team were relegated at the end of last season into Wessex League Division One – that is four tiers below Eastleigh).

Moreover, there is not the merest notion that any of the younger Spitfires will be providing Richard with extra options for his squad any time soon. Therefore, what purpose is being served? The refreshed shape of the club's operation below first-team level will be revealed soon.

When discussing the main men on Thursday (October 24th), Cookie was reluctant to dwell on his currently immoderate workload. McAllister was missing due to illness, but is expected to be resuming full duties imminently. Will's appearance at the ground was merely designed to 'get him out of the house', but the sanguine, easy-going midfielder was in chirpy form. He is optimistic that this knee injury could be of a less serious nature than his pre-season problem.

Still, when he tapped a loose ball at the side of the pitch back to Damian Batt my heart nearly stopped. During the latter part of the session, which included a savage series of five runs through a monstrous figure of eight, I was able to have a long chat with Will. It is becoming the lot of injured by-standers that they end up spending chunks of their working day conversing with me. Call it my contribution towards providing an incentive to get fit… quickly.

Cookie's earlier caution was shown to be prescient. In the very final act of a fiery 9v9, Suvs pulled up, ever so fleetingly, holding his left hamstring. That he did so right under Cookie's nose saved him from himself. Glen was plainly miffed that he'd been spotted, then even more so when he was ordered to go and ice his muscle, which, under duress, he confessed to having felt 'pinch'.

Football daft and uber-competitive, this is the bleakest professional scenario Suvs could encounter. Will asked his captain how much additional time he spends in the gym. 'If I'm not here, I'm there.'

Watching his team-mates run themselves into the ground, Suvs revealed how 'guilty' he feels when he's not doing his bit, before explaining his near obsessive approach to his fitness. 'If you're only doing the same as the next person, it's not enough. You've got to have that edge.'

Michael Green had that 'edge' over his colleagues during the dizzying loop-the-loop death charges. If his manager had asked Greener to press on until dark he'd have merrily complied. The left-back's day was improving. When he was knocked off the ball by Yemi during that 9v9, at the cost of a goal, Richard was ready with his advice: 'Greener, get on the f****** Herbalife.'

By the end of their fifth run every single body was screaming, except that of the aforementioned Green. Eastleigh's players were suffering and doing so in silence. Cue manager: 'Come on. This is where you get round each other. Help your team-mates. If you want to do anything this season, you do it together.'

Collins tried to rouse his wasted comrades, but even this most bubbly of characters seemed as if in a far-off world where pain is king. Then, mercifully, Richard blew the whistle, sparing his players a sixth 'dash' around their wearily familiar course. With individual senses restored, the squad could look forward to a four-day break from club duties.

Richard had been offered by Ray Murphy, the club secretary, in advance of the victory over Staines, the chance to fit in the away fixture at Weston-super-Mare on cup Saturday. The manager's reasons for declining illustrated the speed with which perceptions can change in football.

'We'd not beaten Concord, lost to Ebbsfleet and Oxford City, and then what if we hadn't won against Staines? I'd have been trying to get things back on track with away games at Weston, Sutton, and Dover. Are you trying to get me the sack?'

Even if his team had lost against Staines they'd have remained in top spot. The boss's predicament emphasises again the pressure that every week brings.

While I was sizing up the football I could attend on our blank Saturday, the players were contemplating how to maximise their weekend off. Jai Reason was heading for a break in Liverpool, even if he was insistent that he'd have preferred to be playing – and I believed him. Jai had sought to add to his 'European City of Culture 2008' experience by purchasing a ticket for Liverpool's home match against West Brom, only to be met with a plaintive 'sold out' notice. That'll be the day trippers converging from across the continent then.

I had deliberated on watching Everton at Aston Villa, but, with only home tickets available and an inherent inability to control myself (temperamentally only, you understand), it wouldn't have been the best idea. Havant & Waterlooville it was then. When I had interviewed Jamie Collins on Thursday he said that his strong bond with the Hawks had no bearing on his thoughts when the chance to become a Spitfire arose. Even if he'd have been making the switch directly along the M27 he wouldn't have hesitated. 'As a footballer you have to do what is right for you.'

Still, when I put my £13 into the Westleigh Park coffers I always end up hoping to see an away win, even if the visiting side are Tommy Widdrington's Eastbourne Borough. My money, on this weekend, bought me entry into what was a compelling game, if low on genuine quality, which ended in a 1–1 draw.

The entertainment actually began before we (Dad in the driver's seat) reached the ground. Waiting at traffic lights in Leigh Park and discussing the Twitter follower numbers of Danny Baker (closing on 300,000) and Mark Kermode (above 141,000) in comparison with my high water mark of 116 (the omission of an extra '000' is intentional), and with a deluge from the skies in its full throes, we were treated to the sight of a chap, resplendent in sheepskin coat and gleaming white trainers, crossing in front of us while pushing a lawnmower. For all the progress at the Silverlake, you don't see that down Stoneham Lane.

If Stewart Donald has his way, then in future, when you drive towards Eastleigh's ground down that narrow and winding road, with its blind corners and stream of pedestrians playing roulette with their life expectancy, you will arrive at something considerably grander than what currently exists. This week, interviewing the chairman for the first time, I learned of his Eastleigh FC priorities. Stewart will not, among his club's supporters, find any opponents to his ambition of facilitating the development of a team that achieves Football League status. Similarly, his wish that they make the jump playing in a stadium to befit a higher standing will meet with common approval.

This is no 'long-term' plan of the sort commonly subscribed to in the football world. The only reference to a time-scale for Stewart's goals is 'as soon as possible'. He was especially effusive when speaking about his manager, stating that the owners 'follow his direction and his vision within the boundaries set'. The Spitfires owner will be hoping as much as me that Richard's weekend standing as bookies' favourite for the newly vacant top job at Forest Green Rovers comes to nothing.

Stewart went on to detail the stroke of serendipity that precipitated his taking ownership of the club late in 2011 (the deal was legally completed in February 2012). He had actively been looking to integrate himself further into the football world (his Bridle Insurance Company was then sponsor of Oxford United, where he held a season ticket for near on 30 years). Things became interesting when Stewart received a phone call requesting that he attend a meeting with Glen Hoddle the following day. As a fervent football supporter, a summons from one of the finest players this country has reared could not be ignored.

Hoddle initially wanted to be party to a club takeover, but the initial discussions produced nothing concrete; only the floating of news that Eastleigh might be seeking additional financial backing. When Stewart approached the incumbent board, he discovered what had been increasingly apparent to all Spitfires. Eastleigh FC was ripe for the purchase. Before he knew it, a life-altering project was underway – one that he confesses takes up half of a 'very long working week'.

What shone through all of his responses to my questions was the extent of Stewart's emotional investment in football. Asked if he can relax and enjoy the game, the owner painted a clear picture of the impact that everything Eastleigh has on his state of mind:

'I feel nervous and tense, and am rarely relaxed. I kick every ball, make every challenge. I am a fan, the same as everyone else. I have had plenty of journeys home to Oxfordshire after both home and away games thinking, "What a great result. I am loving this."

'I have also had some at the other end of the spectrum where I think, "What a fool, this was an awful defeat and why do I waste my time, money and effort on such a silly game?" However, when I have calmed down from a defeat or forgotten the last win, I then refocus on achieving the goals we have set at the club. I focus on the next challenge, whether it's Sutton, Dorchester, terracing or the bar staff.'

Stewart, through his own take on the subject, captured in a nutshell the astonishment, bordering on bewilderment, that many people express when they learn of the passion an individual can feel for a non-league football club – so substantiating one of the tenets of this book.

'The passion of the supporters and the strength of feeling they have for the club made a huge impact on me and have been a real surprise.'

There remains an underlying frustration, though, that gates stubbornly refuse to rise towards the four-figure numbers that Stewart craves. He admitted that the hitherto inability of the team to embark on a profile-boosting cup run has dented aspirations to entice a new faction of support. Richard, therefore, has no leeway with this year's FA Trophy.

Oxford City, meanwhile, were summarily dispatched 3–0 at Dover in their

FA Cup tie. That was strangely flattening news. Dover have been handed a 1st round game at Corby Town. Win that, and our home game against the team from Kent – scheduled for second round day on December 7th – will have to be re-arranged. It is the football gods' way of rubbing our noses in it for as long as possible.

The impending away game at Dover is going to be another long drive for the old man. The curiously apathetic take-up of supporters' club away travel has led to Chris Blake cancelling the mini-buses booked for that jaunt and Saturday's journey to Sutton. How much the respective numbers signed up – two for each trip – can be attributed to people genuinely preferring alternative modes of transport and how much to the hotly discussed 'behavioural problems' en route might become more apparent with time.

Back to events at the training ground on Thursday (October 24th) where, after the day's work was over, I was left with a few minutes to kill. The cause of my down-time was Jamie Collins, prior to our interview, having to re-organise the back of his car – which was jam-packed with 'goods' (all legal) that he sells on as an extra cash-generating stream – in order to make it habitable for the trek back to Hertfordshire. While yet another budding Eastleigh FC business tycoon engaged in his heavy lifting, various players who shall remain nameless discussed the merits of assorted vodka and amaretto brands, while others swapped dressing room tales of yore. It was intriguing listening.

If Collins has long since won me over (he'll be made up, I'm sure) then, to paraphrase Jerry Maguire, he completely had me with the declaration that his satisfaction at beating Swansea City on that 2008 Havant & Waterlooville FA Cup run far outweighed any pleasure derived from losing at Liverpool.

That's the spirit of a winner, something Jamie has in spades. To overcome the horrific accident that he suffered when he was nine years old must have required phenomenal courage and resolve. Only the man himself can explain what happened.

'I was on the way to watch my dad's friend play cricket at the local park. The game got cancelled, so we [Jamie and his pal] went to walk over to the shop and saw a car on fire. Being kids, as we were, we stood about watching from about 40ft away. The car exploded, and the rod that holds the bonnet up shot out of the car and went through my leg. It left me with a big hole in my leg. I found out later that if it had gone in an inch higher, I'd have lost my leg from the knee downwards, so I was lucky in one way and unlucky in another.'

A tattoo that covers the entirety of Jamie's calf, and therefore any scarring, is the sole visible evidence attesting to his injuries. That experience, the initial shock and fright, and then a protracted recovery, which included for close to two years wearing a stocking to act as a second skin, must have contributed much to the enchanting, competitive and happy-go-lucky personality we see today.

Another of my recent interview subjects, Sam Wilson, has been loaned to Fleet Town, a side that plays two tiers down from the Spitfires (apologies to the sponsor, but I can't bring myself to write the full name of the league again). Sam is crying out for regular, properly contested football. If he can make a go of it, this spell could propel Sam into Richard's thoughts for the later part of this campaign – when, we hope, Eastleigh will be in the midst of a frantic dual assault on promotion and the FA Trophy.

23

D-DAYS

Sutton United away, 11 weeks into the season. It is not quite a fixture whose Premier League equivalent would be described by a hyperbole-prone sports channel as a 'title decider' or 'winner takes all promotion battle', but it's an encounter of some consequence all the same.

It's now the beginning of a month (Friday, November 1st), which, fit-for-purpose pitches allowing, has the potential to determine whether Eastleigh will, come April, be contesting the league's number one spot or jostling for a play-off position.

Paul Doswell's team have played twice over the course of our unintended two-week break. After throwing away a two-goal lead in their game at Hemel Hempstead on Saturday, they required a Tuesday night replay to reach the FA Cup's first round. It's possible to believe, then, that Sutton wouldn't be averse to the heavens opening, so leaving their Gander Green Lane turf unplayable tomorrow. The Us, understandably, will want to face Eastleigh on an equal footing.

The energy and skill on display yesterday at the Spitfires training ground delighted Richard. He vociferously expressed his pleasure at the standard while the group worked and emphasised to me afterwards how sharp he thought every single individual had looked – adding a word of praise for Damian Batt.

With the players gathered around their manager at 12:20pm, he announced an early finish – 'I've got a fully fit squad and I'm not going to tempt fate' – before forcibly asserting, 'You are better, fitter, and stronger than them [Sutton].'

If the training tempo had hinted that we are on the eve of a humdinger of a match, the boss's demand that his squad come decked out in jacket, shirt and tie was testament to the fact that, from the moment they arrive in Surrey, he wants his men focused and in tune with the significant job in hand.

The calm before the storm; the players go through their pre-season paces in the bucolic surrounds of Wantage. *(JMcN)*

The season's opening day. Jai and Yemi being tightly marked by their Sutton adversaries, but Yemi has his own way of dealing with that. *(Tony Smith)*

We have lift off. Jai's skill has teed-up Yemi to crash the ball home, and win the opening day encounter against Paul Doswell's team. *(Tony Smith)*

While a packed Main Stand – my stand – watches on. *(Tony Smith)*

Chris Dillon in command at Boreham Wood.
Six weeks earlier he was still an Eastleigh trialist.*(JMcN)*

Richard receiving September's Conference South Manager of the Month 'gong'. He
resisted the temptation to do anything untoward with his trophy. *(Tony Smith)*

Green (left) and Fleetwood are crestfallen, after Oxford City spring a surprise to knock us out of the FA Cup. *(Tony Smith)*

Ex-Spitfire Mitchell Nelson hits a free-kick at our goal. By half-time in this game at Sutton, Nelson had been red carded for an unsavoury tackle on Stuart Fleetwood. *(JMcN)*

Jamie Collins has scored a terrific goal against Gateshead. Strevens (left) and Yemi are quickly on the scene to join their team-mate's celebrations. *(Tony Smith)*

Brian Palmer. A popular everyday presence at Eastleigh FC. *(Tony Smith)*

Stu Solly presents Ben Strevens with his richly deserved 'Supporters' Player of the Month' award for December. *(Tony Smith)*

Dover defenders are scattered in Fleetwood's wake, as our Welsh attacker's mesmerising run from the half-way line culminates with him scoring an injury-time winner at 'The Crabble'. *(JMcN)*

Jamie Collins, against the balance of play, has scored the winner against Bath City. The players knew what a huge goal that was. *(Tony Smith)*

Ex-Eastleigh man Jamie Brown, now at Gosport Borough, is typically 'committed' in his efforts to unsettle Jai Reason. *(Tony Smith)*

A chance has gone begging against Gosport. Beckwith is incredulous, McAllister is grounded and Todd reckons he'd have made a better job of it. *(Tony Smith)*

Jai fires in the first of his two penalties in the home meeting with Ebbsfleet; Richard hadn't advised his playmaker where to place these during a captivating pre-match talk. *(JMcN)*

The ever convivial Mike Andrews (left), Sheridan Price (centre) and Chris Blake anticipating another afternoon at the Silverlake. (JMcN)

Cookie (right) is a master of his profession, but if Guy Butters is asking for tips on how to get back to match fitness that might be a challenge too far for Eastleigh's Sports Therapist. (JMcN)

The March of the Condemned. Eastleigh's players, looking strangely downcast, take to the field at Tonbridge, a match which ended a weather-enforced sixteen day break. Ex-Spitfires defender Gary Elphick, seen leading his side out, went on to defend like a Trojan in their 2-1 win. (JMcN)

Beckwith leaping for the ball in a crowded penalty area at Whitehawk. The pitch at the Hawks' Enclosed Ground appears as if chiselled into the side of a cliff. (JMcN)

Ross Flitney in command at Eastbourne Borough.
The 'keeper went on to be the night's hero, when he saved an injury time penalty from
Frankie Raymond to keep the scores level. *(JMcN)*

Fleetwood's reward for scoring a spectacular equaliser at Eastbourne; the attacker is booked
for discarding his shirt amid the subsequent bedlam. Collins (left) and Southam are making
their way back for the re-start after haring over to join the celebrations. *(JMcN)*

The brilliant Ben Strevens rises highest to head a precious equaliser in a crucial late season
encounter away at Bishop's Stortford. *(JMcN)*

Dorchester have just been thumped 6–0, but you wouldn't know it here. Minds are already turning to the next task; in this instance a Mothering Sunday trip to Hayes & Yeading. *(JMcN)*

Macca takes a buffeting every week. His adversary here is Dean Inman, a Hayes & Yeading defender who headed so many balls during this 1–1 draw against the Spitfires that he was lucky to escape with his senses intact. *(JMcN)*

The dogged Adam Everitt engaged in a tenacious battle with Jai Reason throughout the game at Hayes & Yeading. Here, Dan Spence is watching Jai trying to find a way past the ex-Eastleigh defender. *(JMcN)*

McAllister in aerial combat with the Hawks' Sami El-Abd. The pair would go on to have a feisty half-time 'chat'. *(Tony Smith)*

Nothing to see here. Whitehawk were convinced that their goalkeeper, Chris Winterton, was fouled as Toddy headed home a vital leveller on April 5th. *(Tony Smith)*

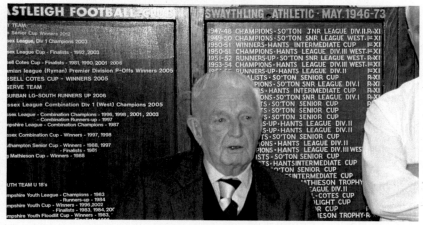

Derik Brooks is pitch perfect as he delivers a speech opening the new supporters' bar named in his honour. Behind the club's Life President are boards detailing the achievements of Eastleigh FC and Swaythling Athletic FC – the original name of the team he founded in 1946. *(JMcN)*

Richard is all ears after we've beaten Whitehawk on April 5th. The manager's son, Dan, is relaying news to the troops of Sutton United's shock defeat at the hands of Maidenhead, and Bromley's single goal demise at Havant & Waterlooville. *(JMcN)*

The Spitfires' travelling support begins to congregate for a momentous night at Bromley. *(JMcN)*

A satisfied Jai leads his victorious side off the field at Bromley, while Richard is interviewed by Jamie Graham. *(JMcN)*

No opponent takes Jai Reason lightly. Chelmsford City were no exception. *(JMcN)*

Mike Wimbridge, Lianne Cavill and Mark Blake (L-R) among an orderly section of Eastleigh's away support at Chelmsford. Mike (t-shirt) and Mark (shorts) haven't dressed appropriately on what turned into a bitterly cold day. *(JMcN)*

Lee Peacock hadn't been on the pitch long when he found himself in the middle of a Chelmsford defensive sandwich. *(JMcN)*

The tea bar provides a story all of its own. Plenty of patrons are after food and drink during half-time of another vital home match against Dover Athletic. *(JMcN)*

A man with his love for football rediscovered. 'Peaks' has scored a thrilling winner against Dover, and inched his club towards the league title. *(Tony Smith)*

Tom Parsons, part of the match day sponsors' entourage, making his way to the 'posh seats' for the game with Basingstoke, is looking more confident than 'in focus' in this shot.*(JMcN)*

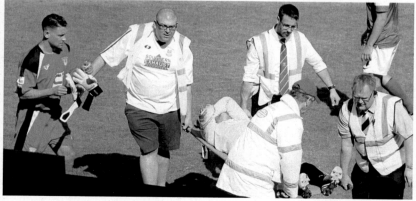

Basingstoke Town goalkeeper Louis Wells, being carried off, has had his gloves unceremoniously yanked from his hands to be handed on to auxiliary replacement Ross Adams. Mike Wimbridge, decked out in old EFC top, is one of the stretcher bearers.*(JMcN)*

'Suvs' meets traffic at the edge of the Basingstoke penalty box, but this surge from midfield led to Yemi's opening goal. *(Tony Smith)*

Ben Wright (number 10) sliding home the second and, ultimately, decisive goal against Basingstoke. *(JMcN)*

Andy Cook, Guy Butters, Ben Wright and Stuart Fleetwood (left to right) might look like they're in the dentist's waiting room. In fact, they're longing for the referee's final whistle against Basingstoke so that the Championship party can begin. *(Tony Smith)*

Toddy looks like he's making the most noise here. The injured Collins (in tracksuit) preferred to watch on as his colleagues shared their delirium. *(Tony Smith)*

Will Evans, receiving his champions' medal, isn't sharing his champagne with anyone. *(JMcN)*

The fruits of two years labour. Derik Brooks and Glen Southam lift the 2013/2014 Conference South winners' trophy. In the background, Yemi proves himself a dab hand with a champagne bottle. *(Tony Smith)*

Who we are (front), what we are (back) and the players who fit both descriptions. *(JMcN)*

Players and supporters come together to salute a historic achievement. *(JMcN)*

A man alone with his thoughts. Stewart Donald with the trophy which signifies that stage one of his mission is complete. *(JMcN)*

Father and son united in joy. Dan Hill knew his old man would be in a decent mood during today's journey home. *(Dan Hill)*

Ray Murphy (left) and John Russell are demob happy on the season's final day. *(JMcN)*

A touch of class. Our local rivals, Havant & Waterlooville, form a guard of honour to welcome the newly crowned champions to the field for an Easter Monday derby clash. *(JMcN)*

The fully fit travelling squad includes, incredibly, Will Evans. Predictably christened 'Lazarus' for the day, Will took full part in every second of Thursday's labours. He confessed to his 'lungs feeling it', but otherwise resembled anything other than a figure who had been carted off a football pitch on a stretcher less than a fortnight earlier.

Saturday's only absentee, therefore, will be Jai Reason – arch-collector of daft bookings. Jai's disappointment is evident, but that uniquely lost and helpless feeling, experienced by a footballer suddenly cut adrift when they are so used to being at the core of the team's plans, didn't adversely affect his training output. Jai asked Cookie to put him through a personal post-training running session to compensate for his forthcoming rest.

I should have been pleased watching Jai preparing for supplementary physical toil. During his weekend stay in Liverpool, he had got himself into the stadium, which once boasted a stand named the 'McDonald's Kop' (I assume that some members of the Somerset Reds cried off with cider poisoning). Jai's confirmation that Liverpool played 'very, very well' (they beat West Brom 4–1), with some force behind the words 'very, very', surely made his imminent endeavours a fair, erm, kop. Notwithstanding that, I'd rather be seeing Jai in his creative guise on Saturday – even wearing the snood that is a standard component of his training ground attire now the cold winds are blowing in.

An afternoon at Sutton's home will invoke personal memories, not of February's 2–1 reverse (the game after which I erroneously wrote off Eastleigh's hopes last season of achieving a play-off berth), but of one of my favourite football days. It was 1989, FA Cup third-round day and I was in my bedroom kicking a sponge ball around while listening in thrall to Radio 2's progenitor to today's 5 Live Saturday sport programme. The afternoon's commentary was delivered from Gander Green Lane, where the hosts knocked the 1987 winners, Coventry City, out of what was then still the greatest knock-out competition of all.

The show finished with John Inverdale interviewing Sutton's manager of the day, Barrie Williams, an eccentric chap with a fondness for using his programme notes to write poetry and whose sheer unbridled joy boomed from the radio. I counted the minutes away until that night's *Match of the Day* (my parents always allowed me the treat of a late Saturday night upon the extremely rare occurrence of football being on the telly). Mere mention of the Us' home immediately brings to mind Matthew Hanlon wheeling away on a mud heap of a pitch after thumping in the game's clinching goal.

Back to the here and now, and early this week Eastleigh issued a press release that stated that the now disbanded reserve team will be replaced by a 'development squad'. Dan Wright's employment at the club has ended. This new initiative will be led by Lee Peacock – a familiar name to supporters of Mansfield, Manchester City, Bristol City, Sheffield Wednesday, and Swindon Town, among others. 'Peaks' will be assisted by Dave Hazelgrove.

No sooner had the announcement been made, than the youngsters were defeating a contemporary Portsmouth outfit at the Silverlake on Wednesday morning. That rewarding start to the new concept's existence was followed the next day by the callow bunch (whose average age is 16) being requisitioned to provide opposition for the first team, so allowing Richard to give his players 20 minutes of full-scale action.

It was like watching, well, men against boys. It was, nevertheless, a valuable exercise for both sets of players, but demonstrated again the immense gap that the hopefuls must bridge to reach the levels of their first-team counterparts. The move to a development squad is designed to help them manage that transition. Regular opposition will come in the form of fellow academy teams. With this Spitfires intake all being in the lower bracket of the 16–18 age-range, time is on theirs and their mentors' side. Certainly, Lee's ascension (he had already been involved in youth coaching at the club, after ending his striking career at Eastleigh once last season concluded) will be a boon to the prospects of the players under his command.

From minute one on Thursday, 'Suvs' had been almost dementedly exhorting his colleagues to operate at 100%; when he failed to match his own demands by placing a ball wide of an open goal from two yards out, our skipper's foot cracked into a post with enough force to make the goal-frame shake. After rounding off the day's acutely focused session with drills centred on formations and tactics, some weary bodies were ready for a good feed.

As if to exhibit how transient every single situation at a football club is, feedback was being sought from the players on the chilli, rice, and warm French bread – which all smelt delicious – due to a company from Oxford debuting their produce after taking on all of the Silverlake's catering duties. The quiet satisfaction as clean plates were decanted into the wash bowls was verdict enough.

Two Days Post-Sutton...

...and Eastleigh's impending contest with Dover can't be hyped as a 'crucial top of the table tussle'. What the Spitfires actually face is a game against their early May play-off bête noir who, after a defeat at Basingstoke on Saturday slipped to 11th – three points behind their vanquishers whose win sees them occupying 5th spot.

But what happened at Gander Green Lane? Firstly, after stumbling into yet more soul-shredding roadworks, causing an excruciating final few miles to my journey, it was a considerable relief to be present for the full 90 minutes. Upon arrival at 2:40pm (ergo, stress levels approaching sweating and palpitation stage), I triumphantly swung the steering wheel of my unremarkable Fiesta into the ground's entrance – only to be greeted by a 'car park full' sign.

Half an hour after abandoning my vehicle precariously on a main road and 20 minutes into the game, Stuart Fleetwood was on the floor banging the turf in agony having been 'topped' by an awful Mitchell Nelson challenge. Our erratic former right-back fully merited his resultant red card. It was the second time this season that the player, who was exasperatingly unpredictable in the Spitfires blue, has seemed uncontrollably fired up when confronted with his last club.

Seventy minutes against ten men, then. Moreover, 11 'better, fitter, stronger' players outnumbering their hosts – it was time for a statement performance and a win. There was no immediate Eastleigh domination, but, thanks to McAllister's emphatic finish from one yard into an empty net, they took a one-goal lead into the half-time break.

Fleetwood, after being victim of Nelson's assault, had spent the remainder of the first period being subjected to a verbal onslaught from an animated home crowd believing our 'over-paid' attacker had hammed up his reaction to the tackle. Fleets continued his theatrics by not playing in the second half, instead re-emerging with his ankle completely bandaged in advance of a trip to hospital to have the wound stitched. All part of the ruse, of course.

Will Evans completed his latest recovery by replacing his limping team-mate and within two minutes was in the thick of the action. During my pre-season induction into the Spitfires' inner circle, I'd have anticipated any combination between Will and Damian Scannell to be wreaking havoc upon

Eastleigh's mesmerised opponents. As it happened, the pair's first competitive coming together – Scans having himself entered the game as an early substitute for the injured Jamie Taylor – won Sutton a penalty. Craig Dundas lashed it high into the goal.

Still, plenty of time to restore our lead. Not so. I don't recall any aspect of Thursday's detailed planning that called for balls to be routinely hit long in vain search of McAllister or Yemi – but that is what materialised. Sutton dominated possession, played the more fluent football, created a slew of chances, and generally gave a lie to their numerical deficiency.

The sound of the final whistle, with the scores still tied, was a relief. It was a strangely disappointing afternoon, despite the outcome being one we'd have all settled on beforehand. Doswell had been his usual idiosyncratic self throughout. He mingled with some travelling fans – who had singled Scannell out for stick concerning his non-selection ahead of kick-off – during the second half's early stages, before heading up to the camera gantry for a bird's-eye view of proceedings.

With a couple of minutes to play, and after Eastleigh's latest aimless forward ball, 'Dossie' – now back in his dugout – strode out to holler across to Richard his judgement on the visitors' style of football, or lack thereof. The sending-off incident had already sparked a fair old ruckus between the occupants of the two benches, as well as a good deal of each side's playing personnel. It is legitimate to conclude that Eastleigh–Sutton relations are as cordial as those between Chelsea and Liverpool.

With our players already down the tunnel, opinions delivered by the good burghers of Surrey on their respective abilities still echoing around the emptying main stand, Richard departed to a personal earful from one disgruntled Eastleigh follower. The dissatisfied customer, as it happens, used to be McAllister's strike partner in the esteemed mid to late 1990s Pirelli unit.

It was a poor showing, but surely we're a long way off any of that caper. That's my view, but a read of the supporters' internet forum, which sees its most frenzied activity at the first sign of everything being less than hunky-dory, revealed plenty of withering words regarding the team's endeavours at Sutton.

Fans of an anxious or reproachful leaning expressed dissatisfaction with certain individuals (Strevens and Evans were this week's chief targets) and the manager's perceived reluctance to alter his tactics in advance of, or during, matches. The continued lack of playing time for Chris Dillon and Ramone Rose is another issue causing consternation – proving again the truism about footballers becoming better the longer they spend out of the team.

My dad managed to become embroiled in a long message board debate about the rights and wrongs of those and other unfavourable comments – his arguments all being in defence of manager and team. While I consider him correct on that standpoint, his assertion that Gander Green Lane's relatively small pitch and poor playing surface were major factors in the Spitfires' display – a topic on which he bent my ear all afternoon – I wholeheartedly disagree with.

Doswell topped off the weekend by giving an interview to *The Non-League Paper* in which he stated of Richard that, 'No one likes their manager, he's arrogant', before finishing his mini-'censure' with the words, 'You talk about respect with people, I haven't got any for him whatsoever.'

Prior to the personal attack, Doswell claimed to have seen Eastleigh's wage bill and declared it to be twice the size of Sutton's. The reference to other clubs' playing budgets is the most tedious form of self-preservation rolled out by managers at every level of the game.

Moving On

Our trip to Dover was preceded by the FA Trophy draw, held at Wembley Stadium. The Spitfires enter at the same third qualifying round stage that they have progressed beyond only twice in the past eight seasons – and they have been dealt a tricky hand this time. A trip to Wealdstone or Maidstone – the latter top the Ryman Premier League, the former are sixth in the same division – ensures receipt of the £4,000 prize money for progression into the first round will be hard won.

The Conference South's standout result over the weekend just gone provided the pre-cursor to this week's main piece of non-league news. Chelmsford City were beaten 6–0 on their own patch by Boreham Wood – the weakest side I've seen this season. Dean Holdsworth, who Richard had believed could operate relatively pressure free during his inaugural term at the Melbourne Stadium, has consequently been dismissed from his job.

Whatever barbs have been chucked his way since Saturday, that is a threat most definitely not hanging over our manager's head. Some respite came Richard's way when heavy rain (and, as uncharitably suspected by some, the home team's forthcoming FA Cup first round tie) saw the game at Dover postponed. In one discerning forumite's view, the cancellation was a good thing as 'the best we could have hoped for was a 0–0 anyway'.

I've now had the opportunity to hear Richard's take on the, in some quarters, scathing reaction to Saturday's outing at Sutton. 'Baffled' is the epithet that most accurately describes the manager's emotion. He does not understand what is inspiring the small band of critics. It is hard to argue with Richard's suspicion that Paul Doswell has achieved the off-field result he hoped for after Saturday. The Sutton boss's public utterances and conspicuously confrontational touchline behaviour have undoubtedly played their part in ramping up the pressure on a man whose team have taken four points from his side and hold a five-point advantage over them in the league table.

Apparently my erstwhile Pirelli colleague was informing Richard that 'you got Dan Wright sacked, you c★★★, and you'll be gone by the end of the season yourself'. Furthermore, the tunnel area, where I had mused at the full-time whistle that I would love to be a fly on the wall, was the scene of some heated dispute during the interval. Doswell and Wayne Shaw (Sutton's goalkeeping coach and a former Spitfires stopper) were intent on making very plain their contempt for Eastleigh's boss.

It can only be a good thing that, unless the FA Trophy dictates otherwise, we won't be seeing Sutton United again for a very long time. Attention now turns to the Conference South's pre-season attention seekers, Farnborough, who come to the Silverlake on Saturday.

Bromley laced Chelmsford to the tune of five goals on Tuesday night and have subsequently opened a four-point gap at the table's summit. 'Boro meanwhile were drawing 2–2 at Maidenhead United, as they completed the task of catching up on the games missed during their aborted start to the campaign. Our Hampshire rivals are a tidy outfit, as I witnessed at Havant – a fact backed up by their 20-point haul.

This is a match that the Spitfires will expect to win, but, owing to the mysterious disquiet that has bubbled up among a vocal minority, it suddenly feels like an encounter that has more than just three points riding on it. Richard's every move will be under the microscope. He confessed to misreading his substitutions at Sutton and admitted that the performance wasn't up to scratch. The only consistent 'failing' of his side this season, though, has been its lack of goals. On that note, it was very interesting to hear the manager tell me that if Jamie Slabber ever decided Sutton were no longer for him, he'd love our prolific ex-centre-forward back at the Silverlake.

Slabber's perceived inertia on Saturday drew some rough critique from his own fans. Anybody who watched the 28 year old – who on the pitch looks and moves like a man born ten years earlier – during his time at Eastleigh will know that he is not wont to zip about like a gazelle. Nevertheless, provided with the quality service of which he would be assured in Richard's team the goals would flow – an Aldi version of Dimitar Berbatov.

My Thursday (November 7th) training visit was curbed by my playing taxi driver for my parents, who required a Heathrow drop-off as they embarked on a voyage to Singapore (a former family home) and Vietnam.

After traipsing across the wet fields to the pitch being used for the day, I was greeted by Richard telling me that I'd just missed the players talking about some of the abuse they received from a few travelling Spitfires when going across to thank the hardy band for their support at Sutton. I have always suspected that footballers don't care too much for the thoughts of the proletarians on the terraces. I was wrong. The players' elevated status in our minds does not shield them from the innate human desire to be liked and appreciated.

Significantly, though, there is an appreciation that the bulk of their fan-base is right with them. Spirits, although still short of the clamorous, buoyant climate of a month ago, remain good. I was struck upon my arrival – after noting the startling length of grass and steadily decaying practice conditions – by the presence of 19 individuals, all fit to labour away in their still sparkling new training kit. Fleetwood, meanwhile, has five stitches in his gashed leg and, judging by his Twitter timeline, is recuperating with the assistance of his television and box sets of American dramas. 'Never a red, ref, he's conned you there.'

The turf might not be such a bother for next Thursday's workout. Maidstone came through an FA Trophy replay, scoring a late goal against their fellow Ryman Premier promotion contenders Wealdstone, meaning we visit Kent next Saturday to play on the Stones '3G' pitch. An absolute godsend in non-league environs, thanks to its preventing the glut of winter cancellations that wreak havoc with even the most painstakingly compiled budgets, the artificial surface requires a bit of getting used to for players. Richard, therefore, is hoping to organise a session at our hosts' ground two days prior to the fixture. McAllister was none too impressed with the idea of a two-hour training commute, but it is another indication towards the degree of professionalism being installed at this club.

Stewart Donald and Mark Jewell both popped over to watch some of Thursday's training. 'Seeing what I'm wasting my money on,' the chairman quipped, before declaring himself happy with the Trophy draw. With his obligation to keep an eye on the bottom line, Stewart is rubbing his hands at the prospect of sharing gate receipts from what he hopes will be an attendance of approximately 1,500.

When he joined the players for their chilli and rice, Stewart responded drily to Brian Palmer's (our septuagenarian club workhorse) reflecting that a within earshot Jai Reason would be free after his suspension to face Farnborough on Saturday – 'We can compensate for that.' Ribbing aside, our playmaker is champing at the bit for some competitive football.

Richard admitted some surprise at the extent to which his team missed Jai's intelligent link-play on Saturday – a sentiment I shared. Jai's focus is matched by that of his team-mates, who are clearly fed up with their poor goal return. With the morning's hard work at an end Suvs had a brief word with Jai, imploring him to start unloading more shots at the target from the edge of the box – 'We've got to stop trying to walk the f****** thing in.'

The same matter was being discussed by Messrs Hill, McAllister, Todd, and Beckwith. There is mutual acceptance that the team must become more forceful and, to use a word with negative connotations for the football purist, 'direct'. This doesn't mean a sudden smashing of balls forward to Macca – rather a readiness to use the big target-man's muscularity as a way to discomfit those sides that camp deep, and in numbers, in their bid to negate Eastleigh's customary wads of possession and slick movement.

One quarter of those talking heads – Todd's – was pounding. He had stumbled out of the earlier practice match after taking a ball flush on the top of his napper. This is the week when Tottenham goalkeeper Hugo Lloris remaining on the field, after sustaining concussion at Everton's Goodison Park, dominated the sports news agenda, until the Champions League turned up and provided some football to write about.

Toddy, like the Spurs Number 1, returned into the fray. When setting off for home later, however, he was looking forward to dosing up on paracetamol and having a good long lie down. His pasty exterior and slightly groggy demeanour had me crossing my fingers that his Renault Clio would return to Devon in one piece.

An Eastleigh player undergoing a more natural change in his outward disposition is Damian Batt. The rust that had been so evident during Damian's bedding in period is progressively being replaced by a smooth polish. His spiky weekend outing at Sutton is being backed up by a concentrated and confident training ground manner. On Thursday he even killed dead the pass that I made damn sure to rattle back to him after retrieving a stray ball — this is no environment for me to let slip that my personal familiarity with a football is dwindling by the day.

Sam Wilson showed no ill-effects from playing in Fleet Town's 6–0 spanking at the hands of Yate Town on Tuesday night — instead, looking sharper for the game time. Ramone Rose would profit from a similar opportunity, but Richard would be loath to have a valuable and versatile option unavailable to him at this testing period.

At least when he does feature again, I'll spell Ramone's name correctly. I have been taking my lead from the official website and team-sheets to call him 'Romone'. It is, he tells me, an oversight that has dogged him since his QPR days. Even I can't blame Harry Redknapp for that.

If Anybody Can

Writing now (Tuesday, November 12th), three full days after the latest possible of victories over Spencer Day's Farnborough, I have had the chance to reflect on where another scratchy performance leaves the side. The lurching fortunes of *Ramone* continued with him not being fit, due to a hamstring strain, to take a place in the match-day squad.

Fleetwood persisted with his dressing up the after effects of his Sutton mauling, but was not spared completely from a bit of weekend club work. Richard sent the Welshman to carry out post-game interview duties with Spitfire TV — perhaps to give our moneyed striker the chance to air his splendidly burgeoning beard to a wider audience. What was a restrained Andre Villas-Boas type effort has now morphed into the full Brian Blessed vintage.

While ruminating on the day's action with Jamie Graham, 'Fleets' alluded to the confidence the team can take from winning in the dramatic style that they had. Farnborough, with the game drifting to its close, actually looked the more likely of the two sides to nick a winner. That eventuality would have left the mini-legion of supporters, who had been at the ground since 10am to rid the pitch of its excess water wondering why they'd bothered. In fact, manager and owner/chairman had both been spied with a fork in their hands joining in the fight against the elements – which continued even as the skies re-opened in early afternoon.

The conditions resulted in half an hour's football during which both sets of players struggled to keep their feet, let alone string more than two passes together. Our controversial visitors did mould together some good stuff in the second half and it was only when going back through my soaked and barely legible notes that I concluded a draw, rather than a Boro win, would have been the fairer outcome.

C'est la vie. Richard, as the game wore on, had fiddled with the team in terms of personnel and tactics. He had to wait for his sustained pursuit of a breakthrough to be vindicated, but, in the nick of time, the moment came. Will Evans and Dan Spence, both 84th-minute substitutes, initiated a move, with the latter injecting some pace into its inception before passing out to 'Greener' who was now operating as a left-winger – having been pushed forward from his full-back role. Greener delivered a delicious cross, which McAllister, at the back post, touched in from a yard. As a famous American TV character was once renowned for exclaiming each Saturday tea time, 'I love it when a plan comes together.'

That plan, conceived to suit the action as it unfolded, had necessitated the hooking of habitual 90-minute men Collins, Strevens, and Todd. It is a healthy situation when every player, and all supporters watching on, know that no one individual is bigger than the greater team cause.

The overall display, in truth, was little better than that served up seven days previously – yet there has barely been a negative word uttered in response. Richard, therefore, has the answer to the question he posed after the draw at Sutton, 'What would the reaction have been if we'd played like that but won the match?'

It was a huge three points. If we'd taken only one, Bishop's Stortford would have been nestled in behind us – two points away and with two fixtures in hand. Bromley, on 31 points and enjoying an idle Saturday, would have relished Eastleigh failing to capitalise on their chance to move up to the 30-point mark.

The Bishops were destined to lose their FA Cup first round tie against Northampton Town in what was Sunday's live terrestrial television offering. More pertinently, though, that occasion was the last on which their prolific 20-year-old centre-forward Kyle Vassell will appear for the club. He has signed for Peterborough United. Bishops will be in economic clover at present owing to the dual boost they'll receive from ITV and Vassell's transfer fee. Nevertheless, if they are to remain a threat to the expanding concertina of sides at the top of the table some of that cash windfall will need to be invested very astutely indeed.

Another interminable deluge has finally relented, enabling the Spitfires' local midweek trip to Gosport Borough – another haven for former Silverlake men – to go ahead tonight as scheduled. Jamie Brown, quite possibly the most committed individual I have ever seen on a football pitch, will sadly be suspended. It is rare to wish a key member of the opposing team were playing, but 'Browner' is a one-off in every sense. The reason for his absence will shock precisely none of what is sure to be a hefty away support.

Time, then, to discover if the high of beating Farnborough in minute 94 spills over into what we witness from minute one in Gosport – and beyond.

24

ON THE ROAD AGAIN

Anybody longing to see an upsurge in cohesion and poise from Eastleigh's play didn't see their wishes wholly realised at Gosport. With Borough's players working like dervishes and making a fine job of clogging up their defensive third, we watched some pretty attritional stuff; football that would have more befitted one of the scruffy, well-worn pitches that backs onto the home side's stubbornly dated Privett Park ground.

A ground I should add that, as a young footballer, I graced on a few occasions. My last appearance on the craggy turf came in 1994 (a stellar cup final victory for Locks Heath under-16s over our Landport '72 opponents) and nothing has changed since.

When I arrived for Tuesday's (November 12th) game, an hour early, of course, I was half wondering when the floodlights might be switched on. They already were, of course. For those of us sitting in the main stand when the action got underway, viewing was made extra challenging by a light failure in that part of the stadium. That's my excuse for not identifying Brett Poate as the man off whom Yemi's shot took a conclusive deflection, sending the ball sailing lazily into the net with the last touch before half-time.

When, nine minutes into the second period, Southam applied an emphatic finish to a sweeping end-to-end move, one that began at Flitney's foot, continued via McAllister's head, and had an incisive Reason pass as its penultimate act, the game was won. The final 2–0 score-line, with a little more care, could have been far more convincing. Nevertheless, having scrapped away and established a lead, a hint of the Spitfires' early season swagger tentatively returned.

Two days after that satisfying night's work (Thursday, November 14th) and having been denied by Maidstone's manager, Jay Saunders, the privilege of a training session on his club's 3G pitch – he claimed that his academy team use the facilities on a Thursday; and anyway, 'I'm not being funny, but most teams train on 3G these days, so they know how it plays' – the local Southampton University complex was the venue for FA Trophy preparation.

Among much animated chatter throughout the session I barely caught any comment on the two victories earned during the past five days. McAllister did ask if, in my account of the Gosport game, I'd noted his late passing up of an open goal from six yards out (Macca shuns any social media sites, forums or match reports, dismissing the lot as 'a waste of time'). For the record, it was a miss that absolutely warranted mention.

Fleetwood was back to work, although still bearing an angry-looking scar on his ankle. Batt and Todd were excused with illness – a wise 'decision' on their respective parts. The bitter wind cutting through the exposed grounds made for a day that might have given Sir Ranulph Fiennes reason to think twice before stepping out of his front door. Indeed, despite my being contented by the locality of the session enabling me to attend, my viewing was somewhat distracted by having to regularly check that my nose was still attached to my face, and all ten fingers and toes remained in situ.

As we have discovered, the players are blessed with markedly tougher constitutions than my own. Their prime focus was on becoming acquainted with what was beneath their feet. Far from being the carpet that one might expect from a synthetic turf, the ball bobbled its way from boot to boot, with loose soil springing up on every contact with the surface.

It was a concentrated hour's work, mainly designed to provide the squad with a taste of moving and playing on unfamiliar terrain. When a match was set up, Guy Butters counselled his charges: 'Right, Fleets is joining in, so don't smash him', before, with impeccable timing, turning to Cookie and wearily instructing, 'Be ready in case anybody smashes him.'

The busy nature of the morning continued when the bulk of those on duty rounded off their labours with an additional shooting drill. Richard headed off with Greener for what appeared an intense one-to-one tutorial. The poor chap had felt the sharp end of his manager's tongue more than once during the preceding 60 minutes – Richard still believes his left-back can do more when in advanced areas of the pitch.

With the shooting in full flow, Yemi asked Cookie to devise him a sharp sprinting exercise, while Suvs and Jamie Collins stood in earnest conversation. The body language and various gestures of the two indicated that it was a chat centred on their job. That is unless they have mastered the football equivalent of the office worker who sits at their computer, with a look spread across their mug that suggests a mixture of contemplation and confusion, while actually choosing their summer holiday or keeping up to date with proceedings in the test match.

Back at the club, and after the most poorly received meal I've witnessed yet – pasta smash was the, admittedly accurate, description of our club's prandial judge (Fleetwood) – I was granted an interview with Dean Beckwith, to my mind the season's outstanding performer to date.

He didn't agree with my assessment of his form, going as far as to say that he's not been at all happy with it. Dean's personal standards are sky-high, but if there is as much room for improvement to his own contribution as he believes is the case, he is good enough to play for England 'C' – the non-league's national representative team. I asked if international recognition was something he'd ever considered. He was genuinely staggered by the question.

Dean shrugged off the criticism that habitually comes the way of team and manager when they encounter a bump in the road – Richard actually interrupted us briefly to demand that the player, who he has described as Eastleigh's 'best ever signing', say something nice about him because 'nobody likes me'.

He didn't need to. Dean had already cited the manager's ideas and recruitment, along with the personal intervention of Stewart – 'It's not often you get chairmen ringing players up, I've certainly never had it in my career, saying that they want you' – for his decision to become a Spitfire just days after seeing with his own eyes 'Bromley away'.

Dean accepted that fans pay their money and so are entitled to their opinion, even if the players don't agree with it. In the next breath he acknowledged how valuable an asset positive support is – to the extent that 'it's 100% better when you've got the fans behind you'.

The cynical pre-July 1st me considered that, in a vast majority of cases, footballers' sentiments with respect to those who pay to watch them fell into one of two categories. They are either idiots to be suffered or a peculiarly obsessive bunch with whom they could in no way empathise. The complete disproving of that personal long-held belief regarding the player/supporter relationship has been one of the revelations of my past four and a half months.

Dean was no different from any of his colleagues when specifying his singular aim for the season – win the league. As one of the men to have a penalty saved – along with Chris Zebroski – in last season's play-off shoot-out at Dover, he is more eager than most to avoid another journey down that route.

From start to finish of our talk Dean was nursing his Herbalife shake. His nutrients for the afternoon were not going to end up residing in a dustbin along with those of many of his team-mates (the unusual offering of shortbread and chocolate biscuits proved more popular than the 'hot dish'). My eyes had nearly popped out of my head when I saw Jamie Collins diluting some Herbalife product with milk. I wasn't the only one. A sceptical McAllister lamented, 'I remember when it was "I need some Foster's" [other fizzy Australian lagers are available], now it's "I need my milk".'

Undaunted, and with Beckwith arguing, 'Imagine how good he'd be if he lost eight pounds', our former Havant & Waterlooville midfielder pressed on with composing his modern-day nectar of choice.

And then, revealing the quietly kept bounteous side of his character ('That's because his missus doesn't let him talk at home,' McAllister had responded to Richard's training ground observation a fortnight ago; 'All you can hear, all the time, is JC'), Jamie left for the day carrying a copy of the paper, which contained his interview with me, having asked if I could find him a spare because his mum would like one.

When I next set eyes on Eastleigh's footballers they were over half an hour into the game at Maidstone. A joyless journey to Kent had brought about my worst footballing nightmare. Even with a relatively fresh perspective on life – my parents' holiday location in Vietnam was last week destined to be the next port of call for Typhoon Haiyan as it left the Philippines having wrought such devastation – it required some effort to keep a lid on my simmering inner temperature gauge while a large chunk of Saturday afternoon drifted by at Cobham Services.

With my dad abroad (the typhoon eventually affected their trip to no greater extent than a slight re-jig of plans and their water-proofs being put to frequent use), I was on the supporters' club bus, along with between 30–35 others, for the trip. The departure time of 11:15am had already got me worried.

What wasn't called for, then, was for our coach, while it was stopped for a 15-minute break, to be subject to a roadworthiness test by the Vehicle and Operator Services Agency (VOSA).

Inclusive of completing paperwork this whole rigmarole lasted 45 minutes. One individual, in particular, among the VOSA team was unquestionably relishing his opportunity to scupper the weekend plans of a coach load of people. So great was his misguided sense of self-importance that he thought it appropriate to respond to Brian Palmer's urgings – 'come on, get on with it, we're going to miss kick-off' – with an icy stare in the direction of the 70 year old, before telling Chris Blake, 'That old man wants to shut up.'

I hope said VOSA employee went home and stubbed his toe on a door frame. Very, very hard.

Brian is a man whose life revolves around Eastleigh. He hasn't missed a home date since being enticed to the club after spotting a poster advertising a game at the outset of season 2005/2006. His match-attending soon progressed to helping with jobs around the ground and some stewarding at reserve fixtures. Now, a man who had followed Southampton throughout his football-supporting life is a Monday to Friday, come hell or high water, presence around the Silverlake.

No task is beyond Brian's remit – other than decorating because 'the missus would go mad if I went home covered in paint when I won't get a brush out in the house'. His dedication to watching the team is such that, against all sensible advice, he clambered aboard the coach for the infamous play-off at Dover when he was evidently not a well man. As it transpired, he spent the majority of his afternoon at the Crabble Athletic Ground receiving medical attention. It was a genuine relief to see his chirpy face about the place when we returned in the close season.

Right, Cobham Services, 1:45pm. We can make this. Engine on. Aaarrrgghhhhhhh. As the VOSA van breezed off to throw a spanner in somebody else's harmless plans, the battery on our coach revealed itself to have fallen flat. It was at this point that my pent-up frustration turned to resignation. I could envisage no way in which we'd be watching any football. It is a peculiar trait of mine that I would almost rather see nothing of a match than dip in late, furiously trying to get a grip on what is happening.

Thanks to the assistance of the RAC we were on our way at 2:45pm. The local radio commentary had kept us travelling contingent apace with the game

– which was waiting for nobody. We knew upon arrival, therefore, that the scores were still locked at 0–0. Immediately on entering the ground – after one last delay when, incredibly, a home steward boarded the coach to deliver his match-day spiel – the sizeable crowd and Football League-scale atmosphere struck me.

I was forced initially to watch from pitch-side, a vantage point that emphasised the frantic pace of the game. At this grounded level everything appeared to be happening at breakneck speed. That impression made McAllister's opening goal, which he finished in some style after beginning a move that also featured three of his team-mates, all the more impressive.

With Toddy not recovered from illness, Chris Dillon was finally given another start – his first since mid-September. He was exceptional. When discussing the game via e-mail yesterday (Sunday, November 17th), Beckwith described 'Dills' as having been 'superb' and 'our MOM'. I couldn't disagree. When he was receiving his rave reviews early in the season I was still in some need of convincing that our bargain centre-half was the real deal. He played like it here, especially during a late onslaught on the Spitfires' goal.

By the time most of the 1,397 crowd were screaming blue murder as their side were denied a last-second penalty, for what they believed was an obvious Dillon handball, we were clinging on to a 2–1 lead. Jai had responded to an equaliser, scored soon after half-time, by slamming home a spot-kick five minutes later. It was a thrilling game, one that an impartial observer could have mistaken for a League One contest.

My personal 60-minute watching experience was firmly in keeping with the preceding motorway shenanigans. No steward was able to smooth my passage to the press area before the interval (with not a seat to be had there was no chance of me following my usual ritual and plonking myself in the main stand here), so I was rushed into a family block of seats.

The half-time break enabled me to head upstairs and furtively avail myself of an executive lounge. It is remarkable what you can manage if you press on with your activities as if they are a matter of everyday course. Employing that tactic I helped myself to a large tea and cowered from the cold for 15 minutes.

Back outside and gutsily braving plunging temperatures I snatched an empty seat – in which I survived for five minutes. My neighbour – late back after kick-off – busily informed me that this location was strictly not for reporters. His clipped words came in a gratingly brash and belittling tone.

With gritted teeth, it was off to stand at the end of the row. Obstructing nobody, and with a fine view, I re-settled and re-composed. For two minutes, until a club official told me that I was in an area they like to keep clear. My final resting spot for the afternoon was next to the local radio commentator (if the sharper ears among Kent's listening audience picked up any background muttering I admit my guilt but plead mitigating circumstances).

Despite the chaotic outcome to my every move, the game had enough quality to keep me totally absorbed. I did note that the 'area we like to keep clear' was populated for the remainder of the match by the very person who had decreed it untenable. I really have never wanted Eastleigh to win a match quite so much. That they did in a fashion that left the Stones faithful incandescent, and consequently giving the referee both barrels as he trudged off, added to the satisfaction of the moment.

I should say, however, that in the clubhouse post-match I was immersed in a long chat with a Maidstone fan who, along with his circle of companions, couldn't have been friendlier. Therefore, when he insisted that Jai should have been punished for inciting the crowd in the wake of his goal (by dancing directly in front of a loaded home end), I nodded along sagely – while inwardly reflecting fondly on the smile that had engulfed my face as the afternoon's match-winner revelled in his feat.

Speaking to Callum, whose re-invention since his self-flagellation post-Boreham Wood continues, I was surprised when he claimed not to have celebrated our winning goal, believing Yemi to have dived to earn the penalty. I wasn't sure about the award either, but that hadn't dented my subsequent exuberance one jot.

'Simulation' is a perennial problem in the game and something I abhor. Yet, presented with a scenario where that very act might have benefitted my team, I turned a blind eye. The overriding opinion among Spitfires was that we've had plenty go against us, so we'll take a bit of luck when it comes our way. Football, assuredly, breeds in a hefty number of its followers a sense of right and wrong that is far removed from their individual day-to-day beliefs – me included.

There has been a lot of discussion since Saturday about the merits of Maidstone's 3G surface. My prior fears about our players' ability to adapt to the turf proved completely unfounded. Many of the Eastleigh spectating horde suspect that it contributed significantly to the high-tempo, high-quality action.

It is curious that, as a result of their pitch, if Maidstone are to win the Ryman Premier League they will be denied entrance into the Conference structure. The 3G is a different animal altogether from the 'plastic pitches', formerly used by QPR, Luton Town, Oldham Athletic, and Preston North End, until the FA outlawed their use in 1988 (although the last three of those clubs retained them, respectively, for three, three, and six years beyond that date).

Those artificial surfaces of yore, with their spongy bounce, produced football that was entirely alien to that which one would typically expect to watch. My only real gripe this time, and it is one that was common in the 1980s, is that the 'grass' was aesthetically disconcerting. It just didn't look 'right'.

For all the financial arguments in favour of allowing lower and non-league clubs to install 3G turf, Mick Geddes offered one essential reason why it should never happen. The surface places heavier demands on players' muscles and joints, leading to a marked increase in incidences of short- and long-term injury. It is at that juncture where the debate is closed.

As ever, there is always something happening off the pitch at Eastleigh. One of Mick's former boardroom allies and all round raconteur, Mike Andrews, has left his position with the club, apparently unhappy with some of the changes taking place. As forecast, a seemingly incidental change can bring wider ramifications. I'm sure, though, that with his passion for local football, and Eastleigh especially, we'll be seeing plenty more of Mike.

Similar clarity of prediction would be very useful to assist in determining how the next TSSC coach trek will unfold. Eastleigh's 'reward' for dispatching Maidstone from the FA Trophy is a tie at Bury Town (a side that plays in the same division as Saturday's vanquished opponents). A hike to Suffolk wasn't what anybody had in mind as we anticipated Monday's draw. In terms of opposition, it could certainly have been worse. Regarding miles on the road, however, well, that's another story.

Yes, inferior foes, tentatively pulling up at the Silverlake, hoping merely to escape with their pride intact – that would have been perfect. A bit like Tonbridge Angels, visitors on Saturday (November 23rd), without a win on the road to their name and sitting uneasily beneath the grim reaper's perforated line at the bottom of the table.

The Angels narrowly avoided an FA Trophy calamity against lowly AFC Sudbury of Ryman League Division One North, conceding a late equaliser at home, before scraping through a replay by a single goal. Richard attended the latter of those games and had already told me during Thursday's training that he was distinctly unimpressed, before he articulated the same message to his players.

'They are not good. The pressure is on you now. We've been saying we can knock a team out. Saturday is the day to do it. Now it's down to you. I'm leaving it in your hands.'

And the task looked to have become even easier when Tonbridge's midfielder, David Ijaha, perhaps getting in the spirit of the broader sporting scene with Carl Froch and George Groves due to clash in a boxing ring later in the day, opened proceedings by giving Jamie Collins a cuff round the ear.

No rolling around clutching his 'wounds' by our Herbalife convert, just an incredulous look at the referee while pointing to his violated body area. He needn't have bothered. The red card was out with a flourish and we had 88 minutes to watch the hapless away team being put to the sword. Tom Parsons, a regular alongside us in the stand, and I even agreed that the sending off would ruin the game.

Anyway, it was simply a matter of when the first goal might arrive, especially with Gary Elphick – a centre-half I was soundly underwhelmed by when he had a brief spell at the Silverlake and who Richard had described during that Thursday training ground dispatch as being 'slower than Guyser [Butters]' – stationed at the heart of the Tonbridge defence.

22 minutes. Goal. Chris Todd's left-foot did the business. But not in the style we had hoped. Toddy's flailing boot directed the excellent Brighton & Hove Albion loanee Shamir Goodwin's shot out of Flitney's reach.

When Germany's football team was unconvincingly stumbling its way through the World Cup finals of 2002, their legendary ex-player and manager, Franz Beckenbauer, was moved to evaluate his countrymen's efforts thus: 'Kahn [Oliver, the side's goalkeeper] apart, you could take all of them, put them in a bag and hit them with a stick. Whoever got hit would deserve it.'

When it came to whom Richard would drag off at half-time, on a day when Eastleigh's footballers, with the exception of Spence and Fleetwood merited assessment similar to Beckenbauer's, every man was vulnerable. To be forced into making early changes was all the more galling for the manager after he had concluded Thursday's work by saying, 'Whatever team I pick, it's not personal. I'm just picking a team to win a game.'

Green had been taken out of the starting 11 – to much consternation among a rather meagre 536 crowd that had seen him receive his October Player of the Month award before kick-off. August's player prize winner, Dillon, had deservedly kept his place, but, playing at left-back, looked a shadow of the authoritative defender who thwarted Maidstone seven days ago.

Dills joined Southam in being hauled off. Suvs had been incessantly rubbing his bothersome hamstring throughout Thursday's session, but characteristically waited until the very last activity was complete before seeking out Cookie for help. The captain spent Saturday's second half shouting encouragement from the stand, his whole body tensing and contorting in a mix of highly strung tension, frustration, and ire, as the seconds ticked away.

With 35 minutes to play, Collins scored an equaliser – a goal that owed a huge amount to Fleetwood's enterprise. The earlier certainty over the game's eventual outcome returned. With Oxford City fresh in the mind and, to an extent, Sutton United, we should know by now that nothing can be taken for granted.

Eastleigh dominated without ever convincing. Elphick excelled and a scruffy 88th-minute set-piece served up the coup de grace. It completed a 2–1 reverse that had been impossible to foresee. Tonbridge, and Elphick especially, were delirious. Fair enough.

My emotions across the entire day had oscillated back and forth; rage to relief, delight to despair. The advent of a Merseyside derby casts a foggy complexion over my every move. This, it seems, will never change. Without access to the subscription channel that was, that lunchtime, screening its latest staging and, of course, being due at Eastleigh, I would be unable to watch, gripped by terror as events played out. Instead, I initially resorted to cowardice and did my best to pretend Liverpool's trip to Goodison was not happening.

By the time I was sat in the Silverlake car park, writhing in my driver's seat, convulsing as I listened to commentary of the match (having given in to temptation and tuned in while driving to the ground), I was a wreck. The score was 3–3 when, during the four minutes added time, I caught sight of myself in the rear-view mirror. My whey-faced complexion and distorted features must have conveyed an outward impression of extreme suffering – not somebody with their radio switched on to a football game.

I was still shaking at 3pm. My trembling at 4pm was due to a whole new internal rage. Not at the Spitfires' half-time deficit – 'We'll overcome that.' I had been agitated when queuing for the full 15-minute break to buy a cup of tea at the last home game against Farnborough. When I offered up my £1 on this occasion I was told that the water was yet to boil and hot drinks would therefore be 'a couple of minutes'.

Now, remember how highly I value the non-league accessories, the little things that are unattainable at a Premier League ground. Chief among these is the ready access to a half-time cup of tea. Laying my hands on this is becoming a more arduous assignment by the week.

As I waited patiently, I heard every request for tea, coffee, or hot chocolate being met with the standard, 'That will be a couple of minutes.' It was becoming clear that the only thing anywhere near boiling point was me. When the teams returned I strolled, empty-handed, purposefully back to my seat, mumbling darkly all the way.

5pm, and it was the football that was dictating my frame of mind. For 24 hours I couldn't shrug off the same stifling dejection that followed the Oxford City FA Cup tie – even if the wireless coverage of Froch's victory over Groves in the hyped-up boxing was a welcome diversion. It had been the televised press-conference ahead of that fight that led to Thursday's clubhouse meal – which received only rapturous reviews having been cooked on site, unlike last week's 'pasta smash', which had been parachuted in from Oxford – being eaten to a backdrop of whispers and a TV turned up to its max.

I dipped out from the 'dining area' that day to conduct an illuminating interview with Dan Spence – incidentally, one of seven players out of 20 on show who opted to keep the freezing training ground winds at bay by donning a pair of tights. Dan, with his erudite manner, is the antithesis of the stereotypical monotone footballer; the one-dimensional, coarse individuals so widely portrayed, but notably absent within this group – although bump into any of them when they head into London on December 7th for the dreaded Christmas party and who knows, you might be in a position to counter my claim.

Dan spoke about the value of his time as a member of Glenn Hoddle's Academy, in particular the influence that specific initiative, if it had been provided with sufficient support to continue, could have exerted towards solving the conundrum of how to produce technically proficient English footballers.

Dan's own accomplished game is evidence of his grounding and reason for optimism in his pursuit of a return to the Football League where he has already played for Reading. As a contemporary of Watford and Scotland's Ikechi Anya at the Hoddle Academy, and good friend of Reading's goalkeeper Alex McCarthy, he's not short of motivation.

Nor, when fit, is he short of form. With his recovery from a torn hamstring looking complete, Dan is proving himself one of the Spitfires' superior players. He looked every inch that during the training session on Thursday November 28th, seven days on from our talk, and five days after the Tonbridge debacle. The workout consisted primarily of a full scale 11v11 match. Richard was pondering the implementation of a new shape into the side and here was an extended chance to work on his ideas – in short form; two holding midfielders providing a platform for four attackers, and two raiding full-backs, to make merry in the opposing half.

The intensity of the practice game was comparable to that in a league fixture. The players are keenly aware that Saturday wasn't acceptable. That was the theme of Richard's closing speech for the week, which was markedly different in tone and directive to his words that preceded the Tonbridge clash.

'We were rubbish on Saturday. A lot of players were doing what they wanted, not what they had been asked to. I've had to look at myself. I've taken my foot off the gas for the last two or three weeks. I've been lazy in training, just letting you have a game and standing there with my hands in my pockets waiting for the session to finish.

'You're all such good players that the temptation is to believe I can leave you to it. I obviously can't. You've been great for me this season, apart from on Saturday – and you were great for 20 minutes then. I've looked at myself. Now you've all got to do the same.'

The floor was opened for opinions, but it was commonly accepted there wasn't much to say other than to agree that a swift improvement is imperative. Richard moved on to remind his players that, when things aren't working, there is no obligation to force the issue.

'Be hard to beat. If you're giving possession away, don't try to make amends by hitting a 50-yard ball – play yourself back into it with a couple of 5–10-yard passes. Take two or three touches instead of just one.'

It is a theory long espoused by the aforementioned Hoddle. Richard refers to his players needing to concentrate on the simplest aspects of their respective games. Only once a team or individual is functioning at the most rudimentary level, are they able to inject an express shift-up through the gears.

The manager's final message to his men came by way of a revelation that pricked every pair of listening ears. Richard disclosed that he had already discussed a prospective promotion budget with 'him upstairs'. I wondered at that juncture whether our boss was hoping to enlist the help of the Almighty in setting affairs back on track.

He had, in fact, been informed by Stewart that, in the event of his club attaining Conference Premier standing, the purse strings would be loosened accordingly. Richard's response, to the players' visible delight when he relayed this news, was to inform the chairman that, should his team accomplish their year's objective, he wanted to retain every single member of his playing staff. Moreover, there would be 'an extra few quid for everybody'.

As a declaration of faith, particularly coming so soon after the season's low point, it is a gesture that couldn't be matched. There was some mirth aimed in Jamie Collins' direction, him being the sole individual in custody of a two-year deal.

Richard had told me at the session's outset that he'd done 'a lot of thinking' during the week. If any of that ruminating was in preparation for his pep-talk – which all at once acted to boost morale, reinforce belief, and massage egos – it was time well spent. It is highly likely that, when the team emerges at Bury Town, there will be casualties of last week's defeat. That, however, is a short-term measure. This is a battle that has to be fought as a group.

When I spoke to Suvs he confirmed that he had undergone all manner of horrors when forced to watch on for the second period on Saturday. He is characteristically upbeat, though. 'We won't lose many games like that. We'll get results at Bromley and Dover.'

Furthermore, he believes Sutton will be on the end of more results of the type they suffered on Saturday: a 1–0 home loss against Dorchester Town – a side that are only just in touch with those above them at the bottom of the table.

On Friday (November 29th), a story surfaced on Sky Sports' website that speculated that Jai Reason is a target for a number of League One and League Two clubs. With its mention of Jai being a free agent next summer, the article reeked of an agent's input. Richard was certainly not enamoured with what he had read. I was staggered when, during Eastleigh's darker period 12 months ago, Jai's flair, guile, and imagination didn't have suitors beating down the Silverlake door. We are yet to see him reach those heights this time around, but he remains a fantastic talent and an essential component of the team.

Additionally, Richard feels that he can coax more from his playmaker. On Thursday, the manager was vocally encouraging his man to run with the ball, to commit defenders and not be afraid to get shots away on goal. If Jai's regal vision and passing are enhanced by a more direct menace, he will be well on his way to fulfilling his authentic promise.

Wembley Via Bury Via…?

The trip to Bury on Saturday, November 30th, took Jai close to his original football home of Ipswich Town. For plenty of a Spitfires persuasion, it represented a right old hike. With the town's remarkably large and popular Christmas Market – who knew? – thrown into the day's mix, a number of the players enjoyed a Friday night's accommodation at Stansted's Hilton Hotel. Richard's side turning up in dribs and drabs throughout match afternoon was not a scenario he was prepared to countenance.

Todd enjoyed double hospitality benefits, having spent Thursday luxuriating in his De Vere home from home – hence, after Thursday's training session, me informing him that 'you'd better win'. That he did, being part of a back-four that kept a clean sheet into the bargain. It was the consummate 'professional' team performance.

Bury had their moments, but at a primitive ground, which nevertheless possessed an inexplicable allure, Eastleigh got back to doing what they are expected to do. Collins and Dillon both dropped out of the starting 11. They were joined on the bench by McAllister, whose reward for staying with his team-mates while his fiancée was giving birth at 2am on the morning of the game was a place among the substitutes. Beckwith sustaining a slight niggle paved the way for Macca to play the second 45 minutes and, typically, he scored promptly after his arrival. Cue trademark Bebeto baby-cradling celebration.

The boss's re-shaping of his side in Suffolk extended to positional and tactical alterations. One of these saw Ben Strevens move into the lone striker's role. Many fans are yet to be convinced that 'Strevs' has the requisite attributes to be effective in the midfield berth he has occupied for much of the season. Mick Geddes, after the game, divulged that the Strevens issue – which has been rumbling away for a while – had been a topic for discussion in the car carrying himself, Ray Murphy, and John Russell to the east.

I'm of the opinion that Strevens is excellent in the middle, particularly in a tightly fought contest. What's more, I rate the standard of Ben's displays, thus far, below only the exemplary Beckwith's – and that is a close call.

There was no arguing, though, with Strevs' two-goal impact up-top that set us on our way to round two of the Trophy. Richard was contented after the plans formulated on the Wellington Sports Ground two days earlier translated into a satisfying 3–0 win and equally buoyed by Strevens handing him another selection problem.

When Ray Murphy's vehicle returned south, Dillon and Green were added to its passenger list. Greener's car – BMW with personalised plate – packed up on the M25 on Friday, so leaving four hacked-off footballers stood at the side of a motorway awaiting rescue. Fair to say that Richard's caution regarding travel arrangements was well founded.

While McAllister found another spare seat in the Eastleigh convoy home, Jack Dovey was condemned to settling himself into the back of our Civic. It was interesting to hear the Spitfires' reserve 'keeper talk about his own career. Far from being disillusioned by a recent personal dearth of competitive football – something that must sting all the more for his eight years spent at Southampton and ongoing friendships with the likes of Saints' James Ward-Prowse – Jack is commendably philosophical with respect to his situation.

He values his thrice-weekly work with Ross Flitney and is bullishly confident that at a mere 21 years of age his time will come. Moreover, Jack is aware that the nature of his unforgiving job in the team lends itself better to later professional development than is true of any other role on the pitch. If total application to the task is a guarantee of success then, judging by what I've witnessed on every occasion I've seen him at work, Jack will be alright.

He'll be helped towards his goals by the level head on his shoulders. Only recently moved into a flat of his own, Jack's most pressing concern is living within his constrained budget, while ensuring he maintains his strictly healthy diet. No longer tending to the greens of a golf course to supplement his income, Jack is spending his spare hours employed by a gym; opting out of the sort of 'social' lifestyle that would damage body, bank balance and professional aspirations in one fell swoop. Chapeau.

Progress in the Trophy provided another of those fabulous Monday mornings, spent counting the seconds until a cup draw. Gateshead away was the fear. In fact, the Conference Premier 'Heed' were pulled out of the hat directly after the Spitfires and will undergo an odyssey to the Silverlake on December 14th. A midweek replay is not the desired outcome from this game.

By Tuesday, December 3rd, my thoughts had turned to whether or not Richard will still be in charge when that cup tie is played. John Gregory, our manager's great friend, has been appointed to the top job at Crawley Town. My concern was that Gregory would ask the boss to join him. That worry was evidently shared by Stewart. I turned up for the latter stages of Thursday's (December 5th) training knowing that Richard would be elsewhere and suspecting that he might be engaged in resolving any uncertainty over his future – as it happened he was driving to Gateshead to watch their FA Cup tie against Oxford United. When Richard confirmed, via text, on Friday that he would be accepting his current club's offer of an 18-month contract I was delighted and more than a little relieved.

The atmosphere among the group in their boss's absence was bordering on demob happy. That had nothing to do with having 'only' Guy Butters watching over them. Naturally, a win lifts everybody, but the real cause for excitement was the impending Christmas party.

The predominantly 'to-the-letter' execution of what had been asked at Bury persuaded Richard to shelve any thoughts of playing a friendly this forthcoming weekend – instead choosing to hold three concentrated training sessions next week ahead of the Heed's visit. The consequent free Saturday means that the players' festivities will commence on that day at 10am in London and take them who knows where, in mind or body.

Before they were eventually excused of responsibility for three days, Guy put the animated bunch through a gruelling running exercise – one that they convinced Richard's assistant to cut short, by virtue of their unified effort put into the sprints and the equally wholehearted badgering of their coach to take it easy on them.

As the players staggered away to warm down their jelly-legs, Suvs confided in me his worry that an incident that looked to have left him badly winded at Bury might actually have cracked one of his ribs. As he spoke I noticed that our skipper was white as a sheet. Indestructible and stubborn, he resolved to be 'ready for next week'.

On this same day *The Sun* newspaper linked Jai with a move to Leyton Orient. Our playmaker protested his ignorance at the story's origins. While his colleagues were showering ahead of lunch, Jai was sat in a Silverlake dugout, still in training kit and deep in conversation on his mobile phone.

Wednesday of this busy week had brought news, after a mighty wait, that planning approval has been granted for the terracing that Stewart wants erected behind each goal. Council wheels have turned at a leisurely rate, but the outcome befits everything that today's Eastleigh FC craves – progress.

The next gauge of that phenomenon can be taken after the team goes for a Conference Premier scalp for the first time in its history. And, in the meantime, I'm sure the players will have a drink, or two, to that particular ambition.

25

A TWIN ROUTE TO GLORY?

It is the misfortune of Eastleigh's footballers that the mind of Andy Cook is stuffed full of a diverse range of exhausting trials by running.

So it was that, less than 48 hours after they were buried deep in a refreshing Christmas celebration, Monday's trainers were subjected to a drill that would have tested the freshest of bodies and minds. They did get the benefit of a wry impromptu post-session round of applause from Fleetwood to mark their attendance, although Richard's subsequent comparison of his player to Arthur Scargill whistled over a few heads.

In truth, I arrived to see a bunch of relatively bright-eyed individuals, totally immersed in preparations for Saturday's impending FA Trophy tie. Richard's 525-mile round trip drive from his home in Oxfordshire on Thursday to take in Gateshead's FA Cup replay against Oxford United had left him impressed.

'The Heed' lost to their League Two opponents only by virtue of a goal deep into extra-time, and the manager felt they were hard done to, having produced an accomplished performance filled with slick, passing football.

The boss's newly garnered information was being drummed into his men early – the right-back thrives on pushing up the pitch, John Oster (a face I remember well from his unremarkable time at Everton) consistently demands the ball to his feet in midfield; they play out from the back, passing and passing, 'but often without hurting you'; the attackers recurrently seek to cut through opposing defences via spritely one-twos – and more.

As well as the focused attention to detail in this work, there was one overriding message from the manager: 'I think we will win, but we need to press together, do everything together.'

The job of beating a high-flying Conference Premier side is not going to be aided by the absence of Ross Flitney. The prime reason for my being at a

Monday get-together was to interview the 'keeper, only to learn that he was at home nursing a severe eye infection. Beckwith, who assured me Saturday's high-jinx passed off in good spirits with controversy avoided, is still struggling with his thigh. A goalkeeper and outstanding central-defender down isn't the way you'd choose to start a week like this one.

When it came to undergoing the latest Cook-inspired ordeal, designed to make up for a few horizontal days, the amount of effort that was spent on bartering for a reduction in exercise repetitions was staggering – and pretty entertaining.

Richard put himself right at the centre of the running zone, urging, demanding and providing stern intervention – 'Two of you, you're cheating, get round my f****** cones.' Whoever the culprits were, they were part of Reason's group, leading to his pleading with his cohorts as they next gathered on the start line: 'Whatever you do, make sure you go round his f****** cones this time.'

Somehow, Cookie was harangued/coerced into reducing the pre-ordered laps of his circuit from six to four. 'Ah, I'd have made the f****** keep going. Bo**o***,' was the boss's verdict on that decision.

Perhaps one reason for the fitness demon's softening stance was the impending friendly at Crawley Town, newly fitted into the week's schedule and due to be played at 11:30am on Tuesday (December 10th). Richard's network of contacts might make him vulnerable to being poached away, but they are invaluable with respect to his ability to, at late notice, line up a test like this – not to mention when it comes to expanding the scope of his own feasible transfer market.

Unable to make the journey to Sussex for a contest played behind closed doors, I had to rely on the manager's synopsis of events. All sounded positive. Having become familiar with Richard's character, I know that he wouldn't bother wasting any words on painting a misleading picture. He relayed news of a fine workout against a League One side that, for an hour, operated at full-strength.

Crawley won the game 2–1, with Will Evans scoring Eastleigh's one to give his comeback a handy push. McAllister had picked up a slight knock in training so missed out, but all others, Beckwith and Flitney aside, got essential game time.

The manager did reveal that during the course of driving from Crawley to

Lincoln, where he would have another look at Gateshead – that's 1,400 miles in five days – he telephoned one of his players to issue a flinty word in his ear. The player's mind, his boss says, is elsewhere.

Richard's opting for Lincoln as his Tuesday night football viewing place of choice, rather than Dover where our opponents next Tuesday (December 17th) were hosting Bromley, substantiates his principle that the next game is always the most important.

It was apparent when the side talked as a group on Thursday that the prospect of playing Gateshead was getting the juices flowing. There is no doubt that ego is a significant determinant in this. As Todd said, 'We all believe we should be playing at a higher level, let's go and prove it.'

A huge factor in the task of winning the Conference South is the necessity to grind out victories against opponents playing with that same steely determination to show themselves capable of matching reputedly superior foes. That number one aim, to finish at the top of the pile, is being made ever harder by Bromley continuing to grind out victories, while the Spitfires go without league football. The target this weekend, though, is to lower the colours of a more illustrious opponent – a role reversal for Eastleigh's footballers.

Richard's theme in what is becoming a weekly briefing – conducted on the training field when Thursday's work is complete – began on a continuation of Toddy's line. 'Now is the time to prove how good you are.'

The manager told his players that, for all their teasing spells of good football, he doesn't consider them to have played well across 90 minutes this term. He met no dissenters from that opinion – only vows that this Saturday is the time for that consistency to be attained. Batt did take his life in his hands when asked for his input: 'You talk f****** bo******, that's what I reckon.' The huge accompanying grin and polished form in which even those words were spoken made sure the light-hearted nature of his reply wasn't lost.

The remainder of Damian's thoughts were akin to those of his colleagues and reflected a man who is growing into this group. In his first couple of months at the club, 'Batty' (obviously) always appeared to flit around the training ground periphery – be that in terms of not becoming appreciably incorporated within the crowd, nor absorbed to the extent of his colleagues by the Spitfires' principles and ambitions.

Today, the right-back cuts a bubbly and assured figure. That could have much to do with his feeling more comfortable now that his fitness is up to speed and he is consequently confident of contributing on the pitch. That he has every chance of starting against Gateshead is confirmation of Damian's Eastleigh evolution.

One man desperate to be in that first-choice 11 is Jamie Collins – dropped for the game at Bury. I spoke to the midfielder after training and, a man who typically embodies the epithets I applied to the present-day Batt – bubbly and assured – was strangely subdued. Jamie, with his team-mates already disappeared for their showers, had spent another 15 minutes on the field with Richard. I subsequently asked if he had received any hint towards his likely involvement on Saturday, but the boss, as always, won't be naming his line-up until kick-off is approaching. A nervous 48 hours ahead for 'JC'.

Ramone Rose will just be happy with a place on the bench, having not even had that of late. What's more, Ramone hasn't endeared himself to his manager by accepting a job that requires him to work on Mondays and Tuesdays. Richard's demands are not for changing. Ramone was present for Thursday's session, but his continued relationship with Eastleigh will, I suspect, be dependent upon his changing of his alternative employment hours at a comparable speed to that with which he accepted them.

The Biggest Test – So Far

When I had spoken to Richard on Wednesday, a day before that final pre-Gateshead training session, the subject vexing him above all others was some fans' (again, the few not the many) disenchantment with Bromley continuing to expand their lead at the head of the table. The gripe would have more solid foundations if our side had played for points at any time across the past three weeks. As the manager intimated, the task of trying to control his own team's fortunes is difficult enough. Exerting influence on any other contest is beyond his job's remit. The boss's concern is that due to events happening away from his own club, an air of negativity could descend over the Silverlake.

An effective way of nipping that particular scenario in the bud would be to beat opponents coming to Hampshire in a rich vein of form and, resultantly, lying just two points outside the Conference Premier's play-off spots –

moreover, opponents whose high quality Richard openly told his players had 'surprised' him. The ideal eventuality would be to win while dominating and delivering that '90-minute performance'.

And that is exactly what happened. A miserly 330 people, including a smattering of valiant troopers from the northeast, witnessed the most complete Eastleigh display to which I, and many others, have ever borne witness. Simultaneously, this was the first occasion on which the Spitfires have toppled an adversary from the division above.

Collins started, was magnificent, and scored a truly wonderful goal. The exceptional Fleetwood added number two in the thumping fashion his manager craves from his players' finishing (Reason's weakly chipped goal attempt during Thursday's training drew an exasperated 'no, No, NO, NOOO CHIPS').

Will Evans imperiously filled Beckwith's mighty absence at centre-half and Batt turned in his finest Eastleigh showing yet – a display that included the execution of a string of booming tackles. Green found himself out of the first 11 once more; Dan Spence shifted across to the left and was outstanding.

Another highlight of a 2–0 victory was Jack Dovey's clean-sheet. After a belated season debut, and having adopted responsibility for replicating the aura of command that Flitney exudes between the Spitfires' posts every week, that's an achievement to celebrate.

And, on Monday (December 16th) the good news continued to flow. Richard has formally committed to his 18-month deal – with an option incorporated into the contract for another year on top of that should Eastleigh have achieved promotion during the initial period. The club couldn't have wished for a better time to announce this development. It will be my duty, on Thursday, to interview the freshly signed-up boss and produce, I would hope, a markedly upbeat piece to back up Saturday's inspiring show.

It will be the intention of Dover Athletic to scupper the 'feel-good factor'. I write an hour before we leave for Kent (Dad and myself that is; mini-bus again cancelled on account of poor uptake – the debate about what away travel should comprise rumbles on).

It will be the first in a mini-series of fixtures against the Whites, for yesterday, while Arsenal were drawing Bayern Munich out of the Champions League hat, the Spitfires were being handed the role of hosts to last season's play-off nemesis for a last 16 FA Trophy tie.

The Trilogy: Part One

'I'm sure if we'd have gone and played in Calais the other night, people would have gone. It takes a lot of commitment to follow a football team at any level. To go to some of the places that we have to away from home takes even more commitment.

'To travel to Dover on a Tuesday night in the numbers they did, in horrible conditions and eight days before Christmas, I think that's quite a feat.'

The words of Richard Hill, speaking to me during the interview to mark confirmation of his and Eastleigh's continuing relationship, two days after our trip to Kent. The numbers who endured that journey on a filthy night were rewarded in the finest possible style.

After the Spitfires had responded with some haste, by way of a terrific 20-yard Ben Strevens strike, to the home team taking a 76th-minute lead, Stuart Fleetwood took it upon himself to deliver my favourite goal – to date – of this ten-month journey. It had every ingredient you could hope for. Exemplary skill, which had defenders splayed in his wake, a beautifully executed give and go with McAllister, and the most sumptuous of finishes that, quite simply, was never in question. All in minute two of three added.

And with that the match-winner was gone, leaving memories of a Maradona-style slaloming dribble that began when he killed Mitch Walker's errant kick from goal on the half-way line – a feat accomplished with colleagues urging him to let the ball drift out for a throw.

Introduced in Fleetwood's place to supplement Eastleigh's rear-guard for 90 seconds of backs-to-the-wall action was Dean Beckwith. A spur of the moment decision on the boss's behalf? No. Here was my latest lesson in the degree of thinking, anticipation, and adaptation that feed into every single action of a football manager – certainly in the case of the Spitfires' version.

From the second that Strevens' equaliser hit the back of the net, Richard was pondering on how best to ensure his side came out of a testing away fixture with at least a point, while correspondingly not undermining their chances of taking all three. To throw Beckwith into the fray, one of the three attackers had to be withdrawn.

McAllister? There would be no benefit to that switch with regards to seeing off Dover's aerial threat, as one towering presence at defensive set-pieces (our opponent's main route of attack on the night) would be sacrificed for another.

The removal of Jai Reason would have freed Chris Kinnear from his man-marking duties on our creative force to wield a positive influence on proceedings.

Fleetwood then? The downside to that move would be the departure from the action of a man who can produce a goal from nowhere. Lo and behold that is precisely what he did, before freeing the way for Beckwith to slot in at the back. Counted among Dean's four touches of the ball (a figure totted up by Richard) was a huge header to clear his lines.

The substitute's contribution spoke volumes for the 'strong bond' at the club to which his manager alluded in our interview. An experienced first-rate professional, the Silverlake's premier Herbalife vendor dutifully accepted a place on the bench. When asked to de-layer on a windswept, cold and wet night for one and a half minutes of football, and what was personally a 'no-win' situation – see out the victory and his appearance is a mere footnote, ship a late equaliser and his introduction would be the subject of keen scrutiny – Beckwith was instantly on his game.

Even with previous evidence to the contrary I expected the following Thursday, after possibly the most fulfilling week of this campaign so far, to find Richard in spirits congruous with the impending festive season. I was met upon strolling over to an already active training ground with the question, 'How crap was that referee?'

It wasn't only the manager still harbouring a sense of bitterness about the officiating at Dover. Southam had been booked for a thundering tackle that won the home team the free-kick from which they opened the scoring. The man himself, his team-mates, and his 'gaffer' were as one in considering the captain extremely harshly done to. 'Suvs' now incurs a one-match ban over the holiday period.

I had been struck during the match by Glen's sustained urgings, beseeching his colleagues to keep pushing for more. An example, with 81 punishing minutes on the clock, clearly audible and accompanied by manic hand-clapping, 'Spence, come on, we've got loads more in us yet, come on. We can win this.'

Indeed, the sense of injustice at the manner in which the team fell behind was attributed, by Richard and every player to whom I spoke on the subject, as the reason why ensuing defeat was never an option.

'Suvs' told me on Thursday that, even after going one down, he could never envisage his team losing. 'I knew we'd win, we were just so much fitter than them.' That inherent belief is all the more admirable given the pressure under which this Spitfires' unit operates – and their recent Silverlake dip against Tonbridge.

This is not a group prone to brooding after a bad day. Nor will it lose focus in the wake of any elation-filled days and nights. From Southam's matter-of-fact attitude regarding the triumph at Dover, through Fleetwood responding to my telling him his goal 'wasn't bad' by saying 'it was about time', to Will Evans chuckling and saying 'it was alright' at my comparing with Marcel Desailly his domineering showing against Gateshead, there is no prospect of anybody here getting carried away.

There is the next battle to be won. For this lot, that came in the form of their customary Thursday (December 19th) practice match. Richard didn't hide the fact that, despite some protestations to the contrary, his players were shattered as the 93 minutes played on a heavy rain-sodden pitch in Kent were coming to a conclusion.

Nevertheless, if anybody was suffering lingering feelings of weariness it wasn't evident during an eight-a-side, played roughly 38 hours after Fleetwood's wizardry at the Crabble Athletic Ground. The game was littered with its usual roared profanities greeting any wasted scoring opportunity or misplaced pass. Reason's chipped goal, executed to perfection in order to beat Jack Dovey who was no more than two yards from his line and which made a delicately sweet sound as it went in off the underside of the bar, was a piece of skill to rival anything I've seen on these fields. No managerial admonishment for that one.

Green snapped back at Suvs who, following his manager's line, had been 'encouraging' the left-back to be more positive in his work – 'Don't get f****** bullied out there, Greener.' Later, spotting his skipper up-field while his comrades in this skirmish defended a concerted attack, Green seized his moment, 'You're alright, Suvs, you just stay up there and we'll deal with it.'

The 16 competing included three goalkeepers. Beckwith's injury continues to restrict him – he cuts a forlorn figure trudging off for his latest lap of the giant Wellington Sports Ground, usually with a new face for company – his previous accomplice back integrated among the throng. Collins, having been unable to play at Dover due to an ankle twist sustained against Gateshead, was receiving acupuncture at the hands of the versatile Cookie. Youngsters Jamie Bulpitt and Ryan Fuller are fit for no more than one-to-one work with the fitness overlord.

For those two fledglings, their bodies might be reacting to overdue regular football. Bulpitt is playing on a temporary basis at Bashley – just one division down from his parent club – while Fuller has a similar arrangement with Wessex League outfit, Folland Sports.

Sam Wilson, however, is back from Fleet Spurs. The teenager's loan was extended into a second month, after the first harvested a couple of goals. The downside(s) of Sam's stay at the Spurs was his suffering a leg injury. That would have been frustrating enough without the red card that incurred a two-match suspension, so rendering him doubly unavailable for what would have been further valuable competitive football.

Things were looking rosier for Sam, back now as a full member of the first-team group and able to train. Until – no more than two minutes after Guy Butters had turned to me and bemoaned the striker's laziness due to his preference for taking a fresh ball from the side-line to re-start play rather than retrieve one that had rolled a couple of yards away – Sam turned in possession and went over awkwardly on his ankle. When he eventually clambered to his feet, it was to return indoors. During the day's feeding it didn't go unnoticed among Sam's peers that their green co-worker had, with the masterful timing of a wily old pro, been stricken with the busy Christmas period just days away.

Ah, food. A team of Paula (soon to be anointed as the new clubhouse manager), Karen Wynne, and Sharon Cavill is combining to apply the magic touch longed for in the kitchen. 'Bangers and mash, get in,' Chris Todd enthused at ample volume for the entire dining room to be privy to the defender's excitement at Thursday's menu.

Without hesitation McAllister countered, 'What are you going to eat on Christmas Day now, Toddy? You can't have bangers and mash twice.'

Prior to the meal-time mirth (a period that exposed Spence and Southam as the latest Herbalife disciples; not many to go now), I asked Ross Flitney about the eye infection that he had suffered – an affliction that had given Dovey his prized break. While Ross's understudy has demonstrated admirable mental fortitude to come in from the cold and play his part in a notable week, the main man was having a dreadful time.

When feeling unwell during the players' Christmas bash, Ross attributed his nausea to the seasonal consumption of daytime beer. By the afternoon he was feeling sufficiently off colour to call his good lady and ask her to collect him from his hotel. Still ailing the following day, Ross's eye became uncomfortable and his vision blurred. After a less than helpful hospital visit, it was to Moorfields Eye Hospital on Monday morning – the agony having become so stark that a man who is 'ok with pain' was in tears.

An infection, so rare that it strikes approximately 100 people in the UK each year, was diagnosed. The specific bug that Ross had attacks the cornea and, without treatment, will lead to blindness. Its origins in his instance are baffling – the best guess being that something untoward had breached his eye while he was earning an extra dime working as a plasterer. Not an activity readily associated with goalkeeping and certainly not a pursuit you could imagine Ross's early career mentor – during two years between 2003 and 2005 at Fulham – Edwin van de Sar, indulging in.

The condition requires continuing treatment and Ross will be attending the hospital for monthly checks. He is, though, back in the ranks – although as yet unable to shower or wet his face after a workout. Baby wipes are a new ally. Goggles are an option if the 'keeper can't resist a proper wash, but – wisely – 'I'm not wearing those here in front of that lot.'

My official interview with our first-choice stopper has been delayed until the New Year – something that has made more of a dent on my agenda than his I imagine. For now, Richard gave me bountiful copy. He had been similarly forthright at the outset of his preparation for Saturday's meeting with Chelmsford. 'Ok. Let's tempt fate. They are f★★★★★★ rubbish. What they are good at is having a go at you. They'll work their b★ll★★★ off.'

The ensuing drills, all with the next opponents in mind, were rendered futile by a deluge of rain that blew in on Friday night and still hadn't let up when the match was called off at 2:30pm on Saturday. That despite a healthy share of the Spitfires' fan-base showing its true colours by working ceaselessly from early morning, in an ultimately fruitless attempt to clear the pitch of its standing water.

I have utmost admiration for their efforts, dedication, and endurance. I was wet through after five minutes at the Silverlake, spent cowering under my waterproofs and waiting for confirmation that we'd be adding further to a fixture jam that is already stacking up.

Gosport Borough's home clash with Eastbourne was called off long before midday. It was only the determination and togetherness, which, regardless of any underlying or sporadic tiffs, undoubtedly exists within Eastleigh's support, that delayed the inevitable in our own case.

The postponement put on ice the direct face-off between Southam and Mark Hughes, Suvs' midfield partner of 2012/2013. The prospect of their coming together is salivating. Glen's opinion of what was then a looming duel? 'F★★★ Hughesy. He ain't my mate on Saturday.'

A Merry Christmas

My own festivities took place in Walton-on-Thames, which, prior to our stay (family time, so both parents accompanied me for a three-night break at my sister's place), had resigned us to the fact that Dorchester away on Boxing Day might be the occasion on which I missed my second match of the season.

After an irrational amount of time across the preceding two days spent checking weather forecasts – and selfishly not being averse to the idea of a call-off – we awoke on match day to news that the game had the go-ahead.

At once invigorated, and slightly chilled by the prospect of watching a match close to our temporary home while the Spitfires were simultaneously in action, the decision to travel to Dorset was taken with little hesitation. It proved a wise move.

Despite it only being nine days since the team last took to the field, the advent of Christmas Day and a brief separation from all things Eastleigh made it seem as if this was a renewing of acquaintances. The men on the pitch displayed no rustiness as they went for the throat of the league's bottom team. A 1–0 half-time lead, earned through another excellent Ben Strevens goal, was doubled soon after the interval by Reason's smart finish to round off a flowing move.

If we were waiting for the floodgates to open we'd still be there. This Dorchester side showed a few changes to the one that I had seen thumped, despite a promising performance, a few weeks earlier at Havant & Waterlooville (while our players held their Christmas bash). The pleasing football remained, but the soft centre was gone. A fantastic strike, delivered by Josh Wakefield (remember the name of this young starlet whose parent club is AFC Bournemouth), brought the Magpies back into the contest. It required some unflinching defending, notably by Todd and Dillon, to keep hold of the three points.

'Dills' was introduced early in the second half after McAllister was afflicted by yet another knock – a kick in the ribs adding to the pick 'n' mix of blows he's taken this campaign. Craig continues to endure what must be the most frustrating of existences for a footballer. Recovery, play, back to recovery, ad nauseam. It is a tiring routine.

Back in suburban Surrey for 7pm, we were delighted we'd made the effort. The win was all the more valuable for Bromley and Ebbsfleet sharing the points in their top-of-the-table meeting.

Dorchester's display, which was way above anything one would expect of a team in their dire predicament, was great cause for excitement among the vocal home crowd. None more so than the two gents sat in front of us, once they had returned late for the second half clutching their plastic glasses re-filled with weak beer and unaware their side had slipped 2–0 behind.

The pair soon put that inconvenience behind them. A blend of rampant partisanship and the spirit unique to those full of 'festive cheer' gave rise to their progressively more vehement rants in our direction. Any comment on my behalf invited the chastisement of one of the duo specifically – and I must admit it was difficult to avoid the temptation to prick his tail. Happy New Year.

My new friends would have been knocked back somewhat by their team's capitulation, two days later, at Weston-super-Mare. Richard's take: 'Dorchester were disciplined and fought till the end. Yesterday [at Weston] they have three sent off and gave up. They would not be bottom if they played like they did on Boxing Day.'

The manager's offering of his opinion on the side we are due to meet again on New Year's Day came at the end of a text conversation. Our exchange was initially centred on the outcome of Saturday's (December 28th) game with Bath City. Bath were exceptional. Strevens, yet again, was the man to make a breakthrough, in this instance entirely against the run of play, by unleashing a bullet header that crashed into the stanchion in the top-right corner of goal.

Undeterred, the visiting team, with their three men in midfield completely overrunning Southam and Evans, continued to dominate. The equaliser, on 29 minutes, had been long in coming.

At half-time I'd have gratefully scurried away with a draw in the bank – even though Tom Parsons, on hearing me say that, made the valid point that with Bromley almost exclusively winning every time they step onto a football pitch (and they did so again on this day) Eastleigh simply have to do the same.

How they did against Bath goes down as one of life's mysteries. A large part of the explanation lies in Richard buttressing his midfield with Strevens and making a couple of telling alterations from the bench. Green, still fighting to regain his spot, replaced Batt and, most productively, Yemi was withdrawn in favour of the far from 100% fit Jamie Collins.

By the time Collins strode on to head in a Reason free-kick and snatch victory from a disbelieving City side, Fleetwood had been sent off for a daft off-the-ball kick at an opponent. It was the most infuriating type of red card – utterly needless and, even though extremely soft, impossible to appeal because the offence is there for all to see. Throughout the half-hour they played with ten men, the side relied on its spirit, commitment and unshakable drive to see them over the line.

Richard thought his players had looked lethargic. That would be understandable given that Dillon was the only starter who didn't feature from the off at Dorchester. What's more, every pitch now is a clone of the one we encountered at Dover – boggy and energy sapping.

The boss conceded that 'we didn't play well' against Bath, but, having read my report, declared me the only person to have given him any credit for his team winning the game tactically. That is exactly what happened. A reporter attached to the away side confirmed how well our last visitors of 2013 had played when post-match he greeted their excellent forward Josh Low by saying, 'Josh, what a performance today. That was outstanding, the best we've played for a long time.'

So much of the Silverlake viewing experience is on the up, largely, of course, because the Spitfires keep winning there. The lone declining element of a home match day is the formerly reliable 'tea hut/burger van'. My latest brush with said food and drink outlet involved standing stock still, approximately 12th in line, in a queue that didn't move throughout the 15 minutes I stayed patient.

I might be more forgiving if Mark Jewell hadn't, in an article in the day's programme, thanked every man and his dog to have contributed an iota of effort to the Eastleigh cause in 2013, including the 'boys in the burger van'. This match reporter was missing from the list.

Mr Jewell's ever expanding role at the club is dictating that his 'Commercial Manager' remit is becoming something closer to that of a Chief Executive. I had wished, therefore, when I was struggling for a half-time drink at the Farnborough match on November 9th that 'Jeweller' was on hand to witness a profusion of punters being denied the opportunity to put some extra money in the coffers.

Of more pressing concern to my Eastleigh supporting counterparts, 'Fleets', just as he has hit blistering form, will be missing for four games (his red came on top of four previously collected yellow cards). During our pre-Christmas interview, Richard passed on – off the record – some cheerier news about our rampaging attacker/food doyen/Herbalife salesman. The boss revealed that Fleetwood will be signing a contract to extend his stay at the club. It is unlikely his agreed wage is of the otherworldly proportions purported by envious league adversaries.

All being well, and fingers firmly crossed, Stuart will be a Spitfire until at least the end of 2014/2015 – an official announcement is due in January. Richard is confident that the same agreement will be reached with every one of his players – all of them taking the view that if they come up short of their ultimate goal this term, to then walk away would condemn the Eastleigh FC part of their lives to being remembered as a waste of time. Stewart Donald concurs with that line of thinking and has promised Richard his continued financial input regardless of how this term concludes.

Our fellow Hampshire outfit, Gosport Borough, meanwhile, are enduring a horrendous week. Christmas Eve's high winds took the roof off their clubhouse. An ensuing prodigious effort to repair the damage enabled the team's match against Basingstoke four days later to go ahead – that was until a power failure caused its half-time abandonment.

We have much to be grateful for, and Chris Blake, in his TSSC guise, must be thrilled that five days prior to the Spitfires game at Eastbourne Borough (and the renewal of Hill–Widdrington pleasantries) no fewer than 25 names are listed for coach travel to East Sussex. My defection from that means of transport continues, unfortunately. Spoiled by the relative peace and luxury of the car and radio station of choice, the prospect of returning to the lively beer-licensed Eastleigh road trips is not the most tempting.

26

AND A HAPPY NEW YEAR?

The answer as regards day one is a resounding 'no'. An incomprehensible amount of rainfall has led to the cancellation of a plethora of fixtures, our hosting of Dorchester being one of the first to go. Even as a confirmed advocate of the idea of English football introducing a winter break, I can't deny that this day off is the last thing Eastleigh need.

Richard has already conceded that his side's FA Trophy involvement, and the consequent demands they are sure to face in order to cram in re-arranged games prior to April 26th, might prove the undoing of this year's promotion aspirations. The only succour to be taken from 2014's dawning with a day of rest is exactly that. It's an opportunity to see off the lethargy that the manager detected in his troops against Bath and, vitally, provides extra recuperation time for Beckwith, Collins, and McAllister.

R&R and Running

A thumbs-up after a 9:45am (Saturday, January 4th) pitch inspection at Eastbourne's Priory Lane was the prompt for Eastleigh's combined forces to hit the road. Minutes after my dad and I had pulled into the car park, an incredulous Southam rolled in, asking of a club official, 'Are you seriously telling me this game is on?' Suvs was desperate for it to be so. This is where he was due to serve his one-match suspension. Any postponement and the skipper would be watching on when we go toe-to-toe with Dover in the last-16 Trophy clash – the trilogy: part two.

Despite continued re-assurances that the playing surface was in fine condition, angry skies and a relentless deluge didn't inspire a great deal of confidence in our hopes of making ground on Bromley – whose fixture had already gone by the wayside. Sure enough, at 2pm and with the TSSC coach trippers entering the Borough clubhouse – all looking like they needed wringing dry after scuttling a full 100 yards from their parking spot – various officials trooped in making cut-throat gestures. They weren't agitating for a scrap, merely confirming what, deep down, we had known throughout a rain-soaked week. Our 160-mile round trip was a waste of time.

When we return this way, and hopefully play, the already intriguing Hill–Widdrington aspect of the game will have extra spice. A few of our players, cynics to a man, suspected that Eastbourne's boss would have been more than happy to leave as late as possible the decision regarding the pitch's condition and might not be overly troubled by the thought of Eastleigh's footballers and manager, for no good reason, devoting a large part of their Saturday to traipsing across southern England's roads.

Richard, though, believed his opposite number fancied the game taking place on a sub-standard surface, which would act as a 'leveller'. Either way, or even if there is no substance to these alternative theories, the seeds for a feisty spring clash have been sown.

Two days after that washout (Monday, January 6th), I made my way into training to discover the players were being run around the lake in a nearby park. With its undulating and harsh terrain, the pre-determined circuit made a standard athletics track look an appealing workplace proposition. The course was run repetitively, with short breaks between each exertion, for close on 45 minutes. As expected, there was plenty of moaning during the pit stops – all typically good natured. Richard noted, however, that uber-professionals Strevens and McAllister didn't utter a single dissenting word.

Macca instead asserted that Dover (our seemingly ubiquitous foe, who we face in Saturday's FA Trophy tie) 'won't know what's hit them'. Beckwith made a humorous aside to the effect that if our opponents were being spared this kind of purgatory it wasn't a bad trade-off. 'Oh, you don't want to get to Wembley then,' jibed McAllister.

Jai Reason was using up any spare energy by demanding the club recruit a sports scientist to move them on from this 'old school' form of training. As ever with Jai, when it came to undertaking the actual runs he did so with some gusto. That he had in common with every one of his team-mates. With just a couple of efforts remaining, Todd enquired of the gaffer as to whether there might be 'a carrot for the lads'. 'The f★★★★★★ carrot, Toddy, is that if you run these last two properly we'll finish when I said we would and I won't have to send you round again.'

With that demand fulfilled, Jamie Collins, who by now looked decidedly green around the gills, went to every one of his colleagues with a high-five or slap on the back for all. Richard, out of his players' earshot, declared himself delighted with their work. He hopes not to have to lay on another hard-running, pre-season-style session until July. That will depend on kinder weather allowing the team to get on with tackling an ever more crowded fixture list.

As we crossed back to the Silverlake's Astroturf pitches I spoke with Ramone Rose – evidently free of Monday employment duties elsewhere. Ramone's attitude was entirely contrary to that of somebody whose sights are set away from Eastleigh. He is utterly desperate to play some football. When I mentioned that, early in the campaign, he'd revealed an aptitude for filling the right-back spot, Ramone effused that he would be happy to take any position in the team if it meant getting on the field.

An ensuing nine-a-side practice game was barely five minutes old when Richard blew his whistle, apoplectic. 'Come on. This is no good. Work, close down. I asked for 20 minutes. Don't take the f★★★★★★ p★★★.' Another five minutes had passed when the manager turned to Cookie and, his voice a mixture of surprise and sympathy, simply said, 'They look f★★★★★.' They did – not that the quality of football on display suffered too much.

Fleetwood admitted, as he made his way through four sausages, roast potatoes, peas and gravy (this is more like it), that by the time of their training match he was 'f★★★★★'. 'I just stood in the centre circle and didn't move.' That's more than he'll be allowed to do over the next couple of weeks. Fleets' four-match suspension is due to commence with Dover's visit.

The Welshman's voracious appetite, and efficient turnaround from training kit to civvies, led to his making the first dent in the day's food – and contributed to the stragglers being denied the meat option on the menu.

Paula was left bemoaning the 'shrinking sausages', which left a few of the workers forlornly filling their plates with spuds and greens – excluding the Herbalife clique, of course – all while Mr Fleetwood, with a beaming smile, confessed to feeling rather full.

Away from the lunch offering, it took Sky Sports' often extremely dull breaking news strap's revelation that Roger Johnson had signed for West Ham to interrupt an animated chat about the opposite sex. Reason and Collins, arch Hammers, didn't take well to news that their favourite club had recruited a player relegated three times in the past three seasons. McAllister was interested to note that his former strike partner Matt Tubbs has returned to Crawley Town, the club at which the pair linked to prodigious effect.

After sausage-gate I interviewed another villain of the piece ('I only had two honestly,' McAllister – 'Yeah, and how many have you got in your pockets, Roscoe?'), Ross Flitney.

The 'keeper confirmed his preference for wearing a white kit, believing it makes an off-putting sight for a striker bearing down on goal. Mild eccentricity is a pre-requisite of goalkeeping, but no more so than a certain sense of sangfroid. Even reflecting on his sending off at Old Trafford when a 21 year old with Barnet, an incident he described as 'difficult and upsetting', Ross said that a few days later 'it was done and dealt with'. Indeed, his primary concern then was that his red card necessitated the substitution of one of his mates – Louis Soares – who hadn't had a touch of the ball.

An extra promotion incentive for the Number 1 is that a resultant increased budget might allow for the employment of a 'keeping coach. That's not to say that Ross isn't enjoying the challenge of working with the Spitfires' promising young crop. He refused any credit for Jack Dovey's assured recent outings, but there was a definite sense of pride emanating from our stopper when we discussed his understudy's performances.

Nevertheless, having been reared at Fulham surrounded by a who's who of his trade – Edwin van der Sar, Maik Taylor, Marcus Hahnemann, Mark Crossley, Dave Beasant, and Peter Bonetti no less – Ross would value analytical input on his game. Furthermore, he'd quite appreciate the luxury of being free to concentrate wholly on his own endeavours.

Playing what he considers to be some of his finest football, Eastleigh's custodian categorically stated that he can operate in 'League Two or higher'. Yet to hit 30, it is a better than evens bet that he will make good on his ambition. The immediate priority, though, is the here and now. 'We're doing extremely well. Bromley, at the moment, have got a bit of a head start on us, but that's only due to the games we've got to catch up on. If we keep doing what we're doing and don't worry about anyone else I think we'll get promoted.'

That head start amounts to a barely credible 11 points, albeit we have three games in hand. The gap is only likely to widen at the weekend when, while Eastleigh contest a Trophy quarter-final spot, Bromley have an extremely winnable home match against Eastbourne.

Preparation for Dover was at full-tilt on Thursday (January 9th). For this session it was back to the 3G university pitches used prior to the visit to Maidstone. I moaned, and moaned, about the cold then, and this was little better. Eleven of today's complement of 20, while being drilled to the nth degree ahead of a match that seems to have crept up under the radar, were adorned in black tights. As it heaves into view, the reality of this cup tie being a rare opportunity to push on towards Wembley is suddenly striking all involved.

The force of Southam, and direct running and ingenuity of Fleets are going to be missed. Notwithstanding that twin handicap, as Richard steadily revealed his hand throughout Thursday's shape and team pattern work, there was plenty to inspire confidence that the Spitfires can compensate for the absence of two star men.

Thanks to the manager's exasperation with one young player taking six touches of the ball before passing during an earlier training match, he proceeded to count for the benefit of those nearby the subsequent number taken by his key men. Fleets was the exception, being a man whose first instinct is to carry the ball forward. It was instructive to stop and digest the metronomic fashion in which the majority receive possession and instantly move it on – Spence and Strevens in particular never wavered from a touch count of two.

Jamie Bulpitt is clearly absorbing the good habits of those around him. I noticed in Monday's leggy kick-about that Jamie was shifting the ball quickly and effectively, a deed he routinely repeated on Thursday. He caught my eye early in the campaign when hurtling himself fearlessly into challenges during a reserve fixture, but, in a matter of months, Jamie's game has evolved appreciably. When I suggested to the teenager that, owing to Southam's ban, he must have a chance of being in Saturday's squad his eyes lit up – he had previously been unaware of the skipper's non-involvement.

After the morning's main work came some shooting practice. Fleets and Yemi larruped the first two digs, from approximately ten yards out, over the (very) high fence behind the goal. They weren't the last culprits. Save the hits for Dover, chaps.

My contribution to the cause for the day was to inform Paula of the slow service being provided at the burger van. Being a woman who I don't imagine tolerates any slip in standards or indeed money draining away on her watch, it is a situation she is already seeking to rectify. I have promised my feedback on Saturday's operation – yes, I really do take this seriously.

Que Sera Sera

On Friday night, news emerged on the internet that Reece Connolly had signed for Eastleigh. Speaking with Richard briefly, after our Trophy clash with Dover (Saturday, January 11th), it transpired that this was a piece of business the club had been determined to conduct well away from prying eyes – mine included.

Before I could chip away at the details of that story, there was at hand the small matter of another titanic confrontation against a team that had won on its five previous visits to the Silverlake. Dover's odds of stretching that victorious run to six looked decidedly long when, with two minutes played, Yemi's shot ricocheted off Jai Reason and past Mitch Walker. For 15 minutes Eastleigh battered a visiting side that was bereft of ideas as to how to stem the tide, let alone able to construct anything to trouble Flitney's goal.

With half an hour on the clock the Spitfires should have been out of sight. Instead, the game was level after a rudimentary Dover set-piece produced a soft equaliser. Momentum appeared to have swung straight back our way when Nathan Elder – a hulking centre-forward, already not enjoying his finest day – was red-carded after chucking his head at Jamie Collins as, with play stopped, the pair grappled for the ball.

There was a sense of déjà vu to the incident. Collins, back in November, talked Tonbridge's David Ijaha into limply swinging at him following a comparably innocuous tête-a-tête. The similarity didn't end there. When facing the ten men of the lowly Angels for the best part of 90 minutes, Eastleigh's football ground to a halt and they ended up suffering an unforeseen home reverse.

With that match still fresh in the mind, as well as games against Hayes & Yeading and Sutton when the team also laboured despite having a numerical advantage, there was no complacency in the stands as a bewilderingly bewildered Elder trudged off.

That mutual sense of caution was replaced by something more sinister when, ten minutes after the interval, the Whites were awarded a penalty, Green having clipped the heels of the outlandishly coiffured Liam Bellamy. Set-piece wizard Barry Cogan walloped the ball in off the underside of the bar.

A healthy away contingent was jubilant (on a topical note, plenty of that boisterous clan had travelled on official club transport that prohibits alcohol). As the Spitfires toiled, with no suggestion that they could muster the intensity or imagination needed to break through a packed Dover barrier, the visiting fans exultantly reminded another sparse home cup crowd (368) that they were winning with ten men.

Batt, whose off-key showing against Bath a fortnight ago had consigned him to bench duty, was thrown on with half an hour to play. Joining him on the field – as Yemi and Will Evans trooped off – was Reece Connolly. Connolly's ability is not in doubt. A centre-forward, he has been fantastic whenever I've seen him. Richard wanted to purchase the 21 year old a year ago, but Farnborough, curiously given their well-chronicled financial issues, were reported to have stumped up £12,000 to secure the player whom they had originally taken on loan from Aldershot Town. Strangely, Connolly spent the last few months of 2012/2013 on loan with Forest Green Rovers.

His 30-minute cameo here was all that was required to inform anybody who didn't already know why this is a man whose presence Richard so covets. Strength, mobility, guile, and awareness are all crammed into the Connolly footballing package.

But, despite the new boy's zest and the additional thrust provided by Batt out on the right wing, an equaliser was far from certain. That was until the re-called Green rapped a half-volleyed pass into our debutant on half-way. Reece's touch and power were to the fore as he sparked a penetrating move. Strevens took over to play a fantastic, incisive one-two with Batt, haring on to the precise return and finishing first-time under Walker.

The Dover 'keeper has an unfortunate personal knack of being culpable for the concession of a goal whenever he faces Eastleigh. He couldn't have done anything to prevent Strevens notching. He could, though, have managed better than spilling a routine late high delivery into his box. Play continued and 'Strevs' was denied his second by a heroic Michael Kamara block that put the ball behind. From umpteen earlier corners the Spitfires had produced nothing – nor looked like doing so. Green swept this one into the box, Todd contrived to knock it goal-wards, and Collins swooped to hook in from barely six yards.

Cue absolute unabashed delirium. Richard was off down the touchline, Yemi back on the pitch leaping about uncontrollably. Every player converged on the scorer and, honestly, the main stand broke into song. Only the old ditty, 'You're not singing anymore' aimed in the direction of the crestfallen Dover horde, but, nevertheless, this was truly a momentous happening.

Slightly alarmingly, my dad was celebrating as boisterously as anybody. Of course, securing a place for the first time in Eastleigh's 68-year history in the last eight of this competition was justification enough for the old guy's slightly out of character evident display of glee. The avoidance of a Tuesday night haul to Kent for a replay was the icing and cherries on his cake.

The manager admitted that, after his team's explosive start, it wasn't a particularly impressive performance. For large parts it was quite baffling. This group continues to find a way though – and that is a priceless habit. Southam, watching on, and wearing as one forumite noted a voice-altering fit of jeans, has seen out his one-game ban and can resume skippering his men on Tuesday when Dover come back for more.

For Fleetwood, that's merely one quarter of his suspension complete. That irritation aside, on a day when the good news just kept coming, Richard made public after the game the news that 'Fleets' has committed to the year's extension he had been offered on his contract. I've been waiting slightly anxiously for confirmation of that agreement since Richard alluded to it in our pre-Christmas interview.

Oh, and Bromley were denied by a waterlogged Hayes Lane pitch from extending their 11-point margin on us in the league.

The gaffer is reluctant to go too far into the 'Reece Connolly saga' just yet. In November Reece was suspended by Farnborough, the club stating that he had failed a drug test carried out at their own instigation. The press release stated that their player had tested positive for cocaine, marijuana, and a 'third unspecified substance'. There is an FA hearing imminent. The situation, therefore, is extremely delicate. We could lose Reece, who has never pleaded his guilt to the offence, almost as soon as he's arrived.

I hope beyond hope that he is allowed to continue with his career. The prime reason for that is plainly selfish. But this is a 21-year-old lad who has been placed in a terrible predicament. Conspiracy theories abound regarding the sudden desire to conduct dope tests at Cherrywood Road. One suspects that this tale might have a way to run. I won't personally discover much from the man himself quite yet. Richard is keen that Connolly isn't interviewed or subject to any publicity until his long-term situation becomes clear. For now, he will be left to focus on his football and, judging by his Saturday night tweeting, that suits him nicely.

My Dictaphone victim this week, with rather handy timing, will be Strevens. Deservedly the victor in Saturday's vote for December's 'Player of the Month' (the first time this season that the recipient has corresponded with my choice), Ben is in rare form. He's delivered crackerjack goals in each of the last four games. Much more than that, his overall contribution from a variety of starting positions has been gargantuan.

There was a Portsmouth FC delegate specifically watching Jai Reason wield his influence during the Dover cup thriller. His all-action showing was noteworthy – albeit the boss wasn't totally won over, still considering his playmaker to lack positional discipline. Strevs, though, was simply outstanding. Still only 33, he could comfortably slot into a League One or League Two side. This is the calibre of player we are watching at Eastleigh now.

If the Spitfires putting themselves two rounds from a Wembley final wasn't enough for one day, I had a half-time cup of tea. And I was back in my seat to enjoy it before the players had returned to resume hostilities. Paula parachuted her son, a chef no less, into the fray. He did the trick. Inertia and procrastination were replaced by energy and efficiency. Please, please let it continue.

One man not in Richard's Trophy squad, or indeed inside the stadium, was Ramone Rose. On Monday, after he had told me of his longing to feature in the team, the attacker's training game performance was full of application and vitality.

Reminiscent of his pre-season endeavours though, when he has the bit between his teeth Ramone can sometimes over-cook things in his attempt to catch the eye. In possibly 'trying too hard' he can tend to select the more difficult option, an ambitious dig at goal or a speculative defence-splitting pass rather than playing the ball to a well-positioned colleague. While the former QPR youngster has already, at 23 years old, been at a number of clubs, given match experience there is plenty of scope to develop his game.

Next in store for Ramone's current employers is the latest Monday FA Trophy draw. Remarkably, Aldershot, Havant & Waterlooville, and Gosport Borough complete a quartet of Hampshire outfits in the hat. Gosport at home, please, football gods.

Balls

At midday on Monday, January 13th, Gosport were dealt a trip to Yorkshire to play North Ferriby United. Havant & Waterlooville welcome Aldershot. Tamworth or Chorley go to Grimsby Town. All of which means that the first and second placed teams in the Conference Premier, Luton Town and Cambridge United, will contest a replay with the prize for the victor a trip to our very own Silverlake Stadium.

We have been spared an epic road trip, but this isn't exactly the dream draw. An away tie against either of those opponents would have contributed far more, by way of gate receipts, to the club's coffers. Moreover it is the pairing that, when assessed coldly, offers the least prospect of progress to a semi-final. Yet, when the game is here it will be a grand occasion, perhaps the biggest in the Spitfires' existence. And, being football supporters, we'll fancy our chances.

By 9:30am on the morning of Saturday, January 18th, with the Silverlake pitch defaced by puddles and Gosport Borough due for the day's 3pm kick-off, plenty more had happened to impact upon the Eastleigh FC machine. And the team hadn't kicked a ball.

Despite Tuesday (January 14th) being a uniquely dry day, the damage already done to our home surface had been beyond retrieval. Dover's latest visit has been re-arranged for next month. Bromley's Courage Stadium was fit to host Concord Rangers and, from absolutely nowhere, the league leader's voracious sweeping up of points was checked by a 2–1 defeat. The result was even more of a surprise for the Ravens' boss Mark Goldberg having, days earlier, acquired Ali Fuseini – formerly of Sutton United and the one time 'missing-in-action' Eastleigh player – to strengthen his midfield.

There is something curious afoot at Mr Doswell's Sutton. In addition to Fuseini's departure, Jamie Stuart left the club in pursuit of regular football at Ryman Premier outfit Margate, that club having recently appointed non-league sage Terry Brown as its manager. More surprising is the clutch of players to have followed their team-mate to the 'Gate's' Hartsdown Park.

While Bromley were slipping up, Cambridge United were winning at Luton thanks to an Ashley Chambers goal. With our opponents for the February 1st FA Trophy quarter-final confirmed, the impression of an immense occasion looming is spreading throughout the club.

There is some disquiet concerning the fact that, due to an expected travelling support numbering approximately 500, fans will be segregated at the game. Those unhappy with the arrangement argue that it's a sad indictment on football that its followers can't be trusted to mingle without the potential for mayhem. The counter view is that the necessity to split the Cambridge congregation from their Spitfires counterparts mirrors what happens higher up the league ladder. That is where we aspire to be and the measures taken to ensure that the day passes off without bother add to the feeling of this being a seriously big match.

Another feature of the FA Trophy tie and the game with Ebbsfleet this forthcoming Saturday (January 25th) will be a temporary terrace behind one goal. It is a first move towards the longer awaited permanent structure that will be put in place once this campaign has concluded. The fee incurred will be £12 for a spot on the newly erected 'home end'. There is, though, a £3 premium to join me in my stand.

Cambridge United's visit is sure, for the next fortnight, to consume the time and efforts of all those responsible for maximising every last drop of revenue from the game's staging. As well as striving for a cash boost on the day, there is an equally essential requirement to put on an afternoon so memorable that first-time attendees are encouraged back for more. For Richard Hill and his players, however, their next Trophy date constitutes a speck on the horizon.

I spoke to the manager on Wednesday (January 15th) in order to prepare his programme notes for the encounter with all those former Eastleigh men at Gosport Borough. In truth, neither of us expected the match to go ahead. Richard was back on familiar ground, lamenting the lopsided fixture calendar that has us due to play 23 league games in 14 weeks. Reece Connolly was still off-limits for discussion, other than the boss disclosing that 'our' new forward faces an FA hearing on Wednesday, January 22nd – after which more might be revealed.

The impending hectic schedule has led to plenty of speculation concerning whether Richard might want to supplement his playing resources. On that subject he was unequivocal. We already have a strong squad of 18. The manager is, therefore, disappointing seven players each week. Injuries and suspensions permitting, it is incumbent on him to leave two men who would be regularly involved elsewhere at this level watching on from the stands.

Richard is only interested in bringing in individuals who could 'add value' to what he already has. Connolly, a player of some repute and reared in the professional environment of Aldershot Town, expressed the view to his new manager that the quality of training that he has stepped into is several notches up from that at his previous employers. Everything is 'quicker, more intense'.

The boss is loath to sacrifice that work ethic and standard, but is confronted with a delicate balancing act. There is an exacting programme ahead, for which Richard wants his men as fresh as possible. Other than the missed opportunity to make up ground on Bromley, the Dover cancellation provided another setback. Fleetwood's ban will run to cover the vital Ebbsfleet clash – and deprive the hungry player of a chance to wreak revenge on the side, or more precisely Daryl McMahon, who left him, in October, limping away with a severe gash to his leg.

The non-availability for such an extended period of a pivotal performer might push some managers into the market. Richard was, again, unmoved. Such a short-term acquisition policy is what leads to the stockpiling of players, so adding to the number of disaffected bodies around a squad. Additionally, it's a sure-fire way of hiking up the wage bill.

The boss's thoughts were given extra weight by the near full attendance of his men when I took in Thursday's (January 16th) training session at the wind-trap, 3G Southampton University complex. Chris Dillon was the odd man out, working with Cookie before taking himself off for some lonely sprinting exercises. Dills' foot, injured during the new year running round the lake, is sufficiently on the mend that he will be ready extremely soon to join the rest of the stir crazy, but uproarious group.

I raised an eyebrow when I saw Ben Strevens scuttling about as usual.

Richard's belief that his current serial goal-scorer might be absent for the week had led me to defer any plans to interview Strevs. As such, I was reliant on the good nature of Craig McAllister to provide me with some copy and my former team-mate came up with the goods.

I have already confessed to my admiration for the way that 'Macca' responded to being out of the reckoning for the first 11 at the campaign's outset. I can recall how downbeat he had been when telling me, 'I'm just not looking forward to the season anymore.'

After fighting his way into the side, to some effect, he was stymied by a string of niggling injuries. The biggest kick in the teeth came at Bury Town, way back in our FA Trophy first-round tie. Craig admitted he has had 'a fair bit of stick' for staying with the squad when his fiancée went into labour during the night before the game. To this ultimate professional, however, 'there wasn't a great deal to think about'. His understanding partner had agreed, telling him, 'Get on with it, it's your career.'

For his dedication on that day Craig was rewarded with a substitute's bench coat. Richard had selected the team he felt best equipped to win the match in hand and his judgement was proven correct. Nobody would suggest that the manager should alter his plans in order to administer a proverbial pat on the head to a player for 'services to his industry'. Macca admitted he 'wasn't overly impressed' to be excluded at Bury, but he came on at the break and promptly scored.

He knows that it is his goals return and overall on-field contribution that will dictate whether he earns a prized contract extension. Craig is rightly full of self-belief, but perfectly embodies the reality of life for plenty of non-league footballers – even with a host of clubs behind him and currently part of an undoubtedly upwardly mobile outfit.

'The pressure comes from wanting a new contract. You need to provide for your family, like any man does. I just know that I need to keep performing and one way or another it will be sorted. It's difficult for me to say whether I'll get it or not. It depends on how well I do in the coming four or five months.'

The fact that he has just passed the health and safety unit of his plumbing qualification indicates how little Macca is prepared to take for granted. Fitness allowing, I'm sure he'll be part of the Eastleigh scene for some time yet. Nevertheless, it can't sit entirely comfortably for a man, permanently engaged in a fight for his place, when he has to witness a string of challengers to his position being brought in. Craig insists that 'it's not a big thought in my mind' and that the personal competition can only benefit him and the team.

Macca's actions back up his words. During Thursday's training Richard interrupted an exercise that was designed to gel the side he had in mind for Gosport. The focus of his attention was Reece Connolly, specifically the forward's body shape when holding off a defender at his back. Who should be straight in, once the boss had completed his verbal direction, to provide a physical demonstration of the correct approach? Craig McAllister. Macca was nearby due to Richard deciding he wants to pair both forwards in his next match.

When I bumped into a jaded groundsman enjoying a warming cup of tea back at the club, with the rain hammering the windows as we spoke, he was pessimistic in the extreme with regards to that next match being at the Silverlake 48 hours later. The photographic evidence of Saturday morning made him right. But the same souls who toiled tirelessly without reward when the game with Chelmsford four days before Christmas suffered a late call-off went resolutely back to work. Somehow, they produced a surface that passed muster – just.

Within 20 seconds of the game kicking off, Jamie Brown, the manic ex-Spitfire, had upended McAllister. It was the prelude to a pure 'Browner' display. He'd have no qualms about telling you that he doesn't have the ability of Strevens and Jamie Collins, his direct adversaries on the day. To him, it matters not one jot. He spent the 90 minutes hassling, harrying, and making life distinctly uncomfortable for anybody who dared wander within his compass. What's more, Brown showed a dash of adventure; commonly steaming into his opponents' penalty area to add clout to his side's attacks.

Across their entire playing unit Borough, with five ex-Spitfires in their ranks, made it a difficult afternoon for the team 20 places above them in the league table. McAllister's brave and skilful early finish, along with Strevens' latest clinical effort (five in five now) was, however, enough for three more valuable points. When Strevs smashed a ball ruthlessly into the bottom corner during Thursday's practice Richard commented that 'he just cannot miss at the moment'. How true.

Before we could relax against our local adversaries, the mix of a sloppy goal conceded, Eastleigh's striking profligacy and Nathan Ashmore's breathtaking escapades between the Borough posts made for a heart-racing final 15 minutes.

The pitch, while playable, was by no means conducive to our team's quick passing and fleet movement. As the match drew to a close the terrain had deteriorated into something resembling a lumpy pudding. That is a concern for the weeks to come. Any manager coming up against Eastleigh, as Richard had suspected was the case with Tommy Widdrington at Eastbourne, would appreciate meeting that task on ground that negates the Spitfires' inherent footballing superiority.

Nevertheless, of upmost importance was chalking off fixture number 20 in efficient style. Bromley, meanwhile, recorded a stellar victory at Bath City – still the best team I've seen up against Eastleigh this term.

Back to Thursday, and Paula informed me that the previous Saturday (January 11th against Dover) takings at the food and drink van had shot up – that despite the poor attendance. When I went for the treasured half-time tea this week – imperative on the coldest day of the season so far – a spiralling queue had already formed. Progress came in the shape of us, after 15 minutes, being in the front third of the line. As players began to trickle out from the tunnel we had to abandon any hope of a successful conclusion to our mission. This is going to run and run.

Acquiring refreshments on Tuesday night (January 21st) at Weston-super-Mare's Woodspring Stadium shouldn't be such a head-banging operation. The Seagulls would be described by football's lazier pundits as having 'over-achieved' across the last 18 months – regardless of that phenomenon being impossible. What Weston have done in that period, despite their lowly crowd figures and sparse budget, is compete at the top-end of the division, picking up some exceptional victories along the way.

Even so, they will have a job on their hands this week to avoid a similar fate to that dealt them last February. That was when the Spitfires ended their away-day misery, which had seen them return from no road trip in possession of three points since August 2012, with a 4–2 win. Glen Southam was outstanding on that night. Against Gosport Borough on Saturday he warmed the bench until the 61st minute.

Twelve months ago, the mere notion that our skipper could be kept waiting to be back involved after a ban would have been derided. The scale of this squad's development was exemplified by more than just Suvs missing out on a starting spot against Borough. Will Evans and Yemi Odubade spent Saturday afternoon wrapped up against the cold; not called upon to strip for action.

When I mentioned to Yemi his joyous reaction to Collins' winner against Dover, springing from the dugout having earlier been withdrawn, he replied without hesitation, 'When I'm not playing, I'm a fan.' That attitude is genuinely common throughout the group. Southam will have been both tormented and smouldering about missing out on Saturday. Regardless of any personal disappointment, there wasn't a trace of negativity in Suvs' outward demeanour. Pre-match exercises were completed no differently than would have been the case had he been readying himself to start. When he joined the fray, Suvs, bringing to mind Richard's pre-requisite for his new purchases, added value to the team.

All the jostling for playing berths, even with Fleetwood still reaping the consequences of his momentary loss of temper against Bath, bodes extremely well for the next three months. The impending itinerary has even instigated a supporters' internet discussion regarding whether or not the sacrificing of promotion is acceptable, if that would smooth the way to the club's first ever Wembley trip.

On that one, I'm firmly with the manager. Just win the next game. That is at Weston. The 12-person mini-bus quota destined for north Somerset doesn't include either my dad or me. The season's petrol bill is escalating. So is Eastleigh's winning run, which stands at seven. Let's have number eight

27

GAME TIME: AND MY FINAL FRONTIER

Weston-super-Mare on an atrocious Tuesday night in January. It's the Conference South equivalent of the type of test we hear champions at all levels come through: scrapping out a 1–0 win at Cardiff City or gritting collective teeth and seeing out a bombardment at Stoke City to nick three points. Those are the results on which Premier League winners look back equally fondly, if not more so, as they do victories over their closest rivals.

With games against Ebbsfleet and Bromley coming into view, this less prestigious contest was the tripwire to be avoided. First up, having driven the 100 miles to the Woodspring Stadium, we had the currently standard anxious wait to discover if the match would actually go ahead. Mercifully, before the heavens opened wide during the players' warm up, referee Mark Pottage had concluded we'd be fine.

By half-time, the travelling band among an understandably paltry 198 crowd was starting to think a call-off might have been a decent result. The Spitfires were 1–0 behind to a sloppily conceded goal – Southam uncharacteristically hitting an errant and eventually costly midfield pass – and had apparently left their 'A game' at home.

Despite the acceptance that it had been a rather miserable 45 minutes, recent form, and the quality within the side, always offers hope that in such circumstances things will come good. It took until the 75th minute for that theory to hold true. Without approaching anything like their real selves, Eastleigh had been, for the preceding ten minutes, progressively turning the screw. When the equaliser arrived it came via a majestic McAllister left-footed strike from 18 yards. The stunning nature of the goal ensured the following celebrations were especially wild.

I was the sole body leaping up in a thinly populated main stand. That left me a sheepish figure three minutes later as I sat noting details of Dayle Grubb's speculative hit that skipped up and over Flitney to restore Weston's lead.

There was no coming back. Evans, starting at right-back, had been hooked at half-time; Green's second-half presence on the left of defence, after he had spent the first period sheltering on the bench, provided the team with a more balanced air. That was small succour though. Weston added a third, consigning Yemi's smart finish with the last kick of the night to be recorded in history as a 'late consolation'. All in all, the most positive aspect of the night, aside from a tasty, warming and cheap Wetherspoons meal, was the chalking off of fixture number 21.

A few of the players had seemed at odds with each other as they'd trooped off the field in Weston, but there was no indication whatsoever of any unrest when I turned up to Thursday's (January 30th) training. Cookie confirmed that the post-match dressing room mood had been one of defiance, not dejection. It had been a setback. The last of those came against Tonbridge and, until Tuesday, we'd won every game since. The prevailing attitude was: 'This is an aberration, now we get on our next winning run.'

The increasingly familiar setting of the university grounds echoed with laughter and buzzed with endeavour throughout a 75-minute workout. After some competitive nine-a-side, the defensive unit broke off to work with Guy Butters. Richard took charge of his attackers. An absence of a clinical edge in front of goal has been a recurring thread in the Spitfires' recent displays – even during their victorious sequence. Fleetwood, regardless of his playing no competitive football of late, was the day's sharpest shooter. Others mixed some dreamy touches and classy finishes with scuffed and soaring efforts aplenty.

Before being part of the back-four drilled by Guy – at times they were operating in tandem as if strung together by a rope – Dan Spence had been taken aside by Richard for a quiet word about Dayle Grubb's strike two nights earlier. The excellent winger who, in my naïve early days of talking to the manager, I had mooted as a potentially wise recruit had cut inside from the left and shot, without Dan getting close enough to apply any pressure. I didn't pick up the detail, but the boss delivered his advice succinctly and quietly to his attentive student.

Back in the relative warmth of the clubhouse and its new manager was guarding against any repeat of sausage-gate. Roast potatoes, Yorkshire puddings and vegetables were available to be piled onto plates at will. The roast beef, however, was meticulously laid onto plates held, Oliver Twist-style, under Paula's nose.

Brian Palmer, whose daily attendance is as reliable as the manager's and players', wasn't shy when letting a few of Tuesday's 'culprits' know what he felt about his own excursion to Weston. 'I stand there all night in the p****** rain and what do you give me? Nothing, that's what.'

Brian's bleating was more teasing than admonishing. The same could be said for Jamie Collins' condemnation of his critic for, prior to the last of the day's trainers drifting in, helping himself to a well-earned plate of food. Safe to say that Jamie's enthusiastically delivered upbraiding slid breezily off its recipient's shoulders.

The only absentees from Thursday's gathering were the ever enigmatic Damian Batt and, once more, Ramone Rose. Since our chat over a fortnight ago I haven't set eyes on Ramone. A face we definitely won't be seeing again is that of one of the two regular 'burger van boys'. Paula's martinet regime, which only began on January 1ˢᵗ, is taking hold. That is a good thing.

Eastleigh v Ebbsfleet United (Silverlake Stadium) 25/01/2014

If there was a fixture that Eastleigh's manager and players could have hand-picked, in which to try and bounce back from their midweek low, this was it. Ebbsfleet, scene of one of the Spitfires' most compelling performances of the campaign to date, but where they were defeated 3–1, were in town for the return encounter. Intensifying the must-win feel of this match – a feeling existent through the entire group – was the over-exuberant reaction of their opponents to that October result. Furthermore, Daryl McMahon's spiky presence always brings something extra to an Eastleigh football match – among a section of our support more than the men on the pitch, it has to be said.

For good measure, Osei Sankofa, one of the men never to wear the Spitfires' blue again after last January's debacle at Bromley, lined up in the middle of the Fleet's defence. Discussing the name, penned on the tactics board, of the ex-

Charlton Athletic player, McAllister was sharply to the point. 'Hang it [the ball] up there and I'll smash the ★★★★.'

There is history between the pair. The portents, for all that unfolded on Sankofa's valedictory Eastleigh day, were writ large when a pre-match changing room disagreement resulted in the now Ebbsfleet player, comically in retrospect, throwing a bunch of grapes at his then colleague.

McAllister made his comment today behind closed doors – so how am I aware of it? This was the day when Richard, showing generosity beyond the call, allowed me unencumbered access to his dressing room. For the men on whom responsibility for Eastleigh FC's fortunes ultimately lies, this is, amid the frenetic bustle of a Saturday afternoon, their hallowed enclave. I was stepping into the one place that remains strictly 'no go' for all but the manager, his staff and, of course, the players.

I had deliberately waited, until I was established as a training ground bystander, to tentatively approach the boss and ask whether I might be allowed a 'behind-the-scenes' match-day view. Richard, at a stroke, agreed to my request.

Driving to the Silverlake in time for a 1:30pm arrival, early even for me, and then pacing purposefully around the pitch towards the tunnel area, I experienced the mild butterflies and sense of apprehension that had enveloped me when I took the same journey way back on July 1st. Then, I was the new boy, still to be introduced. This book was a hopeful vision.

In the meantime, without ever becoming blasé, I have become progressively more comfortable in the players' environment. I would, though, be intruding, here, into the most private of territories.

In truth, it was an awkward assignment. This is these men's place of work. I sought, as effectively as possible, to drift into the background and absorb everything I possibly could. I learned a lot more about the individuals who I have been tracking for the past seven months.

Before I could find my bearings after Richard, with a wave of the hand, had ushered me into his sacred sphere, I was dealt a blow square between the eyes. I had been momentarily overwhelmed by the potent aroma of liniment. The staple smell of football changing rooms across the country; being a regular in those surroundings obviously enables the development of individual resistance to its eye-watering impact. I distinctly remember regularly slathering the product all over my upper legs, prior to going out and employing my cultured left foot to mixed effect. That, however, was a long time ago.

It took a while for my senses to adjust, something they had to manage while being battered on another front. The secondary assault came by way of the head-banging music that began blaring out not long after I had entered the compact room. I didn't investigate who is responsible for the Eastleigh FC playlist (Jack Dovey is the prime suspect), but it's not one I'll be searching out for personal listening.

Well over an hour before kick-off, the air was relaxed. The players' den was a throng of light-hearted chat with Collins even injecting an occasional move (sort of) to the 'beat' of the din. McAllister's choice of 'stag-do' destination ahead of his summer wedding, the Bournemouth v Liverpool FA Cup tie playing away on a television high in a corner of the room, and, naturally, the fairer sex all came under discussion – of varying depth.

The majority of the players congregated on benches that, in an 'L' shape, cover two sides of the main floor area. There is an open plan extension to this space, a development that post-dates my sole playing venture into this realm back in another time. That new-to-me area is where Cookie's treatment bench can be found. There, those who customarily opt to receive a pre-game massage or in need of specific attention took turns to undergo their respective treatment. Collins, McAllister and Strevens were among those to benefit from the sports therapist's renewing touch. Indeed, Strevens was far from ready when, at around 2:20pm, it was time to head out for the group warm up.

Strevs had told me on Thursday that Richard places complete trust in him to manage his own body. 'I've been quite fortunate throughout my career in that I've always been pretty fit. When I was young I was one of those that could run here, there, and everywhere and not get tired. And, to be honest, the gaffer looks after me a little bit in training. I join in with the boys, but I don't think he expects the same from me on a Monday morning or the Thursday ahead of a game as he does from some of the younger lads. He lets me get on with how I want to train to get my body back ready for the games.

'Last year I hardly played at all, so it's much better to wake up feeling sore and tired than to be thinking "I haven't done anything again". I'm tired, but enjoying it. When games are getting called off I'm as disappointed as anyone. I'm not thinking "Great, I'll get a bit of a rest".'

His preparing on Saturday at his own pace didn't vex the manager. Will Evans, on the other hand, helping Strevs with taping on his feet, was another matter. 'Will, get out of here, he doesn't need you f****** holding his hand.'

Ahead of the Guy Butters-led pre-match drills, Ross Flitney took to the shower area for his own idiosyncratic series of warm-up exercises – a routine that lasted a good ten minutes. Todd was next into the makeshift preparation zone to complete a slightly less strenuous round of stretching.

The announcement of the day's starting 11 had been a straightforward process. With a marker pen, on a flip chart in full view of the main benches, Richard meticulously, in formation, wrote out the names of the men charged with responding to Tuesday's defeat. Yemi and Greener were back in. Evans and Reece Connolly dropped to the bench. There wasn't a word from anybody. The news was digested and all were left with 80 minutes to prepare accordingly.

While the players were outside with Guy, the manager filled another two sheets with information, then pinned both to the wall. Again, there was no mention among the team, upon their return inside, of the notes. It was detail to be individually absorbed – reinforcement of the positions each man was to pick up at both attacking and defending corners. These players are good enough, and practised enough, to understand and fulfil their designated roles.

Only just into his kit and yet to begin readying himself for 3pm, McAllister had wandered over for a chat about the televised game – Liverpool cantering to a comfortable win was completely washing over me, my mind wholly consumed by everything in my immediate vicinity. When conversation moved on to Everton it was interesting to hear Craig's views on Romelu Lukaku, a player very much in our striker's ilk. Not playing well, a loose touch, and in need of competition for his spot in the side was Macca's opinion. At this moment in time, he's bang on.

One of the first things I'd heard after entering the dressing room was Richard instructing Guy not to allow any of the players back out through the door until it was time to warm up. The manager did not want any of his men mixing and exchanging pleasantries with the opposition – a number of the members of these two teams have previously been at the same clubs together.

The only person granted exception to the manager's rule, at approximately 2:05pm, was Suvs. Captain's duties include a perfunctory meeting with his opposite number – here, the hulking centre-back Paul Lorraine – and the day's

233

officials. When Southam returned – initially with the news that the referee would be John O'Brien, the man whose performance in the first game between these sides provoked ire from every Eastleigh angle – Richard was able to jot down the Ebbsfleet 11.

Fresh from christening the match official, to widespread amusement, with a less than affectionate moniker, Suvs tapped on the name of Michael Corcoran, listed in the centre of the Fleet midfield, indicating him to be a weak link. The pair spent the 2011/2012 season together at Dover. Yemi also had a view on a tactic the same visiting player might favour – euphemistically described as exaggerating a foul.

Guy, spurred on by Richard's tapping of his watch, which was running a couple of minutes faster than his own, took the players out at 2:20pm. 'Get them out of here.' The manager brought a blessed halt to the 'music', a crisp act that emphasised the contrast between newly tranquil surroundings and the preceding hullabaloo.

It hit me how cocooned from all of the Silverlake's match-day commotion this 'bolt-hole' underneath my stand is. PA announcements and the customary entertainment were barely audible. I was completely unaware of the swelling crowd – which topped 700 and of whom a fair selection enjoyed a view of the action from the newly installed temporary terracing behind the clubhouse end goal.

Richard had left his players alone for a good chunk of the half-hour leading up to their on-pitch loosener. Now, he sat on a bench and spent five minutes tapping at his phone. I was perched a few yards away, staying quiet, not wanting to disrupt one iota any aspect of his mental preparation.

Once the boss's eyes turned to the television I asked if this was his quiet time. 'Yes.' Cue another brief contemplative period. With no Batt or Rose on the team-sheet, or in attendance, I couldn't resist asking the manager if Batt was injured or out of favour.

'Damian Batt's left the football club.'

This was not the time or place to dig further. Richard did say it had nothing to do with the player's attitude, which he described as 'fine'. An individual story that intrigued me, then, that of the 'hard to read' seasoned professional, who opted for a career switch at 28 years old, will have no definitive conclusion.

'Has Ramone left as well?'

'Yes. He didn't want the same things as I did.'

Again, not the moment to pursue this line, but the closing of another Spitfires tale in a season already full of them.

During this quiet time, which felt somewhat akin to the final minutes before sitting a vital exam, Cookie was called back into action. The patient was Ray Murphy, the club secretary, who was having 'a bit of trouble with his Gregory'. Perhaps prompted unconsciously by Ray's neck bother, the regular pain I experience in my back and shoulders escalated. I realised how tensely I was holding my body, as I sat leaning forward gazing through the TV.

Once he stood, in premature anticipation of the players trooping back in, their studs clattering on the floor to a discordant harmony, Richard was restless. Not only that, I'm sure he was nervous. He had commented that, by Sunday afternoon, he'd barely be able to detect the ball on the screen when watching the day's live game on television. I enquired if that was due to an impending big night, but no, the boss would simply be completely shattered.

A lot of that drained energy was spent in the five minutes immediately prior to his team talk. Pacing from one end of the room to the other, and back, and back again, while I stood stock still, Richard was a fusion of determination and concentration. Anxiety radiated off a man immersed in his work. An attempt to relax by lying flat out on Cookie's bench was futile, the tightly bound manager springing back to his feet within 60 seconds.

When they made their way back inside (after what had felt like an eternity), warmed up and fired up, the players were altogether different beasts to the ones that had left under half an hour earlier. Now it was game time. Collins was most vocal of the tribe. His clipped urgings changed in words, but the prevailing message never veered from its narrative.

'Come on. We owe these c****. Remember them at their place, shouting and screaming. That was disrespectful. We're too good to lose two in a row. It's not happening. These c**** are going to know they're in a game. They're going to be the ones to pay for Tuesday.'

Jamie had worked himself into a controlled fury. Plenty of his colleagues followed suit. Southam, Beckwith, and Strevens all had their say. Each oratory contained three key bulletins: the absolute necessity for every individual to be 'on it' from the first whistle, the belief that this is the strongest group of players in the league, and finally, this team doesn't get beaten twice in a week. And a lot of swearing.

Others readied themselves less obtrusively. Spence, as reserved in the dressing room as on the training ground, was quiet, but had an unmistakably steely glint in his eyes. Green could have been preparing to nip out and post a letter. McAllister had the bearing of a man, although totally focused, who has seen it and done it hundreds of times before – which he has.

When Richard took over the talking, his tone was measured and clear. Yes, Tuesday hadn't been good enough. Perhaps he had made mistakes of his own. That's gone. A few individuals were given specific instructions and reminders. The need to retain discipline was highlighted; there could be no repeat of the last 15 minutes at Weston when the side lost its shape and looked 'awful'.

Accept that Ebbsfleet might have periods when they are in the ascendancy and manage those phases of play. Finally, 'relax, enjoy it, and pass the football'. That very last order is undoubtedly the boss's favourite mantra, often to be heard from the side of a training ground or, on match day, bellowing across the pitch from his dugout.

With that, everybody was on their feet, high-fives and good-luck messages all round. Even yours truly received a few firm shakes of the hand.

As the starting 11 lined up in the tunnel, just ten or so paces from the changing room door, there was no sign of their Ebbsfleet adversaries. A timid linesman, questioned by Guy as to why we were waiting, explained that when he tried to open the visitors' dressing room door someone was pulling down on the handle.

When the opposition deemed it the right moment to trickle out, there were a few cordial greetings among familiar faces. McMahon, last in his team's queue, and Reason exchanged the most cursory slap of hands. No words were spoken.

I followed the teams out and hared up to my seat in the stand. It was, without exception, the most peculiar football-watching experience I have ever known. Minutes after being right in amongst the stirring, usually private, heated dressing room atmosphere, I was sat on high in my usual spot, watching the same impassioned men attempting to make good on their resolute words.

The opening 45 minutes passed in a blur. Richard having asked that I be back in the dressing room before the players, I took Flitney's late injury as an opportunity to make a uniquely early dash from my spec. It had been a wonderful first-half display, the only worry being that all we had to show for it was Reason's coolly taken penalty.

Ross spent the 15-minute interval prone, all the time being revived by Cookie. Richard, once the players had collected energy drinks or water bottles and were sat in front of their manager, picked out a few issues that needed addressing. The briefing, a result not only of an analytical mind that had busily interpreted every facet of action thus far, but also of a lifetime's accumulated footballing insight, was exact, concise, and simple.

Beckwith, when on the ball in defence, was occasionally bereft of passing options. The early hit up to McAllister was being over-used. Spence, on showing his winger inside, was not being covered efficiently.

Todd had tried to win one header against the towering Ben May by bustling in front of the forward and, having lost out, been left out of position. 'You don't need to do that, Toddy. You're better than that.' Yemi was told he could vary his approach by seeking moments to drift out to the touchline and provide extra width.

'These are small, small things though. I think you've been fantastic. What I don't want us to do is sit back on this. We've had a few similar situations and tended to just see the game out. Let's go out, take the initiative and win it.'

There was time for a couple of minutes' animated conversation while Guy went round dispatching some individual advice. The bell sounded to signal the resumption was due and off they went.

I tore off back to my vantage point and, on sitting down, discovered I had no cup of tea. My dad hadn't bothered trying. To rub salt into that singular gaping wound, Tom Parsons and his more gallant dad had gone down to the van and had their daring rewarded by being served in an instant.

I'd barely consumed my third custard cream when Billy Bricknell, seemingly having drifted offside, chipped a delightful finish over Flitney. I couldn't help thinking of all the occasions I've heard various commentators refer to a manager's half-time words going 'out of the window'.

The style in which Eastleigh responded was as impressive as anything they have produced this season. Seven minutes after the equaliser, and having spent that time pinning their visitors back, a flowing attack ended up with McAllister's scuffed shot from two yards (RH 'I'm convinced Macca needs glasses') being palmed off the line by the Fleet's right-back Chris Sessegnon. With the defender sent off, Reason cracked his penalty high to the keeper's left – said 'keeper, Preston Edwards, had guessed Reason would repeat his earlier trick, going low to the left of goal.

237

There was never the merest suggestion that Ebbsfleet's ten men would cause the same discomfort inflicted by the same number of opposition players on some of this campaign's less notable days. A lung-busting Spence burst forward teed up Jai to curl in a beautiful third. That ended the scoring, but it could have been more.

After the pent-up pre-match desire, bordering on frenzy, to accomplish exactly what they had, I expected a raucous dressing room. The victorious players stayed out after the whistle for what is now a regular on-field de-brief and warm down. I walked in to see the faces of Fleetwood, this the last of his four-game ban, and Collins. Jamie was forced off early in the second half after rolling his ankle, the same misfortune to befall him prior to Christmas. He was, nonetheless, admirably upbeat – and a much cooler person than the one beseeching and motivating his colleagues from that same seat two hours earlier.

Fleets was checking the Conference South results on his phone, primarily that of Bromley. They had won 2–1. Nobody was surprised. It was the score that all, as they shuffled back inside, wanted to know. The overriding reaction was 'F*** them. We'll do our job and catch them. We're better than they are.'

Flitney was soon energetically explaining to his understudy, Jack Dovey, the circumstances that had caused him to be stranded from his line when Bricknell planted the ball into the back of his net. The 'keepers sit together and stick together. Likewise, the tough as teak defensive pairing – Todd and Beckwith.

Gosport Borough's 1–0 victory at Weston elicited plenty of comment. Most shared Collins' view: 'That'll be because they were f***** and ran themselves into the ground against us.' Jamie Brown had scored the Borough goal, on a day when his picture adorned the front of Eastleigh's match-day programme; Browner executing a tackle on Reason with a boot approximately two feet off the floor. Something of a Spitfires cult-hero, our players don't particularly hold him in the same esteem as their supporters.

Richard, smiling and plainly carrying a lighter mental load than had been the case at 2:45 pm, asked for the Leicester City result (a 2–0 win over Middlesbrough), shrugged off Bromley's latest three-point haul and headed outside. Not once all afternoon, within the confines of these four walls, had the manager raised his voice.

With each of the playing contingent back in their own domains, and full of further hand-shakes for their one-off intruder, the mood was far more 'job done' than anything resembling exultation. Even hat-trick scorer Jai, although looking decidedly cheery, wasn't bouncing off the walls.

The quiet satisfaction even extended to the naturally rambunctious duo of Southam and McAllister. Spence and Green's reserved emotions gave little away. There was a glow coming off Sam Wilson, who had been sent on for the final eight minutes. Connolly (three days on from his hearing at Wembley Stadium and condemned to sitting tight and waiting for a verdict), after an excellent half-hour display, was the first to be showered, into his tracksuit and slipping unassumingly into the night.

It was time, as well, for me to depart. A memorable and unique football occasion was at an end. I left behind a group of very contented Eastleigh footballers, but a group nevertheless whose thoughts were already turning towards Bromley on Tuesday.

While still not tempted to make the journey to southeast London by mini-bus – with 17 takers, a fully subscribed option – I will be back on civilian duty for that match. That is my lot and it is one I am ready to re-embrace. I'll never forget, though, Richard and his players' kindness in extending a welcoming arm and allowing me to lift the veil on Eastleigh FC's inner sanctum.

Back to Civvy Street

It is a recurring tale. Anticipation builds, only for the weather to scupper growing excitement. One final phone call to Bromley, made to confirm earlier news that Tuesday's (January 28th) game was going ahead, stopped us leaving in the nick of time. The pitch had since been deemed unfit. Richard bombed off to watch Cambridge United losing at home to Grimsby Town, but was nonetheless quietly impressed by our next opponents. We now have the tantalising prospect of a trip to our premier promotion rivals on April 8th – less than three weeks before the season's end.

Two days later (Thursday, January 30th) and Chris Todd was extremely relaxed about the call off. 'We had a few lads carrying knocks anyway. We'll just have to do the job when we do go there.' Glen Southam would have 'loved' to have gone and played the game. Two very different personalities, but linked by one burning desire. Indeed, during Thursday's training match, the pair was in fractious mood, the exceedingly laid-back Toddy even berating Guy Butters over his 'officiating'. Guy's crime had been to decide against awarding Todd's team a throw-in on the half-way line.

Jamie Collins, watching on with ice attached to his irksome ankle after a high octane one-to-one session with Cookie, baited Suvs by asking if he was having a 'sticky ten minutes'. 'A sticky hour more like,' came the reply. Collins' 'cheer-leading' included offering congratulations to Ben Strevens for a 'beautiful cross', when his mate had actually executed a sublime chip, from out wide, over the head of Jack Dovey and into the net.

The most unusual sound reverberated out of the Collins/Cook workout. It isn't often an injured player's slog away from the main group is full of laughter. It'll take more than a dicky ankle to keep the phlegmatic 'JC' down. He is optimistic that he'll be fit for Saturday's huge FA Trophy tie (forecast rain allowing; the resilient 8am match-day gang are girding themselves for another long, long pitch-forking shift).

McAllister's present health is not as robust as Jamie's. The main block of Thursday's training was finished off with some short sprints. On run number two Craig pulled up, immediately limping across to where Collins, myself and, tellingly, Cookie were stationed. The strain, which extends from a gluteal muscle down to the back of his knee and which has dogged him all season, had recurred.

Collins tried to make light of his good friend's predicament. A seething Macca was in no mood to be consoled. His left foot (attached to the end of his healthy leg) took an almighty swipe at an innocent water bottle. Cookie's explanation, replete with plenty of scientific words, of what the problem might be was well beyond me. It did, though, in its gist, suggest that Macca is facing another period of inaction.

That blow will have put the tin hat on a day when Richard was already in less than tip-top mood. Completely dissatisfied, a mental state he shared with his players, at how a practice game unfolded, he had sent the 19 men under his charge for a calming five-minute walk.

Inner calm restored, the manager gave a hint towards his line-up for Saturday when specific game preparation began. Yemi, at that time, was not in the first-choice 11. Watching from the side-lines as Richard spent a minute speaking in ushered tones with the player, that decision appeared especially significant. The boss's careful man-management of an individual seemingly set to miss out on a colossal day in Eastleigh's history could prove essential. McAllister's later misfortune could well present Yemi with a very quick reprieve. Reece Connolly, who was electrifying throughout the session, was one of the likely starters.

Jamie Bulpitt was the sole participant of the day's trainers to have tasted some Tuesday night action. The fast-improving 19 year old's outing for Bashley was, however, curtailed by a first-half floodlight failure. Speaking to Jamie, notwithstanding that aborted appearance, gives a real impression that his loan at the New Forest club is playing a pivotal role in his development. It is impossible to wish this amiable youngster, with no shortage of devil in his on-pitch style, anything but good luck. In this era of flourishing sub 6ft midfield players, it feels almost pre-historic to suggest that a footballer would hasten his advancement by bulking up. It is, though, true of Jamie.

When, back in the club, I sat down to interview Suvs, Ross Flitney – in cheerier mode than when hollering in fury after letting a ball slip into his net during some late session shooting practice – generously offered to make the tea. (If only it were that easy on a Saturday at 3:45pm.) Having, like me, politely declined, the captain was honest when I asked him about his exclusion from the line-up 12 days previously against Gosport Borough.

A smile remained plastered across Glen's face as he assured me that, disappointing as that was, he understood the manager's decision.

'I want to play every game – every minute of every game. Even if I'm playing well and have to miss a minute of a game I'm not happy. That's just my mentality, but it isn't always the case that I play all the time.

'We've got a good squad here with a lot of depth. There are a lot of good players and competition all round. It's going to happen. We'd won a succession of matches, but I got a suspension and we won the game I missed [the FA Trophy tie against Dover]. The lads that had played deserved the chance to do so again.

'It's part of football. I was disappointed, but anyone who's happy not playing, I think they need their head testing. I still want us to win and I love my team, so it's no problem.'

The matter of being denied a berth in the side is a sensitive one to broach with any footballer, but never more so than if the man in question is Glen

Southam. Suvs was back in for the games with Weston and Ebbsfleet. He agreed with my assessment of Saturday's win (which Richard has since said was one of *the* performances of his 16 months in charge) as having been greeted in the changing room with certain serenity, as opposed to delirium. Nevertheless, the Spitfires skipper's eyes narrowed a notch when he confirmed that the beaten team had overdone their celebrations after October's fixture.

'I wouldn't say this was revenge, more a feeling of satisfaction. On the night there we played very well and dominated for 90 minutes. We didn't deserve to lose and afterwards we got a little bit of stick from their lads. I think that was a little bit premature considering how early in the season it was. We wouldn't do that. On Saturday, we were calm, we did our job and that's as far as it goes for us.

'After the game, we knew we've still got some catching up to do. We're not content with beating Ebbsfleet. It's just another game and we've got three games in hand yet. We'd have loved to have gone and played Bromley on Tuesday. Until we get to the top of the league I don't think there's a player in that dressing room who will be satisfied and the management certainly won't be.'

Those words perhaps best encapsulate the pervading feeling of fortitude and ambition that I instantly detected seven months ago at Eastleigh FC – and which I have been attempting to convey ever since. Not one single person currently at the club – be they directly involved with the team or furiously burrowing away in the background – has ever hinted at any loss of focus towards the year's aim. It had taken 30 seconds during the day's ill-fated training game for Richard, emphasising this point, to first express verbal dissatisfaction. Unhappy with the tempo and calibre of the play, his brief interjection ended with the words, 'We've come too far to start letting each other down now.'

Even two days prior to a match against the team that is second in the Conference Premier and which by winning would put him a semi-final tie away from a first ever Wembley appearance, Suvs was poised enough to keep his overriding priority in mind.

'The league is still the main focus. If you give me a choice between winning the league and getting to the Trophy final, I'd rather win the league because that's our main goal.'

Collins, to my slight surprise, had expressed a similar view when discussing his fitness with me. He described the league encounter with Dover next Tuesday as more important than this Trophy clash and therefore his main target for a return. On a different note, Jamie continues to ask after this book's progress and even sounded moderately impressed that I hope to have it stocked in actual 'bookshops'. His interest is appreciated!

A measure of 'JC's' joie de vivre on Thursday owed itself to him having spent the previous evening as part of West Ham United's support at Stamford Bridge; the Hammers having earned a fine point in a 0–0 draw with a piqued Jose Mourinho's Chelsea. Jamie, along with a host of his colleagues, defies the characterisation of footballers as having little interest in the game outside their own exertions. This lot can frequently be heard discussing the latest televised fixture – be it a Premier League humdinger or a midweek offering from League Two – and the merits of various players and managers across the country and beyond.

Away from playing preparation, the expected arrival at the Silverlake of roughly 500 Cambridge folk continues to exercise the minds of a good proportion of Spitfires' staff. A pointer to the size of the operation and 'impending big day' was the sight of a number of players asking Mick Geddes about ticketing arrangements for their families. With plenty of police on duty, stewards spirited in from St Mary's Stadium to shore up our usual deployment and more coming from East Anglia to supervise the away hordes, nothing has been left to chance.

It's a match whose staging would have been considered extremely unlikely when I happened upon the Ian Baird-managed local Conference South outfit. My Eastleigh epiphany occurred shortly after a renowned 2009 visit by AFC Wimbledon, on their way up through the leagues, when the away club's travelling entourage swelled the crowd figure above the 2,000 mark. Regardless of their flirting with an FA Trophy run three years ago, the prospect of Spitfires' progress this deep into any cup competition has always seemed remote.

Shifted from my usual seat (back one row), requiring a flask to guarantee a hot drink and sure to be squeezed into a chock-a-block main stand, I will be deprived of a few of my beloved non-league luxuries. Even a half-time skip to the Gents will be a mission. It's a jolt to the system for which I'm ready. I have long since accepted that, if the progress that Stewart Donald, Richard Hill, every single player, member of staff, and so many supporters are striving to achieve for Eastleigh is to be accomplished, some things have to change.

'THE MORE WE WIN, THE BETTER IT WILL BE'

It is exciting to be living through this transformation, a whole other element to my relationship with the club that I could never have foreseen. Cambridge United at home, two rounds from Wembley, is another staging post on this captivating voyage.

28

ONE DIRECTION

That we had any football to watch on Saturday, February 1ˢᵗ, was, yet again, down to head groundsman Tony's industry and expertise – and the dedicated 8am club. The latter's efforts were recorded by Jamie Graham, the club's cameraman and after-match interviewer, for posterity.

The pitch, not too pleasing on the eye but perfectly playable nonetheless, was never going to stage an exhibition of free-flowing end-to-end football. Eastleigh and Cambridge United, though, produced a compelling contest; hard fought, tactical and decorated with flashes of individual and collective skill.

The only shame was an official crowd of 757. That figure's announcement provoked suspicion among the more sceptical minds present. There were, however, more gaps evident at the Silverlake than anybody had hoped to see during the frenzied lead up to the match. From Cambridge, 500 anticipated spectators were, in reality, something nearer half that number. The local police force presence and their insistence on crowd segregation proved needless measures. The away troop was no more spoiling for trouble than I was inclined to stand exposed to the elements on the temporary open terrace, which, incidentally, was where the owner could be found watching his investment.

Sat to my right at the back of the main stand were three generations of a family all paying their maiden visit to the home of Eastleigh FC. The granddad of the clan, a veteran of watching football across the country in the course of following Bradford City and West Ham United, was impressed by the fare on offer (information I gleaned at half-time while simultaneously ruminating on why tea from a flask is never quite the same as its freshly poured equivalent).

My neighbour for the afternoon was equally enthused by the welcome Brian had afforded him when, the previous Monday, he popped into the clubhouse to purchase his tickets. A cup of coffee and a welcoming chat, and instantly the first-timer was being charmed by the Spitfires. As we parted at full-time he suggested he'd be back.

That is why these one-off 'occasions' are so essential. They provide the platform to lure new support with its accompanying cash; the vehicle for the initial seduction that will hopefully lead to a long-term relationship. Extra bodies in the ground and consequent increased revenue are a necessity for any aspirational non-league club.

None of which is any use without a team that fulfils its side of the bargain. Facing such strong, confident opposition was a fine marker for our progress. There was little to separate the sides during an opening 45 minutes in which Eastleigh played the better football. Collins, despite his reservations, was in the starting line-up and went on to be named as man of the match. His imposing midfield display left him with no rivals for the award.

That is not to denigrate the performances elsewhere. Not one of the 11 had an off-day. Therefore, when looking for a player to withdraw in favour of Reece Connolly, Richard was confronted with something of a dilemma. Yemi was the unlucky man and became the first individual in Eastleigh blue this season who I've witnessed show public displeasure at a managerial decision. It was nothing outrageous. Just hands pointedly on the hips as his number 9 flashed up on the fourth official's board and ensuing head shaking. Indeed, once he'd completed his desolate trudge to the dugout, and regardless of his irritation, Yemi shook Richard's hand.

The 66th-minute introduction of Connolly, who I had, of course, expected to play (second-guessing the boss's team is becoming a more futile exercise every week), was a bold move designed to win the game on the day. As it happened, within two minutes of Reece entering the field, the otherwise impregnable Beckwith and Todd allowed a long ball to escape them and send Ryan Bird on the charge at Flitney's goal. The 'keeper flew from his line and, with everybody of a Spitfires leaning inwardly pleading for him not to dive in, rashly went to ground and upended the forward. Luke Berry – some player – scored the penalty and Eastleigh's Wembley dream is over.

'It's a cruel game,' commented a still crestfallen Todd on Twitter later that evening. Certainly, Richard's men deserved more. Even my dad, initially fearing a replay for its Tuesday night long drive scenario, was thrashing about dramatically as he roared the team forward in their pursuit of an equaliser.

News, as we filed away from the stand, that Everton had bounced back from a horrific Merseyside derby cuffing by beating Aston Villa provided a flicker of personal solace. Still, this slender defeat, within touching distance of a national cup final, stung. But, on reflection, with 20 league games between Eastleigh and their principal target for the year, the FA Trophy run, enthralling as it was, might have ended at just the right time.

To emphasise the prize on offer if all goes well from here, the Silverlake was due, until its pitch was considered to have taken enough of a pounding for one week, to play host to Dover on Tuesday night. Cambridge's next Conference Premier outing – a clash with Kidderminster Harriers – has been selected for live television coverage by BT Sport.

The Us' FA Trophy semi-final opponents will be Grimsby Town. Astonishingly, Gosport Borough, whom one Eastleigh player (name withheld) last week described to me as 'absolutely f★★★★★★ useless', won their quarter-final at the Conference North's table-topping outfit North Ferriby United. One of the Borough, Aldershot Town or Havant & Waterlooville is going to Wembley.

In light of our latest postponement, Richard set his sat-nav for Maidenhead to watch Saturday's scheduled opponents beaten 3–0 by Weston-super-Mare. Any prospect, at Thursday training (February 6th), of walking through a tactical ploy based on what the boss had witnessed at York Road was stymied by another furious downpour. The 1 hour 45 minute session was, by necessity, perpetual motion.

There is an argument that these commonplace English conditions are a contributory factor to the country's dearth of technically gifted footballers. Certainly, in the cold and driving rain, there is no appetite for standing still or studiously honing individual craft and touch. Nevertheless, the football on display was not only fast paced, it was bright, skilful and intelligent. Reece Connolly shone and, in scoring one of his goals, tied Dan Spence in knots. Nobody, in the year I've been watching Dan, has managed that feat. Not a man who gives much away, Spence was bristling.

Reece no longer has the title of 'Eastleigh new boy'. That honour belongs to Ben Wright, signed on a month's loan from Salisbury City. The first I, and just about anybody else, knew of this move was when 'Wrighty' (of course) was one of the 21 men involved in this session on the artificial pitches that lie outside the Silverlake Stadium.

Ben scored against the Spitfires during pre-season (unwittingly, when he profited from Jack Dovey smashing the ball into him) and recently had a temporary spell at Basingstoke Town. I was surprised when I saw Wright had been allowed to head for the 'Stoke, especially as he only joined up with Salisbury in the summer. At 25 years old, Ben is an embodiment of the nomadic non-league footballer. Eastleigh, including loan periods, will be his 18th (*eighteenth*) club – and he's been at a few of them more than once. That will be an issue on the agenda when I interview our latest recruit next week.

Ben's training ground playing display was powerful and direct. If his touch failed him or he misplaced a pass, though, there was a tendency towards self-castigation – something that Richard was instantly onto, geeing his player up, instructing him to instantly forget any perceived lapse. It was noticeable that the manager was similarly keen to boost an unusually downcast Yemi, commending his efforts wherever possible. The age-old truth about some players requiring an arm around the shoulder, others a kick up the backside, was evident here as Richard astutely used the former method to lift Yemi's spirits.

While the group worked, McAllister was running encouragingly freely around the pitch's periphery. Cookie, hot on the heels of restoring Jamie Collins' fitness at breakneck speed, appears to be applying his sorcerer's touch once more. With yet another competitor on the scene for his striking jersey, Macca will undoubtedly be working every permissible minute to ensure he is available to Richard extremely soon.

When the manager announced that Thursday's session would finish with a full-scale, no restrictions, ten-minute match, a perishing Cookie turned to me, saying forlornly, 'I'm not sure I can last that long, Paul.' That he eventually withstood the inclement weather was purely down to the quality of what we were watching. With everybody in rare form, fingers are firmly crossed that, against the odds, we can play this weekend.

Speaking to Mark Blake that afternoon, the son of TSSC chairman Chris and somebody who is devoting hours beyond the call to keeping the Silverlake turf in nick, the signs aren't good. As we discussed the sodden ground, Flitney joined in. The 'keeper, discussing the perils of playing on marshland-like pitches, said that he had wanted to put the brakes on his penalty-conceding charge against Cambridge, but feared becoming rooted in the mud should he do so.

Such comic-book plights shouldn't have to enter the mind of a footballer when the stakes are so high. This will be the reality for a while yet. Thankfully, we've got a goalkeeper whose judgement is ordinarily sound and people like Mark – who was at the ground eight and a half hours prior to the Trophy quarter-final kick-off. It is a combination to get games on and won.

One person who won't be on the pitch, regardless of whether the Maidenhead game goes ahead, is Chris Dillon. Dills, though, despite being out of the side since November 23rd due to the sustained fitness and form of Beckwith and Todd, told me that he's loving his unexpected, but well-deserved and hard-earned, opportunity with the Spitfires. After four years on a scholarship in Alabama and a hastily aborted venture to play for Doveton Soccer Club in the Melbourne State League's second division, Chris is delighted to have got a foot in the door at such a progressive club.

Any thoughts of utilising his sports science degree are on hold. Dills is happy – other than spending a bit of spare time working at a leisure centre – to be focusing entirely on his football. The chance to regularly train with this group of players, he says, is invaluable. He couldn't have chosen a more appropriate day, when the standard of work had been stratospherically high and its pace unforgivingly rapid, to express that view.

I dwelt for a second after Thursday's training was complete, as I peeled off my drenched waterproof before heading for the relative glow of the clubhouse, on the fact that I seem to be turning into something of a storm chaser. Following a *Wizard of Oz*-style typhoon that swirled through the Silverlake and shook the main stand roof during our home match against Gosport Borough, I had been at Havant & Waterlooville's Westleigh Park on Tuesday (February 4th) night where our local adversary played their delayed FA Trophy quarter-final against Aldershot Town.

Surrounded in the main stand by mostly away supporters, my dad and I looked on as the Hawks, aided by Shots' Jordan Roberts' mindless first-half sending off, thumped their visitors 4–1 in the filthiest conditions imaginable. The weather could claim an assist in at least two of the home team's goals. Even so, the result was no more than Lee Bradbury's troublingly fast-improving side deserved. Havant & Waterlooville and Gosport Borough will compete for a place at Wembley – you'd have got very long odds on that when we all started out on the Trophy journey nearly three months ago.

The 1,125 attendance for Tuesday's match, swelled by a large Shots contingent, dwarfs the Spitfires' comparative figure for Cambridge's visit. Or it did, until the club recognised an error in their initial calculation and released a statement revising the number of spectators at last Saturday's game from 757 up to 957. That sounds more like it!

Obviously hardened by my trials by rain, I actually stood utterly spellbound for five minutes post-Thursday's training session as Wright and Jai Reason passed a ball to each other across a 20-yard distance. Their mastery of the art was incredible; the ball seemingly on a string, fiercely struck, fizzing and veering this way and that, before landing precisely at its intended recipient's feet. And these two Englishmen play in, effectively, our country's 6th division. Maybe that theory about the pernicious effects on footballers of our chilly temperatures and frequently soggy days needs further investigation.

Nevertheless, when our country takes a buffeting of the type presently being dished out by Mother Nature, there is simply no opportunity for many of those footballers to demonstrate their underrated prowess. Maidenhead at home, as expected, was canned. It was, then, back to the artificial turf for Monday's (February 10th) training – the start of a week in which even Manchester City and Everton were forced by the apocalyptic elements to postpone matches (that on the same night, Wednesday, February 12th, that, to my dismay, I realised Liverpool were going to win the Premier League).

Chris Todd, under the usual murky skies, assumed control of Monday's opening half-hour of activities. This included overseeing some agile, rat-a-tat-tat keep-ball work – during which serial offenders were treated to bouts of merciless ribbing.

He might have responsibility entrusted in him to take these tentative first steps towards his post-playing career (duties that extend to some scouting on Richard's behalf), but Toddy isn't immune to the manager's forthright observations. Richard, having halted a characteristically pugnacious practice match, picked out his defender for having earlier struck an overly ambitious pass: 'Toddy. If I wanted a ball playing centre-half, I wouldn't have signed you.'

A degree of tetchiness developed late in the frenetic game, something Richard addressed with the group immediately after its conclusion. He understood that, when asking them to play at full tilt on a small-scale pitch, tempers are wont to fraying. A few of the players went on to release their pent-up frustrations by firing some session-ending pot-shots at goal. Dan Spence, joining in and sending his first dig wildly off target, caught his manager's attention. 'Get inside, Spence. I don't know why full-backs want to shoot.'

The major issue for the boss, as February begins to mirror July for its lack of competitive action, is that, to use his description of the situation, the players are bored. Matches are in short supply and keeping them interested is a fiendishly difficult job. That is why the plan for Tuesday was to take Eastleigh's footballers for a spinning class (instructor-led indoor cycling; the torture of choice for countless fitness devotees across the country).

Before Ben Wright could escape on Monday, he subjected himself to my questioning. Interview finished, Richard enquired of me what our new forward had said for himself. Reluctant, with Wrighty still within earshot, to discuss the details, I was quickly set straight on the fact that the manager, frankly, couldn't care less who heard what I relayed.

I was able to tell him that Ben attributes his hefty number of clubs purely to a desire to play football. Like Southam, who recently told me that people happy to sit on the sidelines 'need their head testing', Wrighty is not content to stay anywhere he's second choice. This is a man with designs on winning a move back into the Football League, having first made the jump from non-league to Peterborough United five years ago. Talking about his qualities – 'scoring goals and creating chances' – Ben doesn't want for confidence. Equally important, his words were laced with a conviction that this move is going to work.

Unsurprisingly given his track record, a stack of the 25 year old's – I'm still staggered he's got ten years on me – new team-mates double up as old colleagues. Most notably, when Ben had his most prolific season yet – scoring 17 goals for Braintree in the Conference Premier – he was working in tandem with a certain Jai Reason.

One in has been offset by one out. Three goalkeepers clocked in on Monday morning: Ross Flitney, Lewis the Cat and Tom Coffey. Jack Dovey has traded the bleak English landscape for Melbourne and a life-shifting opportunity to continue his career playing semi-professionally in Australia. More prosaically, it's a chance for Jack to finally play regular football. An integral part of the Spitfires unit when he arrived under the tutelage of Ian Baird, it's been an entirely different story for Jack since Richard decided he needed the experience of Flitney in a side with immediate promotion as its target.

I've described already my admiration for Jack's relentlessly positive attitude.

He displayed some ability, and no less in the way of cojones, when he came in from the cold to replace the eye-infected Ross for the pre-Christmas games against Gateshead and Dover. Everybody at Eastleigh is together in hoping that Jack makes a real go of it in Oz – and if he is responsible for that dressing room 'mix tape', I hope our Antipodean cousins help him re-evaluate his music tastes.

Regardless of having 20 games still to squeeze in, this was a blank midweek in Eastleigh FC's calendar. On a related issue, the Conference's member clubs have voted against allowing the installation of 3G playing surfaces, a decision that, in the wake of a near unprecedented spate of call-offs, has attracted a host of brickbats. In the midst of the present chaos, the certainty of avoiding a repeat scenario in future makes the 3G option appear a 'no-brainer'. That doesn't consider the effects on the bodies of the men who will be asked to play on the turf. I readily recall our players still complaining of aches and pains close to a week after playing on Maidstone United's 'artificial' pitch.

Privett Park was – just about – playable for Gosport's Tuesday night (February 11th) game against Whitehawk (the damaged clubhouse is also back up and running – some tarpaulin hastily affixed to provide an auxiliary roof). Prior to kick-off, having been unable to resist getting out to see some live action, my dad and I bumped into Guy Butters on a mission to watch the Sussex outfit – a side we are yet to meet this season. After a jovial chat with the Spitfires' assistant gaffer we watched a very good visiting team win 2–0.

Since their promotion last term, the Hawks have been bedevilled by trouble. Most notoriously, they sacked two players who are due to stand trial in connection with match-fixing charges. On a solely footballing level, the club's manager, Darren Freeman, having in the space of four years dragged Whitehawk from the County league to the sixth tier, was sacked late in January. Now managed by former Farnborough boss Steve King and with a collection of fresh faces in the team, they are a vastly improved unit to that which was being beaten left, right, and centre earlier in the season. And, I repeat, we have got to play them twice.

It was never going to be easy, this title-winning business. Tonbridge Angels, in the relegation places and 2–1 winners at the Silverlake in November, are a reminder of that fact. After waterlogging precluded the return match taking place on Saturday, a mysteriously dry spell enabled a hasty re-arrangement to Monday night (February 17th).

If I tell you that during the training ground review on Thursday (February

20th) Richard began by expressing his regret at accepting the date 'just to fulfil a fixture', you can probably guess how the match went. The boss was furious with himself for allowing a situation to occur whereby Tonbridge had trained on Saturday, whereas his men went into the game after a three-day break and no preparation session.

The result was a messy first half and a second period camped in Tonbridge territory desperately trying to recover a two-goal deficit. When Fleetwood scored after 49 minutes, an equaliser appeared an inevitability. If we were still there now, it wouldn't have come. Shots rained in from all angles and ended up in all places other than the back of the net.

That aspect of his team's performance, and their less than assiduous collective defending when falling behind, the manager wasn't taking responsibility for. His exasperation on the night could be heard from the opposite side of the pitch. A wayward Southam strike at goal: 'SOUTHAM, WHAT ARE YOU DOING? PASS THE BALL.'

When the skipper was dragged off, the dugout in which he'd spend the next half an hour took an almighty blow from his right boot. Suvs' vocal frustration boomed around the Angels' Longmead Stadium. So, laudably, did his subsequent encouragement of his team-mates.

Tonbridge have now collected the best part of a quarter of their 25 points against Eastleigh. This defeat left everybody involved with the inescapable feeling of another opportunity lost. Bromley had played on Saturday – and lost 3–2 at bottom club Dorchester. That 11-point gap refuses to budge.

Will, who was in at right-back, took a bit of after-match stick on the fans' message board. He didn't have a great night, but neither did most. Spence, Strevens and Todd were in the minority in being anywhere near the top of their respective games.

I remain convinced that with his natural, easy ability, towering stature and elegant stride Will Evans is going to be a seriously good footballer. When I returned to the clubhouse after Thursday's (February 20th) training session, Will and Jamie Collins were waiting (one patiently, the other less so) for their lunch, having completed gym workouts. Will's knee, which caused such concern early in the campaign, had been feeling sore. Jamie continues to nurse his ankle. Both are ok to feature on Saturday, but it is plain that Will is going to need some tender care on the way to producing his best in a Spitfires jersey.

Richard had begun addressing the faults evident at Tonbridge by working, once more, with his array of midfielders and attackers – while Guy applied his defensive expertise to drilling that unit. A typical 'fan', I was drawn to the striking group. McAllister, Reason, Southam and Connolly – RH 'Reece, have you got a twin brother?' – had all passed up presentable scoring chances, when Yemi dragged a weak close-range shot against a post. The manager's whistle was slung to the floor as he cried, 'F★★★★★★ SCORE.'

I didn't know where to look when, within 30 seconds, Strevens chipped the next clear scoring chance into Flitney's hands. Richard bit his tongue, waiting until all those under his instruction were bunched together to tell them that they 'go soft' in the penalty box. As if to prove his boss's point, Fleetwood promptly displayed a touch to receive possession that would have graced the San Siro, strode into the area and, from six yards, perhaps in homage to his Welsh roots, scooped the ball over the bar.

RH seething and emphasising every word: 'You have got to score a goal.'

The theme was carried into the later Tonbridge post-mortem. After the manager's mea culpa, Fleets suggested that the team is simply not ruthless enough. That, as they are sure another chance will be along any second, people are lax in front of goal (an issue Flitney touched on as far back as October). Furthermore, the nasty, hard to beat edge to the side, so evident in the campaign's initial months, has disappeared.

Todd wholeheartedly agreed with Fleetwood's second point. He argued that opponents, after watching Eastleigh, will have concluded that surrendering possession to them isn't a problem – their thought process being: 'Eastleigh will have loads of the ball, but they won't hurt you with it.' There had been plenty on Monday night to support that claim.

Strevens advocated the idea of, every so often, being more direct (a tactic discussed a few months back, but rarely used since). Continually playing out from defence, suggested Strevs, gives the opposition time to regroup. When the ball is in the final third we have the players to wreak havoc, so let's not be frightened to get it there quickly. The ultra-professional Strevens was also in no doubt that, in the event of a call-off at Farnborough this weekend, everybody should be called in to train.

It was another discussion that I consider myself fortunate to have been granted access to. How many football supporters would covet the chance to listen in as their team dissect what they believe led to a disappointing result? We all go away with our own opinions and ideas about what went wrong. The easy assumption is that the players won't care as much as us. They do. It was, however, back to relaxed mode over lunch. The positive outcome of the Great Britain women curlers' bronze medal match at the Winter Olympics was eagerly discussed, before attentions were turned to an unflattering picture, used to accompany his newspaper interview, of Ben Wright on his Peterborough unveiling.

Before they had made their way indoors for their meals, Richard had applied the final words to the training ground review. 'We keep saying it will be alright. Well, it needs to start being alright now.' The boss warned his players of his intention to suggest in the local paper that the title is Bromley's to lose. It was time, the manager said, to exert a bit of pressure onto our rivals. He didn't believe the sentiments that he would be expressing for public consumption. It's in our hands. Let's go and do it – starting at Farnborough on Saturday (February 22nd).

What should have been a smooth 55.5-mile journey to that game in north Hampshire became something far more circuitous. My dad's decision to opt for a 'shorter route' offered by his sat-nav (fuel economy being the motivation for this choice) had the entirely foreseeable consequence of leading us out into the sticks of this picturesque county – and headlong into strife. Signs warning of road closures due to flooding were dismissed confidently by the driver: 'Ah, these will have just been left up – nobody's bothered to take them away.' Imagine my (complete lack of) surprise when that supposition proved inaccurate.

Our elongated travel time (roughly 1 hour and 40 very long minutes) enabled us to listen to the entire 95 minutes of Everton's match at Chelsea. Seconds before we hurriedly parked up, Roberto Martinez's men conceded a gut-wrenching late goal to succumb 1–0.

Fuming, my gaze finally away from its fixation on the clock, I had to switch instantly from my petulant, immature worst into a personality fit for a public outing. I think, as we queued at the turnstiles with an impressive number of away fans – all of whom had been luxuriating in the clubhouse after arriving well before 2pm – I just about got away with it.

Once inside, prising a team-sheet from a club official was, in keeping with this progressively more annoying day, less than straightforward. An intervention by director John Russell persuaded the Boro man in charge of their dispensing that I was entitled to one of his precious documents, from what was a not insignificant pile.

The line-up selected by Richard disclosed that Will's knee wasn't going to be risked, even from the bench. A look at the pitch explained why. The Cherrywood Road stadium turf made Privett Park's equivalent look like a bowling green (the players were nevertheless relieved to be playing and not training). The standout revelation in the Spitfires starting 11 was the absence of Glen Southam – relegated to the bench. Connolly was brought in to play against his former club – with whom his relationship remains extremely complex – and Greener resumed left-back duties.

Without Suvs, Collins and Strevens played as a disciplined holding midfield duo, barely breaking forward from their defensive roles. Clearly, although locating an assured touch in front of goal is high on this team's priority list, shoring up the middle of the park is considered equally vital. That, after the way Tonbridge, at times, romped through that part of the field, is wholly understandable.

This was no great spectacle (actually, it was no spectacle), but Farnborough had just demonstrated a fleeting ability – with a fluid end-to-end move that concluded when Flitney pulled off a fine diving save – to overcome the quagmire of a surface, when the away side struck.

Connolly to Fleetwood, cue huge misguided and unanswered home calls for an offside flag, a cool pass rolled across the six-yard box, and Ben Wright had the easiest possible task in scoring his first Eastleigh goal. He did, mind you, appear to get the ball caught under his feet before prodding home from two yards.

On the cusp of half-time, Wrighty went over a clumsy challenge in the area. Penalty; 'an altogether dreadful decision,' reported the home club's official website. Right call from where I was sat. Since an extravagant early season miss against Eastbourne, Jai Reason has been his usual reliable self from 12 yards. Not here. A soft strike allowed Kevin Scriven to get down to his left and push clear.

Strevens and Collins continued their defensive midfield masterclass throughout the second 45 minutes – despite 'JC' grimacing and hobbling his way through the game's closing period. Todd, adhering to his vow on Thursday that this team needs to get back to being horrible to play against, was magnificent at centre-half. Along with Beckwith – captain for the day, with Suvs only featuring for the last 12 minutes – Toddy won a series of aerial battles, thriving on the physical scrap. There were a few scares along the way and more than a few chances to put the match to bed, but 1–0 it finished and that was just fine.

Whatever divergent opinions exist about Farnborough's participation in the league following their early season membership issues, the Spitfires have taken six very handy points from Spencer Day's men. That smile wreathed across the Boro manager's face last January, as he watched Eastleigh's slump at Bromley, was nowhere to be seen here.

This victory, though, did nothing to eat into that stubborn 11-point gap to the top of the table. Bromley are proving as adept as ourselves at responding in composed manner to any stumble. Despite playing with ten men for 65 minutes of their encounter with Boreham Wood, the league leaders won 2–1.

At the aforementioned Privett Park, Gosport followed up their unlikely 1–1 FA Trophy semi-final first-leg draw at Havant & Waterlooville by winning the return clash 2–0. I was both amazed and delighted by that outcome. The thought of Jamie Brown, Danny Smith, Andy Forbes and Brett Poate playing at Wembley is an endearing one. Our conquerors, Cambridge United, having squeezed by Grimsby Town, will be Borough's opponents at the national stadium.

All Spitfires might cast a cursory wishful glance towards events at Wembley on Sunday, March 23rd. It is worth noting, though, that while we continued our chase of Bromley on Tuesday (February 25th), Gosport were losing 2–1 at home against Eastbourne Borough. 'Browner' returned from suspension to be sent off and his team remain rooted to the foot of the table.

Eastleigh's midweek opponents were Maidenhead United, another club fighting against relegation and unlikely to obligingly roll over and hand us three valuable points. I'd love to discuss Monday's (February 24th) preparation for that vital game – whose scheduling allowed only three days' recovery from 90 minutes of combat on that unforgiving surface at Farnborough.

Instead, I suffered my second episode of traffic horrors within 48 hours. My regular 20-minute journey to the Silverlake was, thanks to a jam-packed

M27, extended by a full hour. I arrived to see the final 15 minutes, on the Wellington Sports Ground grass, of what was obviously another high-velocity workout – the ball fizzing from foot to foot in an intricate small-scale match.

Collins and Evans were again sentenced to a morning's labours at the mercy of Andy Cook who, in turn, was the recipient of my post-training questioning. Characteristically Collins' ankle travails did nothing to affect his jaunty disposition. Watching the last of the morning's action unfold, JC was customarily forthright with his 'coaching advice' for Beckwith and Strevens, before earning a rebuke from his manager, Jamie's offence being to continue chatting while Richard was addressing the group. A plea that he was simply chewing gum didn't wash, but was no deterrent to Collins' standing at the side of the pitch and exaggeratedly chomping in the fashion of an enthusiastically grazing cow. His boss couldn't help but laugh.

Richard wasn't so good humoured when reflecting on some criticism that had made its way to his ears. Apparently a 'supporter', after being at the Farnborough game, had been advocating the manager's removal on account of the fact that, not only should Eastleigh be running away with the title, but there aren't enough forwards in the squad.

That rather daft assertion doesn't stack up against McAllister and Yemi appearing only from the bench on Saturday – roles they reprised on Tuesday during a clash that, surprise, surprise, wasn't the stroll we wanted.

Much of that was down to Maidenhead being good; very, very good. For the past couple of years, Johnson Hippolyte, the Magpies' manager, and a man whose other life as a maker of marble kitchen worktops, my mum staggered me by recalling from his time in the spotlight at Yeading's helm, has produced easy-on-the-eye teams. Their high ideals, though, came with a questionable backbone. There was always a suspicion that, when the going got tough, Maidenhead would fold. A Conference South West Ham United (pre-Big Sam).

This version was more akin to the streetwise Magpies' edition of three years ago. Thirteen minutes had elapsed at the Silverlake when Reece Tison-Lascaris, capitalising on some ponderous defending, stole in and put his side ahead. Powerful, skilful, unafraid, and buoyed by handy loan signings from the Football League, Harry Grant and the brilliantly monikered Brentford midfielder Tyrrell Miller-Rodney, Maidenhead looked anything but a bunch with relegation issues to overcome.

In truth, for a good deal of the first half, Eastleigh didn't look like championship-winning aspirants either. Equalising through a sweet Reece Connolly finish and then, on the cusp of half-time, conceding the lead once more was the stuff of a jittery, hesitant unit, not the authoritative, confident group I am so used to watching on match day and, even more so, when training. It brought back a comment made to me by Richard a fortnight previously when I said how impressive a practice session had been: 'Oh, we'd f****** beat anyone at training.'

Richard would speak after the game about a degree of self-imposed pressure perhaps having an adverse effect on his men. Every player feels like it his duty to win this league. That responsibility, in turn, might be encumbering some individual performances.

Talking with my dad and Tom Parsons at the break, the consensus was that we were getting what we deserved – nothing. Nevertheless, I retained my belief that this was one we'd claw back, particularly if McAllister was introduced into the mix. He promptly appeared for the re-start in place of Wright, who had laid on Reece's goal after good initial work by Southam (Suvs made a quick return owing to JC being ruled out following the late injury he suffered at Farnborough). Four minutes on from his introduction and, after more bold and direct Connolly play, Macca was receiving a cross, slowing time in the manner that only the best players can, taking a touch, and rolling the ball across the box for Fleetwood to smash home.

It remained 2–2 with 90 minutes on the clock. My dad turned to me: 'That'll be it now.' 'No, I think we'll get one more chance, I can see Macca scoring,' I replied, more in hope than anything to do with a sudden aptitude for astrology. My words almost anointed me as a football visionary. A Yemi shot was deflected to McAllister, stood yards from the line. He prodded goal-wards – and was denied by a heroic Matt Ruby defensive block. A regular match-goer turned his head back towards me: 'You were nearly right.'

'Definitely 2–2 now,' said my dad. 'Mmmmmm' was all I could muster. Jai hung a cross over from the right. The playmaker was out wide as a consequence of Richard's latest tinkering; our boss had been changing and re-jigging in desperate search of a winner, while 'Drax' Hippolyte had blinked first, chucking on an extra centre-half. From Jai's delivery, Macca's colossal presence forced Elvijs Putnins into a weak punch. Strevens – a holding midfielder – picked the ball up just inside the 18-yard line, manoeuvred it beautifully, spun and crashed an unstoppable shot inside the left-upright.

Bedlam. There were only 445 people in the ground and for a lot of the match plenty of them probably thought they were watching a routine midweek encounter that wouldn't live long in the memory. Ben Strevens changed that. Richard must take a lot of credit for his changes – both tactically and personnel-wise. So must the 'Motorway End' crossbar. Additional centre-back eschewed, Maidenhead raced up the other end, had a looping header sail back off said woodwork, and looked on aghast as Harry Pritchard sent bobbling wide a more than presentable chance to snaffle a stunning equaliser.

It was never going to be easy.

Seventeen games to go and we are eight points adrift of Bromley, inactive while we played Maidenhead and with 15 fixtures left to fulfil. Pulses are quickening, even for men such as Cookie, who discussed in depth with me on Thursday his debut as a teenager for Southampton against Manchester United. The day, in August 1987, when an 18 year old marked Gordon Strachan and faced up to Bryan Robson, Norman Whiteside and Paul McGrath et al.

It was his own startling list of injuries and resultant catalogue of surgery – a discectomy, five groin operations, two on the ankle and one for the knee, with a broken leg and repetitive hamstring problems added to the sorry list for good measure – that sparked our sports therapy expert's interest in the body and its recovery. Some things just happen for a reason and it's fair to say that, through a convoluted and painful route, Cookie is answering his calling.

Like our own Strevs, flat out in the final year of his degree, Andy began his studies while still playing with Millwall – although he declares that part of his career was almost exclusively spent in the treatment room. My latest check on Strevs' progress with his Sports Science course, naively assuming that the two free days a week that he hadn't benefitted from until this season would be of huge assistance, revealed him to be an inordinately busy individual.

Assignment submission dates, as well as the omnipresent need for revision, are rendering the 24 hours in Strevens' days insufficient. Ben can't wait to fully concentrate on the football next year, relaxed in the knowledge that his hard-earned qualification is nestled away, waiting to ease the transition into life after the game.

'Having the kids all day on a Friday' was one of Strevs' explanations for his personal time shortage. That draining end to the week is certainly not reflected when he gets onto the pitch. The stamina and intensity that Strevens is bringing to every performance is astonishing. Even this early (February 27th) I think the name 'Ben Strevens' must be odds on favourite for inscription onto at least one, if not all, of the club's end of term prizes.

Thoughts now move to Saturday (March 1st). In prospect is a hasty chance to avenge January's 3–2 defeat at Weston-super-Mare. Mr Strevens will surely look forward to renewing acquaintances with Ashley Kington. Late in the Somerset clash, the Seagulls' stocky nuisance of a midfielder was chirruping away in Strevs' ear to the tune of his low opinion of Eastleigh's football team.

I saw a hitherto undisclosed side to this most placid of characters as, his face twisted with animosity, he responded to his provocateur with gusto. It required the intervention of Collins and Southam to prevent their comrade's verbal jousting turning physical. I had sat straining, at the front of the tiny stand at the Woodspring Stadium, desperately but fruitlessly attempting to hear what was being said.

On Saturday, actions should speak louder than words. If they do, Strevs will be a mite closer to earning something more for his year's endeavours than the individual awards surely coming his way.

29

MARCH HARES

On the first day of what will be a mad month of fixtures for his team, Richard Hill's photograph, the manager huddled in the clubhouse kitchen frying bacon for the early morning pitch resuscitating volunteers, was plastered across social media. It is an image that accurately represents the current feeling swirling around Eastleigh FC, that of everybody gravitating together for this big two-month drive to reach the league's summit.

When I arrived at the ground ahead of kick-off against Weston-super-Mare and some five hours after Mr Hill had been on cooking duties, everything was in fine order and ready to go. 'Everything' included all players, with the exception of Will Evans, now seemingly ceding to his stubbornly painful knee. The playing turf was messy, but, despite its recent buffeting, remarkably ripe for action.

Not that it saw a great deal during the first half. It wasn't a dull affair, more a cagey duel between two sides with their recent meeting fresh in mind. As I queued, and queued, for my interval tea, I really had no idea how this was going to turn out. The half's outstanding player, predictably, was Strevs' former agitator, Kington.

Just minutes before the break, Jai Reason produced a moment of déjà vu for all those at Farnborough seven days earlier. Fleets was brought crashing down in the box, Jai stepped up, hit to Lloyd Irish's left and the 'keeper pushed clear.

It was 'one of those days' for Jai, when nothing he tried came off. But in adversity you discover the measure of a man. By that judgement, Reason is a strong, determined character. He kept working, running, creating, in the belief that his endeavours would pay off. All around him individual levels were rising. Things were happening noticeably quicker.

Southam was another who displayed a sense of personal fortitude, delivering a stellar midfield performance, one week on from his omission at Farnborough, that won him the sponsors' (on this occasion, The Spitfires Supporters Club) bubbly.

I had thought McAllister might be due a return to the starting line-up. Ben Wright kept his place though, put in a talismanic performance and scored a blinding opening goal on 59 minutes. One rapidly became two when, in the space of one enthralling move, everything that Reason did turned to gold, including his emphatic finish after a sharp one-two with Wright.

Game over? Never. With my dad excused for the day – off being fatherly in Walton-on-Thames – I was sat next to Tom Parsons, who had an eye on making an early dash for St Mary's where the south coast's favourite team would be kicking off at 5:30pm against Southampton.

We watched on as Chas Hemmings nodded in for the most unanticipated of Weston goals. Within minutes, the same player volleyed over the bar. As we have found to our cost at times this season, such lack of killer instinct rarely goes unpunished, even down here in the Conference South. McAllister, not long introduced in place of Connolly, was quickly executing a beautiful lob from distance and the points really were safe. By its end, and with Kington having trooped off early, this display had a real, clinical champions' edge. Nearly as heartening, especially given Weston's miniscule away following, was a healthy Silverlake attendance of 602. Tom's 'beat the rush' escape allowed him to witness his 'other team' being demolished 3–0 by Liverpool.

Somewhat predictably, then, Monday's (March 3rd) was an exceptionally jovial training ground. Richard, who to my surprise wasn't at all impressed with Weston – 'they just came and waited to get beat' – was on particularly good form, notably singling Toddy out for 90 minutes of ribbing. The manager oversaw a session centred on short-slick blasts, all with the ball a central feature, and with an accompanying aim of 'getting the s★★★ out of your legs'.

The day's first passing exercise, when Richard asked the players to 'test each other', saw footballs rattling back and forth at a frightening pace. Toddy's heavy touch began his trial by the boss's tongue: 'F★★★★★ h★★★, Toddy, you had a hell of a weekend.' It was still going when the practice game that finished the morning's work was at full tilt. 'Toddy, you've been a f★★★★★ shambles all morning – you're still on the A303.'

When an ever curious Jamie Collins, having spent the morning alongside Will undertaking his work in the swimming pool, was busy catching up on all that had occurred in his absence, Todd insisted that the manager had been picking on him. JC's enquiry of Dean Beckwith as to whether there was any truth in what he'd been hearing about our centre-half adopting a physical approach to marking Yemi on the training ground elicited a deadpan, 'On the pitch, anything goes. He was running around a lot and I wasn't used to it, so I got annoyed.'

I had taken the short walk, prior to training, from clubhouse to Astroturf with Dean and Yemi. On mentioning to the latter that the next evening's game at Eastbourne Borough would be a big occasion for him returning to his former club, the response was less than enthusiastic: 'A big night from the bench.'

In fact, speaking to Richard later on, I discovered that both Yemi and McAllister will start in East Sussex. Wright and Reece Connolly – Reece looked absolutely shattered when taking his leave on Saturday – will have a rest on the bench. The boss, during Monday's session, remarked in my direction that he suspected Reece was feeling the effects of his recent exertions.

There is little doubt that our exciting, easy-going forward has never been expected to work as hard before as is required by his new club. It's a challenge that Reece is patently putting all he can into matching – always instantly responding to his manager's demands to up his off-the-ball industry. Indeed, one of the more common sounds presently heard through any Eastleigh training ground match is Richard's Clough-like tones 'encouraging' Reece to track back, tackle, and plug gaps. That will continue until fulfilling the 'ugly' tasks becomes second nature for the player. Connolly need not look far for examples of the desired application – he's surrounded by it.

I noticed that as the players took their first stretch on Monday, Richard wandered over to Jai for a chat. I don't know if penalty taking was broached, but after his colleagues had later rushed in to avoid the impending explosion from a sinister cloud that was suddenly shrouding the entire borough of Eastleigh, Fleetwood was busy stroking spot-kicks past Tom Coffey.

As he rushed past me after facilely dispatching every strike, Fleets cheerily proclaimed that he'll be shouldering spot-kick responsibilities from here. 'You can't miss three in a season, Paul.' Our jet-heeled Welshman was certainly more chipper then than he had been half an hour earlier when, after turning his ankle in a tackle with an impassive Connolly, he furiously hammered a ball into the fence before yelping obscenities as he tumbled to the floor.

With Collins and Will in the water, and Strevens and Southam 'off-site' – Strevs' studies taking precedent for a day – young Jack Masterton was called over from the development group that had been engaged in their Monday morning workout under the instruction of Lee Peacock. Jack has a frame that suggests the slightest contact might leave him in a crumpled heap. In actuality, he is much tougher than that. Most striking is the self-assurance that the left-back has, being not the slightest bit fazed by his sporadic elevations into first-team environs. The package comes complete with awareness and decision-making ability on the pitch – all of which has combined to convince Richard that Jack's not far off a first-team run-out.

Collins' ankle has now been injected, hence his non-involvement in a training session taking place on an artificial surface, and he is in the party for Eastbourne. Jamie will journey east a day on from overcoming his suspicions and devouring a plate of post-exercise Thai green chicken curry. JC's avowed preference for something 'a bit more normal, like a tikka masala' and Wright's removal of any trace of mushroom as he scooped up his portion, a manoeuvre executed with surgical precision, had poor old Paula tearing her hair out. 'I should just cook a load of plain chicken and they'd be thrilled.'

The TSSC mini-bus made its way to Tuesday night's (March 4th) fixture at Eastbourne with all 17 seats filled. A relieved Chris Blake, the supporters' club chief, must be equally gratified to see coach seats filling up for Saturday's sojourn to Concord Rangers in Essex.

One of the many regular independent travellers, Mike Wimbridge, a committee man and supporter from way back in the Spitfires' Wessex League days, told me of his disbelief that he had found himself thinking we'd missed the midfield control of Jamie Collins on Saturday. Mike confessed that he'd spent much of the season moaning that JC is too slow and has a limited passing range. Jamie has, of course, long since forced me to revise my pre-season misgivings about what he might contribute to the team – doubts that now seem more incredible to me every day.

After a bafflingly labyrinthine process to secure my entry pass and a complex crusade to seize a team-sheet, it was already time to take a seat directly behind the two Priory Lane dugouts. Watching on from my all-encompassing perspective, I was amazed by how introverted Richard remained throughout what was a high-quality, compelling contest. Tommy Widdrington, by contrast, didn't let any incident go by without booming comment. The spiky Geordie also opted against shaking our boss's hand at full-time, instead purposefully striding onto the pitch towards his players.

As for the game itself, after a pretty bright start, the Spitfires spent a lot of the first half on the back-foot, straining every sinew attempting to suppress some impressively nimble and intelligent Borough attackers – a namecheck for Darren Lok, Chris Shephard, Stacy Long and Elvis Hammond. The last of that quartet shone at the Silverlake earlier in the campaign for Farnborough, the club he left for Eastbourne in January.

Getting to half-time score-less had become the principal objective, when Flitney's poor punch fell to Ian Simpemba. The defender, formerly a Havant & Waterlooville man, acrobatically turned a left-footed strike into the top corner of goal.

Our side returned from their sit-down with more discernible vigour, but couldn't locate any end product. With 23 minutes to play Richard went for broke. Off came Yemi, a curiously subdued McAllister and a head-shaking Jai. Collins, Connolly and Wright formed the three-pronged cavalry sent on to save the day. The manager, on the quiet, hadn't been optimistic about taking anything from this game, but his trio of changes left no question regarding his ambition on the night.

My dad, in pursuit of some goalmouth action snaps, had decamped to a spec behind the goal, leaving me an isolated jack-in-the-box when Wright twice came agonisingly close to equalising. If I was feeling in any way self-conscious as the single away fan in this part of the ground, it didn't stop me jumping deliriously to my feet, and a few feet further into the air when Fleetwood surged down the left and, after a slight ricochet sat the ball up asking for a clobbering, smashed a pearler of a 20-yard shot into the same part of the net that Simpemba had hit so unerringly 34 minutes previously.

Fleets was booked for his shirt-off revelry, a moment he shared with the clamouring Spitfires behind the goal, all surging down to join in a minute's hysteria. And it could have been even better, more chances coming and going in the final quarter-hour.

But it could have been worse. A stoppage-time period of three minutes was being announced as Hammond made a late dash for the penalty box and, to my horror and that of the occupants of the dugout immediately in front of me, went down under Collins' attentions. JC had been absolutely magnificent in his 25 minutes on the pitch, but his coming together with Borough's striker left the match's outcome in the gift of Frankie Raymond – an ex-Eastleigh loanee.

Flitney meandered from his goal to take up a debate with the referee about the ball's positioning on the spot. On it rumbled, our 'keeper's name eventually going into the book. Back on his line, after the lengthy interruption he had carefully engineered, Flitney dived full-length to his left and palmed Raymond's penalty away to safety. On this occasion I was too wrapped up in my own fervour to notice how exuberantly my fellow Spitfires, away to the right at the opposite end of the ground to the drama, reacted to a glorious, and potentially critical, moment in the season.

Bath City had done us a favour on Saturday by drawing 2–2 at Bromley. Now it was the turn of Paul Doswell and Sutton United no less. Tied at two each going into added time and at roughly the same point that Flitney was gloving Raymond's 12-yard strike clear of his goal, Sutton were taking a lead at Bromley's Hayes Lane. The Us hurriedly scored another to win 4–2. That 11-point gap has, within seven days, been sliced down to five. It hasn't gone unnoticed that Sutton, five points in our wake, are appearing in Eastleigh's rear-view mirror, although we hold a priceless two games in hand on Doswell's team, as we do on Bromley.

My main pre-match concern, aside from hoping that Eastbourne's Wetherspoons' food would be up to standard – it was – had been whether Borough's blank weekend just gone would become an advantage late in the game. It proved a misguided worry. I should have heeded Toddy's words, spoken during our conversation the day before. After saying that he's 'enjoying his football more than ever' – some statement after a not too shabby career to date – the defender revealed that he's coming out of games untroubled by any aches or pains. Toddy partly attributes his robust state to slogging up hills near his home in Devon over the recent downtime. That dedication to preserving peak physical condition is paying obvious dividends.

Unfortunately, and to the great consternation of spectacular goal-scorer Fleetwood, we won't see any re-run of the thrilling conclusion to the action at

Eastbourne. Jamie Graham, having been (partially) lured away by Arsenal FC, wasn't in East Sussex to record events. The Eastleigh cameraman's all-weather diligence has impressed the Gunners enough for them to offer him some freelance work, duties that will impact his attendance on Spitfires' match days. That's our PA announcer hired by Crawley and Jamie off to Arsenal. All that's left, surely, is for the match reporter to attract the interest of Barcelona.

While we're in Canvey Island on Saturday for Eastleigh's fixture at Concord Rangers, Jamie will be at the Gunners' Emirates Stadium watching Everton trying to make their way to an FA Cup semi-final. The world moves in mysterious ways. Craig Laird, manager at Weston-super-Mare, would agree with that sentiment. Sacked two days after his side's defeat at the Silverlake — apparently due to budget issues — he was 24 hours later the owner of a new two-year contract with the club.

A family get-together at my sister's had us travelling to the Concord match (March 8th) from Walton-on-Thames. An early departure, with possible M25 chaos in mind, had us parked up at the tiny ground by 1:30pm. The downside of avoiding any 'we're going to be late angst' was that we were consequently able to sit in the small, 'atmospheric' clubhouse at Thames Road and watch on television Everton's FA Cup hopes demolished by three second-half Arsenal goals – the Gunners winning 4–1. Viewing 'highlights' of the game on Sunday night it hit me how little of it I had absorbed in the raucous surroundings first time around. In this instance that was no bad thing, but watching football in a 'pub' will never be my thing.

While we sat with Dan Hill, Richard's son, despairing as the Toffees' trophy-winning aspirations went up in smoke for another year, a host of visiting Spitfires, including the 28 on board the supporters' coach, was streaming in, all buoyed by the sun and a sense of occasion that is now accompanying every Eastleigh match on this run-in.

I wouldn't mind betting that neither Roberto Martinez nor Bill Kenwright had ambled in to chat with Evertonians supping their pre-match drinks across the capital. Here, as I plonked myself in front of the big screen, Richard had pulled up a seat to my left. The boss decided to escape the ground's miniscule changing rooms saying that, with playing kit in situ, the away team's next task would be to cram 16 footballers inside their temporary home. Confirming that he was content with the point at Eastbourne, the manager wouldn't disclose his choice of line-up for the afternoon – an afternoon he expected to be exceptionally competitive.

Stewart Donald, meanwhile, was in convivial mood, breezing in to sit at a table with supporters – although not before offering drinks all round. My dad and I declined as, rather reluctantly, did Richard, even if his chairman mischievously offered to take on responsibility for the team talk.

Once he'd finally sat down with his own pint in hand, Eastleigh FC's owner was hit with the usual barrage of questions. The most interesting revelation arising from Stewart's impromptu forum, and one that would gain legs as the week moved on, was that he and his board are in the midst of agreeing a deal to purchase a stand from their counterparts at Exeter Chiefs rugby union club. The structure, with capacity to house 2,000 people, will cover the side of the Silverlake Stadium opposite my cherished main stand.

There is no denying that the primitive arena we pitched up at in Essex on Saturday, March 8th, is exactly the type to which Richard and his players are desperate to avoid a return. Nevertheless, the Concord Rangers' story, county league Champions as recently as 2008 and now comfortably placed mid-table in the Conference South, is testimony to the charms of non-league football. Furthermore, the opportunity to visit 'stadiums' such as this, hidden away down a succession of mundane back roads in Canvey Island and backing onto a caravan park, is all part of the diverse adventure and joy that is generated by following Eastleigh.

With regards the game, a bare, rugged pitch was going to add another dimension to the challenge in hand. The manager admitted the following Monday that he didn't settle on his starting striking pair until he'd had a chance to study the surface. He went for Connolly and Wright. The twosome, which has nosed its way to the front of the hotly contested race for the team's attacking spots, experienced contrasting afternoons. Nobody expected anything other than an almighty skirmish against a brawny, gutsy unit. As another club labouring under the misconception that their visitors from Hampshire are a full-time moneybags outfit, Concord were furiously galvanised as they set about their aristocratic prey.

There was nothing of the 'Big-time Charlie' about the way Eastleigh bossed the opening 35 minutes. It was at this point that the incident occurred that Richard later told me had 'killed us'. A plastic water bottle was flung from the

Spitfires fans bunched in behind Jamie Butler's goal, landing near the 'keeper's feet. The match was stopped by the referee while, astonishingly, it was left to the home side's manager, Danny Cowley, to make his way across to our noisy horde and request that they move from that part of the ground. That pause in the action, and the absence of a hitherto vocal backing positioned right in the opposing goalkeeper's ear, took some of the wind from our team's sails.

A couple of minutes later Rangers had their first shot on target and, a further 60 seconds on, Sam Collins curled a sublime finish into Flitney's top-right corner. Shortly after a half-time break, in which my dad's explanation to a few home fans that Eastleigh are 'not full-time but train during the day' did more to confuse than clear up the issue, Wright skilfully guided home a crisply struck equaliser.

Things took a nasty turn on the hour. Reece went into a challenge with his boot raised. My immediately offered opinion on the tackle, 'That's a red', was shared by the referee. There has been a welter of debate on the validity of the decision since, but after repeated viewings I've not been swayed from my initial verdict.

Richard's ensuing change, hooking Fleets and sending on Dillon, had me wondering about the negative thinking behind replacing an attacker with a defender. I should have known far, far better. The manager has, after all, said enough times that his job is to win every game. Strevens and Wright played as an authentic front two and Mr Hill's audacity looked to be paying off when Strevs nudged us in front.

To their credit, Concord weren't disheartened and their approach quickly took on an intrepid nature. It was 2–2 on 75 minutes. The hosts' winner, Steve Cawley scoring with an expertly dispatched looping header, came in stoppage time.

In retrospect, this was destined to be Rangers' day and, my word, they milked it. The 'Beachboys' celebrations are unlikely to be massively exceeded by the supporters and players of the eventual title winners. Good luck to them.

Suvs had dragged himself away from the scene of the late defeat, using Guy Butters as a sounding board, railing against the injustice of preceding events. By Monday morning (March 10th), the skipper's spirits were sufficiently renewed to question the state of my, admittedly out of control, 'barnet'.

Richard, too, himself having departed the Thames Road field emphatically informing the afternoon's referee of his multitude of officiating errors during the 90 minutes, was in admirably good cheer. Perhaps the fact that Bromley had, yet again, been beaten, this time 3–1 at Chelmsford City helped to cushion the blow.

I had received a text from the manager on Sunday stating simply, 'Sending off????', perhaps in response to my report, which didn't contest the decision. The prevailing feeling at the start of the week, however, appeared to be that Saturday's was a match to swiftly 'put to bed'.

Once more, a single defeat was not going to be allowed to disrupt the group's morale or sparkle. Richard, as he led a 90-minute session, was no less gregarious in his manner than he had been a week earlier with three straight victories propping him up. Any criticism of his men was directly followed up by praise. Even mistakes were applauded if the intent had been correct.

The players were in similarly ebullient mode. That intangible edge that exists within combative sportspeople, however, is never far away. Seven against seven, with three additional players operating as 'floaters' – the object being simply to keep the ball from the opponents using one touch – sounds an innocuous enough exercise.

I didn't identify the footballing transgression that Jamie Collins had deemed to be committed by Fleetwood. There followed a truculent exchange of obscenities – or one obscenity in particular. Tensions simmered between the pair until it was time for a drink. Fleets bounded over and jumped on his colleague's back, leading to each of the pair taking a rise at the other's ire. Richard had completely ignored the initial fall-out – clearly in the knowledge that this kind of event is unavoidable in such a testosterone-fuelled environment and, more importantly, that the conflict would be resolved as quickly as it had flared up.

The ensuing drill, now 8v8 with goals at both ends and various specific conditions imposed on the game, started with Suvs advising, 'Stay away from Reece, boys.' Back in the clubhouse I asked Reece if he'd felt 'hard done by' to be dismissed for what, he told me, was the first time in his career. The answer was a tentative 'yes', especially given that 50 minutes prior to his ordering off, the striker had needed to briefly leave the field to tidy up a cut lip, sustained when he met with a stray elbow. With the scars from that collision readily visible as he spoke, Reece did concede that his studs were showing as he made the fatal tackle.

Tellingly, despite plenty of our fans remaining steadfastly convinced that the red was errantly flourished, Todd and Fleetwood both accepted that the right call had probably been made. Michael Green's dad, himself a handy former non-league player, held the same opinion when talking about the episode on Tuesday night. It's safe to assume an appeal would be fruitless so, sometime soon, we'll be missing Reece for three games.

The remainder of Monday's training had seemed set to pass without serious incident. Until... Collins tricked his way through a couple of tackles and around Lewis Noice in goal. As Jamie prepared to tap in from a yard, the young 'keeper grabbed back in a last-ditch attempt to scoop the ball away, but only succeeded in tugging at his colleague's problematic ankle. Collins staggered away ten yards before sinking to the floor. Angrily pulling his boot off, the midfielder was in obvious distress, emitting a few pained howls – a mixture of agony and pure rage. 'It had been feeling better than for ages,' he lamented.

Lewis 'The Cat' was on tidying up chores, along with his academy contemporaries, when Richard approached him, light-heartedly saying, 'You can't go injuring our players.' The boss's words took on a sterner tone as he went on to counsel our now number two stopper on the importance of recognising the boundaries for physical contact during training.

'He won't play tomorrow now, he's f*****, he'll probably miss Saturday as well.' If, as a 17 year old, I found myself in a work setting that required having to take an occasional verbal volley from Richard Hill, I wouldn't have lasted a single day. Lewis, though, is cut from tougher cloth. He has continued to advance since his first attention-seizing training ground displays and had, prior to the coming together with Collins, been right on song in this session.

Phlegmatic as ever regarding injuries, the manager was already considering how to re-shape his team for Tuesday night's visit of Chelmsford as we made our way inside – passing a shuffling, forlorn Collins on the way. Richard was less nonchalant with respect to the closing stages of the defeat at Concord. He admitted turning to Cookie, as soon as the home side pulled level at 2–2, to say that the moment we'd snatched the lead should have been his cue to tighten things up – forgoing the two up front and seeing matters out by playing with a more compact 4-4-1 formation. As is his way, the boss made no attempt to shirk his part of the blame – however harsh that analysis is – and repeated his self-critique in the local paper.

A three-day gap between games leaves little time for dwelling on what's gone.

Attention speedily turns onto the next barrier to be hurdled. The intensity of the current schedule, with respect to both its rigorous nature and overwhelming importance, is reflected in the fact that my weekly player interview has now turned away from chat about the subject's wider career. Focus is firmly on the here and now – 14 fixtures to wrest top spot from Bromley, and keep it.

This week's edition with Fleets, conducted after Monday's training, was predictably engaging. The Spitfires' marquee summer signing has long since dispelled any doubts concerning how committed he might be, after a career spent operating in more illustrious climes, to Eastleigh FC and its lofty ambitions. While declaring his otherworldly strike at Eastbourne a personal favourite among the collection of stunners he's produced this season, Stuart also acknowledged that winning the league with this club would match anything that has happened in his football life to date.

That, considering his past achievements, is a weighty statement. He was the Conference Premier's top scorer when with Forest Green in 2007/2008, won himself a move to Charlton Athletic on the back of that feat, appeared in promotion-winning sides at Hereford United and Exeter City, and has been capped at under-21 level by his country – playing alongside men of the like of Gareth Bale and Joe Ledley. Fleets' explanation is that nothing could top being an integral component in a close-knit unit that, with plenty of attendant pressure, accomplishes all that is asked of them.

As I left for the day, clutching my Dictaphone and allowing myself an introspective moment to share in Fleets' vision for late April, Southam and Collins rocked up for lunch. Suvs being last in is a customary occurrence – individual grooming always taking precedence over securing first dibs on the day's fare. Collins had been undergoing the first bout of his latest treatment programme. The pair was greeted by plenty of rice, salad – and a sauce bereft of chicken. A crestfallen JC was none too pleased to discover that his team-mates had snaffled the main course. One of those days.

Bouncing Back

Richard might have regretted not reverting to one up front when he had the advantage at Concord, but on Tuesday (March 11th) Chelmsford were confronted with Ben Wright and Craig McAllister teaming up to lead the Spitfires' line.

Wright is looking more potent every time he plays. Our visitors from Essex couldn't live with his quality – Ben's touch, movement and power all too much for a side that was in every way inferior to ours. It resulted in a routine victory, in all but score-line. Reece went from Saturday fall-guy to mid-week match winner when he headed Fleets' corner past an overworked Carl Pentney in the Clarets' goal.

The breakthrough came in the 43rd minute, by which time Eastleigh should have been out of sight. There were countless opportunities to extend the lead. With none taken, the three minutes added to the 90, somewhat absurdly, became an exercise in clinging on as Chelmsford threw off the shackles and poured forward.

JC watched on from the stand, no less audible than when he's patrolling the centre of the park. Alongside our stricken midfielder sat Jai Reason, serving the second of a two-game ban incurred for the distinction of managing to rack up ten yellow cards, and a still recuperating Will Evans. Toddy, in the meantime, had to be content with a place on the bench. Chris Dillon, who has an uncanny ability to step in after a lengthy period of inactivity and perform as if he'd not missed a beat, had his first start since November 23rd – and didn't put a foot wrong.

Two weeks before this match, when trailing 2–1 at half-time against Maidenhead United, the 11-point chasm to Bromley couldn't have appeared more insurmountable. If one week is a long time in football, then two weeks is an eon. While we were seeing off Chelmsford, the league's top team for so long was being humbled 4–0 at home by Dover. Remarkable. The gap is now only two points – and we have six more points left to scrap for than our long-standing foes. As important, the buffer to Sutton United beneath us has extended to five points – with Paul Doswell's team having played 30 games to our 29.

While our quietly contented band of footballers eased through an early Thursday training session, this coming Saturday's visitors, Bishop's Stortford, were busy later in the day slugging out a goalless draw with Hayes & Yeading. The Bishops' home pitch suffered more than most during the recent avalanche of rain. Consequently, an outfit that looked an early threat to our championship winning hopes is picking its way through a horrendous fixture pile-up and struggling to sustain a fight for a play-off spot.

Sadly, at the end of the week (Friday, March 14th) it was announced that Sam Wilson has signed for Winchester City. As playing opportunities stubbornly failed to materialise, Sam became progressively more frustrated. It is understandable that a promising teenager wants time on the pitch; something that has been very limited since he emerged onto the Eastleigh scene as a green 16 year old. The signings of Ben Wright and Reece Connolly, such a shot in the arm for the club as a whole, really put paid to Sam's chances of tasting first-team action any time soon.

Sam's situation is entirely reminiscent of the type that is commonplace at the very highest level of the game; that of the young local favourite being budged out of the frame by bespoke recruits, able to deliver here and now. The only solution for the player is to go away and improve, to the point where they become a 'go-to' man.

The midweek game with Chelmsford was the first occasion this season on which I've been moved to describe a victory as 'routine'. Against Bishop's Stortford, it was back to the norm – even though the visitors' left-back Jordan Brown offered the Spitfires a helping hand.

I have a bee in my bonnet about the torrent of penalties Liverpool are customarily awarded (ten and counting this season). I wouldn't be surprised if some of our league counterparts this term feel similarly about the number of times Eastleigh have found themselves playing against ten men. Closer inspection would reveal each of the red cards to be just. Brown's was no exception, as he launched himself injudiciously into a 16th-minute 20/80 tackle with Dan Spence.

It was a 'challenge' born of frustration. Strevens, Southam, Wright and Connolly had all teamed up to pressurise the opposition high up the pitch. For all their efforts, the away team simply couldn't keep hold of the ball and, as it ran loose, Brown snapped. The defender's mood was already on the slide as it was, with McAllister having scored the game's opening goal in the 11th minute.

As Spence writhed on the floor clutching his leg, it was impossible to resist glancing down to my right where Dan's parents were watching on anxiously. Their plain expressions gave little away, but, later in the match, our right-back's dad was less discreet. When his son had a short pass intercepted – unluckily and in a relatively harmless area – Dad instinctively flung his head in his hands, prior to throwing his arms up in exasperation. Evidently, watching a close family member in action is not a relaxing experience.

We have long since guarded against becoming complacent when ahead against ten men, BUT, surely, against a side that had played twice during the week and was struggling here to make any incisive impact, this would be a cruise.

Minute 24. A nothing free-kick launched into the box, nodded on by giant central defender Callum McNaughton – resplendent in Basil Fawlty-style head bandaging – and toed home by Anthony Church.

The presence of the aforementioned Wright and Connolly, though, has added something extra to this Spitfires team. There is an indication that, with impeccable timing, the former inability to score the goals that performances have warranted is being rectified. It took Wright seven minutes to restore the lead.

When Bishops equalised for a second time – after Flitney's ill-advised rush from his line and subsequent upending of Cliff Akurang enabled Reece Prestedge to dispatch a penalty – 'Wrighty' was even quicker on the draw. Four minutes had elapsed following Prestedge's 53rd-minute spot-kick, when our loanee, who, of course, informed me that his strengths lie in 'scoring goals and creating chances', continued to make good on his word. A flowing move ended with Spence cutting back from the by-line for his red-hot team-mate to effortlessly stroke home a classy finish. Ben wasn't done there, knocking off for the day with a hat-trick goal after becoming the beneficiary of some scintillating Fleetwood wing-play to smash in from close-range.

A 4–2 win, paying spectators tallying over the 600 mark and, as is becoming their habit, Bromley lost. I had said beforehand that if our long-standing foes went down at Farnborough they really must be on the slide. Dan – Richard's son – was reluctant to agree, a caution echoed by his dad on Monday. Ever impossible to read, Richard, if not downcast, wasn't exactly bouncing off the walls when his side got together for the first time after ascending to the league's summit. When I suggested to the manager that Bromley must be folding, he wasn't having a bit of it. 'We could have lost at Farnborough [to have done so would have been a travesty – they were not good]. Bromley will come again.'

On his second statement, I'll have to bow to Richard's knowledge. It was he, after all, who predicted Bromley's demise at Chelmsford – an outcome I thought as likely as the prospect of David Moyes steering Manchester United to Champions League glory.

Yemi was the butt of Monday morning's (March 17th) humour. His inauspicious last 15-minute cameo on Saturday had included him ballooning a cross over the bar, when under no pressure and with four colleagues having hared into the box.

To the gaffer's distinct amusement, it was a contribution that Jamie Graham included in his highlights package – highlights that Ross Flitney later confessed he had no intention of ever viewing.

'Well, it was his best bit,' said Beckwith. The manager agreed, 'I was quite pleased actually, the ball landed in my garden.'

'Yeah, next to Jai's penalty,' was Yemi's swift riposte, referring to Reason's early season 12-yard effort against Eastbourne Borough that endangered the Spitfire light-frame on the clubhouse roof more than it did his opponent's goal.

On a more serious note, Yemi does seem low on confidence at present. Since being handed a starting shirt in the recent game at Eastbourne, where he was withdrawn in the second half, it has been substitute duties for our usually upbeat forward. By lunchtime, Yemi had certainly had enough of being the day's subject for 'banter' – usually ready with a witty comeback he chose to completely ignore Jamie Collins' baiting. As he strolled out of the clubhouse for the day, with me by his side, the man they call 'Yemdog' said that he felt he'd done ok at Eastbourne, something that was reflected in my report of the game.

He did fade, though, and, as Richard had said to me later that week, the requirement in this squad is for each player to be ready, immediately that they are called upon, to deliver a display that helps the team win. There is no leeway. The ferocity of competition for places is best exemplified by Jai Reason's predicament. If, 12 months ago, you had told any Eastleigh FC observer that a time was approaching when Jai could return from suspension and not be pitched straight back into the team, they would have considered you barmy.

After missing out against Bishop's Stortford, when he was free to play after a two-game ban, Jai was exceptional during Monday's brief practice match. 'You're training like a man desperate to get his place back,' I said to Jai as he trooped off to warm down. 'Yeah, I just hope *he* notices.'

Completing a triumvirate of high-profile Eastleigh footballers currently watching from the bench, rather than playing, is Chris Todd. After a training session bookended by his overseeing the first half-hour of snappy exercises and offering young defender Jack Smith a five-minute tutorial on some specifics of the job, Toddy disclosed that he is hankering to get back on the pitch. If his exclusion against Chelmsford had taken me aback, the player himself hadn't seen it coming. As is Richard's way, Toddy is unclear as to the reasons behind his demotion. A confirmed manager's favourite, the manner of Todd's replacement by Chris Dillon is sure proof that everybody in this group is treated equally.

With Dills coming in and excelling, Toddy accepts that he can't have any complaints — albeit he admitted his frustration that, straight off the back of undergoing a physical bombardment at Concord, he missed out on the fixture against Chelmsford, which he could have strolled through in his slippers. If the team are winning, which Toddy declared to be 'all that really matters', then he says all he can do is bide his time and be ready when he's called back into the fray.

Dillon has mastered that particular skill. From the second he stepped onto the field in the midst of a harum-scarum game at Concord Rangers he's played as if he's never been away, much less like a man that hadn't lined up at kick-off since late November. When I put it to Dills that it is a distinct talent, being able to slip back into action so seamlessly, he was nonplussed. 'I'm just grateful for the chance.' There was no inkling that it had crossed his mind he would do anything other than grasp that chance. Having fallen out of the match-day squad as recently as the game at Tonbridge on February 17th, it is an astonishing personal turnaround and one that says an awful lot about the man's character.

Todd's training exercises at the beginning of the latest session had featured a drill involving 15 players, arranged in a circle, keeping the ball out of reach of two in the middle whose role was to try and steal possession. The duo of Beckwith and Wright were soon being subjected to a 'tunnel of death', this being the day's designated 'punishment', for the crime of being 'nutmegged'. Beckwith had been the unfortunate victim of that indignity when making one of his attempts at winning the ball.

Later, as Southam took his turn in the centre with Connolly, and with a very brief spell scurrying after the ball in mind, he mischievously instructed his cohort, 'Remember Concord, Reece', an implicit reference to the striker's red-carded 'rash' tackle in that game.

The keep-ball had actually been instructive with respect to what happens to sportspeople when the stakes are raised. The hapless twosome doing the chasing, whoever they might be, often had to wait for roughly 20 passes to be completed before they could lay a foot on the ball. When Toddy announced that the least successful pairing for the remainder of this game would contribute a fiver per individual to the end of season 'kitty', the ball was never kept on the outside for longer than ten passes.

That was down to the pursuing couple having an extra incentive to win the ball and those striving to retain possession becoming riddled with anxiety, in the knowledge that they were attempting to set a target that would be easy to defend when their own turn as 'piggy-in-the-middle' came. Only a fiver each, remember – and as far as I could decipher the identity of the eventual debtors was never agreed.

Overall, it was a training session, with regards to contact and intensity that was conducted with the utmost care. Richard believes that his players are tired. He is, however, reluctant to give them a day's break for fear of the negative outside reaction if such a move is followed by an adverse result. Nevertheless, the morning's work was wrapped up in little more than an hour, leaving energy spare for the usual boisterous lunchtime exchanges. Wright, as he re-stocked his plate, was still receiving plenty of grief for his perceived 'bottling' of the 'tunnel of death', when he had effectively – and cunningly – ridden on Beckwith's coat-tails, leaving his nutmeg victim mate to absorb the blows, while ensuring his own easy ride.

Against an uncompromising Whitehawk team on Tuesday (March 18th) Ben will need to stand on his own two feet.

30

TOP OF THE NINTH

After digging deep to pay for my dad's steak dinner at the Wetherspoons in Brighton Marina (well, you don't turn 66 every day), it was over to 'The Enclosed Ground'. This, the home of Whitehawk, is perhaps the oddest football stadium I have ever visited in my life – and I used to watch games at The Dell.

It is found incongruously at the top of a hill, adjacent to Brighton's Caravan Club site, with a pitch that seems to have been chiselled into the side of a cliff. The main stand is situated well back from the playing field, perfectly apt for a ground that has imported some of its seating from the soulless Withdean Stadium at which Brighton & Hove Albion were billeted for an extended spell. This is not a venue to which you would be desperate to travel in search of three essential points. Additionally so given the marked increase in quality of this Whitehawk team since Steve King took to its helm.

Chatting to a few fellow Spitfires ahead of kick-off, the mood was more of hope than expectation. Nobody doubted what a tough proposition our opponents would be – an impression beefed up by their 1–1 draw with Ebbsfleet the preceding Saturday.

We also had a conversation on arrival with JJ Waller, who has been commissioned by Whitehawk FC to produce a pictorial record of their season, in celebration of last year's Ryman Premier League winners now competing at the highest level in their 69-year history.

The serial snapper has clearly become part of the Whitehawk furniture, for without the safety net of familiarity there is no way any man would have risked sneaking a close-up of the steaming Tom Fraser, as the Hawks' midfielder marched down the tunnel shortly after half-time. Eyes fixed unflinchingly ahead of him, Fraser was taking an early leave after an unpleasant late tackle that left Suvs squirming on the floor – an act that rewarded the opposing skipper with a place on this term's quickly expanding list of red-carded Eastleigh adversaries.

Fraser's behaviour as he left the field at half-time had suggested he was on the verge of snapping. The midfielder – actually not a bad player at all – had been channelling his anger, at what he considered a host of poor refereeing decisions, in the direction of our manager. Richard's legitimate response, with hands held up in exasperation, 'What do you want me to do? I'm not actually the person out there making the decisions' did nothing to appease the raging Fraser, who disappeared from view with some lucid instruction from Mike Wimbridge ringing in his ears. Brave or foolhardy on our committee man's part? Tom's grandfather is 'Mad' Frankie Fraser.

It was, though, much more than the referee that had got the home team captain's dander up. The hosts peppered our goal for no reward during the opening 45 minutes. In the same period, Eastleigh had five shots. The fourth of those, a Connolly dig, Fraser blocked behind. McAllister planted his head on Fleets' resulting corner and, with half-time still ten minutes away, the Spitfires led 4–0.

It was thrilling stuff; 'a scintillating spell of counter-attacking football' was the phrase I used at the outset of my report. Wright, Connolly and McAllister were sensational. That trio provided the goals: Wright a sublime free-kick, Reece a clinical, assured finish after a run down the left, and Macca, before his set-piece header, an expertly dispatched strike at the end of a break he had started by rising to clear a Whitehawk corner from his own box.

This might be another match that Flitney opts to leave out of his video collection. During the first half, our 'keeper missed his wild kick at a Beckwith back-pass and saw the ball run on to hit the outside of a post. Late in the game, in a similar situation, Ross made contact, but only sent the ball to Kieran Forbes who strolled forward and rolled in a consolation.

After a couple of shaky games, our 'keeper's form is unsurprisingly a message board subject du jour. A man prone to training ground apoplexy, either in the form of outward eruption or inward brooding, upon committing the smallest error, will undoubtedly be stewing over his recent lapses. Moreover, he'll be desperate to get on with correcting them.

Nonetheless, Ross has still been doing his bit. The penalty save at Eastbourne was a standout contribution, but with the game still live at Whitehawk, he pulled off a terrific reaction stop to prevent Jake Robinson's hard struck close-range shot from going in. 'Flits', as he acknowledged when we spoke after Christmas, would definitely benefit from the presence of a goalkeeping coach, but, for now, that won't happen. His mental strength and inherent ability will prevail.

A 4–1 victory, then, at a venue that, on studying photographs of the action, looks as if it's set on the moon – an image reinforced by the sparse presence of only 135 people. But it won't go down as an entirely successful night.

Aside from my dad being short-changed when paying for our briskly served teas, Fleetwood limped off late on with what, on first sight, looks to be a pulled hamstring. Director John Russell called over to ask Fleets, as our formerly mobile winger shuffled across from the bench on the final whistle, for a prognosis. No words were needed. A shake of the head and mournful look said enough.

Richard's extraordinary foresight concerning events elsewhere shows no sign of diminishing. Bromley beat Eastbourne Borough 2–1. Maybe they're not done just yet. Sutton, though, sail on serenely. They eased to a 2–0 win over Gosport Borough – a Gosport Borough team readying itself for a Wembley final on Sunday.

Those results won't have knocked Richard from his stride. When in his company now, the boss's focus and concentration is tangible. His life is centred on how he is going to get this team over the line. I have been politely asked, interview-wise, to leave the players alone for now. Richard is taking on all media duties where possible, reasoning, 'I don't want to say anything.'

This week's article with Greener, then, will be my last for a while. Sometimes a source of his manager's frustration, our left-back has been 'at it' for the last couple of weeks; Richard even referring to 'the old Greener being back… bless him'. Indeed, I think the only time that Green's been uncomfortable of late is when I asked if he could compare Ian Baird and Richard's managerial styles. A look of pure fear came over the poor fella. After a brief pause, the panic in his eyes never receding, all he could muster was 'I can't answer that'.

Greener was happier recounting his experiences of 2010 and 2011. In the first of those years he was part of an AFC Totton team that lost a Southern League play-off semi-final. They returned, 12 months on, to top their league. The Spitfires quest to do the same takes us next to Staines Town (on Saturday, March 22nd). 'Fleets' is injured. Connolly is beginning his three-match ban. The 'gaffer' will have a plan.

A New Way?

That plan had to be overseen from a seat, not far to my right, in Staines' main stand. Our manager's on-pitch after-match discussion with the referee at Concord, during which he confesses he told the official he was 'f★★★★★★ useless', earned him a one-game touchline ban. It was Richard's first such punishment since he watched the opening game against Sutton from on high – the day when a misunderstanding concerning the specifics of his sanction led to him entering the home dressing room at half-time. Thankfully there was ultimately no fall-out from that indiscretion.

The boss had accepted his latest penalty without contest. Notwithstanding that, he has been slightly dismayed since his 'offence' at seeing other managers escaping any sanction despite making far more withering comments to the men in the middle.

Yemi and Jai were, at Staines, freed from their bench exile to replace Connolly and Fleetwood. Everything else remained untouched. Without the sheer pace and directness of the missing pair, though, the absolute attacking cohesion that we had seen on Tuesday at Whitehawk was missing.

The home team were rather more energetic than a few of us had earlier suspected they might be. A large number of the travelling party, happily inclusive of my dad and me, were early arrivals at Wheatsheaf Park. As we stood discussing the joys of our midweek win and the ongoing implosion of Arsenal at Chelsea (Mourinho's men stopped at 6–0), it was impossible to ignore the incessantly breakneck speed of the Staines warm-up drills taking place before us.

'This lot will be bloody knackered by the time we kick off,' said Mike Wimbridge, shortly before I informed him in just whose direction he'd delivered his Tuesday night oral salvo.

Unfortunately, Marcus Gayle's men sustained their pre-match tempo right through until the whistle was blown on the day's events. The first notable blast on that same whistle arrived two minutes prior to half-time. Beckwith climbed over the back of Jerson Dos Santos, one of Staines' trio of busy attackers, as the Portugal-born man bore down on goal. Penalty.

A second member of that forward line, the usually prolific Louie Theophanous, dragged a horrible 12-yard strike wide of Flitney's goal. Cue my latest bout of exultation in enemy territory. As an aside, the spot-kick miscreant has a side-line as Cristiano Ronaldo's body double, intermittently heading off to Madrid to film television adverts with the peerless Galactico. Piccolo mondo.

Minutes into the second half, McAllister, unmarked and from about ten yards out, sent an effort soaring skywards. It brought to mind many a training ground shooting practice. As we drifted towards stalemate, Richard was growing more and more agitated. With his players unable to resist the urge to get on the front foot, so leaving themselves vulnerable to ending up with nothing for their afternoon's exertions, the boss was desperately, loudly, exasperatedly, trying to relay the message that a point would do just fine.

What nobody had foreseen and I only learned of from the boss's son, Dan, in the car park before the game was youth coach Lee Peacock's name being in the Spitfires' match-day 16. Retired from playing at the end of last season and, by Conference South standards, a relative Galactico himself, Richard decided that 37-year-old 'Peaks', with his 'knowledge of where to be on the pitch', might be a valuable resource in the latter phase of a game. And on Lee came, in place of McAllister, for what he described to me on Monday as 'four minutes of hell' – a watered-down version of John Barnes' one-time declaration, in a national advertising campaign for a sports drink, that playing football is '90 minutes of sheer hell'.

Lee admits to not having enjoyed large chunks of his career, owing to the crushing nature of the pressure that comes with playing the game for a living. Here, though, he was liberated. Without the worries of playing for a contract he could relish his brief return. There was even time for Peaks to play his part in a move that concluded with Suvs volleying a last-ditch chance wide. Regardless, when the whistle went to confirm a dogged 0–0 tie, the overwhelming feeling was one of relief – including, evidently, for the young lad behind me attending his first ever football match. He probably didn't watch with the same manic intensity as those of us with so much invested in the result.

Predictably, living through games with so much immediately at stake is becoming an increasingly jittery ordeal by the week. I mentioned by text message the butterfly-inducing final minutes at Staines to my sister and received the following in reply: 'Squeaky bum time then' – a reference to the off-colour term used by the man who for 26.5 years kept the Old Trafford hot-seat warm for David Moyes, in reference to the nerve-jangling end to a campaign. Not that Richard has any sympathy.

'What do people expect? If you want to win anything, you've got to go through this stage. All you're feeling now is what I go through 42 times a season.'

My contact with the manager on Monday (March 24th) came via an afternoon telephone chat. Upon arriving at training earlier that morning I discovered only Ross and Lewis, of the first-team squad, on duty. The 'keeping pair was integrated into the development squad's session; Lee Peacock back on the day job and in charge. Our weary-boned outfield players were off undergoing a light gym workout. What's more, Richard has decided that Thursday will be a day off, regardless of how we fare against Tuesday night's visitors, Dorchester Town.

He may be short of numbers, but Richard is having none of the idea that he is operating with 'a small squad'. That notion, he says, is 'b★ll★★★s', pointing to the high-calibre individuals frequently missing out on a starting spot – Todd is still to regain his place. 'If I can't keep Sam Wilson happy, then how am I going to satisfy any more top players?' Sam's is an interesting case. Richard certainly didn't want to lose him right now. A touch more patience and the young forward might just have found that the absences of Fleetwood and Connolly tipped ajar the door he has been so desperate to kick down.

Dorchester are next up at the Silverlake and will arrive geed up by a 0–0 draw with Sutton United. While ourselves and the Us had a gridlocked Saturday, Bromley stuck six past Maidenhead. Eastleigh are off top spot, now sitting a point behind the Ravens.

Before Tuesday night's (March 25th) game against that unpredictable Dorchester side, Stewart conducted the latest of his fans' forums. Held in the newly re-developed supporters' club 'den', a room housed inside the main clubhouse, it was a lively affair. First up, we heard the owner's heady vision for the future of the Silverlake Stadium. The mooted purchase of the new covered terrace from Exeter Chiefs is complete. It will be dismantled in Exeter and re-assembled on our own sacred ground over a couple of summer days.

The life of my beloved main stand hangs precariously in the balance. There is the potential for the structure to be extended at either side, in order for it to run the length of the pitch. An alternative, however, would have, as its first phase, the entire edifice razed to the floor. I felt like somebody being informed that their family dog would have to be put to sleep.

Nevertheless, the plans for what would come in the current stand's stead represent serious intent. A vastly upgraded replacement would include 15 corporate boxes, bar, restaurant, club shop and ticket office. All very 'Football League'.

More parochial issues – publicity, ground access, and purchase of extra land around our home – merited discussion. Things became more fevered when the Spitfires' youth set-up came under scrutiny. One dissenter, in particular, was scathing about the current lack of a pathway to the first-team for the club's youngsters.

Bizarrely, the firebrand in question was convinced that Will Aimson and Bradley Fountain – two gifted teenagers previously on Eastleigh's books – might have stuck around longer had they been granted first-team opportunities by, respectively, Ian Baird and Richard. Will was enticed away by Hull City. Bradley joined Bournemouth. No amount of Conference South football could have persuaded either of those lads that their professional ambitions would be best served by staying put.

After 20 minutes' belligerent toing-and-froing between Stewart and his interrogator, a truce was called. The club's youth strategy next season centres on the continuation of a development squad. That group will play matches against their contemporaries from Conference Premier and Football League clubs. With Lee Peacock and Richard working in tandem to reap dividends from this arrangement – a reserve side will again be eschewed – we can hope, in time, to see a steady trickle of locally reared players making the step up into the first-team domain.

Somewhat fittingly, before leaving the ground later that night, I bumped into Sam Wilson who had popped over to watch his former team-mates. Sam left me in no doubt that choosing to leave the Spitfires had been an agonising decision. Regardless of his concerns about dropping three divisions for regular action, Sam just couldn't decline the chance to remind people of his wares. In one month, after all, he will be chasing a contract elsewhere. The 90 minutes that preceded my speaking to Sam probably validated the local boy's decision to move on.

I had stopped half-way through the climb to my seat beforehand to catch up with Dan Hill. We were talking about Nigel Pearson, the manager at Leicester City (the club fervently supported by Dan and Richard), who had been taken ill during his team's game at Blackburn Rovers on Saturday. This is the boss of a side streaking away at the top of the Championship table, yet an almost exclusively prosperous season has administered no antidote to the oppressive nature of his job. Dan understood better than most. He explained how his dad is utterly consumed by Eastleigh's fortunes, the result dictating entirely the mood on their journey home to Oxfordshire.

'He never sleeps on a Saturday night. He won't sleep tonight. If we lose, he won't sleep tomorrow night either.'

Richard will have nodded off ok come lights-out on Wednesday, for 24 hours earlier Eastleigh savagely put away their bottom-of-the-league visitors. Not that the Magpies, a predominantly youthful side that remains steadfastly faithful to its manager Phil Simkin's admirable footballing ideals, didn't pose any problems. This match, in fact, was reminiscent of our opponents' early-season trip to Havant & Waterlooville. As it did on that occasion, Dorchester's slick passing and overall energy at the outset looked capable of chiselling out an even contest.

By the 18th minute, when Toddy steamed onto the end of Jai's corner to head past an increasingly burdened Alan Walker-Harris in the Magpies' goal, that initial impression had been shown up as something of a fallacy. Todd's effort added to Reason's close-range opener two minutes earlier. From there on, the Spitfires were rampant. The gulf between the two teams was exposed amid an Eastleigh display that featured all that is enchanting about this unit.

There was power, pace, fluidity, daring, panache and, that previously missing ingredient, a killer touch in front of goal. For the second Tuesday on the bounce, the half-time score-line read 4–0. Goal number five, with ten minutes to play, completed Jai's second hat-trick of the year. The rout was completed by Yemi. He might have been out of touch of late, but here was the effervescent character we know to be the real Yemi Odubade. He came on at 4–0, with the tempo having dropped from its high-octane pre-interval lick. Full of vivacity, Yemi created Jai's third before adding the coup de grace with a lovely touch, spin and volley. Our popular attacker's customary smile and exuberance were, once more, just as discernible as his unquestioned lust for the game.

The good news kept coming. When the same evening's forum had touched on playing matters, Stewart Donald was able to reveal that earlier in the day his club had finalised the loan acquisition of Dan Wishart. I remember Dan as a fast, potent left-sided player at Hayes & Yeading. He left our Conference South counterparts for Alfreton Town prior to this season, but has since been back at both his former club and Margate for month-long spells.

It is a peculiarity of the game that, for all of Richard's careful honing of his team, myriad shape play sessions, detailed drills, and fine-tuning of the smallest details across the past eight months, a new man can arrive and, hours later, be thrust into action. It was a scenario that Dan Spence encountered last season. Spence's former Hayes & Yeading colleague, when he completed a whirlwind day with a 71-minute debut, was as assured as our perennially unruffled defender ever is. Wishart took the place of the stricken Fleets, of whom Richard has no news concerning any date for a playing return.

I was as in the dark about our imminent capture as any of my fellow 35 or so forum attendees. When we spoke on Monday there was no hint from the manager towards his potential purchase. With these deals being so complex, even more so at such a delicate stage of the season, the circle of those in the transfer know is contracting by the day. Even Dan (Richard's son, not the player himself) knew nothing of our new recruit. Only the men responsible for completing the deal were in the loop.

Wishart, on his maiden appearance, was confident and direct, before coming off to a generous ovation. And still, neither 21-year-old Dan's Silverlake baptism nor Yemi's return to his real self were the most endearing features of this forceful 6–0 triumph. Nor was Jai's individual goal haul or 'Wrighty's' latest glorious strike. Not even Toddy's first 90 minutes for over a fortnight stole the 'high-point' honours – an opportunity handed to the Welshman by Beckwith's tight hamstring. 'I'll be struggling to get my place back,' Dean laughed at half-time, having ambled over from his seat – alongside our expanding hoard of absent stars: Fleets, Connolly and Evans – for a half-time synopsis.

The post-match plaudits were reserved for Jack Masterton. Only recently bumped up to first-team training, the wispy 17 year old was given his chance at 4–0. After the belligerent stance taken by Stewart's inquisitor only hours beforehand and, it has to be said, the scepticism of a few others regarding Eastleigh's commitment to developing young footballers, Jack's debut was just the tonic.

His name has become the most prominent when discussion has turned to possible playing chances for any of the young stock. In competitive surroundings, Jack was the same player who I've seen on the training ground.

Cool and confident, he was the source, with his assured passing from the back, of both second-half goals. His development has a long way to travel, but this auspicious first dipping of his toe in the water made a lot of people very proud. The Eastleigh FC 'Twitter-sphere' was full of congratulations for a new team-mate/precocious pupil/well-received graduate.

All we needed to cap an intoxicating night was glad tidings of results elsewhere. If Hayes & Yeading United 0 Sutton United 0 was a pleasant aperitif, then Staines Town 2 Bromley 1 – a result granted some irony by the identity of Staines' 89th-minute match-winner: Saturday's wayward penalty-taker and Ronaldo doppelganger, Louie Theophanous – was the feast to savour.

Unwilling after our weekend draw to publicly disclose his desired final points mark, Richard, on the quiet, confessed to thinking that 20 more would do the job. Three down, with the boon of assistance coming from other quarters, was a decent way to make rapid inroads on the boss's private target.

No sooner were the Spitfires knocked from the league's summit, than they are back in number one spot. That might change by the time of our Sunday lunchtime trip to Woking's Kingfield Stadium (the landlord club are at home on Saturday) for a game against Hayes & Yeading. This is another return fixture with added piquancy afforded it, thanks to the brouhaha that followed the sides' first meeting in September. Then, Richard was pretty scathing about United's negative approach to their task. More pertinently, Phil Babb's assistant, Tristan Lewis, chose our manager as his object, and the Silverlake Stadium tunnel as the location, when he wanted to vent his frustrations of the day.

The only concern ahead of that match, spiky touchline inhabitants aside, comes in the form of the kick to the knee that McAllister took on Tuesday night – it was Craig's enforced withdrawal that paved the way for Yemi's mini-renaissance.

The Mothering Sunday (March 30th) scheduling of the match might make a small dent in our away support numbers. No such issue when we go to Bromley on April 8th. The 49-seat coach is full and there are sure to be many more in what will be a substantial – and decidedly whipped-up – Eastleigh cavalcade descending on Kent.

The unusual weekend arrangements called for a Saturday (March 29th) training session. I was pleasantly surprised to see all present and correct. Macca's knee, despite having a couple of stud marks embedded into it, is fine. Will was back in football attire and moving smoothly. JC's latest recovery would appear complete, and Beckwith was in full working order – even if, on a marvellously sunny early morning, he was sporting a pair of tights to protect his hamstring.

Fleetwood was working with Cookie – and a minor grilling of our 'Welsh wing wizard' extracted welcome news. His hamstring pull was of 'grade one' severity (the lowest level) and he is targeting a spot on the bench when we host Whitehawk a week from now (April 5th). 'Fleets' was actually in fine spirits, delighted that the side have continued their productive spell of form in his absence. That, he says, eases the pressure on him with regards to rushing back. Not that he's been taking it too steady. Cookie has provided a daily rehabilitation schedule and our sports therapist certainly pushed the patient beyond his comfort zone on Saturday. The sprints, in particular, that Fleetwood undertook, with Cookie tugging at a bungee rope attached to his midriff, didn't look to me the most restful of ways to be out soaking up the clement weather.

It didn't go unnoticed by plenty of his colleagues that Fleets had made it outdoors on a warm day. Nor did they ignore his 'special treatment'. Collins observed, 'What's the story here? Spence was out with a hammy for eight weeks and he didn't see a bungee rope once.'

Regardless of their putting in a double weekend 'shift', there was no mistaking that these players were delighted to be at work. Laughter was the main soundtrack to 75 minutes of nimble, skilful toil. It wasn't possible to pick out the half-dozen players who Richard said recent saliva and blood tests revealed to be 'the wrong end of tired'. Perhaps training just over 24 hours ahead of a match concentrates mind and body.

The manager is well aware that, with his suddenly broader player pool, he'll be disappointing a few with his forthcoming team selections. As he addressed the entire group, bunched tightly around him with the morning's labours finished, Richard divulged that it had not originally been his intention to add to the squad this late in the campaign. Nevertheless, circumstances (injuries and suspensions) dictated that when recruiting an individual of Dan Wishart's quality became a realistic prospect, he couldn't let the chance pass.

Now, the boss admits, 'I've probably got a few more players than we need at the moment. A few of you will miss out, but don't get grumpy. To be honest, I don't care.'

Richard explained that, having been left short going into the second leg of last term's play-off at Dover, he was not prepared to risk a repeat. A couple of his men are two bookings away from a ban and niggles can crop up at any time. The idea that the team's promotion bid could end in failure, for want of requisite numbers, is unpalatable. Not that the play-offs are what this lot want. Not now. RH again: 'You can really go for it now, play like we have been and win it. Or you can just do enough and coast into the play-offs. You've got a diamond Rolex in your hands. Don't let anybody take it off you.'

There wasn't much said in the body of the session about the next day's opponents, merely a warning that their approach remains every bit as pragmatic as that we encountered six months ago. The focus was on enjoyment, relaxing, playing without pressure. A pause in a keep-ball drill had the manager imploring, 'Relax. Don't get uptight. That's my job. You just have to go out and do what you've been doing, moving the ball. Nine more games, you need four wins, five draws, and that's it.'

Later on there was a reminder from their boss of what a strong group this is. 'We've got players here from clubs in higher leagues and they want to stay. Eastleigh is a very, very good place to be. *We... are... good.*'

Of those loanees from the Conference Premier, Wrighty's integration on and off the pitch has been seamless. Dan Wishart fitted in snugly on his first workout with his new colleagues. Dan's consistently top-notch left-wing crossing was a standout component of the day's main exercise, ranking alongside some spectacular goal-scoring, equally spectacular missing, and three barely credible point-blank Ross Flitney saves.

Fleets, his Cookie-inspired exertions complete, witnessed all this while sunbathing at the side of the pitch and loudly likening Yemi's wing-play to that of Norwich City's ex-speedy dribbler Ruel Fox, before bravely suggesting that his manager bears a resemblance to Everton's former gurning Dane, Thomas Gravesen.

It was Fleetwood, in the guise of referee, who, on Richard's instruction, whistled to end the practice match, so signalling that work was over. The sight of Southam taking a hefty thump to the back in a challenge with Connolly prompted the boss to call a halt. It's not the time to be inviting complications. That wasn't a risk Jai was prepared to countenance when the manager asked for some input to round off his debrief. Reason's response to being asked for his thoughts – 'we just need to take it one game at a time' – drew a chuckle from the boss who, after mirthfully chiding his player's borrowing from the cliché manual, told his men that it was time for lunch.

As I prepared to leave, Suvs, McAllister and Todd were on the Silverlake turf going through some self-governed 'abdominal' exercises. Richard was readying himself to drive to Eastbourne, that being where Bromley would be playing. Neither lack of application nor dereliction of duty will cost the Spitfires a single point.

Before setting off I introduced myself to the new signing, unchanged, first into the clubhouse, and ready to dig into the soup and sandwiches. Dan explained that 'the lads' had told him who I was. It would be fascinating to know what shape that description took. I managed to catch my tongue in the nick of time to stop him deciding it should be 'idiot'. When he detailed events of his signing on Tuesday, Dan said that he'd agreed the move and then 'flown down here' to play. Momentarily taken aback that the club had provided aerial transport to smooth their latest acquisition's journey, my brain mercifully clicked into action and informed me not to interpret every statement literally.

Dan made no secret of the fact that, even 24 hours ahead of a match, his introduction to Eastleigh training had been a more strenuous experience than he had become accustomed to at Alfreton. His parent club, he says, are forced by their restricted numbers to keep things 'light'. And it's working, as they compete for a berth in the Conference Premier play-offs.

Nobody's Fools

The first day of British Summer Time, and its resultant thieving of one hour's sleep, left me feeling somewhat 'thick-headed' as we embarked on the 60-mile journey to Surrey – that despite not a dreg of alcohol passing my lips since August last year.

Shortly after we had pulled into the Kingfield Stadium car park, fully 90 minutes before kick-off against Hayes & Yeading, a harassed-looking Cookie and Guy Butters rolled up. As they hurriedly emptied their transport – the battered old 'EFC Football in the Community' van – of all the kit and assorted apparel that make up the modern match-day essentials, the pair were bemoaning an M3 jam that had resulted in their two-hour journey.

When we trundled into the stadium therefore, the sight of a near-full complement of Eastleigh footballers, already outside, resplendent in their shiny blue tracksuits and taking a cursory glance at the jarring surface on which they were due to pound their joints, came as a slight relief. I must confess to wondering which of their number would have forgotten to change his bedside clock.

It was only Lee Peacock, however, running late, another victim of the motorway hold-up and an embodiment of both relief and agitation as he scampered towards the dressing room. Lee was set for a third successive stint on the bench – or to use his jovial take on his role, 'here to offer support'. A mention though for Reece, who clicked through a turnstile 20 minutes before kick-off.

We could have done with Connolly on the field during an opening 45 minutes that veered dangerously close to turgid. That wasn't for want of effort on either side. In fact, the furious intensity applied by both sets of players to closing their opponents and any space made silky passing and off-the-cuff ingenuity near impossible. The state of the pitch, rutted, hard, and looking as if it was parched, rather than having been exposed to months of the type of conditions that saw Noah building his ark, lent itself to Dillon and Todd heading a lot of footballs.

The excellent Dean Inman and, his United defensive partner, Ben Gerring were equally assaulted by a series of dropping bombs. Inman later tweeted to the effect that his body 'was in bits'. Frankly, he should be grateful that his brain was still capable of sensing pain. Although not in the 'footballing centre-half' mould of Phil Babb, Inman is a tough nut to crack. In the third minute of 'a minimum of one additional minute' at the end of the opening half, Wright and then, decisively, McAllister found the sledgehammer to do so. The defender was judged to have fouled Wright halfway up the pitch – one of a slew of contentious refereeing verdicts. Jai subsequently lofted up a free-kick that Macca paced onto, leaping to plant a proper centre-forward's header low into the corner of the net.

I celebrated alone, my dad off to my left and behind the goal where McAllister was taking the acclaim of approximately half of the 204 crowd. My pessimistic forecast of a low Spitfires turnout was proved errant. The mini-bus only carried 14 souls, but many, many more left their mums in peace – or in the case of Dan and Gaz, Richard's sons, dragged her along.

As I bounced down the main stand steps to buy my customary half-time refreshment, I ear-wigged in as two of the hosts' directors vented their spleens – the referee's most recent dubious free-kick award and then his unreliable time-keeping the focus of their angst. The on-field complaints were similarly vigorous. Nevertheless, there was nothing outrageous from Tristan Lewis. I had spotted, before the match, the Hayes & Yeading assistant boss take time away from laying out his cones and other props in order to stroll across to Richard for a handshake and fleeting trade of pleasantries.

Returning to the stand, with dad now in tow, I discovered my carefully chosen first-half seat had been swiped. For a relatively unobstructed view from the dated structure a shift to the right was needed and the second period was spent sat behind a trio of our own directors, as well as Reece – who had spent the interval arming himself with a couple of bacon rolls. Admittedly, one of those was for Fleetwood.

To my dad's right was Brian Palmer, who was still doling out his sweets when Jai somehow swept a close-range shot high into the expansive vacant stand that sits at one end of this ground. As the action played out, John Dunn and Mick Geddes – more exuberantly than his contemporary – offered plenty of opinion about its officiating. Alan Harding adopted a more cerebral stance than any of us, preferring to concentrate on the finer details than become too wrapped up in some increasingly bizarre decision-making.

The second half began with a tasty spat involving Adam Everitt and Jai. A physical tangle preceded an exchange of words less friendly than those the ex-team-mates had shared when they breezily made their way inside from the pre-game warm-up.

When he was brought back for his second Silverlake spell by Ian Baird, Adam was someway short of being a hit. It was Richard's first away game in charge that really did for the scrappy left-back. He had the proverbial 'mare' in a 6–2 defeat at Farnborough. He wasn't the only one, but in the minds of many supporters the die was cast on Adam's Eastleigh career that night. I make no apologies for being a fan of his. He abhors losing and bows to no opponent, however gifted. If your direct adversary for the day is Adam Everitt, be prepared for a battle.

And battle all over the pitch is exactly what Eastleigh's footballers had to do here. Southam's name being among the day's five substitutes perhaps explained, in part, why Richard had felt it necessary to ask that his team selection be met with no dissent. When, mid-way through the half the boss called on his skipper and Yemi, I ventured aloud that I thought Jai was destined for the 'hook'. Mick Geddes trumped me, suggesting Dan Wishart would make way. He did, along with 'Wrighty'.

Suvs, in his 25-minute outing, was full of purpose and running, providing energy where it was needed, with Strevens – captain on the day – and the fit again Collins facing an increasingly demanding midfield task to keep the reins on Babb's men.

I have discussed the fashion in which Eastleigh's players have shot a host of my stereotypes, even prejudices, to pieces. They have shown themselves to be of superior playing quality than I had realised. Furthermore, my former cynical, disparaging theories with respect to an overwhelming majority of footballers and their questionable devotion to their jobs, ambivalence to the team's results, and downright decency, or lack of, have been hastily and comprehensively dismantled.

Nevertheless, in Pat Cox, Hayes & Yeading do have the stereotype non-league Number 9. To the uninitiated, a striker at this level is a whole-hearted, bustling, imposing, niggling, scowling menace. A 90-minute pain in the *rse. Cox's rampaging display fitted each of those criteria. That is not a criticism.

He doesn't have dexterity to match Jai Reason's, the cold-blooded finishing ability of Ben Wright, Stuart Fleetwood's express pace, or Connolly's aptitude for improvisation. But Cox scored a terrifically taken equaliser and without an astonishing late Flitney save – a stop on par with his wondrous training ground deeds the day before – would have struck the winner.

Long before Ross's heroics – the criticism of our 'keeper is ebbing away as quickly as it surfaced – we'd have all gladly made off with the point that a gritty, obstinate display just about deserved. The Spitfires' 1–1 draw matched exactly Bromley's result at Eastbourne Borough a day earlier, while Sutton United, under the perceptive eyes of Mike Wimbridge and his committee ally Stu Solly, had pinched a late equaliser to end tied 2–2 with Bath City.

Quietly satisfied and strangely shattered, my dad and I enjoyed a leisurely early-afternoon drive home, a journey made all the more pleasant with confirmation that Everton, by winning 3–1 at Fulham, had racked up a fifth consecutive league victory.

If only Babb could have returned to the middle of Liverpool's defence later in the day. They demolished Spurs 4–0. My gloomy realisation when the 'red men' beat Fulham in February that they would go on to become champions – and in all probability win every game they had remaining – has given way to resigned acceptance. I don't have it within me to become overly vexed by what they get up to. Being gripped by one title fight is energy-sapping enough. Especially with the next match coming along almost as soon as the last one finished.

With almost indecent haste, it is time to re-convene with a Bishop's Stortford side that didn't exactly blow Guy away with their performance at Gosport Borough on Saturday. Borough won, that for the second time in a week after falling to a 4–0 defeat against Cambridge United in last Sunday's (March 23rd) FA Trophy final. Their 'bounce-back ability' is startling.

The exhibition of that same attribute was essential for Eastleigh to leave Hertfordshire (on Tuesday, April 1st) with anything other than a beating. When Rod Young was gifted a goal to put the Bishops two up after 32 minutes, this was not shaping up to be the facile plundering of three points from an exhausted team longing for the beach – or a simple midweek night on the sofa – that we'd hoped for.

Sat directly in front of me was a Charlton Athletic scout. With the old man off again in pursuit of goalmouth snaps, the Addicks' man was, sporadically, my sounding board for the evening, while also being prepared to offer his own insight. He opined that Eastleigh, for all their quality, 'don't do enough' and that the strike pairing – the now established Wright and McAllister relationship – 'could work harder'.

Those verdicts were, in mitigation, proffered during an opening half-hour in which we simply hadn't got going. Young, a whippersnapper forward on loan to our opponents from Norwich City, was running amok, crossing for his side's 4th-minute opener and lobbing a stranded Flitney for the second.

We needed something back, quickly. McAllister was fouled – a clear pull on his shoulder, even if he told me two days later that he felt lucky to receive the free-kick award given that he had inadvertently handled the ball in trying to hold off George Allen.

Cue set-piece expert Ben Wright. Here was Whitehawk revisited. Our loanee took a couple of languid steps and, almost contemptuously, dispatched his 25-yard strike into the top-right corner of goal.

Rod Stringer, the Bishops' idiosyncratic boss, already a frothing lump of apoplexy with his team two in front, spent the remainder of the game doing untold harm to his blood pressure. The red-faced serial swearer strangely castigated Joe Wright, on suspicion of his goalkeeper not having communicated with his resultantly pole-axed centre-back, Sean Francis, in the process of taking command of his box when punching away from danger.

'He's killing me. Joe's f★★★★★★ killing me.'

Stringer plainly knows what he's doing. He won this league in 2011 when in charge of a Braintree Town side that included Jai Reason in its ranks. Nevertheless, his resignation just over a fortnight after sealing that accomplishment, on account of being asked to make do with a low-price company car for the following year, perhaps hints towards a combustible character. As he became immersed in a row with his right-back Ashley Miller, I wondered if the home gaffer was going to squabble his way through the home side's full 11.

Stringer's earlier imploring 'smell the chances, Rodders, smell them' – Young the subject for that particular direction – was congruous with an evening that had already taken us past a road named after Nelson Mandela, and with a Nags Head pub in close proximity to the Bishops' Woodside Park ground.

'Rodders' was finally withdrawn, completely spent, in the second half. By then we were all square at 2–2, the monumental Strevens having headed in Jai's corner to equalise shortly after the break.

Bishops' manager was eventually happy to take his draw. So was Richard, who had once more – as at Staines and Hayes & Yeading – opted against instructing his men to go all out for a late victory. This is no time to risk throwing away a valuable point and, what's more, Eastleigh have earned the right to caution. The campaign has, until now, been spent attempting to win every single game.

There was, though, on this night, one last nerve-shredding moment. In the game's final passage of play, Francis – up originally for a free-kick – got his head to a crackerjack Matt Johnson cross. I slumped deep into my seat, Concord Rangers away flashing before me, as the ball landed a yard in front of the far post, before taking an odd skip off the turf that took it an inch wide of Flitney's goal.

That single bounce of a football ensured that I arrived home in the dark of night a thoroughly contented soul – rather than a mini-me version of Rod Stringer.

31

AT THE JUNCTION

The one blot on Tuesday's hard-won draw was administered by Collins' ankle letting him down – again. I didn't hold much hope when he took his leave with 20 minutes to play of seeing JC for a while to come. I was amazed, therefore, to see him out among the 17 players on training duty two days later (Thursday, April 3rd). When I expressed my mild shock to Richard at seeing the wholly revived Collins – a complete contrast to the frustrated, hobbling figure of 36 hours previously – bounding around the field, he was typically blunt. 'Ah, he's always hobbling.'

Far less surprising was JC being the individual playfully and plaintively lamenting the absence of 'fun' at the start of the session. 'I'm just trying to keep the lads' spirits up – stop the pressure getting to them.'

'Yeah, they look like they're feeling the pressure, don't they?' Richard observed of his customarily boisterous group, adding, 'If you want to have fun, go to Bishop's Stortford and be happy with a draw. I bet they'll be having fun right now.'

'Oh yeah, happy with a draw… they were two up.' Collins was always going to have the last word, but his manager was right.

Ten minutes from the end of our encounter in Hertfordshire, Rod Stringer had thrown on an extra centre-half to preserve his point. Richard, in common with Todd and Strevens, was absolutely incredulous. It was indeed confusing that a team consigned to seeing its season out with little to play for could be so determined, in those circumstances, to end a match level pegging.

The manager had been similarly struck by Hayes & Yeading's monumental effort on Sunday, so much so that he advised a few of his friends they'd be investing their cash wisely by backing Whitehawk to beat Phil Babb's side on Tuesday. If they trusted Richard's judgement, his confidants will have had a few extra quid to see them through the week.

While we were finishing all-square with the Bishops, Sutton were sneaking a late 1–0 win against Boreham Wood. Mr Doswell will surely be a little bullish as he eyes up what is now only a five-point deficit to his former club.

With Guy putting the squad through their warm-up sprints on Thursday morning, Richard casually picked up the cones used to denote the start line and, without saying a word, marched them a few yards back from their original resting place. Minutes on the training ground are now at a premium; every single one must be utilised to maximum effect.

The ensuing keep-ball had Collins back to the fore; Jai demanding that his team-mate, who owned up to having what he describes as a 'sticky five', be dragged off for his own good. Jamie offered, in mitigation, that the one-touch stipulation they were playing under is 'the last thing a man needs when he's at rock bottom'.

Nevertheless, there was no absence of the regular aggressive bent to the day's work. During the same exercise, Beckwith admonished Wright for a lack of application. He received an equally feisty reply. With the session nearly half an hour old, Richard declared in similar but, for his part, light-hearted tone, 'Wrighty hasn't f★★★★★★ moved yet.' The previously bickering playing pair was soon kissing and making up. After over nine months in this group's company, I have not detected one simmering feud. That is a noteworthy accomplishment among roughly 20 highly charged, ferociously competitive males.

Despite being impressed, and a bit taken aback, by the tempo of their endeavours here, I suggested to Cookie that individual reserves had to be running low by now. 'Don't tell them they're tired,' he instructed, the old pro's knowing smile borne of his understanding of a footballer's psychology.

Having spent 45 minutes taking in the morning's activities I was off, leaving as Richard set up an exercise on team shape and with Cookie miffed that he'd not brought his 'daisy roots' over with him. That was a new one on me. Daisy roots?

The reason for my early retreat to the clubhouse was to conduct a pre-arranged interview with the engaging, infectiously energetic Lee Peacock. Officially titled as the Spitfires' 'Head of Youth and Development', Lee's self-confessed passion for his current job surpasses immeasurably the affection he held for playing the game.

'I hated playing. I loved training. I loved it all up until I was about 17, playing in the youth team and reserves.

'I got in the first team [at Carlisle] when I was 16 and, being thrown in as a kid, there wasn't any real learning curve. I was just dropped in from youth football and the reserves where you can find your feet a little bit. You can find what you're good at and what does and doesn't work for you. I was thrown into an environment where I was told, "That's right. That's wrong. Do that. Don't do that."

'That was it every single week. For some people that's ok. For me, and how I was, I couldn't adapt that well. The player I was on the training pitch was completely different to who I was in a game. I'd do things on the training ground that I'd never do on the pitch. You're out there with thousands of potential critics watching and the fear takes over. You just do the easy thing, rather than trying what you know you're capable of.'

Lee was so disenchanted by football that, throughout the entirety of his playing career, he reckons he watched no more than 12 matches. Now, he's obsessed, trundling through the weekend's Football League goals, routinely rewinding to enable closer inspection of each frame of action. That last revelation was a relief – I'm not the only one.

'Peaks'' unmistakable excitement at being accepted on to a course this summer to study for his UEFA A Licence, exceeds even that of a ten-year-old Evertonian ripping open an envelope on Christmas Day, full with expectation of pulling out match tickets for Goodison Park. Lee is treading in the footsteps of, among multiple illustrious names, Jose Mourinho and David Moyes, by heading to Largs in Scotland in pursuit of his next qualification.

Put simply, it is a coup for Eastleigh to have an individual of Lee's experience, knowledge and newly discovered lust for the game, working to produce and develop young players capable of adding to Richard's armoury. To that end, Peaks was thrilled with Jack Masterton's debut against Dorchester – even more so for the debutant getting the call from the bench while, after his own turn at Staines, Lee remained idle. That's not to say he hasn't got a bit of the taste back for playing again.

'I'd do it again. I'd do it next year, and the year after. I'll be in better condition by then because I'm going to work at my fitness again. I want to be an active coach who can demonstrate what he expects.

'I'm more than happy to do whatever helps Eastleigh. At the moment, everybody's goal at the club should be for the first team to be promoted. If it takes me being on the bench or driving the bus for the first team, I'll do whatever I can to help.'

Despite being a contentious topic for debate at Stewart's recent forum, there is a definite sense of purpose with respect to establishing a solid, transparent structure beneath the Spitfires' first-team squad. One man who won't be involved in its continued implementation is the effusive Dave Hazelgrove, who has this week joined his erstwhile ally Dan Wright in becoming an ex-member of the Silverlake staff.

Regardless of his rekindled enthusiasm, Lee's playing re-birth has been stunted – for now. Playing numbers are back on the increase. Will Evans re-emerged to play at centre-back for the second half at Bishop's Stortford, so beginning the next stage of his Spitfires career. Chris Dillon was the man on the end of Richard's hook. Dills has had a late season run in the side that few people expected, least of all himself. Notwithstanding that, it must have been a blow for our unassuming centre-half to have completed a personal full-circle of fortune. Out of the squad in February, and in the same onlookers role come Saturday, April 5th, for the visit of Whitehawk, via a substitute's remit and seven subsequent starts.

Beckwith is desperate to be back in the side. Toddy, just a few weeks ago wondering when he would get back in, won't be leaving the way clear if he can help it. And, after an intriguing 45 minutes spent inside our clubhouse leading up to the clash with the Hawks, a team we saw off on the back of a counter-attacking blitzkrieg just 18 days ago, I discovered that Will had kept hold of his spot for the afternoon.

An afternoon of even more potential consequence after Sutton had beaten Havant & Waterlooville 3–1 on Thursday night. The Us are now a mere two points worse off than ourselves and have nosed in front of Bromley. A two-horse race suddenly has a third mare in the frame.

If I Was Responsible for Football Days

My dad and I missed our intended 2pm arrival at the ground on Saturday by no more than one minute. Our (his) tardiness caused us to miss the outset of formalities for the official opening of the new supporters' bar. That didn't take away from the opportunity to drink in – metaphorically only – the feel-good atmosphere that pervaded the whole building.

To a background drone of a treadmill humming away, with members of the TSSC completing a fund-raising ten-hour marathon on said disagreeable invention, Derik Brooks, in his capacity as the ceremony's chief dignitary, now 90 years of age, pitch perfect, and with not a single note to hand, addressed a rapt audience.

'Forever Thankful – One Derik Brooks' reads a banner, hung this year inside the Silverlake Stadium. Today marked my first chat with the man who, 68 years ago, founded this wonderful football club.

Surrounded in the now legitimately inaugurated freshly decorated room, by an environment so diverse as to include terrific colour prints of current Spitfires players in action, black and white shots of the very first construction taking place, in 1957/1958, on our Ten Acres site, a plethora of Sharon Cavill's alluring homemade, club-themed cakes, a television screen showing Manchester City beating Southampton, and people clutching pints of beer while dipping in and out to chat or sample 'one more' of Sharon's produce, I introduced myself to Mr Eastleigh.

If your faith is Eastleigh FC, a tête-à-tête with Mr Brooks is akin to an audience with the pope. It was bewitching hearing Derik's tales of the first coming of a supporters' club, known as the 'Bowler Hat Boys', as far back as 1950, and no less captivating listening to him describe the nerves he experiences, to this day, come game time.

Having, in recent years, been forced to forgo his attendance at the team's away fixtures, Derik explained how he'll often telephone our hosts for the day, without letting on whose is the voice at the other end of the line, in order to receive a prompt half-time update. Director Mick Geddes has the privileged responsibility for dialling Mr Brooks' number and informing him of the final score.

Having taken up 20 minutes of Derik's time, and received an invite to interview Eastleigh's now Life President, kick-off in the first instalment, against Whitehawk, of the Spitfires' seven match run-in was fast-approaching. Walking the path from the clubhouse entrance, round behind the goal and towards the main stand, stopping only in the stadium shop to pick up a team-sheet, I spotted the number on Ben Strevens' shorts: 12.

I had asked Cookie, two days earlier, if Strevs has started every league game this season. Neither of us was sure. I discovered on Monday (April 7th – two days after this match), from the man himself, that Ben was indeed in the starting line-up for his side's first 35 Conference South games. Such would have been the scale of accomplishment for Ben to see his ever-present status through an entire 42-match calendar, that Richard broached the topic with the indefatigable midfielder before the mutual decision was taken to give him a rest in this, game 36.

Strevs' body has finally started to groan under its herculean workload. He suffered cramp during the final five minutes at Bishop's Stortford and, with a nod to Bromley on Tuesday, needed a breather. With Collins completing yet another express revival after his own Tuesday night travails and Southam straining to be involved, replacing the convalescing talisman presented the manager with a straightforward assignment. So far, so good.

The Silverlake mood, with the game underway, was in direct contrast to the buoyant hubbub that engulfed the pre-match events. The only occasion I can recall Eastleigh's home ground being comparably subdued, purely because of its patrons being gripped by anxiety, was for the home-leg of last season's play-off tie with Dover.

That fear, bordering on impatience and unrest in some quarters, was perilously close to morphing into resignation when, with only six minutes played, a sluggish start translated itself into a one-goal deficit. On March 18th Whitehawk peppered the Spitfires goal, but barely troubled Flitney. Here, a cool, fluid build-up, and some classy play by Richard Rose, allowed Danny Mills to head his team in front with their first attempt.

It took until the 15th minute for Eastleigh to engineer a dig at the target. Ben Wright took it, hitting a half volley from 25 yards that, if a net hadn't been in the way, would have kept on its trajectory, through the back of the stand behind the goal and for a mile beyond. One-all.

Nerves settled then. Well, not quite. With Evans at his back, Mills fell over. The referee, Daniel Meeson, awarded a soft penalty. Flitney repeated the antics that paid off so handsomely when he saved Frankie Raymond's injury-time spot-kick at Eastbourne – and then some. Our Number 1, who is now in splendid form, procrastinated and postured, before giving his crossbar a hefty smash, leaving it wobbling in Jake Robinson's vision as he steadied himself to strike. There, the comparison with Eastbourne ends. Robinson scored, easily.

Sutton were already one up at Maidenhead. Whitehawk, again purposeful, impressive and looking nothing like a team that should be embroiled in a fight for survival, were playing with confidence and some enterprise. With our players seemingly constrained by the wider importance of the day, the Sussex team must have sensed the possibility for a seismic victory. Without Todd – and it was definitely him, regardless of the hesitancy on the PA that left Chris raising his arms as if answering a school register to identify himself as the scorer – powering his way onto Green's corner, only three minutes after Robinson's penalty, they might have achieved it. The Hawks were furious, believing Toddy to have bundled their 'keeper, Chris Winterton, off his feet in the act of forcing the ball over the line. 'I've seen them given' is a fair assessment of the incident, even if, viewing through my blue and white tinted specs, I considered our old-school centre-half's challenge to be legitimate.

What next? Collins, covering back diligently, completed his job by knocking a pass forward to Fleetwood – and duly pulled up lame. Strevens' 'rest' extended to a period of 38 minutes. I feared at the half-time whistle that McAllister might be about to have some time off himself. Macca became entangled in a scrape with Sami El-Abd, a skirmish that had the hulking centre-half falling to the floor clutching his face. McAllister's use of his nut was comparable to Alan Pardew's recent 'I tried to push him away with my head' moment, when the Newcastle United manager infamously found himself in hot water for butting Hull City player David Meyler, i.e. barely discernible. El-Abd's histrionics did him no favours.

Seeing Mike Wimbridge and Dan Hill at half-time I told both that I thought Macca had been lucky to avoid a red, merely because the linesman had seen the 'coming together'. Officials at this level aren't usually wont to miss any opportunity to escalate their role in proceedings. Mike and Dan held no truck with my view, the pair instead livid at the Whitehawk man's theatrics. Indeed, Macca told me on Monday that the 'referee's assistant' had actually run over and forthrightly instructed El-Abd to get up and stop being so soft.

Amid all of this excitement I'd sub-consciously accepted that my half-time trip to the tea van would reap no reward. I was startled, then, to walk round and find my dad proudly heading the queue – not as startled though as when the very mild shade of Scouse in his accent led to a request for 'two teas please' being interpreted as 'two cheeseburgers please'.

Misunderstanding resolved and back in our seats, it was time for a frankly gut-wrenching 45 minutes. Even shorn of Mad Frankie Fraser's grandson, suspended for his scything challenge on Suvs a couple of weeks ago and sat a few rows down from us, the Hawks were an incessant menace. The visitors' free-wheeling approach, keen to attack and snaffle all three points, prevented the more tightly bound Spitfires from locating any measure of cohesion.

Fleetwood's well-received return to action had been quiet, until Jai – who was outstanding on the day – picked the Welsh food critic out with a low cross. 'Fleets' knocked a first-time effort towards the target. His shot didn't really have the weight behind it he would have wanted, but, no matter, it crept over the line. Fleets told me later that the plan was always for him to depart around the hour mark – he'd left his dent on the game in the nick of time.

Whitehawk never ceased in their search for an equaliser, but a combination of some lax finishing on their part and resolute defending and goalkeeping saw us home. When he was replaced by Yemi minutes after his goal, therefore, Fleetwood was leaving as the match winner. At that time, Sutton, having been pegged back to 1–1, held a 2–1 lead over Maidenhead.

Maidenhead's Danny Green then took it upon himself to assume central billing in a turnaround that, first and foremost, might be essential in his own club's battle against the drop. From our perspective, the attacker made a significant contribution towards Eastleigh seeing off Paul Doswell's team for the year. Green's two goals made him, in my view, the best thing to come out of Harlow – his place of birth – since its post-World War Two inception. Admittedly, I adopt that stance having visited the 'new town' only once, en route to Bishop's Stortford last week. The Wetherspoons was its chief selling point.

His side having succumbed 3–2, Doswell publicly as good as gave up the championship ghost. Mark Goldberg at Bromley hasn't done likewise – that despite his team leaving Westleigh Park on the receiving end of their latest defeat. Our near neighbours' 1–0 win has shifted them into fifth spot. Lee Bradbury lost key players on the eve of the season and has, of late, been encumbered with a conceivably destructive fixture pile-up. I might be going soft in recognising this, but Havant & Waterlooville even being in contention for a play-off spot is some feat.

All told, if a certain beer company was responsible for organising the weekend's football results, they couldn't have managed better than what transpired on April 5th. Not that this profitable Saturday helped our manager enjoy a subsequent sound night's sleep. 'I haven't slept for six weeks,' Richard told me on Monday. When I said that I'd spent a large part of Sunday (barring the two hours when I doffed my Evertonian cap and watched the Blues comprehensively swat Arsenal aside; it was a wonderful thing) studying the league table, the boss replied, 'You've been checking it for a day, have you? I've been staring at it for six months.'

If you want to gauge how much stock the manager had placed on Saturday's game, Richard's revelation that he'd not eaten until 9pm provides the necessary insight. Even satiated, and anaesthetised – not by a product of the aforementioned ale company – rest was unattainable. For his players' part, Richard considered them on Monday (April 7th) to have a freedom in their step of which, prior to the weekend, tension had deprived them.

Indeed, of all the training sessions I have watched, this was undoubtedly one of the most placid. The return of driving rain and dark clouds couldn't dampen what was an atmosphere similar in tone to the demob-happy pre-Christmas air. An ingenious game of baseball played with feet and footballs was Richard's equivalent of a teacher allowing pupils to bring in their monopoly boards on the last day of term. It hit just the right note: fun, competitive, with intermittent bursts of running and ball work.

The following practice match was kept short in length and, again, was contested in comparatively relaxed mode. Cookie's decision to wear his 'daisies' paid off, with Wishart suffering a migraine and having beaten an early retreat indoors – even if Jai was so unimpressed with our fitness guru's performance that he suggested I should strap my own boots back on and have a go in Cookie's place.

With their 20-minute game over that was it. Beckwith was gasping for air. 'I haven't been playing, have I?' he pleaded – 'I don't suppose he told you just then if I'm in tomorrow?' 'He' hadn't. Richard is in lockdown mode. Bromley away, since the re-arranged date was announced, has been shadowing every thought and manoeuvre of the players and management at Eastleigh FC.

The boss did disclose that Saturday's half-time dressing room had been a febrile environment, so displeased was he with a few of the things he'd seen as Whitehawk twice grasped the lead. There was no lingering aftertaste from the rumpus. Richard was outwardly jocular with the group, determined to put them at their ease in anticipation of a mammoth occasion for this club.

Strevs is combining all this with the small matter of getting a degree finished. After I'd congratulated him on his latest gargantuan performance, from which it was impossible to deduce his body is begging for rest, Ben told me that he still had to find 3,000 words for his dissertation. The paper's subject, as far as my bewildered brain could decipher, concerns the ground force generated by wearing different types of football boots. Good luck, Strevs!

Ben's three-year course is finally over on May 1st, five days after – we sincerely hope – Eastleigh round off their season. Needless to say, Mr Strevens would not wish to countenance the idea of play-offs intruding into a summer that is due to include his stag trip to Ibiza and wedding in St Lucia. 'I'll come back from one of those on my last legs and the other totally relaxed.' Let's just hope that happens in the order he anticipates.

Once I headed into the clubhouse, with raindrops still dripping down my forehead and my hands now a definite shade of blue, I was royally looked after by Paula and Brian Palmer, falling over themselves to offer hot drinks, biscuits, chocolate and pork pies. I settled for the chocolate alone, but this was another episode to remind me why I like this place so much – the people, not the assortment of calorie-thick food on offer, of course.

Richard's confession last week, in conversation with myself and Yemi, that 'we're not a play-off team', only exacerbated my fervent wish that we don't have to embark on that route again – although the manager wasn't saying anything that we don't already know.

A 42-match league should reveal its strongest team and that is what the boss believes he has. Reducing course and distance lessens the odds on an outsider prospering. It is why Bangladesh might fancy knocking India over in a Twenty20 cricket game. If the same two countries contest a Test match, the underdogs are lucky to extend it beyond a third day.

Strevens' inclusion at Bromley is the surest bet going. Not only has he become the team's standout performer, the diagnosis on Collins isn't great. I had initially assumed, when he was suddenly incapacitated at the weekend, that JC's ankle was the culprit. It was, in fact, Collins' quadriceps muscle that went. He was told to rest at home on Monday and there is scant chance that the

Spitfires' mischievous lynchpin will be pulling on his Number 4 jersey again before August. But in what division will he be playing?

Tuesday's sojourn to Kent was going to go a long way towards answering that question. It is hard to recall being so excited about a game – ever. All day, this felt as if something special lay in store. Everything invested across the previous nine months, physically, mentally and financially, by such an array of personnel that cares so much for this club and indeed, all that has happened since Stewart Donald and then Richard Hill walked into Eastleigh FC could have its eventual prosperity heavily influenced by this single match.

Bromley

As we took a cursory look at the Wetherspoons' menu, a publication that we can probably both recite to the word by now, my dad and I noticed a few Spitfires already in situ. More followed, in pursuit of sustenance and amber refreshment to see them through a night destined to test the most cast iron of constitutions. There was a palpable feeling that an extremely big football match was impending.

That impression was afforded extra credence when we arrived at the ground to find the overflow car park already filling up. And that was with a large number of the away support still in transit. Our fellow diners, to a man taking advantage of the cut price steak and chips on offer (superfood salad for this nervous gastronome), had heard of trouble on the M25 and been informed that the supporters' coach – fully subscribed to a week before – pulled into its first pick-up point 20 minutes late. Never have I been so grateful to my anal disposition for having us at a ground with an hour to spare.

Speaking to Lee Peacock inside Bromley's Hayes Lane Stadium, I discovered that the motorway mayhem wasn't only affecting a host of Eastleigh's fans. Suvs had been delayed to the point that he was running late for the players' designated mealtime. The best laid plans.

That aberration notwithstanding, Lee said that Richard's demeanour was calm and quiet. When, upon seeing the manager, I offered a quick 'good luck', his brisk 'alright, mate' in reply, and pensive disposition, immediately brought to mind the man I saw pacing the dressing room prior to kick-off against Ebbsfleet back in January.

Two days earlier, I had found myself on the wrong end of the manager's wrath. He took exception to a word I had used to describe the play of one of his men in my Whitehawk match report. A broken Sunday night's sleep ensued, but thankfully the problem was speedily rectified. It is that devotion to knowing, right down to the last word or act, what is happening at his football club that sets Richard apart. One word out of more than 2,000 didn't sit right with him. If there was the smallest chance that could adversely affect one of his players, it needed resolving.

From our seats in a jam-packed main stand, we could see the colourful congregation of Spitfires growing in number, the coach having completed its journey with little to spare. The traffic congestion wasn't discriminating in its choice of victims; Dan Hill had to endure four hours in a car from Oxford in order to be present on a huge night for his dad.

By 7:45pm everybody who wanted to be at Hayes Lane was there. Well, that's not entirely true. Mark Jewell was halfway through a holiday, while Stewart Donald, long before the timing of this fixture was known, had booked himself a fortnight in the Cayman Islands. Who's laughing now, hey? And Derik Brooks, of course, sat at home, telephone number for Bromley FC at hand.

That trio missed a first quarter-hour in which their team came under the cosh – and then some. It had taken Bradley Goldberg all of 30 seconds to send a long-range shot at Flitney's goal that cannoned up off the top of the bar and over.

Then, after 16 minutes, Ben Wright trumped Goldberg's speculative hit. Fuelled, perhaps, by a generous second helping on Monday of Paula's gammon pasta, Wrighty bettered even his wondrous strike on Saturday. Ross, already the busiest man on the pitch, had just thwarted the latest home attack when he punted a routine kick downfield. McAllister's flicked header ran for Wright. But, boy did he have plenty left to do. At 25 yards out, he hit the ball first time on the half-volley, dispatching a shot that dipped in a fraction underneath Joe Welch's bar (how many non-league goalkeepers are called Joe?).

Behind Welch's goal, where the majority of Spitfires were gathered, there exploded a scene of unfettered joy. In the main stand, Dan Hill and yours truly were the only two whose bodies leapt up from their seats, simply unable to control either our delight at a vital strike or admiration for a piece of sheer, magnificent quality.

When I turned, my face a mix of surprise and elation, fist clenched in revelry, to our assembly of attendant directors, I was greeted by the sight of Mick Geddes, John Russell and Alan Harding using every morsel of restraint they could summon to avoid going bonkers.

Flitney was swiftly being called on to continue his shot-stopping master class. Ross reserved his best for this night; the mark of a true champion. All of the other ten starters were immense. That the Herculean Strevens and, in particular, centre-backs Todd and Beckwith – ultimately a 'go-to' man when the stakes are at their highest – were required to perform to an exceptional standard just to keep their side afloat betrays the flow of the game. They knew what to expect – Richard had been warned by Lee Bradbury. Havant & Waterlooville's boss, recounting to his Eastleigh counterpart details of their win against Bromley on Saturday, described the Ravens launching something akin to the charge of the light brigade as they went hunting an equaliser at Westleigh Park.

What's more, in the course of this frenetic battle, Richard's decision to draft Dan Wishart into his squad grew in its sagacity. Chasing a ball out towards the touchline, four minutes before half-time, Fleetwood's hamstring caved in. It was obvious to every one of the 1,011 people who saw him instantly clutching the back of his leg as he pulled up that 'Fleets' wouldn't be taking any further part. After the game, he confirmed the most pessimistic suspicions: 'Yeah, that's me done for the season now.'

Wishart was straight on, taking Fleetwood's place in a team frantically trying to batten down the hatches ahead of half-time. In that aim, they fell at the last. Spence, uncharacteristically, conceded a cheap free-kick at the side of his area. The ball was knocked in and Rob Swaine – a mammoth beast of a man, whose grand rock-hard physique, when he walked past my dad and me long after full-time, seemed superhuman – headed into the back of the net.

The pendulum had well and truly swung. Any talk with our fellow supporters during a hopeless pursuit for half-time tea centred on shared feelings of trepidation. When the sides returned, there was no Macca. Spotting him watching studiously from the mouth of the tunnel, I shouted down to ask the problem. 'Adductor' came the reply, accompanied by an anguished look and rolling of the eyes.

Richard suddenly facing up to being denied Macca's, Fleetwood's, and Collins' respective qualities until next term wasn't on the agenda. That makes especially irritating the timing of Reece Connolly's unavailability. Reece's 25-minute run-out against Bishop's Stortford last week was his last in an Eastleigh shirt – for now. The ability to discuss that situation further in these pages remains constrained by a complex, elongated process.

The interval did nothing to change this game's tide. Dan Wishart and Ben Wright did. After ten more Bromley-dominated minutes, Wright was at the inception of a crisp move. Its ending was abrupt. Wishart drove into his opponent's box, where Dean Pooley cut him to the floor.

Wrighty clinically rapping the resultant, nailed on, penalty into the bottom-right corner of goal sparked a repeat of the hysterical reaction that followed his remarkable first-half intervention – and preceded another unremitting assault on Flitney's goal.

I should be beyond the stage where I can be caught off guard by anything I witness in this league. But Bromley performed with such ferocity, intensity, skill and speed that I cannot fathom how, coming into this match, they had lost on seven of their last 12 outings.

The blast of the whistle that, despite their tumultuous efforts, confirmed the home team had now suffered eight defeats in 13 games, heralded this as an evening a great number of the Spitfires fans present will rank as one of the most memorable of their lives. Football can have that effect.

Typically, on these Tuesday ventures, we're briskly off into the night, conscious that there's a long drive ahead. Here, nobody wanted to leave. That included Richard and the players, all of whom stayed out long after they had received the jubilant acclaim of their clamorous supporters behind the goal.

Those of us hovering close to the tunnel waited, while the post-match huddle and subsequent warm-down were drawn out long past their usual combined ten-minute span. Richard was first over, dragging Dan into a heartfelt bear-hug. The manager was fulfilling on-pitch interview requests as the night's heroes started to file by, every one of them glowing with elation and pride.

Even once the team and its boss had dragged themselves inside we hung around, all with adrenaline pumping and wanting to revel in our own and each other's glee. Plunged into darkness as our hosts hit the off switch on their floodlights, we nattered away undeterred. Mike Andrews was no less thrilled than would have been the case were he still a board member. Once this club gets under your skin, there is no turning back.

Eventually settled in the car, what is usually a 20-minute chat between my dad and myself about the 90 minutes we've just seen, before we drift off into individual thoughts, was replaced by excited babble all the way home.

Well, nearly all the way. Every aspect of this match exhausted, talk turned to Chelmsford away on Saturday. Yemi, who had been Macca's replacement, was limping back to his car when we passed him on the way out. We're running out of players. We need five more points to be sure of the title. The top of the table looks like this:

Eastleigh	played 37	pts. 79	GD 31
Sutton United	played 38	pts. 71	GD 34
Bromley	played 38	pts. 70	GD 29

Perusing that state of affairs from afar, one would consider Eastleigh a shoo-in for top spot. When your existence has become so inextricably linked to the club, however, when you are cognisant of what this means to so many people, your personal antenna is programmed to identify every possible impediment we could encounter. One of those, in the shape of Chelmsford City, looms large.

The Only Way

My first task in Essex (on Saturday, April 12th) was to catch hold of Richard, busy charming the day's match officials as he strolled in from inspecting another unwelcoming, corrugated playing surface. The *Southern Daily Echo* had asked if I could collect some post-match quotes from our players. I asked the question and, within about 15 seconds was informed, via approximately three different terse explanations, that the answer was 'No'.

It was what I'd expected. The manager was unlikely, at such a delicate time, to release the public-speaking shackles he has recently imposed on his players. My Dictaphone's trip to Chelmsford deemed fruitless, it was back to talking to my dad and Mike Andrews, who, encouraged by the morning sun, was cast in shorts while eulogising about the food produce on offer inside the Melbourne Stadium. Cloud cover was now prevailing, the morning warmth giving way to a cold, grey afternoon. The conditions seemed symbolic, given that we walked from the euphoria of Tuesday into an ugly battle, here, to avoid defeat.

When we had sought some shelter on first arriving, we were met with the sight of Fleetwood, Collins and Beckwith, condemned men all, sharing a table in the Clarets' clubhouse. Jamie confirmed that he won't be returning to the field in this campaign. In full club tracksuit, and with wife and two young children in tow, the Spitfires' savvy midfielder is now reduced to a supporting role.

Dean's already fragile hamstring was restricting him late on at Bromley. His fitness, this weekend, permitted the defender to engage in activity no more strenuous than attending a Sunday Herbalife seminar in Brands Hatch. 'Deano's' body was definitely not ready to be pitched into combat against Chelmsford's pugnacious, clever front duo of Luke Callander and Michael Cheek.

Beckwith's absence paved the way for Will to come straight back into Richard's starting 11. A clue towards McAllister's health came when Yemi – who, bearing no ill-effects from his 45 minutes on Tuesday, featured from the outset – came off with 25 minutes still to play. Macca, who told me before kick-off that he wasn't fit – prompting Ben Wright to claim 'yeah, he's injured as well' – stayed rooted to the bench. Lee Peacock made his way on to deliver a battering ram of a performance – not lacking in intelligence for that.

Huddled against the wind in the main stand, I listened in as the trio of home supporters stationed directly behind me took time out from deciding that Wright is 'f****** hopeless' to express their amazement that Lee is still turning out. They don't know quite how pressed for numbers this Eastleigh unit has become.

Not that Chelmsford were hostile hosts. Upon my dad requesting the freedom to take some close-up pictures of the action, he promptly found himself the temporary owner of a high-vis steward's jacket and, with it, permission to patrol the pitch's perimeter at his will. In what is an athletics stadium, and ergo with its stands set well back from the playing arena, it was a handy gift. It was, though, a tad peculiar, looking over in the second half and seeing the old man positioned inside a hammer cage.

All factors considered, a point obtained from a 0–0 draw, even with both Sutton and Bromley winning – the latter owing to a very late goal against Weston-super-Mare – was an extremely decent return.

The manager agreed, but was nonetheless furious about Dan Wishart being denied what were two very convincing penalty shouts. The first of the pair was especially baffling, Dan actually being penalised for the offence of being scythed down as he dribbled into the City box. It had been hard, when I saw Richard talking with all three officials an hour before kick-off, to escape the feeling that the mutual bonhomie might be erased before the afternoon was out.

The home team, for which our former midfielder Mark Hughes was a dynamic force, actually created the clearer opportunities. Flitney made one dazzling point-blank save, while Todd replicated his 'I head it and kick it' (that was how, earlier in the season, he had described his duties to me) resilient midweek display. We deserved our draw, though.

Not that all of the day's away support was completely happy. One told me and my dad that this failure to win our 'easiest' remaining game was going to come back and bite us 'when we lose in three days'. Certainly, a good bulk of the 34-strong coach party, and assorted others, viewed the result in the same favourable light as myself. Some people, however, will only ever be fully content when the Spitfires are summarily trouncing all-comers.

One team that did dish out a weekend hammering was Winchester City. A 4–0 win for a local side down in the Wessex League wouldn't have usually crossed my radar. This was an exception, for Sam Wilson scored all four goals. I was absolutely delighted for him. On the flip side, Jack Smith, an Eastleigh scholar, is playing on loan with Totton & Eling, the vanquished side, and was in direct opposition to Sam. 'Four shots on target and they scored four goals,' he wistfully told me a couple of days later. The life of a centre-half – he'll get used to it.

For all their exertions, and with bodies and minds now evidently entering the 'red-zone' after playing 16 games in a fraction under eight weeks, Monday was a day of rest for Eastleigh's footballers. I barely knew what to do with myself, such has the routine of Monday morning at the training ground become an intrinsic part of my life. It brought home to me how much I am going to miss being so immersed in life at Eastleigh FC – even if my nightly dreams about events at the club are sandwiched by thoughts, before lights out and at sun up, about team selections, injuries, point targets and this book.

Furthermore, my Eastleigh-free Monday is a reminder that I should make the most of the last knockings of this extraordinary ride. Next stop, Tuesday night (April 15th) and Dover Athletic at the Silverlake – a Dover team in sparkling form as they fight to grab the final play-off spot from Havant & Waterlooville.

Meet the New Hero

Kick-off against the Whites was still seven hours away when I called the manager to determine his frame of mind as he prepared for yet another landmark fixture in his season. Richard was quick to admit that he has 'gone into his shell' across the last four weeks, wanting to utilise all his available energy and focus on plotting a way through each test as it arises.

Those tests are extra tough when opponents prioritise their clash with 'big-spending' Eastleigh, even if that means taking a hit in a less glamorous contest. Two days before they played the Spitfires, Chelmsford had been at Bishop's Stortford. Scrapping for points at the bottom end of the division and up against a team that is in a mid-table no-man's-land, the Clarets rested three key men, evidently intent on achieving a statement-making result against the current league leaders.

Richard was baffled, but he's come to expect it. Bath City, still the most impressive side to come to our home this term and incredibly unfortunate to leave with nothing, are out of the play-off running. A fortnight after their ambitious, industrious display at Eastleigh, Richard watched Bath perform so poorly in a match that, overcome by frustration, he left after an hour.

There was no questioning, then, how motivated Dover would be for this tussle. Our players trained at 3:30pm, the lightest of sessions, with the twin aim of relieving any bubbling anxiety and loosening the limbs. McAllister and Beckwith are still unavailable. Richard is taking the pragmatic view that, even if there's a possibility the duo could contribute to a crucial victory, there is more chance right now of a season-ending relapse. He'd prefer to leave open the prospect of them being in sturdier condition for the potentially decisive closing matches next week.

This period is testing the squad's strength like nothing before. The boss is, therefore, unashamedly thrilled by the current sequence of fruitful results. He goes back to last summer and the hard work that went into ensuring his recruitment was spot on. The capture of men like Strevens and Fleetwood, individuals unwanted elsewhere, players who it has since been lazily assumed came to Eastleigh for the money. They came because they had the offer. Nobody, as Richard is keen to point out, does their job for no financial reward. Notwithstanding that, these men came to the Silverlake for the right reasons: to play football, to show they still had 'it', and to prove people wrong.

As Richard told his group after a training session last month, this is a club that players want to be at. He has, more than once, answered his telephone in the days leading up to a game to be beset by an agent asking that our manager keep a close eye on his client during the imminent fixture – that player being keen on impressing the boss enough that he is persuaded to offer him a generous contract. Richard merely wonders why those individuals are only going to perform well against Eastleigh.

For all the erroneous talk elsewhere of the club splurging cash in pursuit of promotion, the manager had to get his calls on who fitted the bill, who was capable of coming in and delivering high-quality performances every week, bang on. There was no slack in the budget for grand-scale mid-season manoeuvring.

Yet still, with so much having been executed according to plan, the manager needs his team to plough deep into their reserves and collect another four points. Richard confesses that his mind is 'playing tricks on him'. Every football fan can identify with that affliction. When our club is within touching distance of glory then every worst-case scenario, however remote its chances of occurring, zips repeatedly through our thoughts.

Such is the pressure right now that Richard is unsure if he could stomach having to tread this same path – striving to take Eastleigh into the Conference Premier for the first time in their history – again.

It's not merely the 42 fixtures, the return visits to those 'tin pot grounds' to which Fleetwood affectionately referred early in the season, his being charged with meeting supporters' ever escalating demands, the team being an even bigger target for shooting down or the mental trauma that would result from failure to capitalise on this current prosperous position. It's the unseen work, all the scouting of future foes and looking for fresh players to come in and take this gigantic step; the garage 'meal deals' and 'filling the car up with petrol again' as he takes these unglamorous road trips.

Not to mention the refereeing, which Richard says, at Bromley and Chelmsford, was reminiscent of some of the things to which he bore witness when working in Kazakhstan. Such intensity of feeling arises purely out of the heightened tension that, right now, surrounds every match that Eastleigh play.

Emotion is comparably fretful in the stands. 'This is ours to lose. We'll never live it down if we blow it now,' was Mike Wimbridge's take on matters in the minutes leading up to kick-off against Dover. Chris Blake, meanwhile, was musing over a dilemma: the supporters club's wish to release a t-shirt celebrating Eastleigh's championship-winning achievement. The fly in their ointment is quite obvious. But, with the four-day Easter bank holiday weekend impending, the mementos need commissioning by Thursday of this week if they are to be ready for distribution at the final home match. A draw would be enough for Chris to push the 'order' button – and risk being left with a job lot of merchandise that Derek Trotter might baulk at trying to peddle.

With nerves, then, bound to be a factor throughout home ranks, I fully expected to see a visiting team coming out bent on attack, primed to exploit their opponents' apprehension. My prophecy was exposed as bunkum in minute one. Five men strung across the back, with two more sat in front of them, suggested this was a Dover unit with caution as its modus operandi.

In fairness, the men from Kent were slightly on top when Barry Cogan went in late, and slightly recklessly, on Will Evans. For his sin, the Whites' midfielder was granted a place on this campaign's Silverlake list of shame. An hour with ten men meant only three things for the away side. Defend, defend, and defend some more.

As Cogan trudged off, Tom Parsons did what football fans do like no other group of people – flew in the face of reason. 'Oh no, we always struggle against ten men.' Adopting an unusually positive stance, I reminded the extremely tanned Tom – a Sunday spent under the bright blue skies in Shanklin and he looked as if he'd come to the game straight from a sponsored sunbed marathon – that the Spitfires' record in these situations was improving markedly. We've had plenty of practice.

Will was actually lucky to still be on the pitch himself. His deliberate handball had prevented Nathan Elder from sprinting clean through on goal. I hadn't seen the incident clearly, but if Dan Hill says Will should have gone, which he did when we spoke at half-time, then that's all the confirmation I require.

When, 45 minutes later, I next saw the manager's son, he was ruffling my hair – uncontaminated, despite Chris Todd last week accusing me of sporting 'product' in my growing locks – in jubilation. 'I love it when a plan comes together,' Dan said as we headed down for the side of the pitch.

When his dad re-signed Lee Peacock last month, the move raised a few eyebrows – and set a few tongues wagging about the substance of this Spitfires squad. Lee came on here, with 13 minutes to play and with the scores still locked at 0–0, to replace Yemi. Within 60 seconds, he had cannily latched on to Greener's right-wing corner and toed in a close-range volley to win the match.

A four-figure crowd erupted – well, most of them. Just like the game at Bromley a week earlier, everything about this night felt 'big'. Anybody who was anybody to do with Eastleigh FC (apart from the still holidaying owner) was present. They all wanted to be there when this club all but guaranteed its ascension to the highest level it had reached in its history.

Brett Williams, our former striker and scorer of 21 Conference Premier goals – and counting – for Aldershot this season, shook more hands than a canvassing politician on election night. Dennis Bundy, the popular former PA man, had news of his attendance broadcast by the man on announcement duty for this evening. The queue for half-time tea snaked from the half-way line to back behind the goal at the clubhouse end. No, I didn't bother.

Once Peaks had done his stuff, there was never any doubt about the outcome. Nobody was going to steal the headlines from a re-born veteran. I couldn't drum up any real sympathy for Dover's inordinately irate followers. They weren't sure where to vent their fury. The referee? Their own manager, who it would appear isn't a fans' favourite? Our manager? Why, I don't know, but Richard was the object for a few of their unimaginative barbs.

Two days later (Thursday, April 17th) and I took on the role of punch bag. Responses to my report – and I did forewarn of its self-indulgence given the seismic nature of the occasion – on the Whites' internet forum didn't speak of any broad approval. The general gist, relayed in colourful terms, was that I described the action from the same perspective as Antony Coggins refereed it – in favour of one team. I'll don my supporter's hat, recall the image of a horde of home supporters baiting Eastleigh's travelling flock after last season's play-off semi-final second leg... and smile.

I'll smile like Lee Peacock smiled when he became the most unlikely hero of this epochal campaign. Who knew that, for all the talent I have watched training and playing over the past nine months, one of the most valuable goals of all would be scored by a retired 37 year old. A man who since hanging up his boots has realised that he didn't enjoy playing football. He loved his 15 minutes on the pitch against Dover – you can be sure of that.

One. More. Point.

32

IF

The first opportunity to secure the title comes against Basingstoke Town – the only Conference South club I'm yet to see play this season. Attending my sister's wedding meant I missed the Spitfires' first defeat of the campaign way back in August. There is a double incentive on Good Friday (April 18th) then. Firstly, it would be nice to right the wrongs of that day, but secondly, and of far, far larger meaning, of course, here is a chance to confirm that the championship is coming to the Silverlake.

The trophy and some of the league's top bods will be in the ground, along with, it is expected, a bumper crowd. Dan Hill will be crossing his fingers for success in the club's 50/50 draw. After buying five tickets at every match he's attended, Dan is yet to have the winner and was aghast that a first-time visitor grabbed the £163 prize on Tuesday. The Parsons will be delighted that the one match-day sponsorship they fork out for each season has fallen on this of all days.

It is likely that the same 11 men, who have gone out and taken four points – without conceding – from the last two games, will be taking up the baton once more. In discussion with Dean Beckwith at half-time on Tuesday, he confessed that his hamstring hadn't been totally right going into Bromley. It was simply a match he was hell-bent on playing – a fixture he admitted had been in the back of everybody's minds for a long time. That makes even more incredible his near flawless performance on the night. My report had mentioned only one lapse between Beckwith and Todd during the entire 90 minutes: describing Dean as having 'dithered' before being harried out of possession in his penalty area.

I was reminded of Ross Flitney being able to detail, in minutiae, the reason behind a transgression of his at Ebbsfleet in October, as Dean recalled at that 'dithering' moment, being unable to hit the ball away first time due to it being on his brittle side. He felt that striking the ball forcefully with his left foot would have caused the hamstring in that leg to tear. It's a fine line to tread, but the best players put themselves up for scrutiny knowing that they'll receive no sympathy if they cry sick in the aftermath of a costly error.

Vincent Kompany, perhaps the world's pre-eminent centre-half, played against Liverpool this week despite being only half-fit and did his bit by way of an uncharacteristically horrible error to help the reds push on in their inexorable, irritating journey to the Premier League title (they even beat Manchester City without their prolific midfielder Gerrard-Pen finding the net).

With numbers still tight Richard decided to give his healthy players Thursday off, so dodging the risk of any more bodies subsiding before, the following day, they were asked to go again against Basingstoke. Ninety minutes prior to that moment arriving, the Silverlake was bathed in sunshine. In fact, there was something of a summer fete feeling inside the ground. An opportunistic ice cream vendor had bagged a spot for his van while, to my astonishment, there was an extra tea and burger outlet on site. Shirt sleeves were the order of the day, but I ducked inside the supporters' bar to plug into the thoughts of Chris Blake.

Thrilled, and to some degree overwhelmed by his club's progress across this season, Chris will this summer be standing for re-election as the Spitfires Supporters Club (TSSC) chairman. Even as the World Cup kicks off on June 12th, the wheels of Eastleigh FC will be turning, that being the date of the vote to determine who takes on what is an unforgiving role for another 12 months.

Chris would be a hard act to follow. He insists that on those appalling Saturday mornings when, beside an army of fellow volunteers, he drags himself into the stadium to clear the pitch of water, snow or whatever else the elements have deposited, he never longs for an easier life. He doesn't wish to follow a team where his involvement extends no further than wandering up to the turnstiles in time for kick-off, before being drained of a day's wages on the way in.

'I love it' was Chris's heartfelt view on his all-consuming devotion to his football club, a commitment that spreads to spending hour upon hour assisting with ground developments. 'I'd work here full-time if I could.' There is no hint of trepidation concerning the Spitfires' exponential growth. Chris knows that, if Eastleigh FC continues to sprout at its current rate, he'll become a smaller cog in an evolving piece of machinery, but he wants only 'the best for the club'.

We all do, which is why an attendance of 1,505 for this mighty encounter with Basingstoke is such reason for cheer. That figure alone is confirmation that Eastleigh FC can be a Football League outfit. It validates the reality of what Stewart Donald has been trying to achieve since he decided that this was the place for him.

As expected, Richard's starting line-up was unchanged from three days previously. Beckwith and fast-healer McAllister made the bench. Director John Dunn was unequivocally calm before the action began – 'nope, never get nervous,' he said when I checked on his pre-game mood. I must confess that I allowed a modicum of rare complacency to creep in, confidently predicting that our guests from North Hampshire would be swatted aside 3–1.

The 'Dragons' had lost 2–0 at Gosport Borough earlier in the week – with Borough then securing their safety on Thursday (April 17th) by beating Hayes & Yeading. Gosport's season's accomplishments have been magnificent, but, nevertheless, if Basingstoke lost there I thought we'd be ok.

However, with the players fighting their fatigue, as well as an opposing side playing some bright, intrepid football, anybody of a Spitfires disposition was content to still be scoreless at the break. Moreover, by the time that the first period finished, the magnitude of the task in hand had theoretically been diminished.

After half an hour, Stoke's goalkeeper, Louis Wells, was stretchered away having come off worse from a collision with Yemi. Without a sub stopper in reserve, Ross Adams, a defender by trade, took the gloves from Wells – literally. As the visiting Number 1 was being carried away in some distress, a team-mate forcibly yanked the gloves from his hands to pass on to his replacement.

My dad and I launched our half-time deliberations, concerning whether or not our players had the legs to exploit their serendipitous advantage, stood a few paces in front of Marcus Gayle. The Staines chief, queuing patiently with us proles for half-time drinks from the additional tea wagon, was on a scouting mission, with his side due to face Basingstoke on the season's final day. A hot drink was a necessity, even at the 40p premium imposed by the newcomers. This being England, the heat of early afternoon was now competing with a bitter chill cutting its way remorselessly through the main stand.

The erratic conditions did nothing to help stabilise Richard's temperature, which, with roughly 75 minutes on the clock, was briskly on the rise – the lethargic tempo of his team's play rousing the manager's fury. Southam, after being on the end of his boss's wrath, took his life in his hands by responding with a 'calm-down' gesture directed towards the bench. Suvs' attempts at pacification didn't have the desired effect, instead sending the manager into frenzy. The skipper, though, had already made a contribution destined to last longer in the memory than any ephemeral spat.

With 24 minutes to play, Suvs robbed Simon Dunn in midfield and flew forward until he hit traffic. The ball ricocheted to Wright, who knocked it to Yemi. From 20 yards the enigmatic attacker stroked home a beautiful, curling first-time finish. And, with the consequent bedlam at its peak, the sun burst free from its cloudy prison to complete the perfect scene.

Fourteen minutes later, Wright was at both ends of a sumptuous move – Reason and Spence playing essential intervening roles – that culminated with him caressing the ball low into the net. Amidst manic ensuing celebrations, an advertising hoarding behind the goal crashed to the floor. Professional to the last, a suited Mick Geddes was soon patrolling round to investigate. The game's breezy closing stages passed by in a blur, an obligation to fulfil before the merrymaking could begin. The densely packed throng clamouring on the terrace, with its now open invitation to escape, remained steadfastly off the pitch.

Basingstoke actually scored with almost the last kick of the match. It didn't matter a jot – except to Flitney. A fiercely proud champion, Ross was incandescent that a clean sheet had been swiped from him at the death. When, seconds later, the now title-winning players congregated in the centre-circle, a human mass of exultation, our 'keeper and Suvs were engaging in a pushing match and trading some spicy words. Tensions between the pair, members of the same 'car pool' and close friends, swiftly receded. But there, in microcosm, was evidence as to why they were about to go and collect league winners' medals.

Very few, if any, of those present on this red-letter day for Eastleigh FC, opted to make an early dart. Everybody had come to watch the champions being crowned.

Collins, dressed once more in club tracksuit, modestly preferred to stay out of the initial triumphant shots. He had no hesitation, though – to widespread acclaim – in drenching his manager with champagne. That manager, a mix of exhaustion, relief and ecstasy, stepped to the side of his bouncing, singing players to draw Dan into a ginormous, extended hug.

After 20 minutes of back-slapping, animated chatter, unsuppressed jollity and some reflection, every player was called forward individually to receive their medal. They all deserved their own moment in the spotlight. Southam was last up, thirsting to lift the trophy that has been this club's singular target for nine months. Our captain waited, though, for Derik Brooks, to a cacophonous roar making his way towards the temporary presentation stand that had been hastily erected in the middle of the pitch. The pair, their respective places cemented in Eastleigh lore, shared in hoisting aloft the gleaming silverware.

My dad trailed the players as they set off on their lap of honour, gleaning as many photos as he could to commemorate a storybook day. Unable to contain myself, I had made for the dugout area, where Mick Geddes, John Russell, head steward Richard Montigue and Rob Castle, the club's treasurer, were dreamily committing everything in front of them to memory. Mike Wimbridge – earlier in the afternoon an auxiliary stretcher-bearer for the unfortunate Louis Wells – and Stu Solly were as proud as they were exhilarated, Mike intermittently gambolling away lost in his own joy. A lot of grown men were very, very emotional.

I was choked. Fleetwood, Evans, Beckwith, Southam, McAllister, Strevens and Todd all came over for a bear hug. I was indescribably elated for every single Eastleigh footballer, their manager, and the owner – back in the nick of time from his Caymans jaunt, as tanned as Tom Parsons, and struggling to comprehend what he'd witnessed. Yes, it's true, Richard Hill, the man he appointed to manage his football team in September 2012, had led them to the Conference South title. On April 18th, 2014, Eastleigh FC became league champions.

The Spitfires' Twitter-sphere later that night was flush with pictures documenting the dressing room pandemonium that had followed the public revelry. The images matched those that had formed in my mind's eye, as we briefly lurked at the back of the stand and heard the din from ceaseless warbling and whooping that a slightly ajar window allowed to seep out from inside those special four walls.

Dan Wishart tweeted, '3-day bender starts here.' He has only been a Spitfire for a month, but Dan has played his part and should cherish his achievement and its associated hullabaloo. As a footballer, you don't know when the next chance will come – if at all.

Mind you, with a derby at Havant & Waterlooville to come on Easter Monday I hope he limits the festivities to two days' worth. After completing his extensive media duties, Suvs, still in full kit, had returned to be with his team-mates clutching two bottles of lager in one hand. Which begged the question – why only two?

As at Bromley, we didn't want to go home. With the 1,505 spectators either inside the clubhouse to continue the party or having drifted off to contemplate everything they'd seen, Richard was stood in the shadows of the main stand, talking to Jamie Graham and a larger than usual press entourage.

We moved to the side of that stand with Tom Parsons, chewing over the day and the season. Inevitably, conversation drifted towards next year: the long trips, the new grounds to visit, who stays and who goes? Chris Blake had ventured that we might need four more players; we thought nearer six or seven. Guy Butters wandered past with Cookie, clutching a near empty plastic glass of champagne. 'The first of many?' I enquired. 'What makes you think it's the first?'

With respect to the perennial travel issues, a TSSC questionnaire will seek to determine a popular consensus for the way forward when Lincoln, Macclesfield, and Wrexham are just three of the exotic, distant destinations on our radar. But for now, this is Eastleigh FC 2014 and, with two games to spare, 'we' have won the league.

33

THE DAY AFTER THE NIGHT BEFORE

And then, we had to play again. Whatever form each individual's first weekend as champions took, be that heavy-duty imbibing, quiet rumination, late nights, or deep sleep, Eastleigh's fans, manager, staff and players were duty bound to be at Westleigh Park for a 3pm kick-off on Easter Monday.

This being a local derby, and with Havant & Waterlooville's play-off hopes still very much alive, there was no scope for slackening off. Not that Richard would countenance the prospect of idly standing by while one of his teams is brushed aside. The idea would horrify him and, equally so, this bunch of footballers. I have detailed throughout the campaign just how competitive any training match among the squad is. No hope, then, of this bunch happily rolling over, having their tummies tickled, and sloping off to continue the party.

The date, April 21st, 2014, though, is one that Lewis Noice, Jack Smith, and Jamie Bulpitt will always recall with some affection. All three of these rookies were handed debuts in the inhospitable environment of our near neighbours' home.

Actually, and I didn't foresee this for one minute, our unexpectedly cordial hosts began the day in rather stylish manner. Eastleigh's players entered the field through a guard of honour, formed by their opponents in recognition of the Spitfires' winning achievement. What's more, all four sides of the ground joined in warm applause when the feat was broadcast in a good-natured PA announcement.

When Jack Smith's mum ambled across the front of the main stand I offered a 'fingers-crossed' gesture. 'Oh, is he on the bench?' she mouthed, in a flash miming as if to be sick with nerves when I provided the 'good news'.

Mum can be proud of Jack's solid performance. Jamie also acquitted himself soundly and 'The Cat' looked perfectly at home dealing with the little that came his way. It's a harsh game though. Lewis erred only once, almost imperceptibly. His positioning, when Nic Ciardini drove a thundering 20-yard free-kick, was fractionally off. The Cat's despairing dive just fell short of keeping the ball from hitting the back of his net.

There was a reminder prior to kick-off of Lewis's tender years. Tom Parsons walked over to offer a 'good luck' to the lad who, just a year ago, he counted as a pupil in his French class at school. 'He was definitely in the zone, he didn't say much,' Tom reported back.

Ciardini's blast going in after ten minutes could have sent the whole house crashing down – especially with a novice goalkeeper playing behind a correspondingly green centre-half. Suvs operating at right-back completed the make-shift look to Richard's line-up. But the manager had no choice – even regarding the 'keeping spot. He needs to find out if 'The Cat' is ready to cut it.

McAllister and Todd were in no state to play, their respective bodies now teetering close to surrender. Beckwith was a token presence on the bench. Dan Spence came on for the final half-hour and shifted about like the tin man. Yet he gave it his absolute everything. They all did.

Despite the mutual gritting of Eastleigh teeth to summon whatever dregs were left in their energy banks and the Hawks' pressing need for the points, here was a match that spoke volumes for the argument in favour of a completely restructured fixture schedule in this league. Both sets of players were running as if in treacle; the will was there, but neither goalkeeper was called on to do anything beyond the routine – with the exception of 'Noicey' plucking the ball from his net.

Richard's first port of call at the full-time whistle was the day's referee, instinct having long since taken over. The boss had begun the match sitting, if not comfortably, then less pent up than we are used to, in the dugout. Within minutes of his team falling behind, our manager's voice, booming from the touchline, could be heard from the other side of the pitch. I can't think of any circumstance that might lead to Richard meeting defeat with a shrug of his shoulders and jaunty march back to the dressing room.

'See you in the Premier,' the home support crooned as we filed out, the 1–0 defeat a footnote to our far wider tale. I'm not so sure they will.

'We're not a play-off team,' Richard had said. I'm not wholly convinced we'd have had 11 men standing if it had come to that.

Thoughts will speedily turn to league match number 42 and, inclusive of pre-season friendlies, the 57th in all for this 2013/2014 season. I will have been at 55 of those and my intimate association with the Spitfires has now officially outlasted David Moyes' reign at Manchester United. Football, eh?

When I met up with the manager on Thursday (April 24th), the game three days earlier wasn't high on the agenda for discussion. Most striking was just how affected Richard had been by a rapturous ovation afforded him when he walked into the clubhouse after the title had been wrapped up against Basingstoke. The boss confessed that he had never received such a fanatical reception anywhere, at any time, throughout his entire career – even when he was scoring at more than a rate of one every two games for a Northampton Town team that were Division Four champions in 1986/1987. Richard was moved enough to describe the adulation towards him as being 'very, very humbling'.

Not that he can knock off for the year just yet – or anytime soon. There had been no training on what is normally the final preparation day for Saturday, but as I waited to interview the manager, he was embroiled in protracted talks with Stewart, Lee Peacock, Mark Jewell and others. Plans for the league above are already afoot.

Now prepared to admit he was convinced that nobody was going to wrench his side off top-spot after the victory at Bromley, it is becoming ever clearer just how much stock was placed on that huge game. Richard had told his troops, when they went in level at half-time at Hayes Lane, that if the campaign was to end successfully, they had to go back out and win the match. The play-offs were no longer an option. 'We had no players left.'

Every single detail of that early April night is plainly etched into the boss's memory. He confirmed my suspicion that, with everything on the line, he had to pair Beckwith and Todd in his defence at Bromley, even if Will Evans was crestfallen to miss out after returning to start against Whitehawk on the preceding weekend.

Any honest intention that Richard held to go and watch a Conference Premier game 24 hours after the emotion of seeing his team confirmed as champions was, rather understandably, stymied by a thick head – the manager and his two sons, Dan and Gaz, moved seamlessly on from the impromptu bash at the Silverlake to a lively night out in Oxford. The 'pressure and expectation' that he's borne since May last year had lifted and it was time to savour the moment.

For such a highly charged individual, a relative moment was all it would be. Summoned by Stewart to take the trophy to his house on Sunday, the pair sat in the chairman's garden, supping beer and discussing potential recruits. By the time we spoke on Thursday, a couple of names on their incipient list of targets had already been scratched out – information had come back that they weren't of the 'right character'.

One full season totally concentrated – often to the detriment of his own well-being and at the cost of time spent with his family – on trying to top the Conference South has left Richard 'very, very tired'. He recalled his friend, the former Aston Villa boss Brian Little, when he was 52 years old, confiding in him that he was exhausted. Our manager was incredulous then, but doesn't mind revealing that right now he is feeling every one of his 50 years. He has absorbed complete responsibility for delivering to Stewart Donald and the club's support the promotion they craved and expected.

When, in December, he was given a contract, the pressure to repay the owner's faith was ramped up further. The exacting demands, though, aren't imposed only from the outside. Richard feels that his players, by consistently proving their grit and ability, turn the spotlight back on him. They are doing their bit, as demonstrated by never once losing consecutive league games. It is then incumbent on the manager to get in his car and navigate his way to wherever the next opponents are playing – even if that is Gateshead on a Thursday night. What's more, if he's going to add to his squad, Richard must procure every possible drop of information about the prospective acquisition. He couldn't chance an individual walking in and disturbing his group's delicately forged equilibrium.

These last two months, the boss says, have been the most difficult of the year. Locating an appropriate balance between scouting opposition, fulfilling every peripheral requirement of the job, and remaining fresh for his side's own games proved near impossible. Jaded and fearing he wouldn't 'perform' on match days, Richard accepted the need to delegate, in particular sending trusted aides to watch impending opponents. It is, after all, for those 90 minutes when he is in charge that the manager's influence is most critically important. A post-training trip to Bishop's Stortford on a Monday night, and its consequent late arrival home, is no recipe for being up and full of vim ready for a crucial fixture on the Tuesday.

For all the esteem in which he holds his players, the manager isn't afraid of rattling their cages when he feels necessary. Richard disclosed he had done just that by accusing them, in the wake of January's defeat at Weston-super-Mare, of not being as good as they thought they were. The gaffer's critique got the response he was after, the polished home victory against Ebbsfleet coming four days later. It is the sort of heat-of-the-moment falling out that is familiar to dads and sons everywhere – an analogy given some pertinence by Richard's description of his role, at the helm of such an experienced, professional group, as being like that of 'a doting father – making sure they're doing what they should be doing'.

When we parted on Thursday, I suggested to the manager that it would make a refreshing change being able to come to the ground at the weekend without the usual tension and expectation weighing heavy. A clipped 'I want to win this' set me straight.

And, true to his word, come 3pm on Saturday, Richard was the same combative, focused figure that had guided the Spitfires through their previous 41 league matches. Riled by his side's inability to inject any real pace or fluidity into their play, against an obstinate, well-organised Boreham Wood outfit, the boss grew more irritable as the afternoon wore on.

The away team scored an early goal, with Will Evans seemingly fouled in the build-up. For all that they wanted to manufacture a grandstand finish to their history-making season, these Eastleigh players had nothing left to give.

It was reminiscent of Everton's sterile match at Southampton's St Mary's Stadium earlier in the day; a 2–0 defeat for the Blues that unfolded, to general apathy, on televisions around the clubhouse. The patrons, all energised by the still palpable excitement at last Friday's fulfilment of a dream, were instead busily engaged in hurried chatter, eating, drinking, and laughing. With the pre-game maelstrom at full throttle, I tactically avoided anything to do with my boyhood heroes, opting to catch up on the grizzly details a day later. Today was about Eastleigh. So many days are.

Ben Wright, speaking to my dad and me after what ended up as a 1–0 reverse, alluded to a strange feeling whereby, however much the mind wants things to click into gear, there is something – when the outcome is of no decisive consequence – that stops the body from going at full pelt, that slows the signals from brain to feet. That undetectable phenomenon indiscriminately targeted many of the year's standard-bearers. Flitney, Beckwith, Todd, and Spence all returned to take a season's bow without being able to influence the result. In fact, the Wood's resolute display perhaps offered an indication towards what a phenomenal achievement it has been for these players to overcome so many similarly minded adversaries across an eight-month slog.

The whistle to signal a home defeat would usually be the prompt for a 'mass' disaffected shuffle away from the stadium. Here, though, a minor pitch invasion and more on-pitch revelry announced the start of another party.

We spent a couple of hours in the clubhouse, where Chris Blake had organised a party for players and fans alike. As I stood waiting at the bar, I glanced through results from elsewhere. Prominent was Dover's win, earned with a late penalty, at Hayes & Yeading. The victors in that game pipped Havant & Waterlooville, who had drawn 0–0 at Tonbridge, to the final play-off spot. After 42 matches, the Hawks missed out due to their inferior goal difference. For Hayes & Yeading, their last gasp defeat was catastrophic, condemning them as it did to joining Dorchester and Tonbridge in dropping out of the division. Whitehawk and Maidenhead United survived with a point to spare.

Before the day's action, in the same building that was now filling with anticipation of the latest Eastleigh FC celebratory shenanigans, I had spoken to McAllister and Fleetwood, the stricken pair doing their bit for public relations with a bit of pre-match mingling. I was made up for Macca when he revealed that he had played the requisite number of matches this season to trigger a clause in his contract entitling him to another year at the club. He has fought his body, a perpetual battle for his place, and a tide of unforgiving Conference South defenders to feature massively in a title-winning season. Macca's post-football plumbing is on indefinite hold. He will be back next year and, I don't doubt, making life distinctly uncomfortable for plenty of grizzly Conference Premier centre-halves.

Fleets, sporting earrings that I had, until now, never seen – 'It's party time' – and Collins are the only others currently tied down for the next campaign. Richard had divulged on Thursday that talks with the rest are impending.

With the evening's festivities in full swing, the duo of Beckwith and Southam was united in the view that there is only one club to which they want to be reporting for duty in July. Wright said the same, but Salisbury City will have a telling say on his future.

The players' table, awash with a cavalcade of drinks, rose in raucous approval when Ben Strevens was asked to the stage to pick up the TSSC's Player of the Year award. He was the rightful winner – a majestic footballer. The supporters present, some of whom wondered what he brought to the side in the season's opening months, vigorously roared Ben's name. As they did Ben Wright's when he collected April's Player of the Month gong.

A glassy-eyed Todd was in his element, speaking of Eastleigh's achievement this term as being equal to that when he won promotion into the Football League five years ago with Torquay United (ironically relegated out of League Two on this day) and on a par with his involvement in Newport County's runaway success in this division in 2010.

The gregarious Welshman was readying himself for a long night, one of the few who, to quote Jamie Collins, had been 'granted a pass'. Beckwith, Flitney, Collins and others were on a tight leash, so obliged to curtail their evening out – a small price to pay when 14 of this squad, courtesy of a grateful owner, are Las Vegas-bound to drink in their success. I won't be there, thank heavens, pen and notebook in hand to record the specifics of that private jolly.

My dad and I scooted off at about 7:30pm, choosing to leave the younger or more resilient to their frolicking. Pictorial evidence of later events shows that a durable hard core – notable mentions for Yemi, Fleetwood, Will Evans, Dan Spence, and Jai Reason – stayed long into the evening, and beyond, mixing freely and merrily with their joyous public. They deserve every single second of their celebrations. These are the days.

Moving On

Before we know it, a new season with its attendant stories, modern heroes, long journeys, problems to overcome, unforgettable afternoons, good days, bad days and, be sure, some absolute horrors will be upon us.

I'll be back in my stand, but absent from the training ground. A supporter above all else. My adventure, in tandem with that of the Conference South title-chasing Eastleigh FC class of 2013/2014, stops here.

Derik Brooks, speaking to me three days after the curtain was drawn on this campaign, captured perfectly how we all feel about Eastleigh.

'I am very proud of the club. We have had our ups and downs, but when we've had our downs we've always recovered and fought back.'

Derik is 90 years old and thought he'd seen it all. Conference Premier football at the Silverlake Stadium, however, will be a new happening for every one of us. Which team is the man, who in 1946 started all this, most looking forward to seeing in action?

'Only my own.'

A revered figurehead, Derik speaks for everybody when he declares his wish for 2014/2015.

'I just want them to do as best as they can. It's going to be an interesting season. The more we win the better it will be.'

The founder of Eastleigh FC strives for excellence, but never at the expense of class and respect. A majority of the people now responsible for the good name and burgeoning fortunes of Derik Brooks' club – from boardroom, right through the management and players, to its dedicated followers – are maintaining those ideals.

Long may that continue.

PS.

A fans' forum conducted by Stewart and Richard on Thursday, May 8th, brought news that all of the championship-winning squad, with the exception of Chris Dillon, were offered contracts for season 2014/2015. Every single one was subsequently signed.

Guy Butters will not be continuing in his role at Richard's side. Macca has been appointed as player/assistant manager, while Toddy becomes player/coach.

On Sunday, May 4th, Dover thumped Paul Doswell's Sutton 3–0 away from home to win a two-legged play-off semi-final 4–1. The final on Saturday, May 10th, was an all Kent affair, Ebbsfleet having overcome Bromley by the same 4–1 aggregate score in their semi-final tie. A second-half Nathan Elder goal was enough for Dover to join Eastleigh in the Conference Premier. It was an outcome that surprised me as much as Liverpool stumbling at the last to finish second in the Premier League behind Manchester City.

On Thursday July 3rd an article on Eastleigh FC's official website stated that the club were 'extremely disappointed' to report that 'Glen Southam has been released from his contract with immediate effect'. Eight days later Glen became a Chelmsford City player.

Ben Wright put his name to a permanent Spitfires contract on Friday July 4th.

Finally, Ben Strevens rounded off his year by completing a unique hat-trick. The Conference South champion, and Eastleigh FC 'Player of the Year', also had his university studies rewarded with the achievement of a 2:1 Honours Degree.

ACKNOWLEDGEMENTS

I would like to express my extreme gratitude to Richard Hill, every single member of his staff, and all the players at Eastleigh FC for welcoming me so willingly into their world. Without Richard's readiness to allow me access to his thoughts and his players, and incredible generosity with his time, this project would not have been possible.

Thank you, Mum, Dad and Rachael. Your enduring support and understanding is appreciated more than you can know. Thanks also to Dad for countless hours spent casting his discerning eye over this book's manuscript and offering valuable insight. His help with my first venture into the intricate world of publishing has been equally priceless.

I am hugely grateful to Tony Smith for providing me with a collection of his excellent photographs to use in the book.

Thank you to everybody at Troubador Publishing for their considerable efforts in seeing the book through to its fruition.

I am indebted to Dr Janet Naylor, Dr Hannah Turner, and Ann Malone. They have all done so much to give me back my life.

And, of course, Eastleigh FC. What a club.